THE POLITICALLY INCORRECT REAL ESTATE AGENT HANDBOOK

THE POLITICALLY INCORRECT REAL ESTATE AGENT HANDBOOK

A Serious How-To Manual with a Sense of Humor

PETER F. PORCELLI JR.

BACKYARD BOOKWORKS
MARIETTA, GA

The Politically Incorrect Real Estate Agent Handbook

Copyright © 2017 by Peter F. Porcelli, Jr.

PICTURE CREDITS:
All photographs contained herein were procured via the Library of Congress, Prints & Photographs Division. The majority of these photos are from the *George Grantham Bain Collection*, dated from the early 1900s through the 1920s. All photographs have been digitally-modified to remove blemishes, enhanced for contrast, and (at times) tweaked to fit content. Digital modifications were painstakingly performed by the author, with love.

Primarily set in Harriet Text and garnished with Playfair Display

Backyard Bookworks
Marietta, GA
backyardbookworks.com

RealEstateAgentBook.com

ISBN: 978-0-9989608-0-7

LCCN: 2017913855
BISAC: BUS054010

Printed in the United States of America

1 3 5 7 9 0 8 6 4 2

FIRST EDITION

There is no shame in not knowing; the shame lies in not finding out.
—wise proverb

CONTENTS

CHAPTER ZERO — FORE WORDS

CHAPTER ONE — BASICS

CHAPTER TWO — PROSPECTING

CHAPTER THREE — VALUATION & PRICING

CHAPTER SEVEN — POTPOURRI

Why I Wrote this Book

It wasn't entirely for the money, but the money is nice.

BY PETER F. PORCELLI, JR.

BORN WITH A STRANGE SENSE OF HUMOR and a desire to share what I know, this book is the natural result of my first fifteen years in real estate sales. During that time, I've seen umpteen agents come and go. Plenty have been successful, but many more were not. And while each had wanted to stay, most of them went.

With its ridiculously-low entry barrier, the real estate sales industry attracts all sorts of people, drunk on all kinds of ambition. The motives of these masses range from building an empire, to funding family entertainment and vacations. For this reason, I have come to realize that real estate success is a journey, not a destination, and is defined by the individual on its path. Therefore, the agent who earns a half-million by closing a hundred transactions per year may be just as successful as the one who closes a half-dozen and earns thirty-thousand. For each, success depends upon achievement of a *personal* production goal. To attain that goal, the agent must routinely acquire clients and close transactions—each of which requires the execution of a long series of tasks. In this way, an agent's *success is predicated upon competency* of task performance.

Of the competent agents I've met, some were conservative and calculated, while others were wacky and improvisational. Some were seasoned veterans and others were fresh rookies. Regardless of style or tenure, competent agents share a single commonality: continued, constructive action. In other words, competent agents keep learning better ways to say and do the right things, at the right times, over and over *and over again.*

Incompetent agents are well-intentioned, but often fall into the trappings of their independent contractor status; left to self-educate, many feel lost. Although classes, workshops, and coaching programs are available, these avenues seem expensive and feel tedious. For those who forego formal training, many find their learnin' via the agent grapevine. Free and convenient, this oral tradition is largely a patchwork of home remedies and tall tales, spun-up and re-told during each summoned session. Depending upon the teller, pearls of wisdom may trickle from its thicket, or the chatter may conjure complete crap. Either way, its impulsive lessons are typically disjointed and full of omissions.

The results have been chronicled: without a qualified advisor, the overwhelming majority of those who attempt real estate sales will not find success and will leave its ranks. Until they flunk-out, these incompetent agents unwittingly flail-about, gasping at clients and bungling transactions, gumming-up the works and spreading distrust of the industry.

My belief is that *the client is best-served by a competent agent* and that competence is easily gained by repeated learning and doing. All agents desire success (competency), but most don't know where to begin or what to believe. Their job is complicated, but it doesn't come with an owner's manual.

So, I created this recipe guide of the most common real estate tasks. Presented in a *tell-it-like-it-is* format, each chapter is based upon an area of real estate competency (as deemed by me). Throughout, the reader is encouraged to forever banish victimhood, seek validation of "facts," and to be direct, but cordial, in all dealings.

Now, anyone can plop-down a few measly bucks, *buy my book*, and discover an offbeat compendium of real estate sales. Hopefully, it will aid agents of all stripes: full-timers and weekend warriors, newbies and wannabes.

Ultimately, this primer is for real estate agents *and their clients.* May you each find success, however defined.

01 October 2017

In Gratitude

Without your help, this book would not be possible.

BY THE AUTHOR

THANK YOU, thank you, *thank you!* You have supported me through active participation, constructive encouragement, or sheer inspiration. Each of you occupies a special place in my mind, in my heart, or in both:

Mom and Dad for fostering a perfect childhood. When faced with life's challenges, your upright example has always guided my cause. My love and devotion to you is eternal.

My siblings Meredith, Matt, and Melissa for being my adolescent best friends. It was with you that I learned to laugh and take life in stride. I love you and your families, too.

S. Alan Schlact for being the inspiration of my real estate passion. Without your tutelage, mentorship, encouragement, and the hundreds of people you've introduced to me, my career would have taken a different trajectory and this book would not be.

Chuck and Audrey Norman for incubating this baby bird. Your nest, with its revolving door of characters from real estate's past, was a great place to learn and stretch my legs.

Tom Norman for showing me the daily routine: search for prospects, put clients first, and never flinch at telling them the truth of the matter. Your example taught me how to take control of my business. It was under your wing that I learned to fly.

Paul Renton for demonstrating just how powerful the use of systems, tenacity, and constant refinement can be to a real estate agent's business. You are the infomercial example of an agent whose results are not typical. Thank you for including me in your journey.

Joshua Thomas for dreaming, scheming, and cavorting with me. You are the perfect mix of sounding board to hash-out crazy ideas and audacious dude to bring those ideas into practical use.

Dave Kubat for endorsing my experimental sales team. When others were skeptical, you stood by my side.

My students for goading me into undertaking this endeavor, my clients for trusting me with your transactions, and my former agents, for trusting me with your real estate roadblocks; the sheer volume and myriad of entanglements within which you ensnared us taught me more than I could have learned in one hundred agents' lifetimes.

The internet for providing access to so many expert resources. You taught me typography, digital photo editing, and graphic design. Without you, this book would be ugly.

The Library of Congress and (in particular) the George Grantham Bain Collection of photographs. Without you, this book would be heavily laden with stick figures.

Arline Kubat for providing a tranquil environment for me to work. Sitting lakeside with a cigar in one hand and a pencil in the other does (eventually) produce a finished product.

Tim Rollins and Bill Hanke for stellar, editorial notes. Your notes were insightful.

Ben Ereddia for playing the devil's advocate. Thank you for continuing to argue minutia with me, long after most would have resigned themselves.

Dad for reading every word of my manuscript. Your editorial suggestions inspired me to add the flow charts and to remove a thousand commas.

Sweet Tiffany for your unwavering support during the laborious, book-making process. Throughout, you provided me stress relief and much needed perspective. You are my ideal companion: you feed my head, my tummy, my heart, and my soul and I love you dearly. Thank you for never complaining about sleeping alone while I stayed up to work on this book. Thank you for sacrificing so many weekend excursions so I could pour over this book. Thank you for believing me each time I said this book would be done at the end of the month. I was finally right this last time.

Effort Meter

You're Gonna Need:

this Book
Open Mind
Thinking Cap
Sense of Humor

How-to
Read this Book

As a humorous how-to guide of real estate sales, this book is not like the others. Its pages are organized by topic and follow a logical sequence, but sometimes the transition from one page to the next will feel choppy. This is because, as a reference manual, each article is meant to be read as either a stand-alone entry or as part of an interwoven system; therefore, some special features are required:

1 Flow Charts

The Flow Chart System is the skeleton from which the meat of this book hangs. Because these flow charts outline an agent's job (and this book), you should familiarize yourself with them before reading further (begin with the *Example Flow Chart* on page 347). For easy reference, the flow charts are located in the back of the book; follow along as you read and take them with you into the field.

tips

The old pictures that grace these pages are meant to remind the reader of three things: 1) real estate sales are predicated upon agents interacting with people, 2) there was a time when political correctness did not hamper communication, and 3) the basic tenets of real estate sales (being prospecting, valuation, presentation, agency, and contracts) do not change; having remained true for more than a hundred years now, the fundamentals of these disciplines are likely to remain unchanged a hundred years from now.[304]

For the sake of space, some words and phrases are not defined the first time they're introduced to the reader, so check the glossary (it's robust).[324]

2 Cross-References

This book is jam-packed with information and it's all inter-related. So, to prevent redundant explanation, cross-references have been added to declarative statements and related topics. You'll recognize them as superscripted, three-digit numbers (referring to another page that further explains the word, phrase, or concept that the superscript adorns). These manual hyperlinks tie lessons together, allowing the reader to weave a customized curriculum, based upon interest and/or need. So, if you're reading along and something seems unclear, then check the glossary[324] and/or follow the attached cross-reference.

3 Quotations

At times, there is dialogue within the text. Following these conversations is simple, because the speakers' typefaces are different:
« The agent is always quoted with this notation. »
« The other speaker is quoted with this notation. »

disclaimer

Real estate brokers represent clients and real estate agents represent their brokers. Therefore, a real estate agent's representation of clients is as proxy for her broker. With this technicality noted (and for the sake of simplicity), this book often refers to the agent as being her client's representative. However, the reader should keep these actual relationships in-mind.

4 Political Incorrectness

This book has nothing to do with politics, nor does it promote being a jerk. Instead, the politically incorrect agent is defined as one who fiercely advocates for clients by continuously seeking the truth,[038] following the rules,[036] and banishing victimhood.[004] She does not mislead, nor does she pretend to be what she is not. She doesn't blindly follow the crowd, but breaks from custom when it benefits her clients.

5 Pronouns

Political incorrectness aside, both men and women participate as real estate agents. The same goes for prospects, clients, and contract principals. Therefore, he, she, him, and her are freely exchanged throughout this book. To keep things congruent, buyers are generally referred to as male and sellers as female, with their agent taking the opposite pronoun. When you encounter a pronoun that does not match your identity, just pretend that it does and keep reading. Geez.

Σ Sigma is found at the bottom of *How-to* articles to provide a simple, single-sentence summary.

How-to
Maximize this Book

You're likely reading this book for self-improvement. If so, you might be hoping that reading a book will make you a better real estate agent. This dream will never happen; however, when used in conjunction with constructive action, *this primer can be the springboard* of your success. To maximize your leap, become familiar with the flow:

1 Read
Some of these entries are stand-alone teachings, and others are building blocks to more-complex lessons. Some passages are sober in style, and others are carved within a groove of levity. Regardless of tier or tenor, each article herein contains the basic information you need to acquire clients and close transactions. So, read this book and then read it again.

Predominant Article Types
- *How-to*: Written in outline for repeated reference, these pages contain the recipes of common real estate tasks and systems.
- *Byline*: As logical arguments in-support of *How-to* articles, these columns are sometimes conventional and sometimes not.
- *Dear Andy*: Common questions from actual agents are rewritten to be clear and concise, coaxing a comprehensive answer.
- *True Story*: The names are changed, but the truth remains in these short narratives, construed to promote lesson recall.
- *Quiz & Puzzle*: The final pages of each chapter are meant to test your acumen.

2 Practice
Attending classes and reading books are like watching football on television. While each will acquaint you with the game, an armchair quarterback remains unskilled at actual sport. To become skilled at real estate sales, you must actively engage in its activities. To hasten success, practice what this book preaches; doing so will yield more touchdowns than bloody noses.

3 Think
Even with the best preparations, you're unlikely to become an overnight sensation. In the meantime, acknowledge your defeats, and ask: *What could I have said or done differently, to get a better outcome?* Then, revise your systems,[070] practice your scripts,[050] and get ready to do it all again.

4 Repeat
Becoming competent at real estate sales is like achieving massive weight loss the old-fashioned way: only a disciplined diet of learning and daily exercise of practice will get you to your goal. It's a lifestyle; therefore, success is achieved by repeating STEPS 1-3 until exhaustion.

Effort Meter

You're Gonna Need:
this Book
Indulgence
Action
Contemplation

tips

Laws, regulations, and customs vary from state to state. Before implementing any lesson, taking any advice, or reading-to another from this publication, check with local laws, regulatory bodies, and custom keepers for any adverse reactions this book may cause you.

Scribble your name on the inside cover, and don't lose your handbook. You're gonna need it!

Cut the spine and spiral bind with thick, plastic coils or the thin, wiry kind. This alteration will allow your open paperback to lay flat (which is helpful when studying the flow charts).

Make notes in the margins, dog-ear the pages, and highlight whatever you deem worthy. Let these words live and breathe.

It's hip to be seen with this manual, so carry it with you everywhere.

Osmosis. Smosmosis. Using this textbook as a pillow will cause a kink in your neck.

Once practiced, you will glean newfound meaning when re-reading these pages.

Σ Repeatedly reading this book and practicing its lessons will produce a real estate agent of competency, capable of success.

Real Estate is the single, most-fascinating promise in America.

She waits in the night,
like a dozen lonesome sirens
aloft a dark, blind coastline,
serenading each passerby
with charms of fortune and adventure.

Of those who heed her beckoning call,
most are at-once swept-under
by currents foreign and foreboding.

Others, carried by waves that break pre-dawn,
succumb to abrupt, jagged stones
laid along her alluring shore.

But, for the few who safely reach her sandy beaches,
she is all that she promises—and more.

Woo her with style and grace;
never wane of her demanding attention.
Dance about her fickle fashion;
cautiouly push against her mounting tides.
Discover her vital rhythms;
pledge yourself to her daily chores:
And ye are bound to court her for years to come.

For she is the sweetest of all the sweethearts.
Real Estate—Let's get it on!

The POLITICALLY INCORRECT REAL ESTATE AGENT HANDBOOK

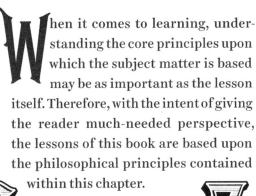

When it comes to learning, understanding the core principles upon which the subject matter is based may be as important as the lesson itself. Therefore, with the intent of giving the reader much-needed perspective, the lessons of this book are based upon the philosophical principles contained within this chapter.

Chapter Zero
Fore Words

Real Estate is like coffee.

Freshly-ground, gourmet beans steeped in a French press makes for great coffee, and so does an old, bulk-packaged brand, percolated over a campfire. Each preparation serves its primary purpose: caffeine coursing through the veins.

However, the quality of bean, the brewing method employed, and the environment in which enjoyed, each in concert, determines the flavor. Just the same, real estate sales may be created in multiple ways.

Real Estate is like a road trip.

With the many combinations of lanes, lodgings, and locomotion to get you there, the specific sequence chosen will greatly impact one's comfort, expense, and time on the road. Similarly, real estate sales may be executed in multiple ways, with varying results.

Real Estate is like skinning a cat.

While it may have potential as an effective fur-removing endeavor, holding Fluffy by the tail while vigorously brandishing course-grit sandpaper as your arms are clawed to shreds, isn't the most efficient manner possible.

When the objective is the same for everyone, the strokes one takes determines the scratch one makes. All the same, real estate sales may be performed in multiple ways.

Real Estate is like... your opinion, man.

This book is full of opinions: *my opinions*. However, the ideas and examples bound by these pages are not mere hyperbole. Together, these selected entries create a catalog of tangible recipes. Each is concocted of numerous books, pamphlets, classes, workshops, and interactions with various colleagues, competitors, and mentors. All that information has since been muddled, mixed, and infused with fresh ideas born from discussions, mishaps, reflections, experiences, experiments, and eccentricities of my own.

The resulting prescription, you hold in your hands. Rest assured, everything in this book has been tested and proven to work by me and by agents and brokers with whom I have worked closely as a consultant, coach, student, broker, team leader, or team member.

Above all else, real estate sales is a practice, similar to medicine and law; therefore, the industry is rife with numerous opinions and methods, all designed to reach the same outcome. This book is but one way to get there.[346]

You Are *the* (Wo)Man!

Everything that happens to your business, whether good or bad, is the direct result of your (in)actions. With this revelation repeating and resonating in the forefront of your mind, may you never again feel like a victim.

You are the thrust of your success.

Nobody holds you back like you.

You are to be blamed or heralded.

Only you can prevent forest fires.

I am what I think.
A strange way to view the world?
Spins heavy and slow.

If I think I can:
I'm right! If I think I can't:
Poo-Poo Creek flows swift.

Thinking, thinking: done.
Where will this process lead me?
Dogs lie. Rabbits run.

Put it to action,
Or the thinking is a waste.
Basking, warm blossoms.

I am what I think.
Wasted thought is forgotten;
My mind is renewed.

HIGH-
FIVE
HAIKU

A Serious How-To Manual with a Sense of Humor

Agent Slogan

Be honest, direct, sincere, and always consider future relationships.

Be Prepared

Being caught with your real estate pants down can be more than just embarrassing. Ill-prepared agents inflict lost opportunity and forfeited income upon themselves and clients, alike. There are many ways by which one may be prepared; make this maxim your motto, and may your real estate days be fruitful.

Be Lawful

Real estate jail awaits those who practice either malevolence or negligence, through either flagrant insolence or latent ignorance. Therefore, playing by the rules is not only the right thing to do, but also a guaranteed protection of your licensure. Keep to the confines of laws and regulations, then sleep easy and never look over your shoulder. In this spirit, always check with your broker, contractual obligations, laws, regulations, and local ordinances before conducting any of the exercises described within this book.[036]

Seek Best Practice

Real estate sales is comprised of many, many subjects. For the sake of you and your clients, always attempt to act as an expert in each of those subjects. In other words, strive for best practice.

Mildly speaking, this endeavor is not without challenge, but is attainable by those who seek expert help, and who continuously grow through the perseverance of on-going education.[034]

Mind the Source

There's an old joke about a door-to-door salesman: approaching a house, he encounters a little boy sitting on the stoop. The salesman asks the boy if his mother is home. The boy answers with a confident, "Yessir!" The salesman rings the bell, and knocks on the door, but no answer avails. Then comes the exchange:

> **Salesman:** I thought you said your mother was home.
> **Little boy:** She is.
> **Salesman:** Then why doesn't she answer the door?
> **Little boy:** Because I don't live here.

When taking action based upon gathered information, it is best to mind the source of that information, and to determine whether or not all pertinent information has been gathered. Assuming information is complete and accurate is not good enough. Validate: always take the time to get it right; always go to the source (whenever possible).

Do not settle for what is overheard. Do not settle for what "seems right." Do not settle for what everyone else is doing. Repeat after me: if my actions go bust based upon incomplete and/or inaccurate information, then more than just egg is on me. Likewise, do not settle for what you read in a single book.

Be Prepared.

Just so you know:
sometimes things do not
go as planned, but a competent agent is
ready when things go awry. Remember,
being prepared for contingency is
more than simply wearing a uniform
and possessing all the tools.

To truly be prepared, an agent must:
learn how to apply the right tool
(or combination of tools) for each job
at-hand, and then master those tools
through everyday use; anticipate both
common and infrequent complications,
and then create systems to safely hike
through each one; and show-up to
work each day, pitch a prospecting
tent, and camp-out with clients.

Along the way, tender-footed moments
will occur; when it happens to you,
contemplate the experience. Then
augment your procedures, so that
the same thing does not
again tie-you-up in knots.

Your Words Matter

What you say, how you say it, and to whom you say it will be the determining factors of your success or failure.

BY LINDA THE LINGUIST

THE JOB OF A REAL ESTATE AGENT is to bring parties together. Often times, these parties need advice and/or guidance on the best way to proceed. While you cannot make another's decisions for them, your words may be used to influence their actions. To guide people towards their best interest (or the best interest of your clients), your words are the best tools to communicate ideas, suggestions, and directions. However, words are only as effective and efficient as *what you say, how you say it, and to whom you say it.*

The English language is amazingly vast and complex, which can cause communication to become complicated. Sometimes the denotation and the connotation of a single word will differ, potentially leaving the listener with an interpretation that is different than was intended by its speaker.

The ability to be understood is also dependent upon your cadence, pitch, inflection, and volume of speech. Mumbling, low talking, accents, dialects, and the use of slang or industry jargon may further complicate message transmission. Words spoken over the phone may be interpreted by the listener differently than the same words spoken face-to-face. Those same words may again be misinterpreted when read via email, text message, or on marketing materials.

A single word or concept may have numerous other words that further describe, enhance, or modify its meaning. Many words carry emotional stigma and/or illicit prejudice. Your listener is forming an opinion while you speak, so be intentional with your speech. Your awareness of and implementation of emotional trigger-words may be either useful or damaging to your intentions, so carefully contemplate the words you use.

Pithy communication is more likely to be received, so avoid adding the unnecessary fluff. Analogies and maxims are wonderful tools for effective communication and will often times make the speaker sound smart. Some words, peppered in the right places, will make the speaker seem *really* smart. Those perceived as smart are more likely to have their advice followed, however, over-use or misuse of these "smart-guy words" may make you seem douchey.

While practicing real estate sales, you will be speaking with (to name a few) principals, those who influence principals, prospects, those who influence prospects, co-operating agents, contractors, and vendors. Always consider the audience when speaking, as this consideration begets what you say, and how you say it, because saying the right thing to the wrong person is a fruitless endeavor at best. At worst, you may compromise a client's position, causing catastrophe to strike.

There is a corollary to the *what you say, how you say it, and to whom you say it* rule, which is *when it's said*—and—*how often it's repeated.* Some messages need to be communicated at just the right time to have the intended impact. Other messages need to be repeated, and at times the repeated message needs to be communicated with different words than previous attempts so that the listener may better gain understanding of your perspective.

Knowledge of the appropriate approaches and the proper methods of real estate sales will allow you to always be comprehensive and truthful. Prepared scripts for common situations allow you to hone your words for maximum influence and impact. Choose your words wisely, considering the listener's goal, your intent, and the connotation, denotation, emotion, grammar, and syntax of words.[048] Then enunciate those words plainly.[051]

Your success is predicated on *what you say, how you say it, and to whom you say it.* And all that having been said, sometimes it's best to say nothing at all. ♠

Life's a Niche

Practice a specialty, or heads will roll.

BY PATTY THE POTTER

IMAGINE A MEDIEVAL SHIRE where life is sticky, and where it has been long-known, far and wide, that the King is prone to bouts of silly whim (and that he is evil). One day, the King's Men snatched a couple of random peasants from off the street, one Bart and the other Murray, to be made participants of the King's latest whim. They were each given a fortnight to make a special pot to hold the King's ashes (he's not dead yet; he's just really morbid and really evil). The King demanded the pot to be tall, with handles and a lid. The peasant who creates the best pot will be rewarded with a new frock, made of golden threads; the other guy will get swift death!

A couple of weeks later, Bart and Murray returned to the King's Court. As each man stood, concealing beneath his cloak a pot of his own creation, the King asked if the pots were completed. He asked if the pots are made to specification. He asked if the pots were the result of diligent effort, representing the best possible pot a novice could possibly craft, given a mere fortnight of creative time. In unison, the men answered YES to each question. "Well, let's see 'em!" the King demanded.

"You go first," the King instructed, gesturing to Murray. So, Murray showed his pot, and what an awesome pot it was. It was tall and bulbous, adorned with a relief carving of the King's likeness. It was made of high-quality clay, with elegant, sweeping handles, and a crowning lid. "Wow!" exclaimed the King, "That sure looks like a tough act to follow. Now show me the other pot. It better be good."

Bart then pulled back the folds of his cloak, mawkishly clutching his handmade pot. "I can't see it," the King bellowed. "Present me with your pot, you pissant peasant!" Acting as instructed, Bart removed the pot from his side and extended his arms, where, clasped in his shaky, out-stretched hands, Bart held the biggest piece of shit you've ever seen!

As the King's Men drug Bart away, he was heard screaming, "But I worked so long and so hard, making that *one* pot! I spent two weeks, without sleep, struggling with that *one* pot!"

Afterwards, Murray was overheard bragging, "Unlike Bart, I didn't stop at just one pot. I made a *hundred* pots! The first dozen or so looked a lot like Bart's sorry excuse of a pot, but then I started getting better at it—much better at it. I learned how to avoid mistakes, make aesthetic changes, and discovered better techniques of attaching the handles. After awhile, I could make these pots in my sleep." While Bart went on to death, Murray went on to run a successful, cottage business called Gold Frock Pottery.

The moral of the story is that mastery takes repetition, and repetition requires niche concentration. Because Murray kept repeating the process of making the same pot, he corrected flaws, progressively producing a pot of higher quality than was the last pot produced, until each pot produced was perfect. Because Bart made only one pot, it was lame.

Rinse, lather, repeat will keep your hair clean, your business a success, and your head securely attached to your body.[042]   🌳

Say What!?!?

If you posses a thick (foreign) accent or a pronounced (domestic) dialect from another region, then correct it (unless it serves your niche market). To adapt a "Hollywood" accent that may be easily understood by the masses, seek coaches, classes, and websites. When you address phonetic changes to pronunciation, *being misunderstood may be avoided.*

Real Estate Sales is for Salesmen

When thinking of salesmen, far too many envision a sleazy, used-car dealer wearing too many rings and a gold chain, laid upon a bed of curly chest hair, framed by the gapping neckline of a loud leisure suit, selling broken products with broken promises. While this may be the perceived epitome of a salesman, it does not describe a *scrupulous* salesman.

Consider another description: a salesman is a person who helps others make smart buying (and selling) decisions. When you embrace this definition, there becomes no reason to shy away from the salesman moniker. After all, real estate agents sell their ideas, notions, and experiences throughout the sales process.

Your viewpoint will (probably) be the reason clients hire you, as they assume you know more about the sales process than they do.

Solid sales techniques may be used by agents to efficiently attract clients, and those same techniques may also be used to help clients achieve their real estate goals. So, if you wanna be a good real estate agent, then you have to be a good salesman. Some agents call themselves consultants or advisors, which is perfectly fine—just remember that you are first and foremost a salesman with fiduciary obligations.[212] Then, adopt and employ sales techniques into your routines; doing so will benefit you and your clients alike.

The Slope of Sales

Each of your salesmanship skills will be put to the test throughout the sales process.[344] Consider that to complete a transaction, at least three, major sales are made by an agent, each of which has its own host of sub-sales.

The Big Three Sales:

1. Convince a prospect to hire you.[077]
2. Negotiate a purchase and sale contract (P&S).[266]
3. Persevere through contingencies and conclusion of the transaction.[221]

Salesmanship Works

Salesmanship techniques will enrich your business; to employ them:

- Use scripts to communicate effectively and efficiently.[046]
- Practice scripts by role-playing, to learn quickly and to stay sharp.[050]
- Use a closing script to incite action upon the part of prospects.[198]
- Prospect daily for new clients, to give your business options for success.[078]
- Practice good, accurate record keeping.[089]
- Know your job, including all aspects of the product[040] and the means by which your clients may attain their desired goals.[154]
- Utilize systems to operate your business effectively and efficiently;[070] attempt to mitigate expense, while ensuring each client gets the exact-same, quality-filled experience.[212]
- Be a proud salesman and speak with conviction.[051]

The Sales Formula

Price + Condition + Exposure = Salability [152]

Each parcel of real property has a condition; to sell one, an agent must simply pick a price that matches the condition,[154] then expose that price/condition combo to the marketplace.[236]

An Analogy to the Wise

A novice chef should follow recipes exactly as printed, otherwise mastery may never be realized. Rudimentary repetition will be his path to mastery, and experience gained through recipe repetition will afford the novice an opportunity to acquire an appreciation for quality ingredients, acclimatize himself to the interaction of those ingredients, and procure dexterity of technique. His repeated implementation of these blossoming tools will result in a product that is superior to its produced-from-the-same-recipe predecessor, until mastery is achieved.

Only once a chef has achieved recipe mastery should that chef begin to improvise and attempt to create a customized product (one that is superior to the original recipe), by swapping-out ingredients, adding spice, and/or applying ancillary techniques.[291]

In contrast, imagine a novice chef mixing a cake. In doing so, he swaps sugar for salt. After all, they do look just the same, so he wonders: *What could go wrong?* That which seems glaringly obvious to a chef with ingredient knowledge may baffle the novice.

Therefore, the novice who cries: *recipe failure!* is either not following the recipe exactly, and/or is lacking the pre-requisite dexterity of technique. Simply put: novice errors lie somewhere between the words on these pages and the spatula in hand.

The Effective & Efficient Tasking of Things

Mindful execution of tasks begets success.

BY ANALOGOUS ANNIE

WHEN IT COMES TO REAL ESTATE sales, there is one, over-reaching, main goal: achievement of a successful real estate sales transaction (that's the *main* job). To achieve this main goal, a sub-goal must first be achieved: acquisition of a client. One begets the other, and each is a task of its own.

In the pursuit of any goal, tasks must be performed.[344] Some tasks must be performed in a pre-determined order,[260] while other tasks may be performed in any order,[252] so long as they *are performed*. Some tasks are performed only when a strategy calls for it,[258] while other tasks are performed every time, regardless of strategy.[170] Some tasks may be scheduled,[186] while other tasks must be completed impromptu,[180] once the need arises. Some tasks are required for transaction achievement,[221] but far many more are "elective" tasks.[193]

For some agents in pursuit of the main goal, some tasks are either unidentified,[222] only partially performed,[226] or ignored as unnecessary,[274] because the main goal is *usually* achieved without that particular task being completed. Other times, agents routinely perform tasks when wholly unnecessary,[237] because those tasks *seem* to be warranted.

Performed tasks are generally viewed as effective or not, but there exists a grayscale. If a white task "never works" and a black task "works every time", then gray tasks "work every time, except when they don't." Therefore, gray is not a color to employ, because gray tasks are only *somewhat*-effective.

In quest of black, you will find that challenges exist. For starters, there are many, many shades of gray, and at times, really-dark grays look like black,[038] and when the light is dim, lighter grays may appear to be dark gray or black.[134] Environmental forces may cause black to fade into gray, without notice.[304] Black is often overlooked because it takes longer to accomplish,[174] costs more money,[230] or is somewhat inconvenient or uncomfortable to perform.[215] For some tasks, black is always the same, but other times is wholly dependent upon circumstance. But the biggest challenge is that some grays, darkened over time by having worked so often, have for many, become adopted blacks.

Strive for black. Don't settle for imitations, and don't stop once you think you have found black; have it authenticated. Black is perfection. Your job is to perform black tasks. If gray is all you have to offer, then disclose—because people assume you're selling black. For best results, use black every time, because black will never return to bite you in the ass, but gray just might.

On the other hand, efficiency is the measure of time and money consumed while performing a task, relative to the time saved and money received once that task is performed. Efficiency is a function of effectiveness, and its gradation is *green*-scale.

Neither black, white, nor gray exist on the efficiency yardstick because, theoretically, a task (or series of tasks) may always be performed more or less efficiently. Really-dark green is the most-efficient a task may be performed, with infinite shades of darker green still unrealized.

Always remain on the lookout for ever-more efficient means to accomplish tasks, without sacrificing any effectiveness, as the efficiency of a task is wasted when that task is rendered ineffective. There is no point in saving time and/or money if an endeavor fails; for this reason, when developing a system, first concentrate upon creating effective elements, then continuously refine it for efficiency. 🌴

Tasks & Systems

A task is a piece of work...

- A task is a piece of work, which may be an unaccompanied, solitary motion.
- A task is a piece of work, which may be comprised of a series of tasks.
- A task is a piece of work, which may be built of multiple series' of tasks.
- A collection of tasks, synchronized to achieve a more-complex task, is a system.

A system is a series of tasks.

A Serious How-to Manual with a Sense of Humor

All Systems Go

Build a strong real estate tower, then check the other guy's work.

BY BILL THE BUILDER

THE WAY IN WHICH a series of tasks is performed, including the order, the depth, and the scope of each individually performed task, is a system.[070] Systems are in all things, but not all systems of a particular thing are created (or maintained) equally.[196]

The mechanical and electrical systems of a transportation vehicle allow a driver to traverse specific terrain. The variety of subsystems employed dictate whether that terrain be air, land, or sea. The effectiveness and efficiencies of those systems determine whether the vehicle performs modestly, zooms along swiftly, or simply sputters in place.[073]

While one may argue that a vehicle that does not move is not a vehicle at all, an agent without an apparent sales system is an agent, still (and in possession of a system). However, a loosely-structured, fly-by-the-seat-of-your-pants real estate sales system is incapable of producing as many transactions as a finely-tuned, tightly-organized one.

While an increase in transactions does not always correlate with more income, an agent with a finely-tuned system does possess the *ability* to earn more money than agents who do not, in two distinct ways. First, a finely-tuned and well-tracked system allows for the identification of bottlenecks (slow-downs in the process), and quick resolution of bottlenecks results in less effort needed to produce more transactions. And secondly, a finely-tuned system may be leveraged by the efforts of other people.[286]

All tasks may be assigned a rate of valuable pay, which is dependant upon the task's importance, and whether or not the task directly influences the generation of revenue. In this way, the performance of some tasks are worth more money per hour than others.

Armed with this knowledge, the operator of a finely-tuned system may efficiently leverage outside services, resources, and people to compliment his system. When one can track and measure every effort in pursuit of the main goal, an advantage is gained by knowing which tasks may (or should) be assigned, a fair rate to pay, and a method of track the results.

In real estate sales, only one achieved task pays money (generally speaking): the successful closing of a real estate transaction. However, the successful closing of a transaction is not a single task, but a series of performed tasks—a variable tower of tasks, which may be called the transaction tower. This transaction tower is built upon a client tower (being a series of tasks performed in acquisition of a client). When there is a co-operating agent involved in a transaction, each has built a client tower, and together the agents build a transaction tower. [Client and transaction towers are outlined on the *Buyer* and *Seller Flow Charts* of pages 344-345.]

A tower builder's competency determines the strength of his towers. Tower strength comes in the form of few, if any, tasks performed by gray means.[012] Gray tasks make a tower wobbly, because gray tasks are not guaranteed to work. Because a transaction tower is built upon the foundation of a buyer tower and a seller tower, if either base tower should crumble, so crashes the transaction tower. While a lopsided tower pays money, sadly, a fallen one does not. Therefore, since you did not build the co-operating agent's client tower, part of your system should be to inspect the sturdiness of their work. If the co-operating agent has built a wobbly client tower, its crashing will wreck your work, causing lost time, effort, and opportunity. Concentrate on building a sturdy tower, and it will be more-likely to stand until closing day.

A real estate sales business grows, stagnates, or falters based upon the effectiveness and efficiency of its systems. An ideal system operates the same way every time, allowing its operator to predict results accurately. With these maxims in-mind, this book was written in pursuit of constructing client and transaction towers with black and really dark green bricks.[012] 🌳

Real Estate is a Bag o' Hats

Headgear rotation makes for a well-rounded agent, and passing outgrown hats to helpers fosters responsible growth.

BY HARRY THE HABERDASHER

A BUSY REAL ESTATE AGENT wears multiple hats of various sizes. The trouble is that new agents have small heads, which causes their hats to slump and obstruct their view. Luckily for them, some hats are adjustable in size, but sadly, others are not. As an agent gains experience, her head will surely swell, and soon she will grow comfortable in each hat. If her real estate sales business becomes *big*, then her head will undoubtedly balloon in capacity, forcing her to pass small hats to helpers.[286] Overtime, an agent may fall in love with a particular hat so much that she rarely dons another, but the ideal agent routinely rotates (or oversees the rotation and the wearing of) perfectly-sized hats.

(fig. 0.1) REAL ESTATE SALES HATS

REAL ESTATE ACTIVITY	HAT	DESCRIPTION
talking about real estate, networking, prospecting, advocating for clients	Fedora	smooth & stylish
giving presentations & negotiating	Top Hat	puts on a quality show
signing new clients	Cowboy Hat	brazen, but in-control during round-ups
client time: showings, closings,..	Ball Cap	comfortable & sporty

ADMINISTRATIVE ROLE	HAT	DESCRIPTION
Marketing Manager	Coonskin Cap	stands-out in a crowd, but remains approachable
Database Manager	Sweatband	constant motion keeps the business fit
Rules Compliance Officer	Halo	always do the right thing
Systems Manager	Helmet	always improving structural integrity
Contract Processor	Welder's Mask	keeps eyes on the job
Comptroller	Green Eyeshade	prevents glare when counting money
Student	Mortarboard	always learning
Analyst	Safari	always hunting for facts
Annalist	Newsboy	steady & accurate record keeping
Errand Runner	Laurel Wreath	swift like the wind
Public Relations Officer	Fez	funny, but formal
Repenter	Dunce Cap	fess-up to dopey mistakes

Ethical Consideration

Are your ethical attitudes and actions a matter of personal preference or professional obligation?

BY THE JUDGE

THERE ARE A FEW ACCUSATIONS that get tossed around way too liberally these days: politicians who allege, "It's the other guy's fault;" girlfriends who exclaim, "You don't love my cat;" and real estate agents who decry, "You can't do that—*it's unethical!*"

These statements hurt, even when true. Of the three, being called unethical is the worst, stinging so badly, it can leave a scar. However, when the accused is actually behaving in an ethical manner, that sting is not only undeserved, but also grotesque.

Ethics are defined as a set of behaviors considered appropriate by a society, group, or profession of people. Each member of our society belongs to differing groups, each with its own ethical code. A family is a group. Bostonians are a group. Catholics are a group. Real estate agents are a group. Catholic, Bostonian, real estate agents, who are also in a biker gang and a knitting circle are a group. In the minds of most, the individual ethical codes of each group they belong morph into one. Therefore, it may be reasoned that the code real estate agents live by is an amalgam of their professional code and their multigroup "morphed" code.

Not all ethical codes are written down, but some are. Being such, it is not uncommon for groups to have members who have either not read, do not fully understand, or do not completely agree with the written code that governs them. The result is a cafeteria-style approach to ethics, which yields group members with very similar, yet personally-customized ethical codes. This reality begs the question: is the ethical code of a group defined by its written definition alone, or as the group commonly behaves in practice?

In the real estate sales industry, several professional organizations exist, each with a written code of ethics. The primary purpose of these ethical codes is to compliment the law, by policing its members actions, hopefully staving-off potential regulation.[036] The largest of these organizations is the National Association of REALTORS® (NAR). NAR's code is based upon The Golden Rule and was designed to act as an agent's guideline for treating all parties of a real estate transaction fairly and honestly. This description is a noble policy, the perfect ethical yardstick. In fact, it seems to be the basis for the ethical codes of all other dignified groups. Therefore, all real estate agents should consider NAR's code—whether or not they are a member.

In keeping with the spirit of fairness and honesty, before branding another with an unethical mark of shame, ask this question: is this person behaving fairly and honestly with all parties? If the answer is NO, then read NAR's code and look at the situation again. Perhaps further scrutiny will reveal some subtlety to squelch your egregious feelings. Of course, there are individuals (of nearly all groups) who purposely break the ethical code for personal gain; these code-breakers should be admonished. However, just because an agent's behavior is not customary does not automatically rule their behavior unethical.

If you don't like parts of the written code, then lobby for support to have it officially changed by consensus. Do not, in the meantime, exercise your own form of vigilante code breaking. And always remember this simple revelation: membership in NAR (or any other group) does not automatically make an agent ethical, nor does non-member status render an agent incapable of acting ethically.

It is advised that you acquire and represent clients with a ferocious style. Treat them to diligent, fiduciary care,[212] and give to all others absolute fairness and honesty; when you act ethically, these two behaviors will never conflict. And Darlin', for as long as I love you, I will also love your cat. 🌲

THE OLD LADIES

When approached with respect and dignity,
full disclosure can be a rewarding experience.

MY FIRST BROKERAGE WAS THE OLDEST in the county and, in its heyday, was one of the largest and most successful. By the time I joined, only a handful of "seasoned" agents were still actively working. Being the junior-most agent by forty years, I was automatically christened the technology director: a job of desperate need.

The brokerage itself was an old, split-level house, decorated like my grandmother's home. Floral wallpaper adorned the walls, wingback chairs graced the entry, and doilies draped tables, which added a bed of elegance to the potted, sun-bathing orchids.

Each morning, three old ladies and I would arrive early, sit in our assigned wingbacks, sip coffee, work the crossword puzzle, and chat about the "good ol' days" of real estate; I really learned bunches from those sessions.

On one such sunny morning, I settled into my seat to find my favorite hens perkish and eager to pick my brain. They had a burning question, but not one wanted to physically ask me.

"You ask him," one exclaimed, "No, you ask him," the prodded shot back. After several volleys of, "No, *you* ask him," I felt compelled to break the indecision.

"Ladies, ladies, ladies...," I murmured, tempering the vivacious vibe. "There's no reason to feel sheepish." I then watched as they bounced animated glances off each other,

as though they were negotiating without speaking. While expecting an embarrassingly-simple techie question, I was caught by surprise when one bluntly blurted-out, "What's tea-bagging?"

Stunned and sitting motionless, I couldn't believe what I was hearing. Imagine three grannies, perched on the edge of their chairs, eyes wide with childish inquiry, oblivious to the sexually-awkward question they have just posed, awaiting my enlightened response. Flabbergasted, I didn't know what to say, when suddenly I realized that we're adults, capable of discussing any topic. But first I needed to make sure I answered the question asked, otherwise the egg would be on me; so came my inquiry, "Where did you hear this terminology used?"

"On the Morning Zoo Radio Show," was their rapid response. With that, my hunch was confirmed, and so I described the act in clinical terms. They laughed like school girls (I remember someone snorting), and I was treated to giggles, sprinkled throughout the remaining day.

Those gray-haired gals taught me a valuable lesson that day: no matter how tough or awkward you think a conversation might be, it's best to embrace the situation like adults. In part, clients pay agents to be non-emotional, so speak frankly and (if necessary) in clinical terms. Who knows, you may even get a laugh from it.

TRUE STORY

This book has a philosophy.

An Agent's Dozen

Assumptions, Maxims, and Aphorisms
to keep in-mind while you read:

1 Your experience is largely
influenced by your attitude.[005]

2 The path to mastery is:
Learn, Do, Reflect, Adapt, Repeat.[009]

3 Getting your way is predicated upon
what you say, how you say it,
and to whom you say it.[008]

4 A real estate sales business grows,
stagnates, or falters based upon the
effectiveness and efficiency of its systems.[014]

5 You are the sole cause of
your success or failure.[004]

6 Real estate sales is for salesmen.[010]

7 Real estate sales requires diligent effort.[019]

8 Mind the source of information.[006]

9 Be prepared.[007]

10 Be direct with your dealings,
and (when in doubt) disclose.[017]

11 The curt answer to most questions:
that depends.[004]

12 Just because you don't like it
doesn't mean it's unethical.[016]

13 Just because it doesn't work for you
doesn't mean it doesn't work.[011]

Ten Little Agents

Not all were vertically challenged,
But in-turn, vanquished by real estate.
Read-on to see how they managed.

Ten little agents:
Promised fruit from the vine.
'Til one couldn't afford her broker,
And then there were nine.

Nine little agents
Offered a commission rebate.
'Til one went belly-up,
And then there stood eight.

Eight little agents
Attended a training session.
'Til one was bored to death,
And then there sat seven.

Seven little agents
Re-posted realty pics.
'Til one was sued for
copyright infringement,
And then there slunk six.

Six little agents
Stood in the street, spewing jive.
'Til one forgot her scripts,
And then there roved five.

Five little agents
Prospected with a knock on the door.
'Til one was answered by a gorilla,
And then there schlepped four.

Four little agents
Argued list price, and could not agree.
'Til one choked-out another,
And then there trekked three.

Three little agents:
Steadily their businesses grew.
'Til one was indicted for
mortgage fraud,
And then there traipsed two.

Two little agents
Showed houses in the sun.
'Til one received third-degree burns,
And then there wandered one.

One little agent
Just couldn't hack the skill.
So, he found full-time employment,
And now there are nil.

Real estate sales isn't for everyone; it isn't even for most people. But for some reason, it seems that everyone either already holds a license, or are thinking of getting one soon. The industry's low barrier of entry and the high profits everyone expects to earn are to blame for the resulting pool party of realty reps. However, most fail because they never realize that an agent's profits come from lots of routine prospecting, and not from knowing the basics of the business. Therefore, this should be stressed: the lessons within this chapter are meant to enhance the reader's ongoing prospecting efforts, and are not necessarily meant to be mastered beforehand.

CHAPTER ONE
BASICS

Day One in Real Estate

It doesn't take much to get your business going; the tools and skills needed to begin are the exact same used to keep it going.

BY CARMEN THE COACH

YOUR JOB IS TO TALK, *talk*, TALK about real estate. Whether you're working for yourself (prospecting)[077] or for your clients (agency),[211] your job is mostly talking. So, on day one and every day thereafter, talk to people about real estate.[084]

Woefully, many new agents fall into the trappings of getting ready to get ready. This occurs when an agent declares she will begin talking to people about becoming clients (prospecting) once her professional pictures are delivered, then once her business cards arrive, then once her website is constructed, then once her yard signs are ordered, then once her scripts are absolutely perfect,[048] then once her car is cleaned, then once her...

Don't be afraid to begin! Jump right in, and become a real estate chatterbox. Call everyone you know and tell them you are now a *real estate agent;* ask if they know of anyone looking to buy or sell real property.[108] Call agents at your brokerage; ask if they have any clients they would like to refer to you.[112] Call For Sale by Owners (FSBO); ask them to hire you.[101]

You only have to open your mouth and speak about real estate. In the beginning, you're gonna say some dumb things, and at times you'll be caught flat-footed. But, don't let these errors scare you to the sidelines.[057] The only way to become comfortable with real estate work is to work at real estate things. You're always gonna make mistakes. However, as you grow, the more often you Think→Do→Track→Repeat, your goofs will occur less frequently.[009]

The best part is that you already have the basic, stripped-down tools needed to practice real estate sales: a telephone, internet access, mouth and ears, and good ol' determination; everything else is just fluff. In reality, you don't need a website nor business cards nor a fancy car. You only need to communicate with people about real estate, asking them to hire you. Once you embrace this simple tenant of real estate sales, you will have a job—*every single day of the week*—for as many hours as you are willing to work.

Your business day should be split into two parts: working for yourself and working for clients; never work at both at the same time. When working for clients, make them your priority, above all self-interest. Any time you're not working for clients, you are free to work for yourself. When you don't have any clients, all day is for you.[078]

Working for yourself (YOU, INC.) has two departments: Prospecting & Administration. Administrative duties may be outsourced,[286] but prospecting may not, and for prospecting, you must do a ton of talking.[086]

Saying the right things, the right way, at the right times, to the right people are what separate an all-star agent from the average.[034] You cannot become an all-star without practice and experience, so start talking today. Nonetheless, most prospects will not hire an agent after the initial contact anyway, so it's imperative you begin the conversation now.[090]

Go talk to people about hiring you. Once you secure an appointment to sign-up a new client, there are gobs of people willing to help with your presentation,[167] and to guide you through the transaction.[221] However, *you* must get the appointment, because no one else will do that part for you.[004]

So, don't delay; act today and each day thereafter. Get into the groove of the *Daily Flow Chart*,[346] and don't stop until you're ready to quit the business. Spread the word that you're open for hire and keep the chatter alive. After all, the difference between a working agent and a mere licensee is a client (or three). 🌳

9 ways To get in The Game

1 Get a Team
Find a group of like-minded agents. Go along when they're doing real estate activities, and ask lots of questions.

2 Office Time
Work from the office; it will get you in the mood. You'll meet agents and vendors, and perhaps some walk-in traffic.

3 Get a Coach
A good coach will help you develop a plan to achieve your goals, and then hold you accountable to those goals.[043]

4 Open House
Clean-up by hosting open houses for other agents. Add to your database,[089] convert buyers,[088] and get it sold.[240]

5 Answer Phones
Volunteer for brokerage desk-duty, or ask a busy agent if you may field their in-bound calls.

6 Get Rejected
If you're not getting rejected every day, then you're not doing it right.[056]

7 Business Plan
It's much easier to get into the game once you have a game plan in place.[062]

8 Learn More
When new, get all state-mandated education requirements completed sooner, rather than later, then keep learning.[061]

9 Get a Client
Once you snag a client, plenty of people are available to help you run the bases and bring ' em home!

A Serious How-to Manual with a Sense of Humor

Effort Meter

You're Gonna Need:

Humility
Introspection
Sobriety
Sense of Humor

tips
It's okay to suck at real estate sales when you're new, but you shouldn't stay that way for long.[034]

Due to its breadth and scope, there will always be *some aspect* of real estate sales at which you suck.

This book alone will not cure your suck; consider it one of many sources you consult.[038]

Some real estate tasks will come easy for you, and others will test your mettle.

Sucking at your job may be tough to admit, but once you acknowledge your skill level, you can do something about it.

caveats
Relax: the insensitive words of this article are meant to grab your attention, and not to call you names, you big *crybaby*.

Osmosis, smoshmosis. Placing this book under your pillow while you sleep will only cause a kink in your neck. However, carrying this book under your arm in public will definitely make you look cool.

Σ Be honest with yourself regarding your current skill level, then go and do something about it.

How-to
Know if You Suck at Real Estate Sales

The first few times you tried to tie your shoes you sucked hard, because tying shoes requires dexterity of digits. When you were learning to swim you sucked water, because swimming requires calmness and fluid motion. Your first attempts at baking soufflé you sucked it up royally, because well-made soufflé requires the meticulous measurement of multiple ingredients, the careful combination of those ingredients, precise heat, and timing.

For certain tasks, you will find that mastery comes quickly, while other tasks take time, practice, patience, and outside help. As a singular task, real estate sales is the latter. Due to its range of topics (valuation, agency, contracts, negotiation, marketing,..), and the sheer volume of tasks that comprise each topic, achieving real estate sales competency can be quite challenging.

Just as learning to serve a perfect soufflé depends upon its chef, the time it takes to go from zero-to-competent will vary from agent to agent. Before chasing real estate mastery, it helps to find-out exactly where you stand:

1 Contemplate Your Experiences
Plenty of real estate license holders suck at real estate sales. To know if you are amongst their ranks, answer the following questions (each YES answer ratchets-up your level of suck):
- Do you show property without first pre-qualifying buyers? [170]
- Do you struggle at asking buyers to sign agency agreements? [186]
  - Do you work with non-signers, anyway? [184]
- Is every listing appointment a new experience? [196]
  - Do you lack consistent presentation? [177]
- Do you defer to co-operating agents for guidance on negotiations and/or contract formation? [266]
- Do you become tongue-tied when prospects, clients, and/ or co-operating agents disagree with you? [052]
- Do most of your listings stay on the market for longer (or *much longer*) than the average? [154]
- Do more than twenty percent of your listings expire? [152]

2 Acknowledge Your Skill Level
Acknowledgement is job one in curing any sucky situation. So, don't fret; this book will help you bunches, so read the whole thing. Then read it again. Follow the flow charts every working day,[346] and then analyze your results. Seek additional resources,[179] education,[061] and tutelage.[044] Keep to a rigorous schedule,[064] until you can answer all STEP 1 questions with a resounding NO.

How-to
Look Like a
Real Estate Agent

The best way for you to let the observant world know of your chosen profession—*without saying a word*—is to look the part. Some would say that the appearance of knowledge is nearly as important as the possession of knowledge itself. To those ends, if you don't look like a real estate agent, then you are likely to be perceived as not being a real estate agent. Which begs the question: *what does a real estate agent look like?* Dress-up the following areas of your business and you are sure to be noticed:

1 Physical Appearance

Unless it's already your thing, there is no need to wear a loud sports jacket or tons of jewelry, as are the now-dated stereotypes. Consider that your look speaks for you before you mutter a single word. Then, realize that a professional look commands respect.

Your on-the-job wardrobe should mirror the type of clientele you wish to attract. If you wish for professional clients, then wear a suit. If instead, you aspire to become the sole representative to the *We're No Angels Motorcycle Crew*, then wear a leather jacket with motorcycle patches and matching chaps. For most agents, the fashionable sweet-spot for optimal real estate mojo lies somewhere between these two extremes.

The real estate sales, physical-appearance sweet-spot:

- Wear clothing that fits and is age-appropriate.
- Wear clean clothing and nice shoes, in well-repair.
- Shower, comb your hair, and clean your fingernails.
- Be scent-free. Doused, splashed, or even spritzed in your favorite scent could cost you business because the smell that makes you smile may turn-off another. Some people are allergic to, or become nauseated by perfumes, so leave the adorning aroma for off-hours. The same goes for smelling like onion, garlic, and/or cigarette smoke.

2 Voicemail Message

Your voicemail needs to mention your position in real estate, otherwise callers may think they've reached a wrong number. If a buyer calls your phone, and your message is a generic, automaton message from your cell phone carrier, the caller may quickly hang up. So, create a voicemail message that incites the caller to leave a response. Try a fun voicemail recording; like this:

Hi. You've reached Agent Andy, real estate agent on a rampage. Leave a message. I'd love to hear your voice.

Effort Meter

You're Gonna Need:
Careful Consideration
Creativity
Mirror
Sagacity

tips
Always consider state regulations when creating your look. There may be restrictions on how you construct business cards and/or voicemail messages.

Consider anointing yourself with a title deserving of your position, but be careful to not overstate your abilities. Fun examples include:
Real Estate Guru
House Hawker
Real Estate Evangelist
Merchant de Mansions
Dream Home Maker
Domicile Dealer
Condo Queen

caveat
Don't try to look like someone you are not. But then again, don't look like the beach bum you actually are, either. If you question your ability to recognize appropriate business attire, consider hiring professional help.

Σ   Put some effort into portraying the person your audience expects to see.

Continued

Consider Live Voicemail: change your outgoing message each morning to reflect your on-going business. This method will demonstrate to callers that you are actually working today. Try something like this:

Hiya! Agent Andy here. Today is Tuesday, April the 11th, and I'm out, busting my hump on behalf of my clients. Because I am in and out of meetings all day long, I will be returning calls today between noon and 2PM, then again after 4PM. Leave a message, and I'll talk to you soon!

3 Email Signature

Your email signature should suggest your position as a real estate agent and should adorn each and every email you send, whether addressed to your clients or to your pet groomer.

Consider the following bits, stacked in logical order for quick intake:

Name
Title
Phone number
Email address
Website URL
Tagline or single-line blurb about your service.

Example:

Agent Andy
Real Estate Renegade
123 - 456 - 7890
Andy@email
www.AgentAndy's website
The guy who makes it happen!

You may also include links to specific listings,[236] to subscribe to your newsletter,[095] or to some other special message. Be creative and memorable, but do not over-crowd the space; there is a fine line between eye-catching display and vainglorious spectacle.

4 Business Cards

Aside from all the normal (and legally-required) markings, your business card should include a picture of you. To ensure this picture actually looks like you, choose one from this decade. For best results, adopt a photo no older than one or two years. Studies show (informal inquires/experiences) that business cards without pictures belong to people who are not remembered. Other studies (real, scientific ones) show that most people have difficulty throwing away a photograph.

Knowing these things, imagine a prospect sorting through her purse, tossing old receipts, unpaid parking tickets, and superfluous business cards. Happening upon your card, will she recall meeting you, and the charming conversation you shared? At this moment, your toothy grin stands a better chance of jogging her memory than any elegant typeface or cheesy catchphrase ever will. Her recollection of you may earn your business card a place of prominence—sandwiched somewhere between her voter registration and favorite gift cards.

5 Name Badge

Contemporary versions come with a strong magnetic clasp that prevent holes in clothing and pricks to fingers. When worn with consideration, the name badge may garnish you more than the occasional real estate-related conversation. Try these tricks:

- Wear it as often as possible: when shopping, volunteering, jogging.
- Wear it on the right side so that it remains visible when shaking hands.
- Wear it upside-down to attract attention. This phoney faux pas will cause strangers to point-out your apparent mistake, sparking a "candid" conversation about real estate.

6 Designations & Certifications

Real estate designations and certifications are awarded to agents for focused study in a particular discipline, including advanced understanding of buyers, sellers, senior living, valuation, property management, negotiation, distressed properties, technology, niche markets, and building materials. When utilized properly, designations may enhance your professional look. Proudly place (no more than two) designations behind your name on business cards, marketing materials, and email signature.

Beware: displaying too many designations at the same time looks like a confusing bowl of alphabet soup. Pick your favorite one or two for exhibition, and leave the rest on your resume. If you feel left-out, bereft of professional designation, then go earn one (or more). Otherwise, consider creating a personalized designation of your own. Possibilities include:

- PGD for Pretty Groovy Dude
- RAL for Rather Astute Lady
- DFA for Damn Fine Agent

7 Car Emblements

The ultimate flourish to garner attention is to splash your vocation all over your automobile. Adorning your car with the markings of a real estate agent may help others identify you. Several choices await your consideration, from the subtle to the audacious:

- *Front-of-Car License Plate*—Can be a handy conversation starter at the gas pump.
- *Bumper Stickers*—Give tailgaters something to read, like:
  FOLLOW ME TO YOUR NEXT REAL ESTATE CLOSING —OR—
  I'D RATHER BE PROSPECTING FOR REAL ESTATE GOLD
- *Fully Wrapped Vehicle*—Be sure to follow state and broker rules regarding marketing display, otherwise you may have to pay for another, compliant wrap job. Also, be careful to convey a real estate vibe, and not one of pizza delivery.

Best practice is to avoid any car emblements that promote a controversial cause or political candidate (unless doing so will attract the express niche you wish to pursue). So, be warned: displaying a stand for or against one group or another will certainly limit your prospect pool.

How-to Wear a Name Badge

Left Side NAME

NAME *Correct Side*

NAME *Clever Side*

caveat

Some will label an agent wearing an upside-down name badge as doofus. If you brave this tactic anyway, then do so mindfully; it wears thin on the people you see regularly.

Effort Meter

You're Gonna Need:
Research
Contemplation
Foresight
Word of Mouth

tips
Before choosing a brokerage, speak with several of its agents. Ask for their personal pros and cons list (all agents have a list).

When you carefully compare several brokerages, you are likely to find one that charges a fair commission split *and* fits your needs too.

When recruiters call, talk to them and explore your options. If you can earn an additional $10,000 per year by switching brokers, then you should at least hear the guy out.

A brokerage should be a two-way street, whereby the agent and the brokerage both benefit by being in business together.

Your clients don't really care about the brand with which you affiliate. They mostly care about what you can do for them.[091]

As soon as you choose a broker, get into the swing of prospecting.[346]

Review all policy manuals and carefully read the independent contractor agreement (ICA) prior to signing with a broker.

Σ   A *one-size-fits-all* brokerage does not exist, so find one that fits you, and you will be happier, healthier, and wealthier for it.

How-to
Choose a Broker

Each brokerage has its own culture and rules regarding its licensees' behaviors. Just because your friend hangs his license there does not automatically make it the best fit for you, too. The only way to know if a particular broker is right for you is to check-out several and compare. When choosing, you should ask:

1 What's in It for Me?
What services are offered? What kind of support is offered? Where is the office? How often must I come into the office? Are sales meetings mandatory? If so, are they worthy of attendance? What technology is offered? Is floor duty required? How are referrals doled-out? What do referrals cost? What type of system does the brokerage have for documentation and contract compliance? Are these systems simple to learn and use?

2 What's in It for Them?
It only makes sense that the brokerage stands to profit from its agents. While you shouldn't choose based upon fees and commission splits alone, remuneration is an important aspect of the broker you affiliate. Ask: what are the commission splits? Referral splits? Bonus splits? Broker price opinion (BPO) splits?

3 What's the Training Like?
Are there mentorship programs? If so, what do they entail? Are continuing education classes offered? If so, what is the cost? Are there sales meetings? If so, how often? What topics are discussed? Are training classes specifically designed to update agents on current market conditions?.. on how to best protect clients?.. on how to make money?.. or is the training mostly vendor-sponsored infomercials (fluff training)?

4 What's the Structure?
Traditional, independent, blended, transaction, discount, new construction, and holding/referral are the most-popular brokerage structures. While each of these types are different, two brokerages that share a structure can be vastly different too. Learn of each structure. Don't pick based upon cost alone. Some structures are designed to be a loose structure within which you may build your business. Others are meant to limit your activities. Each have their merits and each have their restrictions (for details, see *Brokerage Models* on the facing page).

5 What's the Culture Like?
Culture is an often over-looked but important aspect of the right brokerage. You should be around people who are good for you. Choose one that is busy and networks together often. Choose one that follows the rules. Choose one that shares your ideal of professionalism.

6 Does the Broker Compete?

A competing broker is one who runs the shop and also represents his own clients. Many smaller brokerages operate this way, and their agents are happily supported. However, a competing broker may be fishing your best leads from the in-bound buyer calls of your listings, and/or he may not be concerned with growing his agents' businesses. Competing brokers are great, so long as you know what you're getting. New agents need a broker who will inform, educate, and consult; when considering a competing broker, ask detailed questions about the management of your needs.

7 What are the Expenses?

Signs, lock boxes, MLS fees, and errors & omissions insurance are common expenses of agents. While it's typically cheaper to purchase your own equipment and services than it is to receive them in exchange for a high commission split, some brokers offer discounts to agents by means of bulk service purchase. Brokers provide nothing for free; you will always pay for it somehow.[282]

8 What are the ICA details?

Before an agent and broker may collude, they must first make an agreement that regulates their relationship. Comprised of all aspects of your affiliation with a broker, this independent contractor agreement (ICA) is negotiable. However, your leverage to negotiate is heavily weighted in your demonstrated ability to make money (for your broker). The more robust your recent sales activity, the more bargaining power you will have. Regardless, strive to structure an agreement that suits the ideals of your business.

Agents with influence will always have added leverage when negotiating an ICA, because wherever they hang their license, others are sure to follow. Those without clout may consider banding together with other agents, negotiating together. While this strategy is not-likely welcomed by most brokers, there is strength in numbers.

Strive for an ICA that is fair to both the agent and broker. Consider your needs and what you have to offer, then contrast that with what the broker offers. When the two are in harmony, you've found your real estate home.

Brokerage Models

There are as many variations of brokerage models as there are brokerages themselves. The following are generalities:

Traditional Broker provides tools and services to agents, such as a desk, some business cards, a website, lock boxes, yard signs, print/web advertising, and training. In turn, agents pay a high commission split to the brokerage.

Independent Broker provides no tools or services to agents. In turn, agents pay a monthly fee, plus a small commission split to the brokerage.

Blended As a blend of traditional and independent models, the broker charges a monthly fee and a high commission split, until an annual commission cap is reached.

Transaction Agents pay a fixed transaction fee (not a percentage) on sales, regardless of sales price. A transaction *brokerage* is not to be confused with a transaction *broker* (nor the transaction broker's representative: the transaction *agent*).[289]

Discount Operated like a big sales team, the broker charges sellers a flat fee commission at the time of listing. Most of the brokerage's agents field and flip incoming buyer calls that are generated by all the listings.

Builder The builder is the broker, providing all the listings and every service/tool needed. Often times, the agents split commissions with each other, regardless of who was working at the time a buyer walked-in.

Referral/Holding Agents are not permitted to represent clients, and may only earn commissions by sending referrals to agents of other brokerages.

1 Box
Get one large enough to hold everything on this page. Glue some Velcro to its bottom to prevent trunk sliding.

2 Map Book
GPS can fail. A map may help you find your way or identify a short-cut to the next location. Extra points if you learn to read it. Guaranteed to help you outta jams.

3 Common Forms
Keep blank copies of real estate forms for impromptu presentations or emergencies. Don't be caught ill-prepared if technology should fail you in the field (it happens).

6 Plastic Bag
You don't wanna toss muddy boots into a clean car. Stash several grocery-style bags or the thick, tough kind. You'll be glad you did!

7 Flashlight
For showings after dark, when electricity is off, bulbs are out, or exploring dark spaces like attics and crawl spaces. Great any time light needs to be shed on the subject.

8 Batteries
Always keep spare batteries on-hand for that trusty flashlight, cell phone, tablet, and laptop. Power on so you can power on.

9 Umbrella
Even if you brave the elements like a man, having an umbrella on hand is sure to impress clients when the time is right.

10 Water
Stay hydrated! Pack several bottles to refresh yourself and your clients. They'll love you for it (especially on hot days). Good for your skin. Good for your wallet.

11 Food
Keep crackers, chocolate, granola, and/or energy bars on-hand. There will be days when you and client will need a boost to keep on truckin' towards that last showing of the day.

4 Boots
Sturdy footwear is needed when walking property. If you regularly wear dressy shoes, boots in the trunk are a hedge against inclement weather and muddy acreage.

5 Socks
Clean socks may be needed for the boots, or for a refreshing change when the urge strikes. Extra points for argyle or lobster print.

12 Crayons & Books

When needed, this tool is an awesome distraction for children. Consider adding toys, books, playing cards, stuffed animals,... Keep in mind that not all kids are young.

13 Tape Measure

Buyers like to measure everything, but they never seem to have a yardstick handy. Be their agent-on-the-spot, and you're sure to receive more than a smile in return.

14 Chair

Waiting for someone to arrive on the scene, but sitting in your car proves too hot? Not a problem when you've packed a pop-up chair for such occasions. Also great at vacant open houses.

15 Golf Clubs

Perfect for those beautiful days when you wanna blow-off work and hit the links. Don't worry about your broker finding out—you'll probably see him at the clubhouse.

To be prepared when on the go,

Survival Kit

into your auto, these bits you'll throw.

A Serious How-to Manual with a Sense of Humor

Effort Meter

You're Gonna Need:
Curiosity
Internet Connection
Questions
Study Aids

How-to
Speak the Lingo

Real estate lingo can be broken into three primary categories: sales, finance, and construction. Becoming fluent in each category will make you sound like you know what you're talking about. Begin by reading online dictionaries. Cross-referencing as you go, take notes and form questions.[038] Next, take to the field, asking questions and enunciating your words. From your findings, create your own lingo list. Then publish that list on your website, so clients will be able to translate your seemingly babble-filled conversations.

1 Sales
By now, everyone should know that real estate agents speak in code when advertising their listings. Cozy means small, fixer-upper means tear-down, and rustic means no air conditioner. Stereotypical mockery aside, there exists an entire lexicon of language a good agent knows.

Say things like:
Comps, sweat equity, easement, quit-claim, assemblage, market value, parachuting agent, co-op, absorption report, over-priced, conformed contract, and listing syndication.

2 Finance
Learn to speak the jargon of finance and mortgages, and you'll have a better understanding of the topic. Plus, your newfound vocabulary will make for smoother conversations with loan officers and clients alike.

Say things like:
Points, seasoned money, conforming status, locked-in, balloon, amortization, title insurance, LTV, PITI, HELOC, GFE, ARM, PMI & MIP, acceleration clause, pre-qualified, and pre-approved.

3 Construction
Many construction items have multiple terms. Learn them for fruitful discussions with inspectors, builders, contractors, prospects, clients, and other agents. You *must* know the words associated with the product you're selling.[032]

Say things like:
Soffit, fascia board, GFCI, polybutylene, masonite, drip edge, comfort-height, bull nose, R-value, foundation drain, expansion tank, ridge vent, flashing, p-trap, drain field, parquet floor, dentil molding, wainscotting, architectural shingles, and weep holes.

Be On the Lookout
Some people will speak the lingo perfectly, but not understand what they are actually saying. When faced with one of these types, be patient and seek to clarify conversations with a quick recap before parting company. One of these days, you'll be glad you did.

tips
Work in the field will provide many more terms than the best dictionary.

Realty is a two-syllable word; don't add a third.

Never assume terms; always find the correct answer.[006]

If you don't know the words on this page, then now is a good time to go look them up.

When showing or marketing property, refrain from saying *good size*. Instead, say things like, spacious closet, glorious bedroom, and grandiose living room. Save *good size* for candy bars and lap dogs.

Speaking the lingo will make you *seem* more competent than the average agent (and you should take that from wherever you can get it).

caveats
Acronyms abound;[340] don't just toss them around willy-nilly. Be sure clients understand what they mean.

Some things may be described by more than one term—learn them each.

Σ   Speaking the language of real estate promotes enhanced communication.

How-to
Be a Real Estate Buffoon

Real estate buffoons abound and many are quick to join their ranks. Buffoons do whatever they want, whenever they want, around anyone they want to, but there are two problems with being a buffoon: they wear thin their welcome with nearly everyone they work and they jeopardize the well-being of clients. "No big deal," thinks the buffoon, "I'll meet someone new tomorrow."

Effort Meter

1 Wear-Out Your Welcome
Because those around you don't really matter:
- Arrive late to most/all meetings.
- Display an air of pomposity (by using words like pomposity).[008]
- Repeatedly check your phone/email/social media/wrist watch whenever you're speaking face-to-face with people.
- Let your phone ring loudly, especially when in meetings.
- Wait a day or two before returning calls (or never at all).
- Don't bother prospecting when you're outta clients.[078] Instead, complain to fellow agents: *My phone isn't ringing!* Buffoons love to huddle in misery.
- Dismiss recruiting brokers as enemy jerks. How dare they attempt to grow their businesses? [028]
- Tell the fake-buyer lie to FSBO as an excuse to meet.[101]

2 Jeopardize the Well-Being of Clients
Because clients just don't understand:
- Always blame the other guy because it's never your fault.[004]
- State everything as fact, even when you're unsure. You don't wanna look stupid.[038]
- Mirror all of your clients' emotions to co-operating agents. They should feel your pain, too. Besides, you always make rational decisions when on tilt.[310]
- Pricing strategy discussions with clients can be challenging.[154] Instead, list their property at whatever crazy price they want.[212] After all, you can *use them* (their listing) *as bait* to maybe lure some buyers your way.[190]
- Once your listing goes under contract to close, deny any future interest from subsequent buyers. Don't allow them showings. Those idiots may want to submit a backup offer.[274]
- Disclose way more information about your clients than required.[180] Don't worry, it'll never be used to negotiate against them.[266]
- Assume co-operating agents are working on behalf of your client, too. You shouldn't be the only one responsible.[212]
- Insist upon unnecessary contract stipulations in your client's purchase & sale contracts; you've gotta justify your fee somehow.
- Breathe commission breath on everyone you meet.[191]

Be a Great Real Estate Agent

Don't stop short of becoming great at your job; you owe it to yourself, to your family, and to your clients.

BY YOUR GUIDANCE COUNSELOR

JUST LIKE MOST PEOPLE attempting a complicated task, the majority of real estate agents are just average at their job. While having average skill is okay for things like cooking dinner, throwing a football, or driving a car, one should set their skill-possession sights a bit higher when it comes to selling real estate.

A low barrier of entry, coupled with seemingly high profits, causes a constant flood of new licensees into the real estate sales industry. Their independent contractor status, coupled with limited brokerage training and oversight, influence those licensees to remain (on average) not good. Therefore, being a conscientious person of average intelligence is enough for a new agent to begin their real estate career somewhere in the average skill zone.

While it is likely that you will begin your real estate career as average, you should quickly and diligently move towards the good and great zones. Your rapid advance is important because your real estate skill level doesn't only affect your outcomes, but also the outcomes of your clients. Therefore, settling for average agent status is both reckless and irresponsible.

Besides, going from average to good skill status isn't that difficult to achieve, and can be had by most in less than a year.[303] Going from good to great, on the other hand, requires a few years of ongoing, fastidious effort.

To make a quick transition from average to good, simply adopt the actions and routines of great agents.[068] Behave like those you wish to become, and becoming like them will be a natural process. While doing so, keep in mind that a great agent is a problem solver who anticipates her clients needs and prepares for them.[245] She knows the correct answers to most questions, and knows how to get the correct answers to questions she doesn't know.[038] She's an awesome advocate for her clients and she embraces her fiduciary responsibility;[212] she has a network of professional experts to aid her clients efforts;[179] she's innovative and always keeps learning.[061]

In other words, to achieve good agent status, you must learn, learn, learn and keep on learning. At the same time, you must be constantly engaged in the practice of real estate sales.[346] Learning, then putting that learning to practice, will result in accumulated experience. Contemplation of results, then refinement of systems will nudge you even closer to great status. Define and practice within a niche,[042] find a mentor,[044] and hire a coach.[043] Now you're on the fast track to greatness.

The sad thing is that many people are remiss to acknowledge, let alone value, the elite status of a great agent. Instead, they tend to think agents are all the same, and hire the one they most liken to themselves (the same way we tend to elect Presidents and choose Hollywood favorites). Another sad thing is that these people don't realize just how dangerous their decision to hire an average agent may be. Elevate your skill status, and help them to understand their risk; demonstrate to prospects the differences between your service and the service of average agents.[172]

Of course, achieving great-agent status and being capable of superior service does not automatically correlate with making more money than the average, as the two are mutually exclusive. However, reaching such status does make for an ability to offer superior service, by which an agent may charge a premium, or simply conduct (way) more transactions. 🌳

The differences between a good agent from a great one may seem subtle, but within this subtlety resides the kind of service that makes clients *rave*.

DIFFERENTIATION OF SERVICES

AVERAGE AGENT	GOOD AGENT	GREAT AGENT
can help clients draft offers	helps clients develop offer strategies	prepares CMA as part of offer strategy
notifies clients when something needs doing	helps clients prepare for each step of sales process	has foolproof systems in-place, ensuring all clients are prepared
fills-in the blanks on forms and contracts	reads forms and contracts	understands the details and inner workings of forms and contracts
thinks customs and laws are the same thing	knows the customs and plays along	understands customs and willingly breaks them when it's in the client's best interest
does whatever the next agent does	applies innovate practice and current technology	is an innovator, who applies technology appropriately
rides the real estate roller coaster [120]	routinely prospects for new clients	routinely practices scripts before prospecting, and tracks results
reacts to events as they happen	responds to feedback and alters systems	responds to feedback as part of tracking all real estate activities, then alters systems accordingly

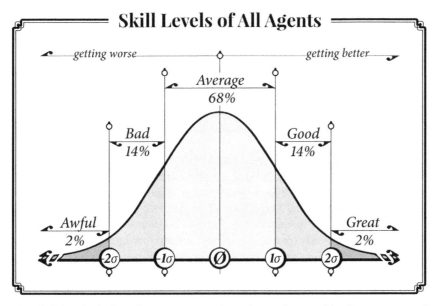

The skill level of all real estate agents (100%) may be graphically represented by the normal distribution of a bell curve. When the absolute average agent represents the mean (Ø), all average agents (68%) plot within one standard deviation (σ) of that mean agent. The farther an agent plots from the mean, the better or worse that agent becomes.

Effort Meter

You're Gonna Need:

Time

Research Skills

Reading Glasses

Lots of Conversations

How-to
Learn the Rules
of Real Estate Sales

Because there are lots of real estate rules, which come from several different sources, one may easily become overwhelmed. When trying to learn these rules, a logical question emerges: *When will I know that I've found them all?*

Start by parsing the rules into three categories: laws/regulations, ethical standards, and customary practices. Next, adopt a strategy to systematically discover each and every rule that binds you. Seek these rules, learn these rules, and play by these rules, and your real estate life will become less frustrating.

1 Laws and Regulations

Each state has different laws, which are divided into two categories:

    1. Legislative laws (also called code): written laws by the State Legislature or the United States Congress

    2. Regulations: written rules by the state's real estate regulatory body (usually called Commission or Board) or by federal regulatory bodies

tips

You can read the laws and ethical standards. Everything else is customary practice. Easy!

Print your state's laws and regulations and carry them with you. Consult this booklet whenever a question arises.

Write a few rules on an index card, and carry it in your pocket. Every now and then, pull the card out and quiz yourself on the rules.

Become familiar with your state regulatory body's website. Check it frequently for updates and proposed changes to laws and regulations.

There are many different regulations and laws that guide your practice. Be sure to seek-out each and every one, and strive to understand each and every one. Then, put systems in-place to become aware of updates.

Local regulations and ordinances may also affect your real estate practice. Seek-out your chamber of commerce, and consult your broker for localized rules.

Don't forget that your actions are also governed by your ICA and brokerage policies.[028]

Always play by the rules.

All laws and regulations are written and are easily accessed, found either online or through the state regulatory body. Best practice is to print these laws and regulations and read them over and over again to become as familiar as possible. It is not necessary to memorize every detail of the law, but you should have a really good understanding of it. Know how to find a specific code when you have doubts or questions.

Reading laws and regulations may seem dry and boring, but it's as necessary to your job as prospecting for clients and delivering outstanding listing presentations.

2 Ethical Standards

Ethical standards are often written by a group to govern its members actions where laws and regulations fall short. In real estate, the National Association of REALTORS® (NAR) has written an ethical code for its members to follow. This code is the ethical standard for the entire real estate sales industry, not just for NAR members. Therefore, if an agent is not breaking any laws and is following the rules of this ethical code, that agent is acting in an ethical manner.

Sadly, the declaration, "That's unethical," is often flung around by real estate agents like monkey poo at the zoo. Just because someone acts in a manner that you don't agree does not mean that this someone is acting unethically.[016]

Whether or not you are a member of NAR, you should be extremely familiar with their ethical code so that you may abide by it; there are classes designed for this exact purpose. Attend these sessions and actively participate in the conversation.

3 Customary Practices

Customs are nothing more than habitual practices that are passed from one generation to the next. They have nothing to do with the law or ethical standards, but if you break custom, you may be met with resistance by fellow agents. Their brush-back is due to the fact that many customary practices are considered the polite way of practice and also because customs are often confused with the ethical standard.

Of the three types of real estate rules, customs are the most susceptible to change. As well, customs tend to be greatly swayed by region or locale. Societal customs may be the currently-accepted length of ladies hem lines, the wearing or not wearing of hats, and/or the shaking of hands versus the giving of hugs. Typical real estate customs may include the leaving of businesses cards on kitchen counters, earnest money,[255] and the treating of buyers like clients, without first signing agency agreements.[184]

Customs can be a source of frustration for the agent who does not understand them. This book often breaks from customary practice (which is one way that it is politically incorrect). However, this book does not encourage agents to blindly break, nor to blindly follow customary practices; rather, it encourages you to acknowledge what they are, why they are, and to determine whether or not they are the best practice.[038]

Breaking with custom may be met with a high five, a scowl, or becoming quickly black-balled by the local agent community. Therefore, before breaking custom, you should carefully weigh the benefits it brings to you and your clients versus the potential stalwarts you may encounter, and the difficulties these roadblocks may bring to you and your clients. After all, you cannot practice real estate sales in a vacuum.

caveats

Ignorance is not an excuse for not knowing the rules regarding your profession and practice.

When it comes to the rules of real estate, don't just take another's word for it. Find out for yourself. Be certain; your license (livelihood) is on the line.

Carefully read the ethical code, then compare it to the customary practices in your local market. Do noticeable contradictions exist? Which standard will you follow?

Some customary practices of real estate sales may be in direct violation of the law or ethical standards; beware of these rouge customs.

Don't blindly break from customary practice, as it may lead to difficulty in representing your clients.

Don't forget about federal regulatory bodies that oversee your actions or the actions of your clients, like the EPA or FHA, and fair housing laws. Consult your broker and/or your state's real estate commission for a full list.

Σ Your reputation for knowing the rules is what separates you from the buffoons of real estate.[033]

Customs remain neither laws nor regulations.
So they may change, but be this noted:
Variations may lead to confrontations.
'Cause to custom adhesion,
     most are devoted.

3 Common Customs

1. Buyer's agents draft purchase agreements.[261]
2. Sellers pay commissions for both agents.[262]
3. Buyers post earnest money.[255]

Effort Meter

You're Gonna Need:

Questions
Resourcefulness
Quick Reflection
Answer Database

tips

A single person cannot be an expert on every subject related to real estate sales. However, a single person may become an expert at finding the correct answers to their questions.

Consult more than one subject-matter expert, because there may be a disagreement amongst experts (or near-experts) on what constitutes best practice. Or perhaps, the explanation of best practice may differ from one expert to the next. If nothing else, by consulting with multiple experts, you will gain a better understanding of best practice.

Some of the stuff on these pages may seem to be self-evident and overly-simplistic. However, real estate brokers will tell you that many agents blindly ask questions that should be directed elsewhere. Therefore, this basic tenet bears repeating: think before you speak, then bother the appropriate person with your question. When you ask someone with imperfect information, you will likely get an imperfect answer.

Best practice is defined as any generally-accepted method deemed superior to any alternatives because it produces results superior to those achieved by other means.

How–to
Get *the Correct* Answers to Your Questions

Acquiring the correct answers to your questions is essential to a job well-done. Follow these tips so your clients may smile all the way to the closing table:

1 Determine Question Category

Whenever you have a question, pause and consider the following:
- What kind of question is this?
  - Real estate specific? If so, of which type, *specifically*?
    - General knowledge?
    - Construction related?
    - Mortgage related?
- May I answer this question on my own?
- Should I research the answer first, before asking someone?
- What tools should I use to conduct my research?
- Should I consult written law and/or regulations? [036]
- Might I find the answer on the internet?
- Who is a subject-matter expert? [179]

2 Consult a Subject–Matter Expert

...not necessarily the agent in the next cubicle. Your fellow agent may be knowledgeable, but he cannot know everything, nor every specific detail that you may need to know about a given topic.
- Got a mortgage-related question? Ask a loan officer.
- Legal quandary? Consult the written law or your state's real estate regulations, or ask a lawyer (but choose carefully).
- Administrative question about your brokerage? Address the administrative person at your brokerage.
- Wanna know how late a store stays open tonight? Call the store.
- Wanna know how much money a repair will cost? Call a handyman or the appropriate contractor.
- Have a general knowledge question? Consult your favorite search engine (but mind the source of your new-found information).[006]
- Have an agency question? Ask your broker or mentor.[044]
- Need details about the a particular home owner's association (HOA)? Call directly upon the HOA manager.

3 Utilize Best Practice

Best practice is the method a subject-matter expert would follow. Write down the best practice method, and then adopt that method into your systems. Sometimes best practice may change; therefore, when learning best practice, ask the expert if best practice has evolved into what it is now, and if they foresee it changing in the future. So that you don't have to ask the same question again, ask for the resource of their answer. Build a database of answers and their sources, so that you may consult this database in the future.

4 Don't Blindly Follow Advice

It is your duty to your brokerage, to your clients, and to yourself to understand the practice of real estate sales. This means you should know the reasons behind the actions you take. Beware of taking advice without understanding the foundations on which it is based, especially when the subject is complicated; doing so may result in future mistakes. Always ask: *Why is it done this way?* Then, keep asking until the lesson is clear.

5 Avoid Asking the Wrong Questions

Before you ask, think-through the issue and do some research, as you may answer your own question. If nothing else, prior research results in a more-informed question. The wrong question may lead to an inaccurate, or wrong answer; wrong answers may cost you money and reputation. Even worse: wrong answers may negatively affect your clients.[212]

6 Don't Take the Listing Agent's Word for It!

Listing agents are great people but you don't know from where they received their information. If you may independently verify the info they give you, then do so. Also, do not assume information contained within an MLS datasheet is accurate. Listing agents (and their assistants) sometimes make data-entry mistakes; we're only human, after all.

7 Don't Take Your Client's Word for It!

Some sellers own multiple properties and keep all the property deeds in the same file folder. In such cases, an error may easily be made, mistaking one deed for another. When a deed of mistaken identity is used to create an agency agreement (and/or a subsequent P&S contract) a legal entanglement may soon follow. For this reason, and hundreds more examples like this one, do not assume your client's assertions are accurate.

Ask questions of your clients, and then validate their answers. Part of your job is to verify everything yourself. In this way, never assume a seller-provided legal description is the correct one (nor the most-recent).

8 Validate

Regardless of where your information comes, go as far as possible to the source. Then, seek to validate your newfound information as correct. Stupid questions do not exist—only stupid agents. Smart agents make sure to pass along accurate, comprehensive advice and information.

Strive to be an agent that people turn-to for answers. You need not know everything, just how to discover the truth of the matter. Hold yourself out as *the* real estate resource. In doing so, the people who call upon your resources will become the same people who gladly send you referrals in exchange.

tip

Great script:
I do not currently know the answer to that question, but I can become certain of it rather quickly. I will get back to you soon.

caveats

Beware answering questions that are outside the scope of your licensure. It is okay to learn the answers for your own information, but do not share specialized information of which you are not authorized and/or qualified. Instead, refer the asker to an expert.

The answers to some questions expire, like interest rates on particular loan programs. Therefore, it is best you know which answers are static and which ones are prone to change.

Asking the wrong question may be as bad as asking no question at all. Carefully contemplate your quandaries before posing your questions.

Keep in mind: there are different types of real estate lawyers. Do not assume that closing attorneys automatically understand the details of license law.

It has been said that there are no stupid questions. While that may be true, there are questions that make the asker *look* stupid. That said, bone-headed questions are okay to ask, just don't be put-off by funny answers. After all, it's better to look stupid for a moment than for a client to find trouble due to your interest of self-preservation.

Σ Correct answers come to those who diligently seek the source.

Know Your Product

It is nearly impossible to competently sell real property without intimate knowledge of the product itself.

BY CAPTAIN OBVIOUS

WHEN IT COMES TO REAL ESTATE sales, product knowledge mastery is probably more involved than you think. To be a good real estate agent, you've got to know valuation,[125] agency,[211] and basic construction. Then, you've got to know forms, procedures, contract creation,[249] and negotiation.[266] Next, you've got to know the law,[036] the ethical code, and some problem-solving skills.[038] Even with all this knowledge, you cannot sell real estate alone, by your lonesome self.

Because your client will require the services of various vendors throughout the transaction process, your job, in addition to those aspects described above, is to understand enough of these ancillary industries to properly advise clients of which services to seek, which particular vendors to hire, and how much their services are worth.[179] Knowledge of the inner workings of these supplementary vendors is not just good service to clients, but also required by law.[212]

You owe clients fiduciary duty and reasonable care. The former means you're to put clients' needs above your very own. The latter, whose definition is constantly changing, is loosely described by courts to mean that you must advise clients on matters that they may not know, of which *you are expected to know*. In short, the law requires that you learn all these other guys' jobs too.[179]

While you are not expected to know everything a loan officer or home inspector should know, you are expected to possess enough general knowledge to know how their roles fit into your clients' goals. These jobs of ancillary industry, of which you should have some knowledge, are (to name a few): appraiser, loan officer, transaction closer, warranty seller, insurer, home inspector, builder, remodeler, handyman, and stager.

If you outsource parts of your job, such as taking listing photos,[230] writing listing copy, data entry, and other administrative duties, your product knowledge is applied through your final approval of these tasks. Basically, any task or job that affects clients is under your purview and—hopefully—your scrutiny.

Your understanding of these jobs will come from experience, internet research, and speaking directly with subject matter experts. The more you know about each of the myriad of parts that assemble into a real estate transaction, the better you will be able to deliver superior service to clients.[245]

Keep in mind that while these vendors may deliver excellent service, they will each treat your client as a customer. You are the *only one* charged with the responsibility of fiduciary care to your clients. So, stay involved in the conversations your clients have with vendors. As well, be mindful of the vendors you refer, as their service is an extension of your own.

Just as the real estate agent's job changes with new legislation, regulation, technology, and innovation, so do the jobs of ancillary industries.[304] You cannot simply climb this mountain of information, and then sit upon it for the remainder of your career. An agent will maintain good or great agent status only through continuous and diligent learning of *all things* that are in their clients' real estate interest. Because without this knowledge, he will more often fail his clients by lacking the ability to properly prepare them for all aspects of their unique transaction.

Altogether, your product is agency *and* all the other services that clients may need. It may be a tough task to learn it all, but you can do it. Remember, you're supposed to help clients make decisions; having an informed opinion is the least you can do for them.

It's Soooo Easy to
Keep Clients in Tune
When You Already Know the Song

1 Construction
You need to know basic construction materials, terminology, and be able to spot whether fixtures are original or remodeled.[134] *Ask: Does this look right to you?*

2 Mortgages
You need to know the mortgage process and how popular loan products affect a pending purchase. *Ask: Does this loan product limit properties, based upon condition?*

3 Home Warranties
You need to know what each available warranty covers, how much each costs, their deductables, and the reliability of each. *Ask: Does this company have a history of repairing systems that need to be replaced?*

4 Insurance
You need to know about hazard and title policies, and their costs. *Ask: Are there riders available for special conditions?*

A Serious How-to Manual with a Sense of Humor

Effort Meter

You're Gonna Need:

Map
Pencil
Contemplation
Decisive Action

How-to
Define Your Niche

While a driver's license allows you to operate only specific types of vehicles, your real estate license allows you to sell any type of real property you desire (but that doesn't mean you should). A single agent has the ability to sell a condo, a fixer-upper house, a piece of land, a gas station, and a shopping mall. Each of these types of sales are completely different from each other and require acute, specialized knowledge to navigate a successful transaction.

Since the heap of knowledge needed for each type of transaction is so steep, it is best to limit your business to a niche concentration.[009] When you dance this two-step, you're sure to high-step into the money:

1 Geographic Boundary

You cannot possibly sell real estate across the entire state without either going nuts or running yourself into the ground. Choose a physical boundary within which you will restrict your sales activities. Get-out a map and draw a line; box yourself into this region. This zone is your stomping ground, so get to know it well. Learn everything you can about this region, like school info, political forces, zoning specifics, recreation areas, shopping, routes, neighborhoods,..

2 Concentration

By what criteria will you focus your expertise? Will you be the one to guide first-time home buyers? Investors? Short sales? Do you wanna list foreclosures? or lakeside homes? Will you become a relocation specialist? Residential assemblage expert? What price-range will you concentrate? Where will you find clients?

You may choose two over-lapping areas of concentration, but more than two will stretch your knowledge and service-giving abilities to dangerously-low levels. The agent who tries to do it all will likely fail to do any of it well.

For the Undecided and Overwhelmed:

You don't have to narrowly define your niche in the beginning. Explore the areas of real estate that seem the most interesting to you. Interview agents and other specialists within a given niche, conduct several sales within that niche, then decide if it's right for you. During this time, concentrate on only one niche at a time. Once you choose, pick a niche-specific mentor.[044]

Top Reasons You Should Pick a Niche

1. You're more-likely to develop a strong referral network.
2. It makes your job easier and adds fun.
3. It fosters passion; no one likes a heartless niche.
4. It's more dignified than picking your nose.
5. Specialists usually make more money.

tips
An agent who restricts herself to niche concentration is likely to reach expert status quicker than an agent who does not.

Whenever you discover prospects from outside your niche, refer them to other agents. Don't forget to ask those agents to refer into your niche.[341]

Together, your contiguous geographic boundary and a single, niche concentration determine your super macro shopping zone, within which several macro markets may exist.[148]

caveats
A niche is a specialty or narrowly defined realm of service. Don't stretch yourself so thin that you give mediocre or down-right terrible service.

You must be disciplined to refer business outta your niche, especially when you are low on clients. At these times, be careful not to stretch your niche too far; doing so may be detrimental to your clients.

Σ 'Tis better for one's reputation, one's disposition, *and one's wallet* to conscientiously concentrate upon one thing, than it is to erringly neglect many things.

How-to
Poach a Coach

Athletes, politicians, and corporate executives all use coaches to focus and improve their efforts through the tutelage of a qualified, unbiased eye. We often turn to fitness trainers, financial planners, ecclesiastic exemplars, and marriage counselors for guidance in our personal lives; why should our businesses be any different?

Through one-on-one sessions, a real estate coach can help you set and reach goals, implement growth strategies, and widen business bottlenecks through planning, encouragement, and accountability. Topics covered by coaches are the same as found in this book—and more.

Because good coaching is customized to fit each student's needs, agents of all skill levels may benefit.[035] Because its outcome is heavily dependent upon the student's input, coaching allows you to control your own rate of growth. And because many brokers expect agents to supply their own training, hiring a coach may be the difference between an agent finding success and discovering a new career path. Follow these steps, and meet your new guidon:

1 Check Qualifications
Hire a coach with a strong real estate background, who understands the current market trend, as well as strategies that work well within it. Choose someone who is creative, able to diagnose your current strengths and weaknesses, and embodies a style that meshes with your personality.

2 Jibe on Style
Coaches implement various styles to achieve results. Be certain to choose one who communicates in a style that you will not rebut. Typical styles include drill sergeant, cheerleader, consultant, and therapist. Choose wisely, as a gung-ho agent may need a therapist type, and the best fit for a meek agent may be a benevolent drill sergeant.

3 Agree on Structure
Some coaches require a year-long agreement, while others go on a month-to-month basis. Sessions may be an hour long or half-hour in duration, offered weekly or twice a month, via telephone; still, others offer face-to-face discussion. Either way, expect to pay hundreds of dollars per month for a coach who's worth any money at all.

4 Be Committed
Before coaching may be effective, you must first commit to the experience. Follow your coaches suggestions, implement the homework assigned, and prepare for your sessions. A great attitude and an open mind will make your coaching endeavor worthwhile.

Effort Meter

You're Gonna Need:
Research
Ambition
Cash
Commitment

tips
Coaching services are offered from national and local groups and individuals.

As an accountability partner, a coach is not your friend, so choose accordingly.

If/when coaching becomes stale, consider hiring a new coach, with a different strategy and/or teaching style.

Aside from live sessions, many coaches offer access to online training materials (scripts, forms, systems), seminars, webinars, and referral partnerships.

caveat
The real estate sales industry is great because it allows you the freedom to run your practice as you see fit. This liberty can also be a trap, stagnating your growth.

Σ Because it's difficult to see the entire playing field when you're mired in the trenches, a coach keeps his head up so that you may keep yours down.

Effort Meter

You're Gonna Need:

Self-Assessment

Investigation

Frank Conversations

Desire to Succeed

tips

A mentor is a terrible thing to waste.

Mentorship requires considerable charity; in return, ask your mentor what you can do to help them. Perhaps that something is for you to mentor another.

Pick more than one: you may have mentors for different aspects of your business.

caveats

A mentor is not someone who treats you like a go-fer or errand boy, rather a protégé.

A mentor is not the same thing as a coach. Yoda is a coach. Obi-Wan Kenobi is a mentor.

Σ Because you're bound to step in *it* every now and then, embracing a skilled path-cutter will likely keep you on the road and outta the ditch/gutter/rut.

How–to
Embrace a Mentor

Whether you are new to real estate or have been trudging through it for some time, the right mentor is likely to help you improve upon your efforts. Don't just pick anyone who looks the part, rather choose someone who will cast a deliberate shadow for you to fill.

1 Understand Your Needs

Depending upon your niche,[042] experience, and personality, a prospective mentor may be knowledgable and willing, but not right for you. To aid in finding the best fit, make a list of your goals, current skill level, and short-comings; then, go in search of a mentor to match.

2 Research

Your selected mentor should be knowledgable of the subject and a good role model who tells it like it is. Ideally, your mentor is situated within a vast network of people from which he is happy to introduce you. To find your match, check-out several prospective mentors and learn of their exact experiences. Show each of them your list from STEP 1, then pick one who is willing and able to assist you.

3 Give It a Trial Run

Before committing to a mentor, ask them for some specific help, and then gauge the interaction. Was it effective? Does the mentor communicate well? Does it feel like a good fit? You should feel comfortable when in their company, free to ask any question. If you don't jibe, find another to ascribe.

4 Show Initiative

Your potential mentor does not want to waste time with someone who is merely dabbling in real estate, so show that you are "all-in." Implement their directives, heed their advice, and put forth concerted effort. Show your mentor that their efforts are not merely lip service. Be grateful and open-minded.

5 Don't Become Dependent

An ideal mentor is someone who will help you but doesn't demand that you do things their way. This dynamic is best avoided by giving your mentor some appropriate space. Don't bother them with every piddly question; don't turn helping you into a job for them. If you need day-to-day, hour-by-hour help, then hire a or coach[043] or join a sales team.[290]

My Mentor
My mentor is for big picture guidance and strategy.
My mentor is for perspective and reason.
My mentor is a beacon in the night,
  and perhaps a friend in the fight,
  but never a shovel in the shite.

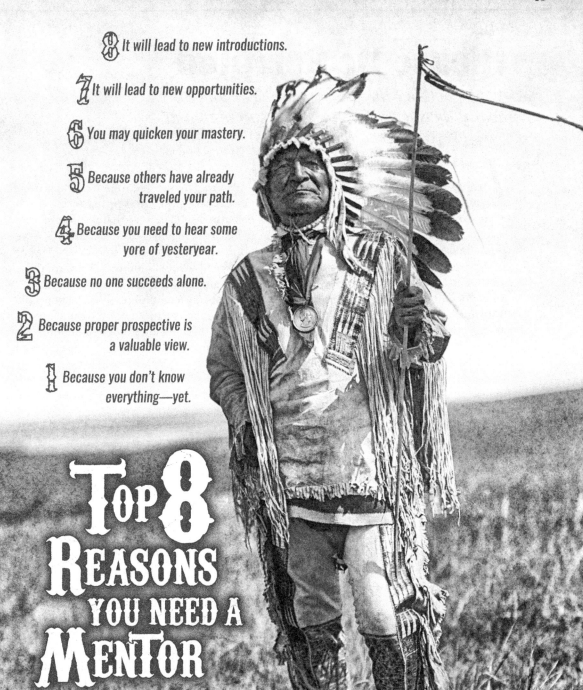

8 It will lead to new introductions.

7 It will lead to new opportunities.

6 You may quicken your mastery.

5 Because others have already
traveled your path.

4 Because you need to hear some
yore of yesteryear.

3 Because no one succeeds alone.

2 Because proper prospective is
a valuable view.

1 Because you don't know
everything—yet.

Top 8 Reasons You Need A Mentor

A Serious How-to Manual with a Sense of Humor

Please Be Scripted

Agents act-out the same scenes over and over again; the successful ones show-up prepared, with pre-conceived things to say.

BY CARL THE CLIENT

I HIRED YOU FOR TWO REASONS: first, you appear to have a superior knowledge of navigating real estate transactions,[221] and second, I assume you will be able to clearly communicate its concepts to me.[008]

You basically talk for a living, so you might as well be good at it. Many of your conversations are commonly-occurring and will be repeated from one client to the next. If you anticipate my questions and objections ahead of our meetings, and you already have responses prepared, then you can actually listen to what I'm saying to you. Otherwise, you'll spend that time scrambling for a response, missing my point; you'll be waiting to speak, instead of sharing a true dialogue with me.

I've met some agents who are afraid of using scripts, saying they're disingenuous and phoney. In actuality, the opposite is true. When you refuse to prepare, I'm the one who suffers. As your client, I deserve your best. I expect your advice to be poignant, pithy, and comprehensive. Your long-winded, rambling explanations are boorish and incomplete.

Two people can say the same thing, in different ways, with different words, and get drastically different results. Your words, their cadence, and their concepts are the primary factors that determine whether or not I hire you, list at your suggested price, or accept an offer to purchase. So, learn some anecdotes, witty analogies, and a few cautionary tales. Help me understand your perspective in a way that I can easily grasp.[272]

Those who practice scripts are better able to communicate the points they wish to convey. You wouldn't want to see a play if the actors didn't rehearse, nor a stand-up comedian without jokes, nor a waiter who couldn't coherently explain the answers to menu questions.

When we're together, you're onstage. Your job has you either presenting to me or on behalf of me. If you were giving a presentation in a boardroom full of top managers, you'd certainly rehearse ahead of time, ensuring your words had maximum impact. Why are those jokers any more important than me?

Scripts are a natural response from people who frequently experience the same conversations. Because of this phenomenon, we have scripts embedded into our psyche and use them every day with people we routinely encounter. When someone asks, "How are you?" most of us have a stock reply. When someone says, "Have a nice day," we have multiple scripts ready to dispose.

These scripts are so ingrained that we sometimes misuse them. When boarding an airplane and the gate agent wishes us to, "Have a fun flight," and when our waiter opines with, "Enjoy your meal," our auto-response is usually an asinine, "You too," as though the speaker is about to embark on the same experience as us.

The fact here is that your subconscience has already embraced scripting. So, why do you resist? Perhaps you think rehearsed scripts sound robotic,[205] like when a telemarketer dryly reads driveling line after monotonous line, hoping to sell a vacation home or newspaper subscription. Ever meet the telemarketer who doesn't sound like he's reading a lifeless, tedious script? Here's a bubble burster: *he is reading a script*! He's just much better at reading scripts than is the next guy.

Always remember this: whether you're speaking directly to me or you're advocating on my behalf, your words may just be the deciding factor between my success and my ultimate failure. So, please be scripted. Do it for yourself. Do it for me. Do it for us. ♟

A Serious How-to Manual with a Sense of Humor

Basics 047

Get Scripted

15 Great Reasons to Embrace Scripts

1. Internalized scripts allow you to listen.[189]
2. Specific scripts, used in specific circumstances, may facilitate smooth sailing and soothed senses.[052]
3. Being scripted benefits your clients.[214]
4. Scripts are the best tools to effectively communicate your viewpoint.[046]
5. Because having words prepared ahead of time is being responsible.[007]
6. It sure beats grasping at straws.[198]
7. Mentally-secured scripts have been known to kill butterflies in the belly.[057]
8. Scripts might save your bacon.[272]
9. Nobody ever looked dumb after saying the right thing.[055]
10. Effective scripting improves conversion ratios.[204]
11. Because scripts are your friends.[102]
12. Practicing scripts is doing your job.[049]
13. If you're gonna open your mouth, you might as well have something meaningful to say.[051]
14. Great river guides anticipate rough rapids and nimbly navigate relieved riders into calm waters.[111]
15. Because being scripted is fun.[050]

8 Times You Should Be Using Scripts

1. While prospecting.[077]
2. During presentations.[174]
3. When negotiating on behalf of clients.[266]
4. When negotiating your fee.[172]
5. When your client wants to do something stupid.[214]
6. During frequently-occurring conversations.[107]
7. When you need to quell emotions.[188]
8. Anytime you're talking about real estate...[084]

3 Standby Starters for Your Toolbox

Make these words your lead-in phrases, and your listeners will surely pay attention to what comes next:

1. *Would you be offended if...*

This starter seeks the listener's permission, before you take further action; it's usually meant to keep a relationship on-going.

« ...I called you again in a week? » [086]
« ...I called you if/when your listing expires? » [100]
« ...I signed you up for my newsletter? » [095]
« ...I shared your phone number with my mortgage gal? » [170]

2. *If I could show you a way...*

Use this starter to make a quick bargain.

« ...that doing [fill in the blank] is in your best interest, would you consider doing it? »
« ...to save time and money by paying me a commission, would you hire me? » [053]
« ...that minimal repairs would make your price more competitive, would you be interested in listening? » [200]
« ...that paying the buyer's closing costs will net you more money, would you consider doing so? » [268]

3. *In my experience...*

Use this starter as a polite nudge towards their best interest.

« ...those who wish to [fill in the blank], usually act in a [fill in the blank] manner. »
« ...those who are serious about [buying a house] usually [hire a single agent to guide them through the process]. » [176]
« ...those who wish to [sell during a buyer's market] usually [price accordingly]. » [154]

Effort Meter

You're Gonna Need:

Experiences
Pen & Paper
Role-Reversal
Heart

How-to
Create Great Scripts

For the sake of effective/efficient conversations with prospects, clients, co-op agents, customers, and other people, you should plan ahead: develop a clear objective to your engagements. In doing so, anticipate their objections and decide upon the best way to explain yourself.

There are already more written scripts than there are stars in the sky. To start: search-out and read these scripts; study their reasonings and understand their strategies. Then modify them to reflect your own voice, and make them your own. But, despite the industry's bounty of script books, you will sometimes want/need to create one from scratch. When that time comes, obey these steps to sire your scripts with style:

tips

Some real estate conversations will be conducted over and over again, with lots of different people; scripts prepare you for these situations. Other real estate conversations will be had rarely; scripts prepare you for these situations, too.

Before making a phone call, write down your objectives so that you don't leave anything out. Script your intro and voicemail (in cases of no-answer).

Keep all your scripts in a journal or digital file, creating a script library that you may grow and consult.

Sometimes scripts are a dialogue and not a simple retort to a trigger phrase. When this is the case, treat the script creation the same as you would for a single objection—follow the steps on this page.

Some people will never agree with you, regardless of what you say to them. When you meet these types, bid them a fond farewell and be on your way. If they waste your patience upfront, they're likely to waste your time in the future, too.

Σ   Think through new scripts on paper, considering your objectives and their objections.

1 Identify Objective

The first time a situation gets you tongue-tied, write-down the objection, concept, system, process, or procedure that you were attempting to explain or overcome, but instead caused your eyes to widen and tummy to hurt.

2 Jot an Outline

Think of a logical argument that will satisfy your objective and their objection. Jot your thoughts with bullet points. Next, put yourself in the listener's shoes: what are their likely responses to your bullet points? Write all possible responses. Then, ask yourself: *Why is it in the listener's best interest to agree with me?* Record your thoughts with more bullet points. Arrange the bullets in an orderly fashion and number them from best to worst. Be comprehensive.

3 Refine

Rework your outline into coherent sentences. Use descriptive words for color and emotional response.[008] Consider listener responses and work them into your script. Use analogies and stories when appropriate, but most importantly, use your own words to compose your scripts, otherwise recital might feel awkward. When crafted with wit and anticipation, your scripts should garnish quick cooperation from most people.

4 Create Alternates

Even the best scripts fall flat every now and then. Reasons for script failure are numerous: some people might not understand the concept you are attempting to convey; others will understand you, but will not be convinced by your first script; and some people just like to argue. Therefore, you should create two or more scripts for each objection, and then prioritize these scripts for each occasion.

Some listeners will seemingly deplete your arsenal of scripts by objecting to each and every one that you pull from your bag. When this happens, remain calm, slow down, smile, and try again. You may be rewarded by an objector who appreciates tenacity.

How-to
Memorize Scripts Quickly

You've got scripts in hand;[048] now it's time to get 'em into your noggin. The steps outlined below will allow you to quickly do so by utilizing your body's muscle-memory function. With this process, memorization is achieved by rapidly and repeatedly forcing your tongue and lips into the precise, sequential shapes needed to recite each script. The result is that you will quickly learn the words, in proper order. Once you have learned your scripts, you will have more time for prospecting. Fantastic!

Effort Meter

You're Gonna Need:

Scripts
Flashcards
Mouth
Rehearsal Time

1 Create Flashcards
Acquire a stack of crisp flashcards (or items similar) and dedicate one script to each card. On one side, write an objection or trigger comment; write its prescribed script on the flip side. Since there exists more than one script per objection, multiple cards may be made per.

2 Lift the Script
Once you have prepared a flashcard, hold the script-side up to your face. Get the card close enough to read and to obstruct from your view any nearby people leering in jest.

3 Read Fast
Read the script out loud—*fast*—five times in a row. Don't worry about internalizing the words; just make certain you enunciate each word clearly and loudly. When done properly, you will undoubtedly make funny faces, as your mouth is stretched to its pliable limits.

4 Recite
Put your flashcard to the side and then recite it from memory at the normal speed of your speech. Recite the script a second time. Then do it once more for thoroughness.

5 Repeat
Either move onto the next flashcard and repeat these steps, or have another go with the same flashcard. You'll find it eerily easy to memorize scripts this way, which turns this otherwise dreaded task into fantastical fun. Awesome!

For Further Internalization of Scripts
- Give your flashcards to another and ask them to test you.
- Role-play.[050]
- Practice the fine art of script-bombing with fellow agents.[050]
- Record your voice while reciting scripts, then listen to the recording while driving or sleeping. Play along to test your memory.
- Tack flashcards onto doors, walls, mirrors, and inside the cabinets and drawers of your home; whenever you encounter one, recite the script.

tip
Practice your scripts: when telemarketers call, trying to sell you a newspaper subscription or a time-share condo, flip the script around and sell them some real estate, or pump them for a referral. Warning: repeated practice on telemarketers may get your number removed from their lists.

caveat
Simply creating scripts without attempting memorization is like taking a shower without soap. It might make you feel good in the moment, but you still stink.

Σ   Muscle memory aids with script recall.

Effort Meter

You're Gonna Need:

Deft Partner
Scenarios
Scripts
Inclination

How-to
Role-Play
the Right Way

It may seem goofy to involve yourself in role-play, but it's a really great way to perform your scripts in a real world simulation. Find a real estate agent who understands your plight and make him your role-play buddy. Take turns alternating between Prospect and Agent (or at times, Agent and Agent). Set the scene, then *action!*

Consider role-playing the following scenarios:
- dialogues with FSBO,[101] EXPIRED,[100] and WITHDRAWN sellers,
- front-stoop powwows when door-knocking your farm,[104]
- polite parlays over purchase-offer negotiation-sequences,[266]
- and many more...

tips

When speaking with prospects and co-op agents in the field, imagine you're role-playing. Doing so may remove jitters.

If your scripts are good but role-playing continuously leads to a dead end, then it's time to change partners; choose a deft one.

It's okay to use flashcards during role-play. However, you should attempt to go "off book" and internalize scripts ASAP.

caveat

Be mindful of role-players who are unfamiliar with the situations you rehearse. Their inexperience may lead to less than fruitful results, or it may lead to new insight.

Σ Real life conversations with prospects and co-op agents are never the same as role-play, but this reality is no excuse for showing-up unprepared.

1 Be Real

Act in your role as you would if you were the character whom you portray. Use the words they use. Adopt the mannerisms they assume. Employ the temperament they exude. Become your character and you will become one helluva role-player.

2 Be Committed

Whether it's your turn as Agent or Prospect, remain in character throughout the exercise. If you stumble or become flustered or forget your scripts, remain calm and stay in the moment; no one likes a chortling chum when there's work to be done.

3 Be Creative

Real life is full of curve balls, so don't be afraid to go "off script" and rift scripts impromptu when you're tossed one. The only way to prepare for the unexpected is to rehearse the unexpected. And while role-play should be a tough game, a role-play partner is kind to remember that an Agent with good scripts should win every now and again.

4 Be Happy

Don't tie an end point to each exercise. Instead, see where it goes; be in the moment. Role-play with serious intent, but don't take yourself too seriously. This time is for trying things out, so allow yourself to be vulnerable. Do it right, and productive role-play is like money in the bank.

Script Bombing is an unexpected call from a friend, for the sole purpose of posing an objection. Speaking only within your role, you must deliver scripts to overcome the caller's objection. This game works by catching you off-guard, forcing impromptu recall of memorized scripts. By thinking on your feet, and calmly handling their objection, your conviction will eventually become solidified.

How-to
Say It Like You Mean It

Whether you are engaged in a listing presentation,[196] a difficult negotiation,[266] or an impromptu conversation at the deli counter, simply remembering your scripts won't cut the mustard; you must open your mouth and spew forth a string of sounds that *feel* logical, genuine, and reasonable to the listener's ear. After all, if it's worth saying, then you might as well say it like you mean it.

Effort Meter

You're Gonna Need:
Timing
Supposition
Poise
Chutzpah

1 Practice
The only path to consistent, desired results is to practice, practice, practice your scripts under various scenarios. Practice with flashcards.[049] Practice by script bombing. Practice by playing games[058] and with role-play.[050] Practice until you can say your scripts like you mean it.

2 Speak with Conviction
Projecting physical cues while speaking displays confidence, and tends to instill faith in speakers and their listeners alike. Be in the moment, and say it like you mean it:
- Speak clearly; don't *st... st... stammer*.
- Keep eye contact when speaking and listening (if face-to-face).
- Project your voice, enunciate your words, and don't mumble.
- Don't phrase your statements like questions; it makes you seem uncertain.
- Don't mutter *er, eh,* or *um*. Instead, remain briefly silent, which will make you seem attentive and sober.

3 Avoid Robot Voice
Sounding too rehearsed, or like you're reading from a script, is sure to fill your listener with doubt.[205] Slow down, and say it like you actually mean it:
- Create a cadence to your speech that is natural.
- Breathe.
- Deliver each script like it's the first time you've ever said it.
- Give pause . . . in proper places, of course . . . for a bit of dramatic effect. . . Give your words space . . . to breathe, . . to bathe over their ears, . . and build towards something. . . You've got a point to make . . . and you have my attention, . . . but don't be a drama queen about it.

4 Believe
Before you can say it like you mean it, you must first believe that what you are saying is both true and in the listener's interest. Take time to understand the purpose of your scripts, and craft them with care. Don't blindly repeat a script written by another if it makes you feel uncomfortable. Instead, find the intent and purpose of the script, re-draft the script to match your voice, and then own it with pride.[048]

tips
Practice breeds confidence.

When delivering scripts, imagine yourself as an actor on stage. Now direct yourself to say it like you mean it.

It's okay (*encouraged*) to read directly from scripts when on the phone. If they ask: *Are you reading?* answer: *Yes. I read my scripts to ensure everyone gets the same experience. I don't wanna accidentally forget something that might benefit you. That's a good thing, right?*

caveats
When prospecting, don't tie an outcome to your conversations. When you do, a tendency to sound desperate, anxious, and/ or hurried emerges (as does commission breath—yuck).

Always use your script spouting skills for good, and never for nefarious causes.

Σ Once you believe your words are truthful and helpful, your scripts will become convincing.

Effort Meter

You're Gonna Need:

Scripts
Patience
Practice
Moxie

tips

Remaining calm and engaged in dialogue is subtly spreading on the smooth.

Having prepared scripts allows you to truly listen to objections, because you are not trying to think of a rebuttal as the objector is speaking. After all, they may object to something completely different than you anticipate.

NO means NO, but anything other than NO is, well... not NO. So, handle that objection until you hear a solid NO. It's worth the effort, but don't be a pest about it. If you pester people with your objection handling, then you may overcome their objections, but lose to them altogether (because they think you're a pest).

For most people, their objection means, "I'm not yet convinced that what you're suggesting for me is best for me." Typically, once someone has decided against, they'll let you know by saying, "No, thanks."

caveat

Skipping Steps 1 & 2, and jumping straight into your script, is about as smooth as a stop sign.

How-to
Handle Objections, Smooooooooothly

Has anyone ever objected to one of your suggestions? It happens to real estate agents all the time. Buyers will object to becoming pre-qualified and to signing an agency agreement before seeing houses. Sellers will object to your suggestions of list prices and your commission rate. Prospects will object to hiring you because they have family in the business. Agents will object to the stipulations of your purchase offer. Your broker will object to paying you more commission. And your friends will object to your choice of lunch destination.

People will object to your real estate suggestions at every turn; this happenstance is not just human nature, but also part of the job. In this way, your job is to be good at your job *and* to have the words to overcome objections, convincing objectors to see it your way (because your way is the way of best practice, as far as you can justify it).

You are your client's sherpa throughout the transaction. You know the safe passages and the dangerous ones. Your words can prevent clients from going over the cliff's edge, or your words may encourage them to take a flying leap. Follow these steps, and stay on solid ground:

1 Acknowledge

By simply acknowledging their objection, you are taking a huge step forward with your objector. Skipping this STEP may cause them to think you are not listening. Wait until the objector has finished speaking, then acknowledge their words. Doing so is your attempt to confirm that both parties are talking about the same thing.

Scripts that acknowledge:
« I understand how you might feel that way. »
« I hear you. »
« I acknowledge your concern... »
« So, what you're saying is... (echo their objection back) »

2 Isolate

When you isolate, you create a foothold by eliminating distractions, and by removing all other objections from consideration. Otherwise you may become stranded along the route, ensnared in an objection trap, debating every pebble in the path.

Isolate objections with a question that poses agreement. If you are unable to isolate, then begin again with STEP 1.

Scripts that isolate:
« If we can agree upon (fill in the blank), will you (fill in the blank)? »
« Is this the only objection you have to (fill in the blank)? »

3 Respond

You've cleared the way, and now it's time to bring 'em to safety with your carefully chosen words. Unleash your argument and deliver that script like you mean it.[051]

Sample Objections, Handled Smoothly

1) Suppose you are negotiating a sales contract, representing the seller:

Seller « I paid my own closing cost when I bought this house, so I don't wanna pay the buyer's closing costs now. »

Acknowledge: « I understand how you feel. »

Isolate: « If I can show you how paying the buyer's closing costs would be a benefit to you, would you agree to do so? »

« Sure thing. I gotta hear this. »

Respond: « What's more important to you: the contract price or the amount of money you put into your pocket from the sale? »

« The amount of money I receive at closing. »

Respond: « Great! Then let's consider adjusting the contract price to reflect the concessions you make to the buyer. So long as you receive the amount of money you desire at closing, does it really matter who pays the closing costs? »

« I guess not. Let's adjust the price. »

2) Suppose a potential buyer refuses to sign an agency agreement:

Buyer « I refuse to sign an agency agreement. »

Acknowledge: « I hear ya. »

Isolate: « Is this the only objection you have to working with me? »

« Yup. I know of other agents who do not require it. Perhaps I'll just work with one of them. »

Respond: « What if I showed you how it's to your advantage to sign an agency agreement, protecting yourself and the agent throughout the sales transaction? What if I showed you our state law, which requires a signed agency agreement before an agent can provide agency, negotiation advice, valuation, and/or strategy? Not every agent will insist that you to sign first, but do you really wanna work with an agent whose first inclination is to either knowingly or unknowingly break the law? »

« Wow! I guess not. Where do I sign? »

3) Suppose you have a hankerin' for hamburgers, and a friend protests your choice of lunch destination:

Friend « I don't wanna eat at the Burger Princess again. I'm trying to watch my weight. »

Acknowledge: « I know it, Buddy. Your fancy for fried foods has hijacked your waistline. »

« You guessed right! »

Isolate: « If the Burger Princess had some healthy menu options, would you consider eating there today? »

« I guess so. »

Respond: « Well, guess what? They sell salad in a cup! Grab your wallet—you're paying! Aww... don't look so sad. We'll dine at your favorite carrot stand next time. »

tips

Sometimes an objection is just a nice way for a prospect to tell you to booger-off. Overcome that objection with grace and reason, and the objector may change his mind about you.

Objections are a good thing; they signify an agent at work, doing her job. If you never hear objections, then you're not working.

Listen carefully to the entire objection before you speak. You might be surprised at what you hear.

Because people don't always say what they actually mean, listen for the reason behind their objection. Since you cannot overcome an objection that is not addressed, STEP 2 is meant to uncover their true sentiment.

If your script fails to inspire agreement, then try another, and possibly a third. When three attempts fall short of hand-in-hand harmony, consider the possibility that STEPS 1 and/or 2 were not performed correctly. Or, perhaps your scripts are crap.

Handling objections is helping them to make smart decisions.

Remember, not all objections may be overcome, nor do all objectors always behave in their own best interest; know when to pack it in and move on.

Once you've become proficient at overcoming objections, an earned confidence will wash over your efforts. Nothing can stop you now.

Σ To acknowledge, isolate, respond (AIR) is to AIR on the side of an effective & efficient communication style.

If I take tons of great pictures, list it in the MLS, and syndicate it across the internet (thereby notifying the world of our listing), then it becomes impossible to sell your house for less than it's worth. If our price is indeed too low, it will compel every serious buyer into action. Everyone will be talking about it, and several offers will be quickly made, pushing our price higher. So the question becomes: Would you rather pick a price that creates demand or one that simply adds to the supply? [154]

Is there a price at which you love one of these houses? Seriously, is there a price that would make you feel good about buying the best of the worst? Let's offer your best price on a few, and see what happens— you just never know! [257]

Your suggested list price is just too low. I won't go for it.

After looking, I don't like any of these houses, so I'm not gonna buy one now.

4 Hurdled Objections

What you need is an agent who sniffs-out all the information available on your house, including the neighborhood. Using that, I select The Right Price, and then aggressively market it to the right buyers. Hire me, and I'll be a bloodhound on your block, and a bulldog on the clock.[091]

When you find what you like, you must be ready to strike. Without pre-qualification, you're a lame duck. No seller will wanna kiss you if you're not looking good. You can't put the cart before the horse, then expect the horse to walk backwards. Besides, everyone else is doing it! C'mon, let's call 'em together; it will take just ten minutes.[170]

I need a listing agent who has experience selling houses in my neighborhood.

I don't wanna bother with loan pre-qualification. I just wanna see some houses.

Rejection Doesn't Have To Hurt So Stinkin' Bad

Rejection can be hurtful.
Rejection can be gut-wrenching.
Rejection can be a real bitch!

BY SALVADOR THE PSYCHIATRIST

A WORKING AGENT'S DAY is full of objections to her conceptions and rejection of her suggestions. Although objection may feel like rejection, the two are not the same. This distinction is often blurred because the road to rejection is usually paved with objections. The possibility that rejection may be waiting on the other side of an objection may allow an agent's fear to overcome her before an objection is even raised. An agent drunk on this fear may be rendered impotent, rarely prospecting for clients and missing-out on a slew of sales opportunities in the process.

What many fail to realize is that *the road to success is also paved with objections.* For this reason, there have been many routines written and methods developed, each meant to prepare an agent to overcome objections with words. However, this preparation rarely addresses the physiological changes that can be triggered by the mere thought of rejection and its resulting fog of emotions like anxiety, nausea, befuddlement, combativeness, and (in rare cases) diarrhea. Working in a foggy fluster is arduous at best; for objection-overcoming preparation to work most effectively, an agent's mind needs to be free of fog.

While fear festers in the unknown, it falters with familiarity. Therefore, regular engagement in a rejection-based activity will acclimatize one's brain to emotionally-foggy operations, and in doing so the brain will learn that the emotional fog it produces is unnecessary and will cease to produce it (or produce less of it).

In an effort to promote a fog-free lifestyle, I have devised a rejection-based game that is low-risk/high-reward, über-competitive, and devilishly-fun. The game is simple in construction and brilliant in its execution: you and several friends take turns approaching total strangers, asking strange questions. The idea is that each question is designed to elicit rejection. The result is that sometimes your questions will not be rejected, but surprisingly embraced.

Over time, game players will be rejected again and again, but they will also be occasionally embraced. Soon, players will learn that it's often not the question that strangers embrace but the way the question is asked.[008] This realization should give the astute players a morsel of confidence: if delivery influences a stranger's response, and brain fog negatively affects delivery, then the fog is what clogs a player's chances of winning.

Because game questions are low-risk and supremely silly, frequent gameplay doesn't really hurt so much.[057] Repeat players will quickly build earned confidence.[051] Their conviction and increased control over the game will lift the emotional fog that surrounds, and soon these fog-free players will be prepared for conversations with anyone about anything.[017]

Remember, there is a difference between rejection and the fear of rejection. While no one is immune to the former, the latter may be conquered. Now, go play *The Rejection Game* and make rejection your bitch! [058]

Don't Be So Scared,
You Big Wimp!

Do the thing you fear, and the death of fear is certain.
-Ralph Waldo Emmerson

We fear things in proportion to our ignorance of them.
-Christian Nestell Bovee

He who has overcome his fears will truly be free.
-Aristotle

To fight fear: act. To increase fear: wait, put off, postpone.
-David Joseph Schwartz

Fear is static that prevents me from hearing myself.
-Samuel Butler

The cave you fear to enter holds the treasure you seek.
-Joseph Campbell

Nothing in life is to be feared; it is only to be understood. Now is the time to understand more, so that we may fear less.
-Marie Curie

Anxiety is the dizziness of freedom.
-Søren Kierkegaard

The only thing we have to fear is fear itself.
-Franklin D. Roosevelt

A Serious How-to Manual with a Sense of Humor

The Rejection Game

1 Gist

Players take turns asking strangers ridiculously-uncustomary (but not impractical) questions, that seemingly warrant rejection.

2 Players

Two or more players are needed, with no limit. Ideal gameplay is four or five players. During gameplay, players take turns as a(n):

- Challenger = player who poses the Question
- Asker = player whose turn it is to ask the Question
- Watcher = any player who is not the Asker
- Chicken = any player who fails to ask the Question

4 Chickens

Any Asker who fails to ask the Question within 90 seconds becomes a Chicken. Chickens forfeit their turn as the Challenger, passing the Question to the next player in line. If the next player becomes a Chicken, the Question is passed again. If the Challenger becomes a Chicken, then the next player in line become the Challenger, and the game continues with a new Question. Chickens must wear a funny hat on their next turn.

3 Rules

Gameplay is conducted in a crowded, public arena. Players establish a home base, and all gameplay must be conducted within eyesight of that base.

- Questions asked must be of the YES / NO variety, and may be asked of strangers only. When strangers say YES, the Asker must perform to earn points.
- Askers get 90 seconds to ask the Question, and may not tell strangers about the game.
- After Asker asks the Question, he becomes the Challenger, posing the next Question.
- Watchers watch gameplay from home base, and may not interfere with the Asker.

Sample arenas: shopping malls, public parks, gymnasiums, state fairs, cafeterias.

Sample Questions:
- to a person near the front of a long line: *May I cut here in line?*
- to a bartender: *May I have a free beer?*
- to a lady with an ice cream cone: *May I have a lick?*
- to a cop: *May I drive your squad car?*
- to a mother: *May I hold your baby?*

5 Scoring

Score is kept by the players, and points are awarded as follows:

1 point to any Asker for asking a Question that results in a NO

3 points to any Asker asking a Question that results in a YES

-1 point to any Asker who becomes a Chicken

-3 points to any Challenger who becomes a Chicken

6 Winning

The first player to earn 10 points wins. Kudos to the winner.

- The winning player gets a meal of his choosing, paid-for by the losing players.
- Losing players must adorn a funny hat and parade proudly through the crowd, until the winning player is no longer amused by such malarkey and shenanigans.
- Because each player has faced their fears, all players ultimately are winners (sorta).

Your Business is
Your Business

Not only do you get to do it your way, you're forced to.

BY PRESTON THE PRAGMATIST

AS THE OPERATOR OF A SELF-EMPLOYED business, your body is shared by the boss and the employee, which makes you the CEO and the line worker. This dualism leaves you responsible for the development and the execution of all policies, tasks, and events undertaken by your business.

You decide it all: you decide how much and what kind of education you receive, whether or not you accept over-priced listings,[190] and whether you concentrate on a niche,[042] or adopt a shotgun approach. You decide how often you work, what you say and how you say it,[008] and the resulting number of transactions you close. You dictate, with each person you associate, with each client you sign, with each vendor you refer, with the advice you give, and with the advice you take, the direction your business goes.

Jekyll & Hyde agents are those who are a good boss but a bad employee (or vice versa); your aim should be to avoid this moniker. To achieve your goals, you must acknowledge and actively manage both roles: boss and employee. Find the time to do both jobs, and take strides to be good in both roles.

Every business has stakeholders, to whom the boss is responsible. Your stakeholders include the people you live with, the charities you patronize, your broker, the agents affiliated with your brokerage, dependents, clients, and employees. A boss who allows the employee to routinely arrive late, take long lunches, and knock-off early is acting irresponsibly to his stakeholders.

Be a good boss: don't overwork your employee. Set hours of operation, the same way a retail store does, but don't be afraid to work overtime either, especially when your business is new. Create a plan of action and a daily schedule, allowing your employee to easily stay on-task during daylight hours.[064] Oversee an appropriate public image and properly tend to the finances, the way big companies do.

Be a good employee: don't fart around or blow-off work just because the day is sunny.[300] Stick to the daily schedule and be attentive. When you notice something lacks effectiveness or efficiency,[012] notify the boss. Then allocate time to stay up late, if necessary, reading about real estate and concocting new or improved systems.[070]

You are not only responsible for giving clients great service, but you are also competing with other agents for those clients, many of whom are currently better at real estate sales than you; strive for continued betterment.

Only you can drive your business. In the beginning (or during a business revamp), you must alter your life to get your business up to speed. You must make plans to work longer hours, study more, seek more help, ask more questions, and document your growth.[303]

No one will tell you when you're slacking. Just as few, if any, will tell you when you're doing it right. The ultimate judge of your efforts will be commission checks and how often they come.[120] If you've struggled to increase your current income, or to get the same income from less hours worked, then you just might be a Jekyll & Hyde agent. Look deep. Seek the truth. Judge yourself.[024]

Your actions today alter your future circumstances, so don't just flit about, responding to things as they happen. Time spent putting-out fires that could have been avoided is a colossal waste; instead, plan and do. Think and act. Have a mission. Be on purpose. Make the boss proud. Your family is counting on it.

6 Ways to Be a Learned Bird

1 Continuing Education (CE)
Complete the first-year, state-mandated education requirements, ASAP. From then on, choose classes that help your business (regardless of cost) not just the dopey, free ones.

2 Coach/Mentor
They're out there,[043] and they're willing to teach you.[044] Just remember that you get what you pay for.

3 Classes/Seminars
Regularly, attend classes that teach you to be better at your job. Don't hold out for only those that give CE credits.

4 Internet/Books
Read books/blogs and watch videos by those in-the-know. Remember to mind the source.[006]

5 Mastermind
Get together with other agents and discuss stumbling-block topics. Copy and steal what others are doing right.[068]

6 Experience
Newly-learned material sinks-in better when you've got something to compare. So, go do it!

A Serious How-to Manual with a Sense of Humor

Effort Meter

You're Gonna Need:

Personal Stats
Calculator
Pencil & Paper
Realistic Desires

tips
If you don't know your turnover rates, begin tracking them now. After three months of data, create your business plan.

This plan calculates *gross commission income* (GCI) amounts. *Net income* is determined by subtracting expense.

The creation of your business plan does not have to be a harrowing experience, requiring fancy software and thoughtful mission statements. Nor should it be created, then placed on a shelf, only to be perused each blue moon, or worse: never again.

elephant dishes
Trunk Tartare
Elephant Burgers
Pachyderm à la King
Tusk 'n' Grits
Mastodon Roll
Moo Shu Phant
Mammoth à la Mode

turnover rates
are calculated by dividing one real estate activity by another. Formulas found under the elephant (next page).

Σ Daily activity tracking and a half-hour of monthly math make for bites you can sink your teeth into.

How-to
Eat an Elephant

They say the best way to eat an elephant is one bite at a time. If *they* are correct, then knowing how-to, when-to, and the order-to take those bites will hasten a steady progression towards the digestion of an entire elephant. When the elephant is your annual income, a business plan is your meal plan. Eat your scheduled meals each day according to the meal plan and you will have no problem finishing your elephant, trunk and all. And since pachyderm may be prepared in various ways, utilizing a customized menu makes finishing your plate a walk in the zoo.

1 Annual Meal Plan
To dice your elephant into bite-sized pieces, begin with an annual gross commission income (GCI) goal. Choose a number that will challenge your efforts in a realistic way.

2 Monthly Meal Plan
To fully consume your elephant on schedule, your meal plan must be re-written (revised) each month. To do so, subtract the money you've earned thus far (GCI to date) from your annual goal, then divide that number by the number of months remaining in the year. The result is your remaining GCI goal. Next, sequentially divide key metrics and turnover rates to determine your monthly real estate activity goals.

Key metrics and turnover rates, in sequential dividing order:[063]
- average commission rate (ACR)
- average transaction price (ATP)
- client turnover rate (CTR)
- presentation turnover rate (PTR)
- discussion turnover rate (DTR)

3 Weekly Meal Plan
Make a pocket schedule at the beginning of each week;[064] with monthly goals in mind, block time for real estate activities.

4 Daily Meal Plan
To determine your daily discussion goal, divide your monthly discussion goal by the number of work days in the month. If your metrics are accurate, achieving your monthly income goals (and thereby, annual goal) will be reached by simply eating your prescribed, daily meal.

5 Track Your Dietary Habits
Keep the weekly meal plan in your pocket, and take it out when prospecting. Mark the page for each discussion had, presentation given, and client signed. Tally the weekly marks on a monthly basis and calculate monthly metrics. Reconcile the metrics on a quarterly basis, then use these quarterly figures when monthly meal planning for the next three months.

(fig. 1.1) MONTHLY BUSINESS PLAN (SAMPLE)   063

STEP	CALCULATION	RESULT	EXPLAINED
1. take annual gross commission income goal	N/A	$100,000	= annual GCI goal
2. subtract GCI to date	− $0	$100,000	= remaining GCI goal
3. divide by months remaining	÷ 12 months	$8333	= monthly GCI goal
4. divide by average commission rate (ACR)	÷ 2.5%	$333,333	= monthly sales volume goal
5. divide by average transaction price (ATP)	÷ $175,000	1.9	= monthly transactions goal
6. divide by client turnover rate (CTR)	÷ 60%	3.2	= monthly new clients goal
7. divide by presentation turnover rate (PTR)	÷ 40%	7.9	= monthly presentations goal
8. divide by discussion turnover rate (DTR)	÷ 2%	396.8	= monthly discussions goal
9. divide by work days in month	÷ 25 days	15.9	= daily discussions goal

Using Agent Andy's statistics (shown here calculated for the first month of the year), if he discusses real estate with 16 people per working-day, then he will earn $100,000 by year's end. Your ratios, and therefore your results, will vary from this sample.

(fig. 1.2) METRICS CHART

METRIC	CALCULATION
ACR =	$\dfrac{\text{GCI}}{\text{SALES VOLUME}}$
ATP =	$\dfrac{\text{SALES VOLUME}}{\text{TRANSACTIONS}}$
CTR =	$\dfrac{\text{TRANSACTIONS}}{\text{CLIENTS}}$
PTR =	$\dfrac{\text{CLIENTS}}{\text{PRESENTATIONS}}$
DTR =	$\dfrac{\text{PRESENTATIONS}}{\text{DISCUSSIONS}}$

Turnover Rates & Conversion Ratios

...are two sides of the same coin.
Turnover Rates are the inverse of Conversion Ratios.
Conversion Ratios are the inverse of Turnover Rates.

———◆◆◆—— *Example* ——◆◆◆———

Agent Andy gave twenty PRESENTATIONS, and as a result, signed eight CLIENTS. Therefore, his PRESENTATION-TO-CLIENT *conversion ratio* is twenty to eight (20:8). The inverse of this ratio is eight divided by twenty, which is a PRESENTATION *turnover rate* (PTR) of 40%.

Effort Meter

You're Gonna Need:

Planner System
Scrap Paper
Fortitude
Alarm

tips
To avoid riding the *Real Estate Roller Coaster*,[120] schedule only D-blocks before noon.

Get your body into rhythm with your mind. Set all routine activities on a schedule: sleep, rise, meals, and exercise.

Use your weekly schedule to track the activities used in metric calculations.[062]

Through trial & error, determine the number of hours required to meet your daily discussions goal. Then, time-block accordingly.[063]

If the administrative parts of your job begin to take away time from prospecting, presentations, and client time, tighten your systems and hire some helpers.[286]

caveat
As an independent contractor, no one is going to tell you what to do; you must choose for yourself, each moment of each day.

The problem with a digital schedule is that it's easy to (innocently) ignore; a sheet of paper in your pocket is ever-present.

Σ   Use two schedules: one for long-term plans, the other for this week only.

How-to
Create & Keep a Schedule

If you're doing your job correctly, it's the same thing every week: prospect for presentation appointments, give presentations to prospects, provide agency the clients you already have, and conduct administrative duties.[346] Keeping to a schedule will ensure you devote considerable time to each task, preventing each from colliding, or becoming neglected. To be productive, live by your schedule; keep it in your pocket, and edit it constantly.

1 Use a Planner System

There are many digital applications and paper planner systems for sale. Some come with training for your ultimate organizational pleasure. Whichever one you choose, stick with it, live with it, love it, and learn to use it well. Begin by first inserting vacations, days-off, training classes, and special events; schedule everything else around these dates.

2 Block Time

Use scrap paper to make a weekly schedule: divide the page by daily columns and hourly rows. Transfer all events from the long-term planner in STEP 1, then fill each block with letters that correspond to real estate activities:

- D for DISCUSSIONS: Plan to spend several hours per day dedicated to talking to people about real estate (AKA prospecting),[077] making presentation appointments.
- P for PRESENTATIONS: Because some time blocks will expire, allocate half of your monthly presentation goal to each week.[063]
- C for CLIENT TIME: Dedicate the appropriate weekly hours to showing property or otherwise spending time with clients.
- Ad for ADMINISTRATIVE TASKS: Schedule this time for all the jobs that could be outsourced: paperwork, data entry, brokerage compliance,..

Spend D-block time trying to convert P-blocks into actual listing and/or buyer presentations. Upon expiration, empty P-blocks automatically convert into D-blocks, forcing you to spend that time prospecting.

	SUN	MON	TUE	WED	THU	FRI	SAT
10 AM	X	D	D	D	D	D	C
11 AM	X	D	D	D	D	D	C
NOON	C	Ad	P	P	Ad	Ad	C
1 PM	C	P	P	P	P	P	C

3 Test Yourself

Create a second weekly schedule, sectioned into half-hour blocks. Set an alarm to sound-off every thirty minutes. When the buzzer buzzes, jot your activities of the previous thirty minutes; repeat this every day for two weeks, and this system should correct distracting behaviors.

How-to
Stay Safe Out There

Some wackos wanna hurt agents, and that is no laughing matter. Like bullies on a playground, bad guys are more likely to target easy prey. Show predators what difficult prey you are and you'll lessen your chances of attack. Safety first!

Effort Meter

You're Gonna Need:
Preparation
Awareness
Vigilance
Buddy

1 Use the Buddy System
Buddy always tags along when you meet fresh prospects/strangers. When Buddy is not available, he knows (at the least) where you are and with whom you're working. Because he cares, Buddy always calls fifteen minutes into your solo appointments. If in distress, you give the unsuspecting code phrase: *Let's watch a movie tonight.*

2 Identify Everyone
Before going anywhere together, snap some pictures: include your prospect/stranger's face, their driver's license, and their car (with tag). Text message the pictures to Buddy. Check their driver's license for authenticity, ensuring the picture and physical description match the person standing before you. Bad guys are not likely to oblige this step.

3 Show with Care
Be mindful of your actions and the actions of those around you:
- Don't show after dark.
- Drive separately from buyers.
- Park on the street for quick getaways.
- Enter vacant property carefully, after first walking around the perimeter, looking for signs of forced entry. Avoid squatters.
- Don't surprise them. Yell out *REAL ESTATE!* upon entering property.
- Always meet strangers in a crowded, public place for the first meeting—preferably at your office.[171]
- Bad guys don't usually talk to loan officers, so only show property to pre-qualified strangers.[170]
- Keep strangers in front of you at all times. Leave a door open. Locate all exits. Avoid confined spaces like basements and attics.
- Keep your phone in-hand throughout showings, so that you may dial for help.

4 Keep Private Things Private
Don't place personal info on business cards, marketing materials, or the web. Home phone numbers, addresses, and family member information should not be part of your business persona.

5 Trust Your Instincts
Mind your gut. If something doesn't seem right, then get outta there. It's better to be embarrassed than to be dead. It's better to run than to fight.

tips

Never risk bodily harm over a measly commission (nor a large commission, for that matter).

Consider mobile safety apps when in the field.

Potential weapons: pepper spray, knife, stun gun, pistol; if you carry one, learn to use it properly.

A basic self-defense course may prove handy.

Always report suspicious activities to your broker. Make others aware that a potential bad guy may attempt to strike again.

Plug into a system that alerts you whenever the real estate community puts-out a bad guy warning.

Don't be flashy: avoid jewelry and showy clothing. Wear clothes you can run in. Leave your purse in the trunk.

Hey, tough guy reading this: heed this page, as this article is not just for the ladies.

Σ Remain diligent in your efforts to stay safe by employing known techniques that deter bad guys.

Effort Meter

You're Gonna Need:

Common Sense
Due Diligence
Discerning Eye
Standards of Practice

How-to
Discriminate (Lawfully) in Real Estate

When discrimination is properly utilized as a tool, it can dramatically pad the bottom line of your real estate sales business; doing so will foster a higher prospect-to-closing ratio.

1 Discriminate Based Upon
...merit and other lawful reasons, as best practice.
- Discriminate against sellers (when representing buyers) by:
  - the terms of their offer.
  - your buyer's criterion.
- Discriminate against buyers (when representing sellers) by:
  - the terms of their offer.
  - their ability to obtain funding by the closing date.
- Discriminate against prospects by:
  - their desire to buy or sell real property.
  - their willingness to sign an agency agreement according to your terms (including list price).
  - their ability to acquire funding by closing date (buyers or short sellers).
  - their willingness to follow your system and pay your fee.
- Discriminate against brokerages (that you affiliate with) by:
  - the fees/commissions-paid-to-brokerage to services-provided-by-brokerage-to-agent ratio.
  - the amount of creativity allowed in your practice.

2 DO NOT Discriminate Based Upon
...class status or other groupings of people. To do so is either unlawful, unethical, or just plain stupid. Numerous acts of Congress and state legislatures have created protected classes of people, whom real estate agents may not blindly discriminate against. Federal law makes it a crime to discriminate based upon race, color, religion, national origin, age, sex, citizenship, familial status, and disability. For a list of your state's protected classes, consult your broker.

Other, dumb reasons to discriminate:
- the type of car they drive
- hard to pronounce surnames
- political affiliation
- their sex life
- their favorite football team
- the college they attended
- the way they pronounce "potato"
- their tacky wardrobe
- their peg leg, wooden eye, pigeon toes, or crew cut
- their steely stare (maybe you should discriminate against this guy)[065]

tips
Your business success is predicated upon the people with which you choose to affiliate yourself. So, discriminate lawfully and with gusto.

caveats
Local statues may provide for protection of classes that are not currently protected by federal law, including sexual orientation and political affiliation. Consult your broker for the full, local list.

Mind the company that you keep: be choosy with whom you sign agency agreements, as well as the vendors you recommend.

Do not approach discrimination in a willy-nilly manner: read and follow all fair housing laws and other regulations that govern your license.[036]

Σ Best practice is to discriminate based upon a prospect's willingness to cooperate, sign an agency agreement, price accordingly, and pay you your value.

How-to
Get Paid as a Real Estate Agent

Effort Meter

There are several, different jobs for which a real estate agent may be paid, but there is only one thing that stands between an agent and a paycheck: *the agent.* To get paid for your work, make this two-step an habitual rite, and you'll dance to the bank every time:

1 Negotiate Your Fee Upfront

Your job is as an independent contractor; therefore, you get paid by the job. So, before beginning each job, make it your duty to speak with the prospective client, and together delineate exactly what that job shall be, how much money you will earn in exchange for the job, what time you will be paid, who shall pay you, and by what means. In other words: do not do any work (not even a little bit) for a client until you have first negotiated your fee.[181]

2 Get It in Writing

If it's not in writing, then it doesn't mean squat, and your work may be for naught. Never take clients at merely their word that you will get paid (even if the client is your mother). Paper may fade, but not as quickly as memories do.

The commission paragraph is what gives teeth to an agency agreement. If you feel uncomfortable discussing your fee with potential clients, then learn to overcome your fear, or you will (at times, for certainty) become very disappointed when your work results in success for clients, yet you receive zero dollars in exchange.

DO NOT skip-over the commission paragraph in agency agreements!
DO NOT leave the commission blank blank!
DO NOT write Ø or *N/A* in the blank!
DO NOT cross-out the commission paragraph!

Ask your broker to provide forms and guidance, to ensure you get paid. After all, your broker cannot receive payment unless you do, so it's in her best interest to help. Embrace the commission paragraph and insist on payment in exchange for your promised results; unless you're running a real estate charity, of course.

You're Gonna Need:

Negotiation Skills
Gumption
Tact
Reason

tips
Unless your broker gives written permission to accept payment directly, all payments for your work must first go to your broker.

Agency is full of challenging conversations.[215] If you are uncomfortable discussing your fee with clients, then you're probably not the right person to be representing them.

caveat
Each and every commission agreement is negotiated individually. Therefore, never discuss a "going rate" or "average commission" for commission fees. Doing so is a violation of the Sherman Anti-Trust Act.

Question:
How much does this particular job pay?
Answer:
It pays the fee you have negotiated.

Question:
What fee should I charge?
Answer:
That depends on the service you provide and how well you provide it.

Σ   Whether or not you're paid is entirely up to you.

A Dozen Jobs that Pay Agents

1. Buyer representation[176]
2. Seller representation[192]
3. Landlord representation
4. Tenant representation
5. Selling CMA & market studies homework[157]
6. Selling listing appts.[288]
7. Transaction services[289]
8. Broker Price Opinions (BPO)
9. Retainer fees[181]
10. Referral fees[112]
11. Expert witness fees
12. Administrative work[221]

Copy & Steal Everything

Nothing is new. Everything has come before.
Grab what works and leave the rest behind.

BY PENNY THE PICK-POCKET

THERE EXISTS NO GOOD REASON to reinvent the wheel of real estate. All the bits you need to operate a successful, organized business are already out there, waiting for you to grab and mix into your routine, making them your very own.

Think of each real estate transaction as a wheel, built from scratch and customized to each client's need. Just as a wheel can be made of various materials and assembled in a variety of configurations, so goes the real estate transaction.[004] For each to reach its destination, the wheel and the transaction must travel a road. And just like a transaction, some wheels (based entirely upon their construction) will ride bumpy and others smooth.

There are basically three tasks {wheel parts} that must be sourced and assembled, in successive order, to make real estate money: 1) get a client {wheel hub} 2) get client under contract to buy/sell real estate {wheel spokes} and 3) get client to the closing table {wheel rim}. Every potential bump and pothole that may surface while driving these tasks has been seen by other agents, many times before.

Because others have come before, a bevy of methods and solutions have already been devised to build a wheel that is able to withstand bumps, and/or to steer the wheel in a manner that avoids bumps altogether. These methods and solutions are out there, awaiting your sticky, sticky fingers.

The challenge for newbies is that every agent's wheel-assembly advice is somewhat different. With so many voices touting so many ways to build the real estate wheel, information overload makes the appropriate selection and ideal assembly of parts difficult to ascertain. To add further difficulty, lots of the good stuff isn't written down anywhere. You won't find it in (most) books or on the internet because it resides as trade secrets, and the only way to access to these secrets is

through active conversations with agents in-the-know. So, go where agents go and talk to them. Hunt them down in the office, at sales meetings, and in classrooms. Seek them in the field, after co-operating on transactions together, and at open houses. Ask about their ways, their means, and their results.

A fast way to pilfer proper parts is to join (or create) an agent mastermind workshop, where agents meet regularly to discuss wheel parts, their construction, and the navigation of bumpy roads (in other words, their successes and failures). This support group is prime for plundering, full of bits to collect and try out, but be mindful of the people you pinch. Not just anyone can build a smooth ride, but many profess an ability to do so.

When you see something you like, take it. And don't swipe from just one agent; steal from anyone who has stuff worth stealing, but be mindful of junk because junk parts don't work well, if at all. Also, if you steal something valuable, you should learn how to use it. Valuable stuff that is squandered or misused by you is the same as junk—to you, at least.

For this reason, when you're new, stick to the fundamentals: the stuff that definitely works (and works simply). Build your wheels from basic, proven parts (the stuff that everyone agrees works). Then, once you've built several working wheels, explore nuanced details that will enhance your systems and services.

Keep in mind: you could read every book written on real estate sales and still not get all the information you need to become a well-rounded agent. With so much nuance to consider, some of your learning must come via on-the-job experience and through meaningful conversations with other agents.

Note: this article does not endorse client theft. *Never steal clients from your fellow agents;* doing so is unethical, unlawful, and downright uncool.

6 THINGS TO COPY & STEAL

1 SCRIPTS
Always listen for scripts that are better than yours, especially when your turnover rates are low. Swipe the fresh ones for yourself.

2 SYSTEMS
Your systems are probably in need of a tune-up. Ask other agents what makes them efficient, then abscond with their best efforts.

3 SERVICES
Those extra touches can go a long way towards past clients giving you referrals. Ask agents what makes them special, then appropriate the stuff that will help you shine.

4 PROSPECTING METHODS
With over a hundred ways to prospect,[084] there's always bound to be one more. Grab the great ones and leave the rest.

5 MARKETING GIMMICKS
Watch-out for the eye-catching efforts of others. Then snatch the ones you like. Look for: giveaways, pic tricks, social media stunts, and novel email campaigns.

6 NEGOTIATION TACTICS
Like boxing, it's best to practice with someone better than you. Plunder their moves, and use them to your advantage. Gems include: the Reverse Offer[263] and the Dear Seller Letter.[269]

Effort Meter

You're Gonna Need:

Contemplation
Time
Tools
Tenacity

How-to
Create Superior Systems

Systems are the means by which one performs tasks.[012] For an example, think of the *Daily Flow Chart* as a system of systems.[346] From it springs several other flow charts and (through cross-reference) how-to articles; from each of these systems, multitudes of sub-systems, and sub-sub-systems may be created as you get into the nitty-gritty of system creation/refinement. It's a safe bet to guess that your current systems likely need improvement, so get started today:

1 Identify It
All tasks may be systematized. Think about your business tasks for a minute, then pick an important one.

2 Build It
Create a robust outline for this task: include every sub-task, sub-sub-task, and sub-sub-sub task. Determine the exact order of performance, level of importance, and skill required for each.

Next, create tools to standardize each task (or group of tasks). Common tools include forms, flow charts,[347] templates,[073] scripts,[048] checklists,[173] database,..[089]

3 Implement It
Standardization is the goal for routine tasks, so incorporate your tools (from STEP 2) into your daily real estate activities. Keep in-mind that the performance of some tasks in a system are worth more money per hour than others. When outsourcing tasks, delegate the lowest hourly jobs first. Provide your documented systems for helpers to follow. Doing so will save you time, money, and hassle.[286]

4 Refine It
Track your real estate activities and resulting turnover rates.[063] First, refine the systems associated with the lowest turnover rate. Once refined, set your sights on the systems of the next lowest turnover rate.

Ask yourself these questions and refine accordingly:
- How effective is it? Does it work the same way every time? If NO, refine.
- How efficient is it? Could it be less expense? Could it require less time (without sacrificing effectiveness)? If YES, refine.
- Is it scalable? In other words, will it grow with your business and still be effective and efficient at all stages of growth? If NO, refine.

The ideal system is written and includes *all* steps; complete with explicit instructions for the completion of each task. Plan for the future by assigning job titles to each task.[015] This tactic allows for efficient growth when hiring helpers; you'll already know which tasks to assign, and as they assume these title roles, helpers may easily follow your system(s).

tips

Systems are the lifeblood of your business. Without them, you will go nowhere.

Think of your systems as being a checklist of checklists of checklists of checklists...

Once you create a system that others can follow, hire some helpers.[286] Spend your newly freed-up time prospecting (assuming growth is one of your goals).

Anytime a system fails, refinement is required. Fix it so that it (the specific failure) won't happen again.

Superior systems allow you to spend more time working on real estate activities, and less time working on administrative tasks.

Some tasks need to be performed by the leader (you). Other tasks may be completed by someone with specialized skills. Still other tasks may be completed by anyone with half a brain. Be mindful of each when creating/refining systems.

When systems are standardized, their effectiveness and efficiency become consistent and trackable.

Σ Thoughtfully-implemented systems produce consistent client service and an increase of hourly income.

How-to
Forge a Winning Website

The purpose of your website is to generate leads and to reinforce your brand. To do each, simply ask people to visit your site, then give them a reason to stay/return.

Effort Meter

You're Gonna Need:
Relevant Content
Consistent Style
SEO Smarts
Singular Purpose

1 Give Logic to the Layout
The design, color scheme, navigation, and imagery you choose should remain consistent throughout your website and should not change with the season. If you change these things frequently, returning visitors may feel lost or on the wrong page. Place social media links at the bottom or side of each page. Keep it simple and organized; don't overwhelm with a cluttered design.

2 Feature Fantastic Listings
Place pictures and data of pretty properties in a place of prominence.[229] First featured should be those in your niche,[042] priced right.[154] Whether listed by another or belonging to your clients, these niche listings are meant to lure lookers from your newsletters,[095] flyers,[233] and other marketing efforts.

3 Blog Routinely
Profess your knowledge, announce your listings, promote your charity drives, relate your experiences, demonstrate your value,[090] and forecast your predictions.[150] Post at consistent intervals, encourage reader feedback, and stay engaged with your audience.

4 Give Others a Voice
Include a page of videos full of people saying nice things about you.[314] Send this testimonial link to prospective clients.

5 Pay for Quality IDX
Internet data exchange (IDX) is a real estate (listing) search engine embedded into your website. Your favorite MLS probably provides IDX services. Some provide nationwide listing data. Choose one that features enhanced searchability through login access.

6 Implement Good SEO
Search engine optimization (SEO) is the process of making your page appear relevant to the internet's search engines. SEO guidelines are constantly changing, so learn and implement the basics, then pay someone to do the rest.

7 Incite Action
Give them reason to contact you. Briefly, state your case on the homepage. Treat each hyperlink as a supporting argument for your agency. Ask visitors to exchange their legitimate contact info for your valuable, insider info (geared at real estate principals). That value may be an auto-email of strategy,[094] or login access to enhanced listing search, or a customized CMA from you.[140]

tips

Consider keeping the same design forever: it's your online persona.

Even if you intend to hire a professional to run your online presence, spend a few hours learning about it yourself.

Don't be boring!

If you build it, and promote it, and maintain it, *they* will make contact.

caveats

Use of a broker-provided website may save you money in the short-term, but your broker will always own that site. Create your own and you don't have to start over if/when you change brokers.

The MLS may offer you a free site. If so, use it as a directory, providing links to all your other sites: main site, social media, blog...

Ensure brokerage reciprocity agreements are in-place before displaying listings that belong to other brokers.

Never greet visitors with music on auto-play. Doing so is being an internet jerk.

Σ　Leads come via websites that offer what clients want, and from websites that people actually visit.

1 POST-CLOSING CHECKLIST
Ensures you properly remit documents to your broker, pleasantries to your clients, and updates to your systems relevant to each transaction.

2 CONTRACT TIMETABLE
Calculates deadlines in a new purchase and sale contract, allowing for immediate confirmation with all parties, ensuring no future misunderstandings.[221]

3 ELECTRONIC FILE CABINET
Stores all your documents in the cloud, methodically labeled, and logically sorted.

4 PRE-OFFER CHECKLIST
Acts as a bank of common and rare stipulations, contingencies, and exhibits, ensuring all options are in plain sight when constructing offers.[252]

5 OPEN HOUSE CHECKLIST
Contains advertisement templates, promotional procedures, sign-in sheets, signs, pens, apple pies, and any other task/tool used in the open house process.[240]

6 CURRENT CLIENTS BILLBOARD
Chart the transaction progress of clients and other pertinent details. Designed to be viewed *at-a-glance*.

7 CURRENT LEADS BILLBOARD
Chart the progress of prospects, sorted by hot, warm, and cold statuses. Designed to be viewed *at-a-glance*.

8 FORM LETTERS
Filling in the blanks makes common communication a breeze. Includes such hits:
Thank You for the Listing Appointment
Thanks for the Closing
Client Experience Survey
Attention Buyers: We've Received Multiple Offers

9 CHECKLISTS FOR CLIENTS
Full of task reminders and bring-along items, these forms help clients prepare for each approaching situation. Includes such gems as: Getting Ready to Move, Getting Ready for Closing Day, Getting Ready for Listing Day, Getting Ready to View Property...

9 SYSTEMS YOU NEED NOW

Bestow upon yourself solid systems, and ye shall have a smooth business.[070]
While they do require considerable time to construct and cultivate,
comprehensive systems payoff in the end (big time). For a well-oiled machine,
create systems for everything, then constantly tweak and refine them
until they suitably match the superior service your clients deserve.
For bonus points: make your systems paperless.

Chapter 1 Quiz

What should you do on Day One in real estate?

1
- a) order business cards
- b) get a name badge
- c) prospect for clients
- d) set up your website

Which of the following is a good reason to be scripted?

2
- a) it allows you to remain calm
- b) your ideas are conveyed clearly
- c) it lets you listen to speaker
- d) all of the above

Why is a business plan a good idea?

3
- a) it puts your goals on paper
- b) it troubleshoots bottlenecks
- c) it outlines daily tasks
- d) all of the above

What is the primary function of your website?

4
- a) an outlet to discuss your dog
- b) your chance to look like everyone else
- c) to show pictures of your latest listing
- d) to generate leads

What is the best way to ensure you get paid?

5
- a) with hope and a prayer
- b) carry a pistol
- c) by crying a little bit
- d) always get it in writing, upfront

What is the best way to overcome rejection?

6
- a) avoid conversations
- b) stay at home
- c) there's no avoiding it, only acceptance of it
- d) just give up, already

Which of the following should an agent copy & steal?

7
- a) leads
- b) clients
- c) systems
- d) am/fm cassette players

When should new agents complete first-year, state-mandated education?

8
- a) whenever it's convenient
- b) ASAP
- c) just in time
- d) all of the above

When should an agent break custom?

9
- a) whenever it benefits their client
- b) whenever the mood strikes
- c) once others do it first
- d) never

Who determines an agent's fate?

10
- a) their coach
- b) their mentor
- c) their broker
- d) that very same agent

Find the best answers throughout this chapter and on page 322.

Crypto Quip

Centuries ago, a wise man
foresaw the fate of many
modern-day, realty reps.

Break the code to read his quote.
Hint: W = E

Answer on page 322.

RQS AWOQ WYZOZW OMWLZY LWVWA SHW.
UOLC DRTYWY BRUW OLS MR,
OY ZDWC YQRIQC MARI QHYZQWYY.
—BRLJTBHTY

Just as river panning is one of many methods employed to find gold, there are numerous ways to find real estate clients. Similar to searching for glint in a stream, hitting real estate pay dirt requires one to spend time sorting through muck and mud. Handling objections and rejections, tweaking strategies and methodologies, and crafting new scripts are the toils of tilling real estate soil. There are no shortcuts: it takes continued effort to uncover clients that will pay gold. Happily, there are proven ways to hasten those nuggets.

This chapter is intended to show the reader how to lay claim to his own fortune: by approaching the client-search process in a systematic way, an agent can logically refine tactics, thereby procuring more clients, more often. After all, if a *qualified* client is real estate gold, then possessing the skill to routinely procure prospects for consideration is hitting the proverbial mother lode.

CHAPTER TWO
PROSPECTING

Get Addicted to Prospecting

When prospecting feels good, it's likely to become routine.
When prospecting is routine, it's unlikely to become neglected.

BY PAULY THE PUSHER

EVER NOTICE HOW YOU ALWAYS find time for your addictions? Morning coffee, guilty-pleasure TV shows, and three-martini lunches are a routine part of your life, and you can't get enough. That's because when it feels good, we want it more and *more*. When the thing that feels good is also good for us, our lives change—for the better.

Routine prospecting is good for you *and* it's good for your clients. Habitually speaking to lots of people about real estate gives you options, allowing you to be choosey when selecting new clients. Signing only the most-qualified principals (instead of just anyone who says YES) leads to a higher client turnover rate (CTR)[063] and increased client satisfaction. You will make more money with less hassle and your clients will think you're good at your job. Happy clients are more likely to refer your services to others,[108] which further pads your prospecting efforts, giving you even more options. Plus, an agent with a steady flow of potential clients is unlikely to provide desperate agency, pushing clients into closings just to cash-in a commission. Therefore, a healthy addiction to prospecting keeps commission breath in check.[326]

All good junkies have a ritual. Make yours challenging,[098] rewarding,[104] and fun.[114] Retreat into your prospecting booth with only your prospecting kit: phone, numbers to dial, pen & paper, your scripts, your goals, and your weekly schedule. Leave your personal life and business woes outside the door. Clear the booth of clutter and distraction; only you and your precious addiction are invited in.

Get out your scripts, give them a refreshing read-thru, then display them neatly for quick reference. Look at your daily, weekly, and monthly goals.[062] Make needed adjustments, then post your daily discussion goal on the wall, written large, with thick marker. Unfold your weekly schedule and place it within arm's reach, making mental note of its P-blocks.[064] Your pulse should begin to quicken; pick-up the phone and dial the first number. A rush will wash over you: anxiety, excitement, and hope.[056] This mix of emotions may be uncomfortable at first, but it's completely healthy. Don't worry. You've prepared for this moment,[050] so relax, but keep an edge. Stay on-task, and document every effort.

Just like anything else, the more you prospect, the better you will become. The better you become, the more likely you are to become addicted, doing it everyday. When you're new, don the façade of the addicted. Realize that each call won't be perfect, but you must be present each time. Give yourself to the experience. When it hurts, laugh it off. When it's good, get some more.

It's only once you're ensconced daily, for hours at a time, that you will begin to feel confident and in-charge of the situation, each and every phone call. Eventually, you'll feel a jones for the phone zone. Don't stop now. It feels good and you want more.

Prospects come in all types, shapes, and sizes. Try them each and find the kinds that really do it for you, but be careful: don't give-up too quickly on a particular type, as the most challenging prospects are usually the most fruitful. Fruitful results will keep you going.

Aside from the financially-fruitful, the stress-relieving, and the sweet, endorphin-releasing benefits that daily prospecting provides,[346] some agents require additional motivation to keep their addiction.[300] If this is you, try self-gifting and reward yourself when weekly goals are achieved. Perhaps you thrive on challenge. If so, find other prospecting junkies and make friendly wagers on results.

When you prospect daily, everyone wins: you win, your clients win, and your family wins. So, grab your kit, settle into your booth, and spread some good about. It feels great! 🌳

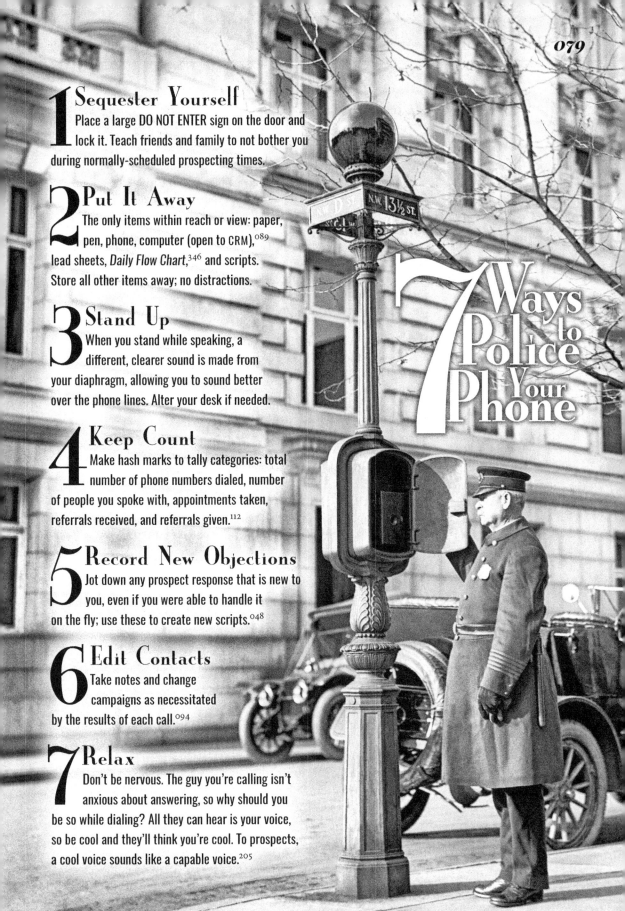

1 Sequester Yourself
Place a large DO NOT ENTER sign on the door and lock it. Teach friends and family to not bother you during normally-scheduled prospecting times.

2 Put It Away
The only items within reach or view: paper, pen, phone, computer (open to CRM),[089] lead sheets, *Daily Flow Chart*,[346] and scripts. Store all other items away; no distractions.

3 Stand Up
When you stand while speaking, a different, clearer sound is made from your diaphragm, allowing you to sound better over the phone lines. Alter your desk if needed.

4 Keep Count
Make hash marks to tally categories: total number of phone numbers dialed, number of people you spoke with, appointments taken, referrals received, and referrals given.[112]

5 Record New Objections
Jot down any prospect response that is new to you, even if you were able to handle it on the fly; use these to create new scripts.[048]

6 Edit Contacts
Take notes and change campaigns as necessitated by the results of each call.[094]

7 Relax
Don't be nervous. The guy you're calling isn't anxious about answering, so why should you be so while dialing? All they can hear is your voice, so be cool and they'll think you're cool. To prospects, a cool voice sounds like a capable voice.[205]

7 Ways to Police Your Phone

Effort Meter

You're Gonna Need:

Phone
Phone Numbers
Scripts
Chutzpa

tips

When you honestly feel like you have value to give, and the desire to help people with their real estate issues, call reluctance will subside.

Be a person. Be yourself. Be confident. Be the one they need, even if that need is to recommend a service other than your own.

Always have a voicemail script ready to read, should they not answer your call.

If the fear of rejection is too much, play the game.[058]

Call reluctance can be licked by those who role play[050] and know their lines.[049]

Keep in-mind: that which defines *the appropriate script* will vary by the type of prospect you're calling, so select and practice those specific scripts just before you dial. For quick reference, keep them on your desk or tapped to the wall. This practice will instill confidence.

caveat

If prospecting feels like begging, then you're doing it wrong.

Σ   Don't be such a wimp; the person answering your call isn't nervous, so why are you?

How-to
Overcome Call Reluctance

The most efficient way to prospect is with a telephone. For many, it's also the scariest way, leading some to shutter at the mere thought of doing so. However, the telephone gives you an advantage: the prospect's image of you is created by only the sound of your voice, the things you say, and how you say them.[008] They can't see when you're reading. They can't smell your breath. They can't see you squirm, but they sure can hear it.[051] The same way a physically-repugnant phone sex operator can conjure a caller's wanton desires, you can paint a similarly enticing picture, with a real estate twist. So, put your game voice on. There's no reason to be apprehensive when you follow these steps:

1 Know What You're Gonna Say

Once you repeat the same conversation over and over again, you will grow comfortable being part of that particular conversation. So, prospect to a niche and the repetition will ease your worry.[042] And always remember: prospecting is but a small demonstration of your value and a request to meet, so that you may further explore whether or not you and the prospect are a good fit.[168] For this reason, your scripts should be straightforward: state their problem, your solution, and a call-to-action.

2 Psyche Yourself Out

Begin by realizing that call reluctance is silly; use logic, reason, and if necessary, physical violence upon yourself until you believe it. If you need further persuasion to make this leap of faith, then chant a soothing mantra, play energizing music, or post a motivating image nearby.[300] Perhaps it's best to sit quietly, and perform the ritual of reciting scripts.[049] You know what works best for you; do that thing and psyche yourself into believing that the call isn't scary at all.

3 Get on the Horn

Don't think about it now. Just dial the number. Take a deep breath. You're feeling good, because you are good. Perform with conviction.[051]

4 Repeat

It is not uncommon for a seasoned prospector to feel nervous as he awaits a stranger to answer his call. The anticipation of what might happen next can be exciting. Because each prospect is another human, able to react in any way, each call will be like playing jazz music—the whole thing is an improvisational back and forth. And just like an experienced jazz player, an agent may find comfort in the fact that he can play his notes in a way that provokes a harmonized response from most accompanying players. Once the duet begins, this truism triggers calmness in seasoned prospectors. It's the glory onstage that shatters stage fright. So, dial again.

How-to
Build Rapport

You're gonna need to build rapport with prospects, co-op agents, vendors, and many others. Of these, rapport with prospects will garnish you the most opportunities to earn money, while playing nice with others. When they know you, like you, and trust you, they're much more likely to say YES to you.

1 Establish a Time Constraint
Ever been out shopping and a stranger strikes up a conversation with you? Most people feel awkward in this situation because they don't know when the interaction will end, allowing them to go about their business. When approaching strangers, establish a time constraint upfront and your impromptu conversations will be welcomed and feel more natural. Say something like: *I've only got a quick minute, but I wanted to ask you a question...*

2 Mimic Them
Adopt a similar tone, speech cadence, and body language as the people with whom you speak, but don't go overboard. Most people will naturally act this way when with those they feel comfortable. Your mimed efforts are simply hastening the inevitable.

3 Ask Questions
Ask about their goals, their family, their livelihood, and/or their real estate desires. Upon hearing their response, ask another question that takes the conversation deeper. Seek to understand their perspective and relate to their experiences. They're starting to like you now.

4 Find Common Ground
Topical discussion of mutual passion flows naturally between paired people, so search for items of common interest. This tactic becomes easy when you prospect in places that attract people of common bond. Try the flea market, bowling alley, or gun range.

5 Use Humor
Don't take yourself too seriously, but don't be overly (or at all) self-deprecating either. Be friendly. Be fun. Be humorous, but don't tell jokes; jokes are for buffoons.[033]

6 Be Yourself
Always be yourself, unless you're a really, *really* weird person, then be someone else. Weird is okay, but really, *really* weird is not likely to garnish much rapport.

Lead the conversation by keeping it on track. Don't be afraid to assert your opinions, even when speaking with bullheaded types. As a real estate professional, you are expected to have opinions. Just ensure you opinions are well founded and not blustering hearsay.[038]

Effort Meter

You're Gonna Need:
Personality
Interest in Them
Something to Say
Sense of Humor

tips
To re-establish rapport with someone you've lost touch, discuss the issue that separated you (in a forthcoming, honest way).

Rapport is best built over time, as a relationship progresses.

When someone knows you, likes you, or feels a common bond with you, they are less likely to say NO to you.

Document all newly-gained rapport in your database; your ability to read that history will prove resourceful in the future.[089]

People like it when you show interest in things they find interesting, so listen-up and actively participate in the conversation. Don't just wait for your turn to speak. Keep eye contact and nod your head when appropriate.

caveats
You must build rapport before adding a prospect to your database. To do otherwise is less civilized and largely a waste of time, as this person surely feels invaded by you and your real estate vomit.

Those who make friends easily may find this article less helpful. But for those who struggle...

Σ   Relate to people as the unique, human creatures they are.

Effort Meter

You're Gonna Need:

Mouth
Valuable Incite
Personal Stats
Engagement

tips
Most people don't care about you nearly as much as they care about themselves, so show them what's in it for them.[090]

Billboard, radio, TV, and print ads of your face are expensive, so be sure to track their results.

For most agents, advertising money is most-efficiently spent showing-off listings, not their smiling face.

Don't assume the people you know are aware of your involvement in real estate sales. Remind them with a blurb, until they can recite it at the mere thought of you.

Track your methods for attracting clients: record time and money spent, as well conversion ratios and tactical effectiveness.[063]

caveat
New agents are often the target of advertisement salesmen, hawking the virtues of your face on grocery store buggies, the reverse side of printed receipts, and bus benches. Beware of these "opportunities" to part with your hard-earned dollars. You'll always get more bang for your buck when you open your mouth and talk to people, instead of your mug shot staring them down while they pick produce.

Σ Once you engage people with your real estate mouth, you'll find prospects lurking *everywhere*.

How-to
Expose Yourself (to the Market)

Some say: to sell real estate, you must sell yourself. This pseudo-axiomatic saying smacks of prostitution, so to be clear: selling yourself (the way by which one fishes for prospective clients) may be exercised by either of two means—advertising or prospecting.

Advertising is quick and easy, but requires a steady outflow of money to keep leads coming your way. Prospecting, on the other hand, requires time and toil. Of the two, (effective) prospecting is more efficient because, due to human nature, people tend to hire professionals they meet through "organic" means, like face-to-face encounters or introductions through friends.[108] People tend to respond to advertising when looking for a transactional relationship, like when shopping for gasoline, microwave ovens, or a house to buy. Therefore, your best play to receive a steady supply of inbound leads is to engage people first-hand through prospecting and to advertise your listings (not your face) to attract buyers.

1 Talk to People (with Your Mouth)
Meeting people always leads to knowing more people. Some of these people will become clients, some will refer clients to you, and others will provide products and services that you and your clients will want. The more people you know, the more people will know you. Therefore, to keep meeting new people, you must perpetuate current relationships by being the one who initiates conversations. So, inject yourself and propel your notions of real estate sales into their consciousness.[086]

Speak individually with people, like neighbors of your listings and friends of your buyers. Prospect to those who have heard of you or have seen your yard signs. Go to your seller's workplace, and make an announcement: anyone who introduces a visiting buyer gets a prize (check the rules before giving gifts).[036]

2 Connect People
Be the guy who introduces people to each other. When you meet someone looking to buy a car, hook them up with your favorite automobile dealer. When someone says they love to dig in the dirt, tell them of the garden club to which a past client belongs. When you discover someone in need of a real estate vendor, introduce your posse.[179] Connect people (without immediate gain to you), and people will come to know you and love you. Helpful and genuine for the win.

3 Advertise Your Listings/Statistics
Use your listing inventory to attract buyers. Treat all callers as fresh leads for plundering: pre-qualify them,[170] then lure them to your lair.[171] Advertisement of your face can be tricky because not every agent can claim to be *number one*. Even so, the top slot is a subjective one. Instead of claiming generic greatness, broadcast your statistics and services, and be specific about it: champion your short listing periods, average DOM, SP/LP, and CTR.

1 RIFF SOME STATS

Oozing market statistics from the mouth is one of the sexiest things an agent can do! It simultaneously demonstrates intelligence and competency. Extra points for relevancy.[146]

2 SPEECH! SPEECH!

Standing before others, espousing your knowledge and beliefs, is a sure way to garner attention.[090] Afterwards, many people are sure to approach you (unless you're boring). Various groups are always looking for speakers. Volunteer!

3 GET OTHERS TO TESTIFY

Word-of-mouth is the best kind of mouth there is. Record video testimonials, then plaster those videos in appropriate places.[314]

4 BUMPER STICKERS

If it's written on a bumper, then it must be true! Make your own and stick 'em everywhere. Example: *I Brake for Agent Andy*

5 PRE-LISTING PACKAGE

Send 'em a gift bag before the listing appointment. Include tons of valuable stuff. Extra points for sending it to their workplace.[193]

5 WAYS TO TOOT YOUR HORN

105 Ways to Meet Prospects

TALK to PEOPLE

Everyday People in Everyday Places
They're just people, and they have houses to buy and/or sell

1 on an AIRPLANE
2 at the FARMER'S MARKET
3 at the DOG PARK
4 in the GROCERY STORE
5 at CHURCH
6 at the COFFEE SHOP
7 by KNOCKING ON DOORS

Pros You Patronize
You give them business, so they should return the favor. They have clients, too; it's always worth the ask.

8 DOCTOR
9 DENTIST
10 TAILOR
11 VETERINARIAN
12 FORTUNE TELLER

Industry Pros
Other real estate agents often have overflow leads that they cannot handle. Or perhaps, are outside of their niche, or they just don't like them.

13 RESIDENTIAL AGENTS
14 COMMERCIAL AGENTS
15 BUSINESS BROKERS

Pick-Up the Phone
Ring 'em up, and chat 'em up.

16 Call people in your CELL PHONE
17 Cold call from the PHONE BOOK

Oh So Clever!
Use public records to identify and contact these owners. Chances are good they need to sell sometime soon.

18 SHABBY PROPERTY OWNERS
19 OUTTA-STATE OWNERS

★★★ VENDORS & SUCH ★★★

20 LOAN OFFICERS	25 APPRAISERS
21 REAL ESTATE LAWYERS	26 MOVING COMPANIES
22 HOME INSPECTORS	27 GENERAL CONTRACTORS
23 ESCROW COMPANIES	28 HOUSE PAINTERS
24 WARRANTY AGENTS	29 ROOFERS

These folks know the score. Reach-out to them for meeting new buyers and sellers, and you'll know the score too.

★ ★ ★ ★ ★ ★ ★ ★ ★ ★ ★ ★

Social Media
Keep an eye out for these events, as they often accompany the need for home buying or selling. Then do some socializing

30 WEDDINGS
31 NEW BABIES
32 DEATHS

Trade Shows
Stick your neck out at these events, and you will attract people willing to chat about buying/selling. Then do some house trading.

33 WALK AROUND
34 RENT A BOOTH
35 MAKE A SPEECH

⚙kid events⚙

36 BIRTHDAY PARTIES	39 SCOUT MEETINGS
37 PLAYGROUNDS	40 DANCE RECITALS
38 SPORTS GAMES	41 PTA MEETINGS

Since you're gonna be there anyway, might as well hit the other parents up for some real estate sales.

GOOD OL' STAND-BYS

Easy Listings
They're ready to sell, and ready for your help. Give 'em a ring-a-ding!

42 FSBOs
43 EXPIRED LISTINGS
44 WITHDRAWN LISTINGS

Investors
You can meet investors in many places. Here are just a few:

45 STOP BY THEIR PROJECTS
46 ATTEND INVESTOR CLUB MTGs
47 HOST A SEMINAR

Host a Seminar
Get a space, advertise, and teach them something new.

48 FIRST-TIME HOME BUYERS
49 FORECLOSURE AVOIDANCE
50 HOW-TO BE AN INVESTOR

Financial Nerds
These folks always know of people that need to buy or sell.

51 ACCOUNTANTS (CPAs)
52 ESTATE PLANNERS (CFPs)

BIG (WO)MAN ON CAMPUS

Spread the word! There are many ways to prospect on college campuses. Many loan products allow for a non-occupant co-signer. This means Mom can help Junior buy a house, and rent to his buddies. Nearly-free rent for Junior, and accumulated equity at graduation. 53 SURVEY: College students love giving their opinion. Ask: "What is your opinion of the current real estate market?" Then: "What if I could show you a way...?" Don't forget to get Mom's phone number. 54 SPEAK WITH PROFESSORS: Professors are people with steady jobs and open office hours. 55 GUEST LECTURE: Speak at a seminar or in a class about real estate. The speaker/expert always gets attention from the audience. 56 GRADUATION: Mill about after the ceremony and speak to new grads about crash pads.

Home Builders
Builders are always looking for competent agents to help sell existing inventory, or find the next project. Track them down, and make your pitch.

57 DRIVE BY THEIR PROJECT
58 ATTEND BUILDER MEETINGS

FSBO Lookout Squad
Enlist the help of those that frequently drive through neighborhoods. They notice any and all changes to yards. All you need are cell pics of the FOR SALE signs in those yards (the phone numbers). The rest is up to you.

59 BUS DRIVERS   60 DELIVERY DRIVERS
61 LETTER CARRIERS   62 GARBAGE MEN

...Just to Name a Few

for Better OR WORSE

These events beckon an agent.

63 WEDDING PLANNERS
64 DIVORCE ATTORNEYS

GOOD OL' NEARBYS

Hobbies

Turn your hobbies into ways of making money. You're gonna be there anyway, so let people know what you do.

65 BOWLING ALLEY
66 SPORTS LEAGUE
67 QUILTING CLUB
68 SHOOTING RANGE
69 WATERING HOLE

Networking Events

If you're gonna attend, don't just stand around talking to people you already know. Mingle. Ask, "What can I do to help your business?" Join these groups and go during lunch or after work hours.

70 CHAMBERS OF COMMERCE
71 SPEECH CLUBS
72 SMALL BUSINESS ADMINISTRATION (SBA)

1-800 Number

Buy a toll-free number and market it to niche buyers and sellers with "free recorded information." When they call, the system captures the inbound number so you can call them back. Niches include:

73 FIRST TIME BUYERS
74 EMPTY NESTERS
75 STUDENTS
76 FORECLOSURE AVOIDANCE

DON'T FEAR THE REAPER

Dead men don't need housing!

77 MORTICIANS
78 INSURANCE AGENTS
79 PROBATE ATTORNEYS

Are They Getting Ready to Move?

Check the local listings, then stop-in at these type of sales. You'll get a new listing or a new dinette set.

80 ESTATE SALES
81 YARD SALES
82 ANTIQUE DEALERS

Start a Farm

It takes a long while to get it going, but once your farm is established, this source of leads is never ending.

83 SUBDIVISIONS/NEIGHBORHOODS
84 SENIOR CITIZEN NEIGHBORHOODS
85 APARTMENT COMPLEXES

Attend Festivals

Most communities have an annual snozzberry or whatnot festival. Some communities have weekly events in quaint downtown locales. Find these events and go happily-a-prospecting.

86 SET-UP A BOOTH
87 HAND-OUT CLEVER MARKETING STUFF

88 Past Clients

You worked hard to get 'em the first time, so you might as well work at keeping them as future clients and as referral sources.

Open Houses

Guess who looks at open houses? People do! If you don't have listings, borrow one. Get other agents involved for a caravan of open houses, and give prizes to buyers that attend every one.

89 YOUR LISTINGS
90 HOST FOR ANOTHER

Auctions

This is where you will find an abundance of people interested in buying and selling real estate. Spend some time here and get to know the rules, while getting to know the participants.

101 PUBLIC AUCTIONS
102 PRIVATE AUCTIONS

SPECIAL PROGRAMS

Loan Programs

There are special loan programs available to those that serve the community. Learn about these loans, then meet the qualified where they work.

91 TEACHERS
92 FIREFIGHTERS
93 COPS
94 MILITARY

Financial Education

The Neighborhood Assistance Corporation of America (NACA) is a non-profit organization dedicated to teaching borrowers about affordable and responsible home ownership. Agents completing the program are afforded qualified, educated buyers. Sign up today!

95 NACA

ONLINE EFFORTS

96 Purchase Leads Online

You can always buy leads from internet sources. Some of these leads are good and some are bad and some are sold to multiple agents. Before you try this route, be sure to fully investigate what it is you are actually buying. Before signing an annual agreement, attempt a one-month trial.

97 Online Marketing

Agents are allowed to market HUD Listings online, anywhere they wish (not just their personal website). Buyers will call.

Foreclosures

Who says you can't list foreclosed properties? Visit 98 LOCAL BANKS, as their foreclosure department is local. Look-up 99 REO COMPANIES and get on their list to receive listings. Scour 100 PUBLIC ADS for properties in foreclosure, then approach the distressed owners for help selling the property before their dooms day comes.

Get Nutty with It

There are many ways to be creative with prospecting. 103 CRAZY VAN is when you and a bunch of fun agents drive around looking for FSBOs. When FSBO answers the door, each agent becomes busy taking photos, measurements, and notes of features, as the lead agent entices FSBO to list. 104 MOBILE OPEN HOUSE is when a group of agents get a bunch of buyers onto a bus and tour several available houses. When a particular buyer becomes interested in making an offer, one agent stays behind and drafts the documents. 105 SANDWICH BOARD is when agents take turns wearing an old-fashioned sandwich board touting the benefits of home ownership. Gnarly!

People Don't Often Think About You

Ideally, when they do think of you, they're also thinking about real estate... and vice-versa.

BY BARRY THE BALLBUSTER

JUST LIKE YOU, people have their own lives to live; they think mostly of themselves, and rightly they should. Each individual sees their life as being more important than yours. That's not to say people are completely without thought of others; we are humans after all.

As humans, we associate words, thoughts, concepts, feelings, sensations, and people with other words, thoughts, concepts, feelings, sensations, and people. The stronger the connection, the more likely we are to associate.

When we hear the word ice, we think of coldness. When we see a baby, we think of innocence. And when we taste bacon, we think of heaven. Likewise, when the people you know think about real estate, you want them to simultaneously think of you.

Your problem is that an overwhelming majority of the people you know (and will ever know) are mere acquaintances, not friends. People don't usually associate real estate with an acquaintance, unless there is a strong connection between the two. Because of this, the people you currently know probably also know several other real estate acquaintances, but won't think of a single one of you when they're thinking of buying or selling real estate. Instead, they tend to think only of themselves. They're even less likely to think of you when someone they know is thinking of buying or selling (your referral opportunities).

You cannot blame them for not thinking of you, because it's not their fault. Their lapse of memory is not on purpose—it's because their association between you and real estate is weak.

Capitalize upon each of your relationships by fostering those relationships: call people you know and tell (or remind) them that you are in real estate sales. Tell them of your dream that one day they will associate real estate with your name, and your name exclusively. Tell them why doing so is in their best interest.[212] Tell them to call you with all their real estate questions, concerns, and comments: you wanna be their real estate resource.[038]

Explain your knowledge of mankind's inherent forgetfulness of his acquaintances' occupations. Say: *It's okay—I'm not offended.* Ask if you may strengthen your connection by calling every so often, asking if they know anyone currently looking to buy or sell real estate.[108] Ask if you may add them to your newsletter[095] and ask them to call you with real estate issues, big and small.

Repeat this conversation with every person you know at least four times per year. When your acquaintance is a likely buyer or seller, call on them more often (especially the FSBO, EXPIRED, and WITHDRAWN sellers).[098]

Likely buyers and sellers are thinking about real estate constantly. They're searching real estate online, they're talking to people about it, and they're looking for solutions. The one real estate-related thing they're probably *not* thinking about is you. They're thinking of themselves and how they're gonna solve their real estate issues. Sadly, regardless of their existing relationships, most people hire the agent who is standing before them when their real estate needs arise. However, those who strongly associate real estate with a particular agent are likely to call that agent.

Insert yourself into the thoughts of your acquaintances with repeated reminders. Tie yourself to their real estate conscience and keep the relationship alive. Give them a call right now—you'll be glad you did.

Whether or not you realize it,
social media networking is the exact same
as all forms of analog networking, except for one major
difference: you may interact with others when they are not physically
present. For this reason, this book will not go into explanation of
which social networks to use (as the preferred ones are subject
to change), how to use them (as their formats vary), nor their
customs (as regular social norms and niceties should control).

In the stead of in-depth analysis, remember this simple gentility:
treat social media interactions the same way you would
if you were standing face-to-face with your audience.

Begin by creating a business account, separate from your personal one, and
invite people via customized messages. Before sending a connection request to a
stranger, explain who you are, how you are connected, and why you wish to associate.
Blank requests to become "friends" will be fruitless, dispassionate, and impersonal.

Keep all content on-topic. Forgo those cute kitten posters and sensational
celebrity stories—unless they're real estate specific, of course.

Post much more than only the gorgeous pictures of your latest listing and its accompanying
open house invitations. When each of your broadcasts appear to be self-serving, your
audience will view referral requests as more splattering of vainglorious vomit.

Interact. Converse. Exchange ideas.
Show more. Be creative. Demonstrate your value.
For 'tis far better to have a small, engaged audience
than a large one that ignores your bullhorn.

A Note on Social Media

A Serious How-to Manual with a Sense of Humor

Effort Meter

You're Gonna Need:

Bravado
Cheesy Script
Capture Device
Money

tips

As an agent, it is your job to be the one that initiates contact with people (each and every encounter), and not the other way around. Never rely on prospects to call you.[086]

Your hesitation may be the loss of a wonderful relationship. Ask for their engagement when it feels right. If it never feels right, then you're doing it wrong.

Asking someone to "share" information with you will be more warmly received than the command of *Gimme your phone number.*

Σ Let them know that you respect their privacy and your desire is to become their valuable, go-to real estate resource—not a telemarketing thorn in their side.

How-to
Get Contact Information

Since you need to communicate with prospects, acquisition of their digits is a daily activity with which you should be comfortable. After all, it's pretty darn hard to communicate with someone when you don't have their phone number(s) or address(es).

1 Ask for It

Remembering that there are multiple ways to ask for things,[008] open your mouth and invite a new relationship. Pre-built rapport should ease their hesitation, as well as your reticence.[081] So, when you're speaking with someone, and feel the conversation winding-down, and you get a nervous feeling at the thought of asking for their contact information, take comfort knowing that their potential rejection is not a reflection on you.[056] Besides, you may never see this person again, so why should you care if they say NO?

2 Barter for It

When someone rebuffs your original request to collect contact information, offer a trade. Say something like:
« Let's swap cards, »
as you extend your palm-sized billboard. To this they may reciprocate, or they may say something like:
« I don't have one. »
To this response, smile and offer a solution:
« That's not a problem for people with pens.
   Let's make one for you now, »
you could say, extending a second, down-turned business card, dressed with a heavy pen. This novelty seems silly, but boasts a high conversion ratio (so long as you say in with a cheesy, non-patronizing tone).

Variation:
« That's not a problem for people with thumbs, »
you could say, extending your hand-held, electronic device with the contacts app glowing on-screen.

Regardless of how you receive their information, ensure they are comfortable with the transaction. Reassure them of your honorable intention to develop a mutually-fruitful real estate relationship.

3 Pay for It

When it comes to acquiring contact information for large groups or for specific types of prospects, paying someone else to do all the selecting and organizing is an efficient method of procurement. You may find online providers peddling FSBO, EXPIRED, and WITHDRAWN seller leads. You can purchase prospect data for specified neighborhoods, zip codes, and school districts. If you look carefully, you'll find lists for organizations like teachers, government workers, club memberships, and online communities.

How-to
Create & Keep a Database

A phone book is a list of names and phone numbers, but a database is a list of *relationships*. When that database is customized, categorized, and organized, it can become the single greatest tool for a continuous, steady flow of prospect-to-client conversions.

1 Customize

Customer relationship management (CRM) software is a tool designed to manage data, streamline communication, and propagate client conversion. Hundreds of vendors offer CRM solutions with varying levels of application. Dozens are designed specifically for real estate sales; some of these CRM offer robust, customizable features while others do not. Inspect several before choosing the right one for you, and remember the old adage: you get what you pay for.

Along with member data, create and upload campaigns.[094] This customization takes tons of time to complete, but is well worth it, so don't scrimp on the details during creation.

2 Categorize

Assign members to categories and your database becomes searchable. For each member, apply at least one category from each of the three main entries listed below. All subsequent categories will be dependent upon your niche(s).

1.x Do You Know Them?
2.x How Do You Know Them?
3.x What Campaign Are They On?
4.x, 5.x, 6.x,.. Special Designations

Categorization is critical. For example: suppose you get a hot tip on a rehab project. With the push of a button, every investor you know pops-up on-screen; your quick action is the difference in a sale, or not.

3 Organize

Think of yourself as a doctor and all the people in this world as potential patients. Each time you see a new patient, a new medical record is created and every time you speak thereafter warrants an update to the record. Campaigns are your current prescriptions.[092]

Make contact with each member at least once a month.[095] Follow prescribed campaign formulas (as shown in the column: 3.x Campaigns). Those who are not on a campaign will likely become lost in your database. Your mission: never leave a database member behind.

4 Scrutinize

Your business is your database; daily maintenance promotes efficient communication, so live inside it and keep it clean and organized. For example: once a buyer-prospect has become a client, it doesn't make much sense to continue sending him emails designed to convert him into a client.

Effort Meter

You're Gonna Need:
CRM
Members
Daily Maintenance
Stick-To-Itiveness

tips
Some CRM include a mobile app that allows for updates while in the field, away from your desk.

membership categories
1.x Met Status
1.1 We've Met
1.2 We Have Not Met
1.3 We Should Meet Soon

2.x Relationship
2.1 Friends & Family
2.2 Current Client
2.3 Past Client
2.4 Referral Giver
2.5 Advocate
2.6 Investor
2.7 Real Estate Agent
2.8 Vendor
2.9 Hot Prospect

3.x Campaigns
3.1 Just Met
3.2 Newsletter
3.3 New Client Buyer
3.4 New Client Seller
3.5 Prospect: Short-Term Buyer
3.6 Prospect: Short-Term Seller
3.7 Prospect: Long-Term Buyer
3.9 FSBO
3.10 Expired Seller

4.x Farms
4.1 Church
4.2 Bowling Alley
4.3 Kids Activities
4.4 Subdivision #1
4.5 Subdivision #2

Σ   An organized database that fosters steady client conversion is a valuable asset that may be sold, leased, or converted into a part-time referral business upon retirement.

Give Value First

Be authentic, be passionate, and be consistent. Lead with valuable information and watch your client intake increase.

BY GLENDA THE GIVER

GIVE QUALITY VALUE. Go deeper than the average agent. Give quality value upfront. Don't wait until they're clients. Give quality value for free. Tell about the market, tell about recalls, tell about community. Go into more (relevant) detail. Share the insider stuff. Let them see behind the curtain. Be their curator. Your commitment to disseminating quality information will certainly make you stand out from other agents.

Every group has a special interest. Discover the interests of your niche market and publish the interesting knowledge they crave. Reach them through various outlets and keep giving it away. Give more to get more. Give in-depth reviews, and provide recommendations of products, services, strategies, and concepts. Explain laws and customs. Clarify the purchase process and spotlight items of community interest. Don't show them only what they need to know, but also what they want to know. Your insight will build within them likability and trust of you.

Give value by doing more homework, by knowing more, by caring about their needs, and by helping them make informed decisions. Teach the good stuff. Enlighten. Make it simple to digest. Use emotion *and* logic to show them what's in it for them.

Be consistent in your message, delivery, and approach. When blogging, give information weekly, on the same day of the week, each and every week. Soon, your audience will grow to expect your message at that time, with that same look and style.[071]

To ensure you're giving them what they want, ask for feedback (to their face, by telephone, in your newsletter, through online comments in your videos,..). Once your efforts gain steam, don't change the look or the pace by which you give value, otherwise you may lose some of your audience.

When you give substantially upfront, prospects will expect that you give even more value to clients. When people (prospects and fellow agents) see the quality and depth of your knowledge, they'll assume you know more, deeming you an expert; everyone wants to work with an expert.

Prospects are apt to hire agents who give away valuable information because when they consume your knowledge, a sense of reciprocal obligation overcomes them. They will feel compelled to hire you once they feel enriched by your upfront efforts. Their compulsion is not a dubious trick on your part; it's a testament to your transparency and your commitment to truly help others with their real estate needs.[245]

Your true value comes from your ability to smoothly guide a high percentage of your clients through successful closings; echo this value and this value only. Recipe cards and tablespoon-to-cup conversion magnets miss the mark. You wouldn't take gardening tips from your mechanic, so don't expect people to digest kitchen tips from a real estate agent.

Because real estate transactions are complicated and full of difficult decisions, people often feel overwhelmed and apprehensive. Settle their fears by shining light on their unknown options.[207] Anticipate their interests, their questions, and their concerns. Think of what they want and what they need, then fulfill their order before they even ask. Do this and you'll become the one they think of when they're thinking of real estate.[086]

Your generous giving will cause people to feel that you not only care for them, but that you are capable of delivering quality service. When this happens, prospecting becomes fun and conversion ratios increase.[063] So, don't be afraid to give it away—just be certain it's of true value and that they notice it. 🌳

When a prospect's only objection to hiring you is that of your brokerage affiliation, they're most likely lying through their teeth. There are people who cling to brand recognition, but those are extremely few in numbers. The brand name brush-off is really just a nice way to say, "I don't want you." Their intent is to find a seemingly-impossible-to-overcome objection, saving you the sting (and themselves the explanation) of an outright rejection. Similar brush-offs include (after asking of your tenure), "I need an agent with more years of experience," and "I need an agent who has sold property in my neighborhood previously (or recently)." When you hear these excuses, they either don't like you, don't trust you, feel like you don't know what you're doing, or they simply don't believe the words that are coming from you mouth. Once a prospect disguisedly declares you unfit for hire, your next best-move is to address their actual concern; honest dialogue will sometimes coax their agreement. If that doesn't work, you may then offer to co-list or refer your objector to an agent who fits their description.[112]

Very Few Care: the Name of Your Broker

A Serious How-to Manual with a Sense of Humor

Mix It Up

Don't be a broken record; blend campaign formats and more of your audience will listen.

BY DJ LEADZ

YOUR LEAD-GENERATION CAMPAIGNS are the songs your business sings. Those with a catchy chorus will encourage throngs of people to either hire or refer your services; dullard ditties will repel them in droves.

Depending upon the type of prospect(s) you're playing to, your songs may be either short or long in duration, fast or slow in rhythm, detailed or brief in content, widely or narrowly focused in scope. Regardless of style and scope, every member of your database should be on a playlist,[089] listening to one song or another at all times. Since nobody wants to hear the same thing, *the same way*, over and over again, keep the beat going, but vary the tempo and melody.

Develop campaigns for the purposes of informing targeted groups of people:[094] newly-met people, newsletter-getters, short-term buyers and sellers, long-term buyers and sellers, FSBO, EXPIRED and WITHDRAWN sellers, investors, new buyer and seller clients, repeat clients, recently-closed clients, newly under-contract clients, advocates, vendors, neighborhood-specific prospects, niche market prospects, and several more.

Because each prospect is an individual, overall response to your compositions will be varied. For this reason, your campaigns should be tuned to the average prospect's ear.

You'll hook some by sounding smart and showing statistics. Others will hop to your value as a resource, and some will swing to the style of your rap. Weave each of your endearing attributes into the mix and most folks will jump and jive in kind.

Get the party started by developing a theme song. Play it as the first song newly-met people hear (play it for everyone when you're a new agent). Your theme tune introduces you, establishes your value as a real estate professional, demonstrates your hustle, and all that jazz. Make this intro-campaign short and sweet, then spin its notes into the basis of all your other campaigns.

Email is the best delivery method by which to beat your drum, but for noteworthy campaigns, you should create a fusion of styles by mixing media formats. Mix-in phone calls, snail mails, text messages, videos, door knocks, party invitations, links to blog posts, online resources, and testimonials.[314]

Embed video into your newsletters, but don't ramble-on about nonsense. Send postcards and marketing tchotchkes in the mail, but don't send boring stuff that goes unnoticed or into the trash. Add telephone calls, but don't call without an agenda. Ask your prospect: *Are you receiving my communication? Is it helpful? Any questions? Got referrals? Ready to sign an agency agreement?*

Each step of a campaign should be strategically timed in content, style, and frequency. Keep yours exciting and inspiring by blending your best efforts into a conga line of specific messages designed to enlighten, demonstrate value,[090] and spur action. Don't simply draft campaigns, consisting solely of emails, setting them to drip, then forgetting all about them. When you let campaigns lose on auto-play, and then fail to monitor effectiveness or solicit feedback, you're likely to miss the lowdown on your own hoedown.

Your campaign songs should all have the same message: *Hire me!* Repeat this chorus in various ways, by various methods, with various verses, motifs, and anthems. Spend considerable time crafting and calibrating your campaigns until your groove produces acceptable conversion ratios.[063]

When your songs inspire them to dance, they'll be lined up, around the corner, clamoring to get in. When you keep a velvet rope at the door, barring all but the most-qualified, money will soon line your pockets. Now, face the music and rock on! ♣

Get 'Em DANCING to Your Campaigns

Sample Campaign Mix Tape:

1 email
Start with compelling, valuable info.

2 phone call
Confirm email delivery.

3 text message
Quick fact with supporting link.

4 email
Send valuable info.

5 email
Introduce your posse.

6 phone call
Have voicemail script ready to deploy.

7 link to video
Testimonial of satisfied client.

8 email
Send valuable info.

9 handwritten note
Your personal touch goes a long way.

10 phone call
Invite them to either meet for presentation, sign agency agreement, or send referral. Depending upon their response, switch them to another campaign or re-start this campaign. To those who duck your jive: boot their butts from your database.

Campaigns are meant to incite action. To do so, disseminate valuable information with supporting arguments to hire/refer you. Then, make phone calls to personally ask for their hand in agency. For maximum effect, keep everyone on a campaign—at all times.

A Serious How-to Manual with a Sense of Humor

Effort Meter

You're Gonna Need:

Content
CRM
Upfront Time
Maintenance

How-to
Wage a Campaign

Everyone you know and meet is a prospective client and/or referral source. Some are hot prospects, likely to buy or sell soon. Others are warm prospects, likely to someday buy or sell, and likely to hire you at that time (so long as they don't forget you first).[086]

Your ongoing campaigns to enlist these people as clients will become more efficient through preconceived, yet personalized communication. When you begin with a solid plan of action, you're bound to win their hearts, their minds, and (hopefully) their dollars.

1 Conduct Reconnaissance

Create campaigns for specific purposes. A narrow focus with clear and consistent call-to-action will encourage increased conversion ratios.[063] Customize your campaigns with regard to recurrence, duration, and mixture of communication methods.[092]

2 Ready Your Resources

Whether you create the content yourself, or use already-generated content, edit it to reflect your voice. Each email should be single-themed, concise, and (when appropriate) bullet-pointed. If your emails are long, few will read them. When done with forethought, your content will read like you composed each message custom, specifically for the recipient. Include links to your website's MLS search page, previous blog posts, or other outside content that will enrich their experience.

Write telephone and voicemail scripts to validate and reinforce the purpose of your campaign. Ask: *Are you receiving my emails? Are they valuable? Are you ready to sign an agency agreement?* Then recite the *Referral Script*.[108]

3 Take Aim

Always seek the permission of people prior to placing them on a campaign. This practice is polite and it invites a warm reception to your advances.[081] Maintain your campaigns daily, checking progress, and placing prescribed phone calls.

Keep everyone you know on a campaign at all times (but only one at a time). Once a campaign ends for a given member, assign them to another campaign. Eject from your database those members you foresee no hope of future relationship.

4 FIRE!

Once you've drafted and titled a series of pre-written emails, phone scripts, voicemails, and postcards, load them into your CRM[089] and set to a systematic delivery schedule. Doing so will allow you to send correspondence automatically, with the push of a button, providing alerts for phone calls and snail mails. Your upfront effort to construct campaigns will save time in the future.

tips

Email alone cannot assure prospect conversion.

A campaign set to autopilot is said to "drip" on recipients. Drip campaigns allow you to set it and forget it, because you're reminded to not neglect it.

Campaigns can be utilized for endeavors other than prospecting.[089]

Offer website visitors the ability to opt-into specific campaigns.

To show your value as a resource, spotlight your posse within campaigns; they may even pay to be included.[179]

On each member's profile in your CRM, keep track of their past campaigns. This will prevent you from doubling-up on a single member (unless they need it).

Add a personal touch by placing a phone call to end each campaign.

caveats

A member without a campaign is lost in your database. Don't waste.

This article assumes you use a customizable CRM.[089]

Σ Because you're likely to wage the same campaign over and over again, create specific, valuable content one time, then deliver that content to a target audience whenever appropriate.

How-to
Construct a Newsletter

Because rapport increases conversion ratios, an emailed newsletter is the perfect, inexpensive and dynamic tool to build a positive association between you and the topic of real estate. Besides, a monthly demonstration of your real estate value is just enough of you and your jibber-jabber for most people to consume.

Since most people aren't interested in real estate on a monthly basis, your challenge will be enticing your audience to open and read your newsletter each month. To encourage ongoing readership, make each newsletter as intriguing as possible and leave-out the boring. Short and sweet construction is best delivered in three distinct, cascading sections:

1 Local Events and Happenings
Provide ten or so hyperlinks to local events like evening cocktails at the botanical gardens, the blueberry festival in the town square, bat night at the local ballpark, and free concerts on the village green. Consider links to locally-proposed legislation and/or ordinances of community impact. When done properly, these hyperlinks will be the reason people (other than your mom) will look forward to your email each month.

2 Brief Blurb about Real Estate
The second section should be a written article that further demonstrates your value as a real estate professional. Consider real estate topics that people will find interesting even when they're not in the market to buy or sell; write about market trends, home maintenance, and/or technology.

Provide only the first paragraph or two, then a *click here to continue reading* link that directs readers to your website/blog.[071] At your site, they may continue reading the featured article and/or find related articles written by you. If you do not have any writings, then copy someone else's work.[068] Always get written permission prior to posting stolen articles, and then be sure to cite your source.

3 Featured Listings
Spotlight a "Listing of the Month." If you do not currently have any listings, then borrow one from another agent. Pick a well-priced one[154] with lots of interesting photos.[230] Supply select details, with a link back to your website for additional information. Details to provide: price, number of bedrooms/bathrooms, unique features, and an address (address could be just the street name, city, *or* zip code).

Showing only one or two pics, plus limited data will serve readers in two ways: 1) your hyperlink directs curious readers to your value-filled website,[071] and 2) your abridged newsletter appears lean and mean, without bloat. Bloviated words and goofy clip-art may lead to being ignored, or worse—cancelled subscriptions.

You're Gonna Need:
Template
Local Research
Content
an Attractive Listing

tips

Find software to help with your newsletter format—or if you know how and are creative—do it yourself for a truly unique look.

Once you select a template for your newsletter, do not change the look. People will grow accustom to the style and arrangement of your newsletter; changing your look may render you unrecognizable.

To save time, create your articles several months in advance (in one sitting) so that you may insert the work as needed.

Encourage feedback by asking readers for their opinions. Then give them what they want.[090]

Your brokerage may provide a pre-formed newsletter aimed at a national audience, but that might not be what you need; your readers want *your* opinion and a local touch.

Keeping your subject line consistent from month-to-month will keep your emailed newsletter recognizable.

To remain legit, always include a conspicuously-placed unsubscribe button in your newsletters.

Σ A monthly, emailed newsletter is an effective and efficient way to continuously demonstrate your real estate value to a large audience.

Buyers Are Attracted to Listings, Always Listings

Dear Andy,
I have a top-of-the-line, state-of-the-art website, but I'm not getting any leads from it. Where am I going wrong?
—*Lamented by Leads*

Dear Lamented,

Agents often fall prey to the latest and greatest promises of a new website, pledging to deliver hot, fresh buyer leads by the dozen. However, your website alone, acting all by itself (no matter how great it may be), cannot automatically bring you an abundance of quality leads. Only an agent's ongoing, fastidious efforts will produce leads.

First, realize that neither seller nor buyer prospects shop for agents online. Instead, they're searching for information. At times, these prospects will have questions regarding information they've found and will contact whichever agent appears to be the provider of that info. All you have to do is provide the content they desire, then lure them to your content.

Sellers want to know the value of their property and buyers want to see listings. Due to their need of highly-customized content, steadily snaring sellers from online methods alone is more than challenging. On the other hand, buyers are looking for data (listings), of which there is ample supply. For this reason, buyers may be caught with bait and hook.

To snag these buyers, use listings as your bait and a call-to-action as the hook (doubling as a hyperlink). Remembering that attractive listings get the most bites,[153] experiment with images and content until you get the formula right. Post your bait/hooks (daily) in a variety of online places, including message boards, yard sale and social media sites,[087] email campaigns,[094] newsletters,[095] and within your email signature.[026] If allowed, add your link to your MLS datasheet.

Implement the latest SEO techniques[071] and consider buying space on national, third-party syndication sites that specialize in real estate content. Track clicks with analytical software to hone your efforts.

Get as much traffic flowing to your site as possible, then give them a reason to stay and come back again.[090] Provide info, insight, and rich MLS data. Buyers want to see listings, so show them listings with lots of pictures and tons of data. Offer visitors the opportunity to put themselves onto email drip campaigns.[092] Consider a prominently-placed button that reads: CALL NOW 24 HRS. Remember, your site is one of thousands and most of them look alike, offering the same generic stuff. Make yours stand-out by giving buyers the content they want and need, making you a valuable resource.

If you are without listings, go get one, as these are the best tools for attracting buyers! When you're without, borrow attractive listings from other agents and use them to your advantage.

Most prospective buyers will look at online content for weeks before making their first telephone call or sending an email to inquire about a specific listing. The agent they call is either the one who has provided them the most value while window shopping or the agent whose name appears next to the listing they like most. When these buyers are on your site the day they decide to make that first call, your phone is going to ring, my friend.

✳✳✳

Dear Andy,
Buyer prospects sometimes dodge my calls. Other times, I seem to be playing phone tag way too much. How can I get these folks to answer my call?
—*Frustrated by Flakes*

Dear Frustrated,

A buyer will dodge your calls when he has changed his mind and no longer desires the listing which drew his initial interest (and thereby has no need of you). Little do these dismissive buyers know that you hold a key that opens every listing in town.

Not only so, but you are also the perfect agent to help them find the right property for the best price and terms. You'll work hard for them and they would absolutely love you for it; your problem is: they either don't know this fact or they don't believe you when you say it. Your job now is to demonstrate your value in a way that will grab their attention.

Customize your next call and have a witty voice message ready if they don't answer. Show and tell them why it's in their best interest for you to be involved in their transaction.[212] Still no reply? Send a text message:

I'M HERE FOR YOU. DON'T DO IT ALONE.
CALL ME TODAY AT 10AM. -AA

During that conversation, discuss the merits of your system for finding and purchasing property. Stress the point that you can find the good listings, perhaps getting them a 'first look' at properties prior to going on the open market.

Explain your ability to help buyers narrow their search to exactly what they're looking for, honing efforts, eliminating time wasted and opportunities lost.[174]

Still no reply? Don't fret. You cannot win the affection of every passing purchaser, regardless of your promise and their potential. Once you've given your best efforts, leave them alone for a few weeks, then dial their number once more.

If they dodge your call again, pass their number to another agent as an outbound referral.[112] Sometimes, flaky prospects will react more kindly to another's personality.[119]

✽✽✽

Dear Andy,
Once engaged in live conversation, I'm pretty good at converting buyer-prospects into full-fledged clients. So, how can I use my listings to speak with more buyers?
　　—Chipper for Chatter

Dear Chipper,
Every listing should attract at least one buyer-prospect who eventually purchases property as part of another transaction. Your desire is to be the agent they hire, and your odds of agency increase each time you speak with a live buyer. You may bolster the rate of this occurrence when your initial contact with prospects are face-to-face meetings. To do so, simply insert yourself into more situations that allow you to discuss your listings with people, face-to-face. For instance: if you've got a vacant listing, consider conducting your daily prospecting from the front porch, so that you'll get a chance to speak with lingering neighbors and passersby.

Not everyone you meet and speak with will be a potential buyer, but they just might know someone currently shopping for property in your market. Therefore, dismissal of non-buyers is a mistake. Court these influencers in a manner similar to hot prospects.

To increase your contact with buyers (and their influencers), host an open house. Make it a blow-out! Invite everyone you meet, knock on the doors of neighboring properties, and ask:

DO YOU HAVE ANY FRIENDS/FAMILY
YOU'D LIKE TO HAVE AS NEIGHBORS?
NOW IS YOUR CHANCE.

Knock the same doors on open house day. Re-invite the neighbors and others on your list, and post lots of directional signs the night before your event. The idea is to market your open house prolifically so that many people attend.[240] Don't just post flyers; invite people with your mouth.

Go to crowded places near your listings and pass out flyers. Talk to people about their real estate needs. Invite them to your open house. Make it a party! When you are excited, others will act the same. The absolute, most-infectious excitement will be generated by the open houses of attractive listings.[229] If you don't have any listings, offer to host on behalf of another agent. Be selective of these borrowed opportunities, then treat them like your own.

When you routinely engage in this live-invite type of prospecting, highlight your efforts as a valuable service to sellers. Not only is it true, but it's every seller's dream to see their agent directly hyping their property.　　　　-AA

Likely Sellers Are My Top Priority

I dig where gold is known to be. I'm sure to get swarming competition and plenty of pushback, but so what?!

BY STEADY EDDY

THERE ARE TONS OF PROSPECT TYPES out there,[084] but only so many hours in a day to engage with them. Therefore, I prefer to spend my time talking to people who want to sell *right now.* I'm talking about FSBO,[101] EXPIRED,[100] and WITHDRAWN sellers.

Because their addresses and phone numbers are published, these likely sellers are easy to find, which creates plentiful (and sometimes tough) competition. However, while lots of agents dabble in FSBO and EXPIRED prospecting for a short time, relatively few make it their niche (their primary source of listing clients). Most agents quickly abandon this bountiful niche due to one, teeny-tiny, little obstacle: the impatient, impolite, curt, snippy, and downright-rude nature of these prospects.

You see, these people are frustrated; they're dissatisfied and they don't know how to solve their real estate problems.[207] They've trusted an agent (or three) previously, but things didn't work-out as expected. They don't mean to be rude, but they're scorned, disappointed, and leery, perceiving bluster in the words of all future agents.

On the day after their listing expires, it's not uncommon for EXPIRED sellers to receive a dozen or more phone calls from hopeful agents—*all before noon.* When asked, these sellers tell me that agents usually ramble and fumble their words, as they boast about being the greatest agent in town. Geez; what a turn-off! FSBO sellers tell me that most agents call them once or twice, then never again. Lack of determination is transmitted *loud and clear,* and frustrated sellers don't wanna hear braggadocios rhetoric—they wanna hear solutions.

What they don't know is that all EXPIRED sellers have the exact same problem: their price is too high to attract reasonable buyers.[152] FSBO sellers usually have the same pricing problem, but also suffer from lack of market exposure (they're in neither the MLS nor syndicated websites). Convincing soured sellers of this reality is *the* most challenging endeavor most agents will ever undertake.[154]

I'm different than most agents: all I do is stay in the conversation,[189] constantly demonstrating my value,[150] offering a logic-based solution to their problem,[153] and showing my determination to help them succeed;[078] for this, I'm likely to get a listing appointment.[196]

Fellow agents tell me these conversations are full of rejection, leading to fright and rattled nerves.[056] I don't have this fear, for two reasons: 1) I understand their plight and I make it known, and 2) I don't hang all my hopes on a single phone call. When peeved prospects act rude or dismissive, I simply remind them of their problem and then offer my best solution.[129] If our chat goes sideways, there's *always* another prospect to call.

At times, prospects will say to me: *You sure are a persistent person.* To that, I say: *All this doggedness is to earn your listing. Just imagine the bulldog I'll become to sell it!*

If they list with someone else: no problem; I wish them luck, and I truly mean it. But, if they expire again, I'll be the first familiar voice they hear (which has always been a warmly-received call). Some of my all-time favorite clients were listed after I called them nine or ten times, or after they first chose to list (unsuccessfully) with other agents.

My concentrated efforts earn me at least one listing appointment *everyday.* Because of this frequency, I have control over how many listings I have at a given time,[120] and I am able to select only the sellers that will list at the price I think is best for them.[154]

1 Mean People

There will be some who say harsh things to you. All you can do is remain professional and get a laugh in. Say: *Sounds like you're frustrated. I have a plan that'll tickle you pink.*[153] *Wanna hear it?*

2 Shutting You Out

Some people won't let you speak. Instead they keep talking with hopes of getting you off the phone. Re-assert yourself when they take a breath or at sentence end. Say: *Give me two minutes and I can outline a new plan to get you sold.*[154] *Wanna hear it?*

3 Hang Ups

Occasionally people will flat-out hang-up on you. When this happens, call them back immediately. Say: *We musta been disconnected. I have a special plan to get your property sold fast.*[155] *Wanna hear it?*

4 "I Don't Like Agents"

When you hear this objection to your advances, simply agree with them. It's hard to argue when you're on the same page. Say: *I don't like agents either. Let's team-up and face 'em together.*[172] *Whatdaya say?*

En Garde

Get this: after fielding fifty of their crappy calls in a single day, some people will become combative with calling agents. Your prospecting success with these people will be predicated upon your ability to fend-off their steely knives—without pulling-out any of your own. Don't poke your eye out over their apparent rudeness. Instead, say something that gets their attention.

Effort Meter

You're Gonna Need:

Script Agility

Stamina

Plan of Action

Uniqueness

tips

Some expiry sellers are surprised to learn their listing has EXPIRED—it's a total shock.

For higher answer rates, begin your calls early in the day, as most people are getting ready for work.

Before calling, check to ensure your prospect has not yet re-listed. Also, watch for those who have EXPIRED yet again (the ones you spoke with the last time). Save time: purchase your leads from a provider that will checks statuses for you.

There are books and websites dedicated to EXPIRED seller scripts; find them, learn them, and love them.

Create a flow chart for your phone chats, based upon typical objections.

When your voicemails contain humor and energy, people are more likely to callback, or answer your next call.

Don't argue the finer points of listing strategy over the phone,[152] as these attempts usually fail hard.

Sellers who withdraw their listing before selling are often doing so to break-up with their agent; ask them for a date, too.

Σ   You must possess tenacity and thick skin to win the hand of an EXPIRED seller.

How-to
Woo Expired Sellers

Your market is full of would-be sellers, hidden from view until they list with an agent. At that moment, these sellers make their property-selling intentions known to the world. When their agency agreement expires prior to selling, the world is again notified via the MLS, with a status change from ACTIVE to EXPIRED. Because their goal has not changed, the majority of these sellers will sign another agency agreement, re-listing with the MLS, restoring their ACTIVE status.

Most EXPIRED sellers will re-list within a week of expiry. This brief, status interlude is your opportunity to become their agent. All you have to do now is join the chorus of suitors looking to woo their re-listing. Best results come from being different.[099] Calm and steady wins their hand.[098]

1 Sympathize

Imagine yourself as an EXPIRED seller: frustrated and disenfranchised, expiry day becomes a firing line of agents looking to "hook-up." Your phone rings incessantly and your voicemail becomes engorged with drab, droning messages from (mostly) boring agents spouting successes and promising to re-hang the moon. Day two isn't much better, as your phone continues to ring; you are bombarded by agents, and most of them sound like more of the same. You just wanna sell your property and the phone to stop ringing.

2 Campaign[094]

Your first hurdle will be getting their attention for long enough to have a quick conversation. Concerted efforts to demonstrate your value should do the trick.[090] Communicate your unique message via voicemail, email, snail mailers, and/or door knocks. Each day, call on all new leads first, followed by the leads that were new yesterday, and so on. Day 1 leads hear the same script, Day 2 leads get a different script, and so forth. If they haven't re-listed by Day 7, go knock on their door.

3 Engage

Your sole objective is to schedule a listing presentation.[196] However, asking for a date without first building rapport is usually met with rejection.[081] So stay curious and don't argue.[189] When they claim to have re-listed, ask if they've signed anything, because without an agency agreement, they're still up for grabs. Ask if the property is still for sale. Ask their opinion of why it hasn't already sold. Ask if they have a plan to ensure a sale this time. Tell them that *you* have a solid plan, but it requires homework prior to presentation.[125] Set a date.

4 Routine

Willy-nilly attempts to woo EXPIRED sellers will likely result in humiliating slap-downs. To make EXPIRED prospecting your thing, give it three months of dedicated effort. The experience will make you a more confident agent, or it will leave you sobbing in surrender.

How-to
Stalk a FSBO (For Sale by Owner)

Effort Meter

Owners who attempt to sell real property on their own are usually intelligent, do-it-yerself types with a strong will. However, a novice trying to sell his own house is like a guy trying to cut his own hair, *while riding a bicycle*. The result is rarely a pretty one, and if he happens down a gravel road or hits a pothole, disaster is sure to strike. But FSBO is determined to give it a try, for one of two reasons: 1) to save money, and/or 2) they think agents suck at their jobs.[235]

Sadly for them, nearly 80% will fail at their attempts to sell FSBO, and will eventually hire an agent. Their failure to find a suitable buyer is due to one or more of the following: their price is too high, their market exposure is too low, and/or their lack of knowledge regarding real estate sales customs interferes with their ability to create, negotiate, and navigate a sales contract. Therefore, the agent who stays engaged with FSBO, successfully demonstrating value,[090] and consistently repeating a compelling call-to-action,[094] is poised for a new listing.

1 Meet with Them
Find FSBO phone numbers via lead providers, internet/newspaper ads, in the field, and/or enlist the help of delivery drivers and mailmen. Call FSBO on the phone and meet them in person. Never falsely-claim to have a buyer, just to gain rapport or to set an appointment.

2 Level with Them
FSBO is persuaded by examples and analogies; therefore, discuss FSBO failure rates and your desire to list if/when their doomsday comes. Ask: *Why FSBO?* Ask how they determined their price. Address their needs and request a listing appointment. Tell them about the Sales Formula.[152] Share market statistics[146] and compare them to your own.[063] Justify your fee with solid agent performance statistics.[181]

3 Plan with Them
Help FSBO create an exit strategy. They should have a sixty-day, all-in strategy to sell. If day sixty finds them still bereft of buyer, their efforts to save money are becoming lost to carrying costs, and it's time to hire competent help. Lucky for them, your specialty is helping people sell real property at top price, without hassle.[236]

4 Support Them
Go to their open houses. Tell them about disclosure statements.[180] Refer a loan officer for the purpose of qualifying buyers.[179] Share your open house checklist. Show a strong work ethic by speaking with them several times per week. Call them Fridays, asking about their weekend plans to snare a buyer. Call them Mondays, asking about their weekend successes and woes. Offer a reduced fee to act as a transaction broker,[289] should FSBO find a buyer. Ask: *If I continue to support your efforts, while demonstrating my value, may I be the first agent you consider if/when you decide to hire professional help?*

You're Gonna Need:
Scripts
Perseverance
Genuineness
Logic & Reason

tips
Be the first to speak with a new FSBO. Welcome them to the market, and wish them luck (they're gonna need it).

Specialty scripts are needed to overcome FSBO objections; keep yours honest.[048]

Most agents who call on FSBO give-up after only a few attempts. You'll earn FSBO admiration by staying engaged.

Even if FSBO picks *The Right Price*,[154] their lack of market exposure will lead to difficulty in selling.[236]

Once you convert a FSBO into a successful sale, you may have also won-over a new advocate.

caveats
Falsely claiming to have a buyer (just to gain an appointment with FSBO) is a transparent lie, and you won't be fooling anyone but yourself (as you lose creditability).

Some FSBO sellers have been FOR SALE for years. Their price is sky-high because they're always willing to sell anything to anyone—anyone willing to pay a premium, that is. Leave these types alone.

Σ To win a FSBO listing, you must remain engaged, providing honest value, and a continued call-to-action.

THE RECEPTIONIST

Some of life's toils are best dealt-with by hiring a trained professional.

HAVING ONE'S TEETH CLEANED by a dental hygienist, and checked-over by a dentist every six months is the foundation of maintaining healthy teeth and gums. Hence, the staff at my local dental office knows me.

After such a visit, I stepped to the front desk and paid my bill. Before scheduling my next appointment, the receptionist said to me, "I'm thinking of selling my house."

Upon hearing this declarative statement, I just had to invent a script on-the-spot: "Oh, really? Well, guess what? I've got shiny teeth and a real estate license, so why don't you hire me for the job?"

"Thanks anyway, but I don't think I'm gonna be needing a real estate agent."

"Why would you say that?"

"Well, I bought my house fifteen years ago, on my own, without an agent. I've lived there every day since, and I know it better than anyone else. I was there for the kitchen remodel. I'm the one who removed the old wallpaper and had the chimney cleaned. Besides, I've seen the TV shows and I've read the internet. I know what needs doing to sell my house."

"Makes sense to me," I smiled. "With logic like that, it seems that you don't need my help." She returned my smile with a sentiment of understanding and pride. A quick, silent moment passed, then she said, "Let's book your next appointment for six months away. How about a Tuesday morning in April?"

"There's no need for that," I said nonchalantly. "I'm not coming back here again."

"Why would you say that?" the baffled receptionist asked, with furrowed brow and puzzled gaze.

"Well, because I've had these teeth for thirty years, and I know them better than anyone else. I brush my teeth every day and floss nearly as often. I've chewed countless meals and bitten plenty of bullets. I know how each tooth leans and which ones to show when I smile. Therefore, I am the best person to clean my teeth."

Her puzzled gaze was long-gone, replaced by a smirky grin. "You're a real smart-ass, aren't you?"

"Yepper, and I'll gladly trade your help cleaning my chompers for a chance at selling your house," I bargained, mirroring her grin.

With a chuckle, she asked, "Are you available tomorrow afternoon?"

TRUE STORY

3 Ways to Prospect in the Field

1 Knock on Doors
Some FSBO and EXPIRED sellers are more likely to receive you on their doorstep than over the phone.

2 Talk to Salesmen
Salesmen are usually chatty folks, which makes them easy to approach. Discuss referrals. Discuss value.

3 Garage Sales
Garage, yard, and estate sales are often a sign of listing preparation. Be the first agent to inquire and you may soon place your sign in that lawn.

A Serious How-to Manual with a Sense of Humor

Effort Meter

You're Gonna Need:

Walking Shoes
True Value
Dedication
Longevity

How-to
Cultivate a Farm

As a grouping of niche properties within a geographic boundary, a properly cultivated real estate farm will provide you with listings for many harvest moons to come. However, creating and maintaining that farm requires diligent effort and dedication. Working the fields takes hours of monthly labor, but suckling its sweet reward is worth the toil.

1 Pick a Farmable Area

Choose an area with a high activity rate (found by dividing the total number of ACTIVE listings within the last year by the total number of properties in the farm). It should be geographically small enough to knock on every door, three or four times per year. Next, define your mission of superior service in *one sentence*.[245] Let this mission become your mantra, as you become a neighborhood expert. Know the schools, local activities, planned development, and history. When you learn something new, share it with your farm.

2 Plant Seeds

Knock on every door in your farm, and introduce yourself. Explain your mission,[245] ask if you may add them to your newsletter,[095] and leave some value.[090] Collect various bits of info: names, birthdays, hobbies, phone numbers, email, ownership tenure, etc. Learn everything you can about each property and its inhabitants, then add it to your database.[089] Show interest in their lives and their community.

3 Feed Your Farm

Just as crops need sunlight, water, and fertilizer, your farm needs strong, continued demonstration of your value.[094] Show them your expertise over and over again: mail them updates on sales activities,[146] email your newsletter,[095] host neighborhood gatherings, start an online message board so they may foster community, and knock on each door every ninety days.

4 Reap the Listings

Whether your listings sell quickly, at top price, or lazily languish until they die on the vine, your planted seeds and budding crops are watching. For this reason, jump at every listing presentation opportunity in your farm, but remain choosy of the ones you actually list.[152] Don't allow pride to over-ride your over-priced rule.[191] Let over-priced sellers list with another agent, then be their first call on expiry day.[100]

5 Till the Soil

You may gain some immediate success with your farm, but real cultivation comes over time, so don't become discouraged when a few months pass without harvesting any listings. Instead, spend more time working on the farm: demonstrate your value, ask for referrals, and demonstrate your value. You will always reap what you sow, so demonstrate your value some more.

tips

When someone new moves into your farm, be the first to stand on their doorstep, welcoming them to the neighborhood.

Identify investor-owned properties in your farm, and market to the owner/investor. Also, market toward the tenant.

Go inside each new (competitor's) listing straight away. Make it your goal to know every property in your farm.

Introduce your posse[179] to your farm, then work those fields together.

If your farm already has an online message board, become a sponsor.

caveats

When done properly, everyone in your farm will know your name and face. Therefore, they will pay special attention to your listings within the farm. Your reputation is being tested now, so don't disappoint.[153]

Beware of farming your own neighborhood (the one you live in now), because work-related misunderstandings may follow you home and on after-dinner walks around the block.

Σ A good farmer is an adopted member of a community, ever-present and lending value.

Four Farms, Fresh from the Fringe

Traditional farms are subdivisions and neighborhoods with contiguous boundaries. Because these farms are easily identified, competition may already be saturated. However, there exist farms that are un-tilled, un-planted, over-grown, and for the taking.

1 Outta-State Owners

Search public records for owners whose tax bill is mailed out-of-state. Mail value and call-to-action to the same addresses. Oversized postcards are most likely reviewed by these prospects.

2 Office Parks

Full of people living somewhere, office parks are prime farming ground. Get to know these people on their way into work and during their lunch breaks. Be on campus. Provide value. Sponsor gatherings. Host seminars. Feed them. Get management approval, then be their real estate go-to.

3 Schools

Teachers often subsidize classroom materials to cover budget holes. Sponsor their supplies and gain their admiration. In return, they will refer friends, family, neighbors, and students' parents. Dust their erasers and school them on your value.

4 Apartment Complexes

A localized area with a high concentration of potential buyers is perfectly fertile ground to cloister some clients. Provide mortgage info and espouse the advantages of ownership. Get a loan officer to sponsor your efforts.

A Serious How-to Manual with a Sense of Humor

Your Friends Are More Than Happy to Help

Feel funny asking friends and family for referrals? Don't be silly.

BY YOUR FRIEND FREDDIE

SUPPOSE A FRIEND OF YOURS opened a flower shop. Would you refer to her brides to-be? Would you send senior prom goers her way? Would you go as far as introducing her to relatives of the deathbed doomed? Of course you would. After all, we're talking about friends and family here, and you'd happily go outta your way for friends and family, right? Well, so would your friends and family. Duh.

First, ask us if we're willing to help (we're gonna say YES). Explain what a big deal it is to get a referral from us and how just one referral can make all the difference in your world. Don't just assume we already know how to best assist you; get our buy-in, then guide us through the steps. Teach us what to look for in conversations: instruct us to keep an ear open for co-workers and neighbors who are moving, getting married, divorced, or contemplating the purchase of investment properties.

If a prospect has never (or barely) met you, they're unlikely to call when given your card, especially if they have been presented with cards from other agents, too. So, don't ask us to pass out your business cards, as this practice is largely a waste of time and a waste of business cards. Statistically, the first agent to directly speak with a prospect has the best chance to earn their business. Therefore, teach us the Friend Script: *My friend is a resourceful real estate agent. Would you be offended if s/he called you?* When it's put this way, most people will happily welcome your call. Then we'll collect their phone number, and send it your way.

Don't allow us to qualify the prospects we meet; tell us not to judge their situation whatsoever. The qualification of a prospect is always the agent's job;[170] when this task is left to friends, you will suffer lost sales and missed chances to refer prospects to other agents.[112] Say to us with passion, this crucial bit: regardless of property type, value, quality, or quantity, if they have real estate aspirations (inclinations large or small), *please just recite the Friend Script.*

To really cash-in on referrals, you need to remind friends and family with a monthly call: reiterate your referral request and rehearse the Friend Script with us until we know it well.

Strengthen your strategy by devising a monthly referral goal, and then communicate that goal to us. Once we know of your plans, we're more likely to help. Through these conversations with us, you will notice that some of us are quite eager to help. These faithful friends are your business advocates, and we are willing to routinely go outta our way to find you new clients. Spend extra time with your advocates, and treat us special.

Another great way to elicit our friendly help is to connect people. Listen when you hear of another's toil, then introduce them to someone you know who can and will help them. When you make an effort to help others, they will look for ways of returning the favor.

It is said that the average adult knows three people per year who either buy or sell real property; this happenstance makes you only one person removed from these potential sales. Some of your friends and family are probably already referring their acquaintances to real estate agents. Those who receive referrals are the ones who deliberately and continuously ask for them. Don't miss your opportunity to do the same and don't feel weird about asking for our help either. We're happy to assist, so long as you *ask* and then show us how.

One last thing: if your friends and family think you're flaky, then they're probably not gonna share their referral love with you. If this describes your case, then demonstrate your value to us and show us that you are seriously good at your job, and we'll eventually come around to joining your referral racket. 🌳

*G*enerally seen as a mere salutation or a small-talk starter, this colloquial question can be answered several ways. Some agents relate personal experiences, or launch into a somber soliloquy on the tenets of home ownership. The showmen amongst us opt for the colorful, "Unbelievable!" This declaration (best sold with elongated enunciation) is meant to humorously hide the market's volatility; because a market's value is conditional, relative to one's status as a buyer or seller, the current market trend could be interpreted as unbelievably good or unbelievably bad.

While these responses keep the questioner engaged, each fail to capitalize on the potential opportunity hidden within. When the question, "How's the market?" is answered with a curious, "Why do you ask?" that otherwise lost opportunity quickly ascends to the surface. The questioner may claim simple curiosity, or the conversation may bloom into, "I've been thinking of buying an investment property." or "We've been thinking of changing school districts. Is this a good time to do so?" or "My brother has been trying to sell his house for months. What the hell is he doing wrong?"

So, How's the Market?

Simply reply: "Why do you ask?" And then watch opportunity blossom, as you wake-up and smell the listing appointment!

A Serious How-to Manual with a Sense of Humor

Effort Meter

You're Gonna Need:

People
Scripts
Working Mouth
Follow-Up

tips

Always attempt to get the referred party's name and number. Don't wait; call them now.

Mentioning the new car and disco music concept to people will help them remember your referral inquiry.

Track your efforts with a systematic approach.[070]

If the Referral Script garnishes you referrals that are outside of your niche, refer those referrals to another agent (and earn a commission).[112]

When you ask, *Do you..?*, the answer can easily be NO. The only appropriate response to *Who do..?* is a name.

If you ask *Who do..?* ten times every day, your business is sure to flourish! If you ask *Who do..?* fifty times a day, you're gonna need to hire some helpers.[286]

When you ask *Who do..?*, you are planting a cerebral referral-seed. Over the next few days, this seed may blossom into a referral-flower. You must then pluck that flower before it wilts, but leave the roots in-place, so that you may pluck that same flower again.

Σ The more often you recite the Referral Script to a specific person, the more likely that person is to provide you referrals.

How-to
Get Referrals from People

Have you ever learned a new word, or decided to buy a specific new car? Once your mind has a new conception, you begin to notice it everywhere. You suddenly hear that new word several times in casual conversations throughout the following week. You seem to see that desired car at every intersection and in every parking lot. These observations are not unlike an annoying disco song, stuck on a ten second loop inside your head. Whether or not you like it, once that beat gets cerebrally thumping, it's nearly impossible to make it stop!

1 Talk to Someone[084]
It doesn't really matter whom it is. Call someone. Knock on a door. Have a casual encounter. Potential someones include: friends and family, advocates (these are people who rave about your service), people in your cell phone, past clients, vendors you know,[179] database members,[089] professionals you frequent, the guy at the convenience counter, neighbors of your listings, the gal that works the drive-thru window,..

2 Recite the *Referral Script*
When calling on the phone, get to the point; don't waste time. People are busy and so are you. With friends, conclude all catch-up chat within a few minutes. With acquaintances, you will garner more respect by getting right to it. Recite this script:

Referral Script Part I
« Hi. I need your help. *Who do* you know that is currently looking to buy or sell real estate? »
They will say (either):
« Frustrated Fred! » (go to STEP 3) —OR—
« I cannot think of anyone. » (go to Part II)

Referral Script Part II
« No worries. You may think of someone within the next a few days. Would you be offended if I called back in a week and asked again? »
(typical response): « Not at all! I look forward to your call. » (go to STEP 4)

3 Collect Referral Information
You want the referred party's phone number, so ask for it. Don't rely upon others to make your introduction. To earn your referral, you must initiate the call.[111]

4 Call Them Again
Whenever someone's stymied response to STEP 2 causes you to skip STEP 3, return calls to them as scheduled, as you are bound to receive many more referrals when you do. Otherwise, repeat STEPS 1, 2, and 3 to the same person every thirty to ninety days. For best results, repeat on schedule.[094]

MUCK IT UP!

Three simple ways to acquire clients:
1. You can advertise to the masses
   (and hope someone calls),
2. You can prospect to individuals directly
   (and put your skills to the test), or
3. You can sleep with a builder or two.

Of the three:
Advertising is the least challenging,
   but the most expensive.
Prospecting is the least expensive,
   but the most time-consuming.
Prostitution is the least time-consuming,
   but the most challenging (assuming a conscience).

When done to perfection:
Advertising relies upon others actions,
Prospecting relies upon your actions, and
Prostitution relies upon you getting action from others.

Silly jokes aside, this book does not disparage advertising, which can be a helpful accessory to prospecting, nor agent/builder spousal relationships, which are an occasional happenstance. Rather, it acknowledges that by keeping an agent engaged in a constantly-evolving marketplace, daily prospecting produces a consistent flow of leads from which the agent may be choosy. The advantage of being in the field, sorting through the muck with your own hands is options, options, options.

Simply put, prospecting places you in control of your business.

Effort Meter

You're Gonna Need:

Current Client

Referral Script

Incentive

Smile

tips

If you offer clients an incentive to refer prospects, your arrangement to do so should be inked at the same time you and client sign the agency agreement—never after.

Do not expect people to just refer prospects to you. You must ask. It is said that your friends, family, and past clients are already referring buyers and sellers to agents—*to the agents who ask!*

caveats

Don't pester current clients for referral requests. Only ask on the three happy days.

Check with your broker and your state's regulatory body before offering a discounted commission in exchange for referrals. Not all brokers nor locales allow for this incentive.[036]

Σ When properly timed, your referral requests can be maximized and realized, now and in the future.

How-to
Get Referrals from Current Clients

Current clients are a great source of referrals. They know you, they (hopefully) like you, and they (probably) know several other people. Do a fantastic job representing their interest and ask for their kind referrals. Follow these steps to leverage your efforts:

1 Acknowledge Happy Days

Take notice: clients are most happy with you on the following days:

1. At time they sign agency agreement (the day they hire you)
2. At time they sign purchase and sale agreement (the day they go under contract to buy or sell)
3. At time of closing (the day their life goes back to normal)

2 Offer Incentive

Everyone likes getting something for giving something, so reward the clients who give you referrals. At the time you sign an agency agreement, offer to discount your current commission to buyers and sellers who supply you with referrals. The caveat being: to earn a discount, the referred party must go under contract to buy or sell prior to the referring client's transaction closing (that's totally fair). This stipulation mitigates the potential loss of discounted commissions, traded for referrals that never close. Remember to put a cap on your referral discounts, otherwise you may end up representing the first client for free.

3 Ask for Referrals

Recite the *Referral Script*.[108] If they come up empty, let it go and do not proceed to Part II of the *Referral Script*. Ask them for a referral on each of the three happy days, do not skip asking on a happy day, and do not ask on any other days during the term of agency.

When you ask a client for a referral on the three happy days (and only on those days), that client will hopefully associate your referral requests with being pleased with you. Ideally, your referral requests will henceforth conjure happy recollections of you and all the wonderful bits of service you've rendered. After closing, put them on a referral schedule[094] and turn these good vibes into money in your pocket.

4 Capitalize of Good Vibes

Aside from your regular campaigning, memorialize the anniversary of their closing by mailing a hand-written card each year on that date. A week later, call them for a chat. Your check-in should be two-fold: (genuinely) ask if you may be of real estate service and ask for referrals. Through proper campaigning (and by asking for introductions), aim to become their family's go-to real estate agent. After all, referrals come to those who ask and referrals come often to those who often ask.

How-to
Get Referrals from Reluctant Recommenders

Some people you meet will have the perfect referral, but feel that divulging another person's contact information is an invasion of privacy. Their sense of protectiveness may prevent you from earning well-desired referrals and that's a real stinker. Whenever you reach this roadblock, change your proposition to one which only the fussy would refuse.

1 Use Your Scripts

Restate your referral request in a way that no one may resist. After all, giving-up a friend's identity cannot be an invasion of privacy once that friend authorizes the event.

« I've got a friend that's thinking of selling her house, but she's just not sure how much it's worth. »

« Sweet. Gimme her phone number. I can help with those figures. »

« I don't feel comfortable giving-out my friend's number. I'll just give your number to her, and then she can call you. »

« In my experience, if we do that, she'll never call me. How about this: tell your friend that you know a super-helpful real estate agent. Then ask if she would be offended if I gave her a call. »

« Okay. I can do that. »

« Awesome and thank you! »

2 Follow-Through

You have almost succeeded, but you do not have the referral in-hand, just yet. If you stop now, that phone call may never occur, so continue to seek their referral with a simple suggestion:

« Let's call your friend right now. Put your beer down and dial the phone. Our chat will take just a minute. »

If you get resistance to this approach, try a slight nudge:

« I would feel bad if your friend received inaccurate information from another source because we delayed. Your call will only take a minute and it will make us all extremely happy. »

Garnish this script with a smile!

Pickin' Apart the Script

Some folks feel this line of dialogue to be manipulative action against friends, family, acquaintances, neighbors, and occasional passersby. However, when you genuinely believe your service is superior to a principal acting alone, the manipulative angle fades to nothing. You're not trying to trick friends into bolstering your income. You're helping their friends achieve goals with amplified gratification. When you stick your qualified nose into their business, everyone wins!

You're Gonna Need:

Logic
Reason
Emotion
Composure

tips
You cannot be expected to win every possible referral out there. However, with a bit of effort, you may snare many more than a passive agent would.

Many people are reluctant to commit social miscues. Save them embarrassment by showing them a way to help their friends without harming anyone's reputation.

caveat
When you allow a potential referral to twist in the wind, another agent is likely to pick it up. Be the cool breeze, and seize every possible referral moment.

Σ   Crafty scripts (like those depicted on this page) will help you gain where others would falter.

Effort Meter

You're Gonna Need:

Real Estate Agents
Scripts
Referral Contracts
Follow-Up

How-to
Trade Referrals with Real Estate Agents

As a real estate agent, you should have two defined niches: a geographic boundary and a specialty.[042] To optimize time and effort, you should refer prospects out of your niche and receive referrals into your niche. Once the referrals begin to flow, refer to the *Referral Flow Chart*.[341]

1 Call Agents Outside Your Niche

Repeat this sequence to earn their referrals:
- Search-out agents who work outside of your geographic and specialty niches. Any agent will do, but remember that high-volume agents may have more referrals to give.
- Tell these agents of your plan to become Referral Buddies.
- Agree to trade prospects with each other and to eventually become exclusive within your respective niches. Exclusivity should be had only once a Referral Buddy has proven herself as an agent who closes referrals—*and* frequently sends quality referrals to you, too.
- Call often, ask for referrals, and strengthen the relationship. A systematic approach will be the most efficient.[070]

2 Call Agents Within Your Niche

Sometimes agents become frustrated by their clients and/ or prospects. When agents refer these "problem people" to you, they may salvage a referral commission from an otherwise loss of time and expense. Use the following scripts when offering your assistance, and you're guaranteed at least a chuckle. Sometimes their response will be: YES, *please take my burden from me!*

Sample scripts:
- Got any pain-in-the-ass buyers that I can take off your hands?
- Remember that listing you've had for a year now? Wanna bet that I could sell it in thirty days?
- I'd gladly pay you Tuesday for a referral today.
- Got any listings set to expire? Refer me as a fresh perspective.

3 Do Your Homework

Some referral agents (or vendors) will want to sell you leads instead of negotiating a portion of the commission earned from closed sales. Before you give money in exchange for prospects, ensure the referor is lawfully licensed to receive payments from real estate-related transactions. Then scrutinize the value of paying upfront for yet-to-be-qualified leads, versus payment made only once the prospect has completed the transaction.

Prior to referring prospects to another agent, interview that agent to ensure you share the same professionalism, performance quality, and work ethic. Your reputation and your wallet are each at stake when referring prospects. Always remember: if the agent you send referrals to cannot close sales, you will get nothing in return!

tips

A Referral Buddy is one you trade referrals with on a regular basis.

There is no "going rate" for referrals between agents. Before you agree on a split, consider the time you may spend with the referral, and the number of transactions that may be had from this one referral.

Track all referrals traded with agents (names, dates, conversion ratios, commissions earned,..). Future trades may be considered by these statistics.

You may occasionally be referred a prospect that is outside of your niche. Upon permission of the referring agent, you may become a middleman, referring that prospect to a third agent (splitting the commission three, appropriately-proportioned ways).

Get all referral agreements in writing, ASAP.

caveat

Check your state's laws/ regulations regarding referrals between agents.[036] Some states require a disclosure, signed by the person being referred, acknowledging the commission being traded between agents.

Σ   Because there's no way you can service every prospect, trading sales opportunities will leverage your income.

A body prospecting

tends to

stay prospecting

A Serious How-to Manual with a Sense of Humor

Get Creative with Prospecting

There's no wrong way to do it—as long as it works.

BY GARY THE GURU

ALL THE ASSORTED real estate nuts and gurus essentially teach prospecting methods. Each profess a different niche or approach. Some methods work quickly, generating results right away,[116] and others take time to cultivate or organize.[104] Here's the secret they're not telling you: *they all work!*

Many, many, many different prospecting methods work for generating listing and buyer presentations.[084] Find what works best for you, then stick with it.

You are likely to attempt several methods before finding the right one(s) for you. Just remember, there is a difference between something not working,[011] you not liking it, and you not giving it your full effort.[019]

Don't give up on a given method without first blowing at full gusto. Do your homework, attempt to understand its challenges, plan ahead, practice, and study scripts. Then refine your scripts and procedures as you go. Challenge yourself and track results. Create conversion ratios and analyze their meanings.

Once you understand the basics and become a somewhat-competent prospector, tweak some of your methods in major ways. Do stuff that's recognizably different from other agents. Do stuff that grabs attention. Be a spiked mohawk in the orchestra pit. Say things to prospects to catch them off-guard. Be unconventional in a way that serves their interest while demonstrating your skills. Act in a manner that garners notice.

Your unorthodox tweaks could be the means by which you communicate,[008] the things you say,[046] the events you host, your marketing methods, the niche you pursue,[042] and/or the value you offer,[090] and the way by which you present that value.[094] Use humor, but don't be jokey. Have fun, but remain professional.[033] Be different, but operate by lawful means.[036]

When your prospecting methods are both effective *and* creative, others are sure to take notice. Your award-winning, wiley ways will surely be imitated by competing agents. It's easy to become bitter or angered by these copycats, but don't allow wasteful emotions to invade your day.[315] Their clone of your work is but a mere caricature of your masterpiece.

When you are a true innovator, rivals will always be a step or two behind, so use their emulation as an excuse to continually develop your methods. You can always be better. When your prospecting methods cease to evolve, your competitors may surpass your potential, by making your creation even more effective and/or efficient.[012]

When you innovate, there will be lots of people to tell you that it won't work. Often times, these killjoys are the old veterans of our trade, stuck in their molds. Other times, the sourpuss will be an unimaginative peer, unable to perceive of novelty. Disregard each.

Suppose the only creative bone in your body is the shape of your skull, and as a result, you've been sporting the same silly haircut since junior high. There's nothing wrong with your antiquated coif. It still functions as a frame to your smiling face and a cover for your dented dome, but the era it was born into has moved-on. If your do no longer turns heads for it's originally-styled intention, update your look by observing creative agents. Copy and steal their best. If it works for them, it can work for you, too.[068]

If prospecting was easy, everyone would be good at it. Get an edge by being different than the average. Keep your eyes open to novel opportunities and seize those moments with customized efforts. Forgo the naysayers, as there are many ways to earn appointments.[167] Have fun and go get 'em! 🌳

Using children or pets in real estate advertising is *cringe-worthy*, at best. You're basically **making a mascot of your offspring** for the sake of making a buck. Your child's cute factor **is not** a differentiating factor of your business. It doesn't make you a better agent, it's not creative, and it doesn't mean you're worthy of anyone's listing.

That gap-toothed grin that makes you smile ain't really padding your bottom line. Not to mention the fact that your kid is now in college. You've had that toddler's face on your business card and/or billboard for several decades now. In a child's hand-scribbled font it boldly states, "Please hire my mommy to buy your next house."

the **Random Rantings** of an **Angry Agent**

It might as well say, "My mommy doesn't have any skills, so she's hoping you take pity on my hunger." You don't see other professionals acting the same way. Imagine if your dentist ran an ad that said, "Let my mommy brush your teeth so she can afford to put braces on mine." Consider the outrage over a therapist's ad that read, "Let my mommy examine your head so she can put a roof over mine." Visualize the newspaper ad of a charity-baiting taxidermist, "Let my daddy stuff your dead Fluffy so he can stuff my belly." It's gross. It's turning me off. And it's unbecoming of our industry. You look amateurish, and people are laughing at you. And while I'm at it, another thing: the number of kids you have, how long you've been married, and for whom you voted in the last election should not be on the *About Me* page of your website—it's equally unprofessional. I know many agents are extreme part-timers, making a cottage business of real estate sales, but this display ain't folksy; it's an invasion of your privacy, which may very well dissuade a prospect from choosing you. After all, if you don't mention your private life, people cannot discriminate against it. Besides, you have far more to offer clients than the fact that you love your kids, so show your value to prospects and keep your dignity intact. At least that's the way I see it, but I could be way off (as I often am).

Effort Meter

You're Gonna Need:

Minivan
Friendly Agents
Listing Supplies
Infectious Energy

tips

Crazy Van can be deployed
on various types of
prospects, including FSBO,
EXPIRED, WITHDRAWN, pre-
foreclosure, garage sales,
over-grown & dilapidated,...

Deploy Crazy Van on the
FSBO prospects you've only
met over the phone. Their
reaction is priceless!

caveats

Without demonstrable
excitement and energy,
Crazy Van loses it's
compelling call-to-action.

You cannot list a client via Crazy
Van, then deliver lackluster
service. Doing so is disingenuous
and a form of false advertising.

Don't use this ploy as an
excuse to be a buffoon. It's a
Crazy Van, not a clown car.

It may seem a silly concept
at first, but once you see the
results of Crazy Van, you'll
wanna do it again and again.

Σ   Crazy Van is a show of
force, demonstrating your
ability to rally a team, and bring
value to selling property.

How-to
Deploy the Crazy Van

Do you need an excuse to have fun at work? Then Crazy Van is for
you! But be warned: it can be extremely addictive. For optimal impact
and intensity, don't go Crazy Vanning more than once per week.

1 Get a Van
Someone you know drives a minivan. Borrow
those wheels and clean out the clutter. Crazy Van has
no room for baby seats nor old french fries.

2 Fill the Van with Agents
All ride-alongs must be of similar mind-set.[034] The more the
merrier, but don't overfill the van. Everyone needs a seatbelt and a
cup holder. Cram some real estate stuff in with the people. Bring
along yard signs, listing agreements, blank disclosure statements,
lock boxes, camera, digital devices, clipboards, measuring tape,
and any other items needed to list property right on-the-spot.

3 Drive Around
For maximum effect, the windows should be down and the
music blaring. Everyone should be singing and getting amped-
up. The van should be (literally) a-rockin' at all stop lights. There's
a reason it's called Crazy Van; don't just sit there like rag dolls
listening to NPR. Excitement and enthusiasm win the day.

4 Seek and Deploy
Everyone is on FSBO watch.[101] Once one is spotted,
screech to a halt and unload curbside. Everyone assaults the
property, with gusto and frenzy. Knock on the door, then take
the place by storm. As the owner and lead agent discuss the
merits of seller agency,[224] another agent is snapping pictures
of *everything*, while another is measuring the property, as
yet a third agent takes notes and fills-out MLS data forms.

The standard result is an impressed owner. When a seller sees
the organizational and comprehensive interest your "team" has
in his property, he is sure to become attentive and persuadable.
Ask him to list now. Once he signs, plant a FOR SALE sign in
his yard. Immediately thereafter, with your newest client
watching from his front stoop, everyone knocks on neighbors'
doors, spreading invitations to next week's open house.[240]

5 Repeat
Pack up your stuff and do it all again. Keep the energy up! Take
turns, as each agent gets the lead role. Spend several hours on this
mission every week and you're sure to increase your listing intake.

Even if the seller refuses to list on-the-spot, you have made one helluva
unique impression upon him. Use this goodwill to begin stalking.[094]

How-to
Host a Mobile Open House

Are you bereft of listings but still wanna make a splash with sales? Are you spending Saturdays traipsing one buyer around town when you've got room for ten? If so, the mobile open house just might be the drive for you. Try this: load a horde of buyers onto a bus, then take them on a tour of several listings—each of which match their purchase criterion.

The listings on your tour should share the same theme: same general locale, similar price range, similar condition, and similar attributes. This harmony amongst listings will attract a niche audience.

1 Get a Bus
You need a vehicle that will carry a throng of people comfortably, so rent a bus, or borrow one from your church, your favorite youth sports team, or your local prison yard.

2 Get Additional Agents
There's no way you can handle a dozen or more prospects at once, by yourself. So, find three or four additional agents to help; you'll need their support answering buyer questions and drafting purchase offers.[252] Helper agents should follow the bus in their own car.

3 Advertise
Begin advertising ten days before the event and enlist the helper agents to do the same. Tell everyone about your event and pass-out flyers, posting them where people gather. Your handbill and online ads should describe the listings on-tour and utilize a strong call-to-action:

WANNA TOUR 5 HOUSES THIS SATURDAY?
NO OBLIGATION. EMAIL FOR RESERVATIONS.

4 Fill Bus with Buyers
To ensure your productive efforts are monetarily realized, all riders must sign agency agreements before boarding the bus (covering—*at the very least*—all the properties on tour). Have a loan officer on-site to pre-qualify buyers.[170]

5 Drive
Between stops, outline the purchase process to those on-board.[176] Describe current market conditions[146] and discuss real estate customs.[036] Show them your value.[172]

6 Show & Sell
Once the bus stops, everyone gets off. When a given prospect declares interest in a specific property, assign them to a helper agent. Together, they will drive back to the office, and prepare an offer while you stay with the group until the end. Afterwards, check-in with these buyers to ensure all is well.

Effort Meter

You're Gonna Need:
Bus
Helper Agents
Vendor Participation
Driver

tips

Before the event, sign referral agreements with your helper agents. Together, decide who will represent the buyers that make on-tour offers and how to divy-up those who don't.

Afterwards, attempt to sign full-on agency agreements with the buyers that don't make on-tour offers.

Bring along all the tools needed to draft purchase offers and don't forget snacks!

Get vendors to pay for the event. Loan officers and home inspectors have extra budget for these types of things, so let them climb aboard and possibly drive the bus. Then, happily share your prospects—it's only fair.

The harmonized listings on your tour may belong to various agents; get written permission from these agents before advertising their listings.

Σ Once the tour is over, all prospects should have been fully exposed to your value; now, convert them into clients.

Effort Meter

You're Gonna Need:

Venue
Vendor Helpers
Niche Presentation
Giveaways

How-to
Throw a Seminar

Filling a room with like-minded prospects is efficiency at its finest. At once, you can deliver a single, comprehensive presentation that is both entertaining and engaging. Because they have a real estate decision to make, your niche prospects are in attendance to learn, so provide the help they want and need. Once people feel helped by you, they're likely to hire you.

1 Select a Target Audience

There are several audience types from which to choose. Some groups will desire information with broad appeal, while others will seek specific knowledge. Lucky for you, would-be prospects yearn for a forum where they can engage in specific real estate discussion.

Choose a niche in which you are able to legitimately profess:

- first-time buyers
- green-energy buyers
- new construction buyers
- specialty buyers
- specialty financing

- foreclosure avoiding sellers
- empty nesters
- investors
- niche investors
- and many more...

2 Recruit Helpers

Vendors of appropriate stature may enrich the content and experience of your seminar, so enlist the help of your posse.[179] Instruct them to prepare a statement about a specific topic (of your choosing, not theirs) for a short duration (don't let them be boring). Do a *great* job boosting attendance and vendors will be happy to share the expense (so long as they can share the prospects too).

Knowledgeable vendors to consider: loan officers, home inspectors, attorneys, construction contractors,..

3 Find a Venue

Free is best, and may be found with a little effort. Consider hosting seminars at your brokerage office, your church's rec room, in a school cafeteria, at the VFW, at one of your vendor's offices, or in the living room of your latest, vacant listing.

4 Invite Your Audience

You must fill the room, because too many empty chairs will dampen your affair. So, hype your seminar with vigor. Place ads *everywhere* and talk about it when prospecting.

5 Organize & Execute

You are the ring leader of this circus, so act like it. Keep the runtime under an hour, otherwise you'll lose audience interest. If the topic is complicated, consider extended Q&A time. Collect contact and other information from your audience. Get their feedback. Offer a reception and attempt to sign as many clients as possible.

tips

When vendors pay money or donate food, the seminar becomes free to you (except for your time). If you make the seminar BIG, you might even profit from the event itself.

Offer raffle prizes or giveaways for attendance or in exchange for audience member contact information.

To boost attendance, team-up with other agents and share the prospects.

If your event generates more prospects than you may responsibly service, refer the extras to your Referral Buddies.[112]

You decide how long a guest speaker speaks. If a vendor runs too long, or wanders off-topic, or is causing snores, then *cut them off*.

Hosting a seminar at a vacant listing is a fantastic way to promote that listing (as well, get the neighbors talking). Before sending out invites, secure written permission from the property's owners.

Σ Seminars create an efficient environment to showcase your value to a room of like-minded prospects.

How-to
Set a Prospect Free

Prospects come in all shapes, sizes, personalities and temperaments. Some will click with you right away, and others never will. Sometimes that prospect who jibes with you is also qualified to act in the role of real estate principal, and other times they're not. Sometimes, that jibing, yet un-qualified prospect can be rehabilitated, molded into the perfect client. And others, regardless of how hard you try, never will.

Some seller-prospects will weigh their options for an extended period of time,[207] and some buyer-prospects are just tire-kickers. Once you've spent your patience and they're still on the fence about you, nudge them from their perch, to one side or the other.

Effort Meter

You're Gonna Need:

a Prospect
Spent Patience
Exhausted Resources
Dignity

1 Have a Serious Conversation

Ask them to make a decision. Outline the pros and cons of each choice: *To hire me, or to not hire me? That is the question.* Seek their true objection. Sometimes, an influencer of a prospect is thwarting your agency agreement. To find out, ask them directly. If your suspicions are confirmed, invite a meeting with the influencer, and re-deliver your full presentation.[167] If they still won't choose you, ask: *Why not?* Regardless of the answer, don't throw them away just yet.

2 Put Them on the Back Burner

When the only obstacle to hiring you is a matter of qualification,[170] help them to qualify.[189] Whether your prospect's woes include bad credit, no credit, lack of funds, cloudy title issues, or relationship clashes (divorce), refer them to an expert who can correct their malady.

3 Check-In

After some reasonable time has passed, re-visit old prospects. For sellers, watch for their current listing to expire, then be the first voice they hear on expiry day.[100] If this prospect has not listed with another, ask them to reconsider you and attempt to win their confidence. For buyers, call to see how things are going. Until they sign an agency agreement, all prospects are still up for grabs.

4 Eject Their Ass

Once you've fully exhausted all efforts to convert a prospect (to no avail), or if you feel that the mutual fit is not comfortable, abandon ship. Let them go and wish them warm and genuine success.

5 Refer Them to Another Agent

Some prospects will stop taking your calls because they're tired of finding new ways to tell you NO. Perhaps they don't like your style, or maybe they hired another agent. Whether or not you know the reason for sure, you have a way to help them while getting paid for it: refer them to an agent better suited.[112] Arm the referred agent with a script: *Agent Andy says you're buying a house. Tell me more.*

tips

When you find an old lead behind a desk or stuck in your wallet, don't throw it out. Call them! There's a chance they still need your help. You could be calling at the perfect moment, but you'll never know if you toss it.

You don't have to withstand prospects with bad attitudes. There exists a plethora of Goldilocks clientele waiting to meet you. Keep looking for them, and then meet their friends.

When they're on the fence, ask direct questions. You've got nothing to lose: *Are you serious about buying/selling real property? What is preventing you from becoming my newest client?*

caveats

When you're desperate to make a sale, prospects can feel it. Don't breathe your stinky commission breath onto them. Nobody wants to work with desperate people.

Treat everyone the same way. Speak to all alike. Sometimes you're willing to tolerate shenanigans for the promise of a bigger pay day, and sometimes you're not. When all parties have an equal and respected voice, things tend to develop agreeably.

Σ Even the most robust system to qualify and sign new clients will fail to convert them all, so refine yours to catch the majority, and part with all others on the best of terms.

Don't Ride the Real Estate Roller Coaster

Daily prospecting mitigates the ups and downs and loopty-loops of commission-based work.

You prospect every day. You talk to lots of people and you take on clients. You're excited now because things are happening! Then you neglect prospecting time, opting instead to work on behalf of clients, tend to life's other demands, or goof-off. Soon, your clients close transactions, you cash some commission checks, and you're riding high. Until the next day when you realize that you have no clients, no pending transactions, and no commission checks on the horizon. So you begin to prospect, as you know you should, only to repeat the process... You're riding the Real Estate Roller Coaster.

When your paydays come in spurts and you sometimes run out of money, you're riding on the real estate roller coaster. Daily prospecting straightens-out your path ahead, ensuring your business progresses steady and smooth,[346] because daily prospecting gives you control of the throttle. This lever allows you to determine whether your business grows or slows, as you choose only the most-qualified prospects for yourself and trade the rest to other agents.[112]

A Serious How-to Manual with a Sense of Humor

Chapter 2 Quiz

After choosing a broker, what should you do on Day One in real estate?

1
- a) order business cards
- b) get a name badge
- c) prospect for clients
- d) set-up your website

How many ways are there to prospect for clients?

2
- a) a few that work, the rest suck
- b) more than may be counted
- c) 105
- d) three

What is the best time of day to prospect?

3
- a) during rush hour traffic
- b) during the lunch hour
- c) in the morning
- d) after dinner

When should you give value away?

4
- a) upfront
- b) sometime in the middle
- c) at the end
- d) never give anything away

How's the market?

5
- a) it's pretty good!
- b) it's rather lousy!
- c) it's unbelievable!
- d) why do you ask?

To what are buyers most attracted?

6
- a) a good-looking agent
- b) listings
- c) well-priced listings, with lots of photos
- d) kitchens and bathrooms

When are your friends likely to give you referrals?

7
- a) when you ask
- b) when you teach them how
- c) when they feel you're competent
- d) all of these

To optimize prospecting, to which database members should you campaign?

8
- a) the newest ones
- b) the ones with intent to buy and/or sell soon
- c) every last one of them
- d) the ones you like most

What is the best way to avoid riding the real estate roller coaster?

9
- a) by prospecting habitually
- b) by prospecting only when you're short on clients
- c) by prospecting when the mood strikes
- d) by prospecting once all your systems are in-place

Why should you get creative with prospecting?

10
- a) to give you an edge over the competition
- b) to evolve your methods and tactics
- c) to keep your job exciting
- d) all of these are right

Find the best answers throughout this chapter and on page 322.

WordSearch

```
C F T P I R C S U B A G E N T R
N O I S S I M M O C M L S E M I
A P N X W E I V E R P P A S B O
M E B T E Y E K N R U T C U N D
S N H R E R U S O L C E R O F U
T H E A O M U S K X D B I H I O
F O R L G K P P N I S T A N X B
A U N Z P E E O P E C A T W T F
R S A D C M N R R E H K S O U S
C E I T R B I C P A R C B T R X
C A R P O R T S Y W R L T A E O
T C O N T I N G E N C Y I I C B
R R T X N I Y A W E V I R D K K
E W C W A C V H A L F B A T H C
N A I G R O E G N I S O L C Q O
D Z V P G N I T S I L P O O C L
```

You become the inspector as you search for real estate terms going up, down, left, right, and diagonally.

List of 36 terms found on page 323.

When it comes to pricing listings and negotiating purchase agreements, real property valuation is a handy skill to possess; it's also a challenging one to acquire, because each individual property and its sales transaction are unique. In essence, valuation is the attempt to predict a future event, using past events and current statistics as a crystal ball. Once an agent is able to accurately identify a property's condition, and thereby its comparables, that agent will come to understand that valuation is part science and part art, and that *with practice*, any agent may become an accurate guesser of value.

This chapter shows the reader how to interpret the value of any subject property, and (with confidence) select a price that will attract reasonable buyers, making reasonable offers.

CHAPTER THREE
VALUATION & PRICING

What is Value?

Value is determined by the individual principals of a transaction.

BY CECIL THE SEER

WE ALL NEED CERTAIN THINGS to maintain life: air, water, food, shelter, love, & medicine. Because we need these things, we are willing to trade our resources and abilities to get our hands on them, which are: time, money, other goods, credit, labor, relationships, knowledge, and (for some) integrity. Once our basic needs are met, we begin to desire things that will augment these needs, thereby improving our quality of life. These desires are specific to us as individuals, and are often motivated by safety, pride, status, quality, personal/financial growth, entertainment, nostalgia, and/or relationship maintenance.

Each buyer comes with his own unique personality, influences, ideas, needs, desires, fears, greeds, assumptions, and opinions. Sellers are built the exact same way.

For each buyer and each seller, specific needs are determined by that person's current circumstances. The current needs of some principals will compel them into immediate, rushed action, while the needs of others are less urgent, allowing those principals to spend ample time considering all choices. The needs of these individuals influence the resulting value of a given transaction.

Given such, there are numerous reasons for which a buyer will acquire property now, such as divorce, a growing family in need of more space, or perhaps eviction from mom's couch. Similarly, urgent needs abound for sellers too, like job transfers, down-sizing to a smaller living space, or in an extreme example, a combination of lots of equity, but no cash, bad credit, insufficient health insurance, and an expensive, pending surgical procedure.

For reasons like these, sometimes value is paying the highest price ever, and at other times, value is selling at the lowest price ever. It all depends upon an individual principal's needs/desires at an exact moment in time.

Consider these scenarios: a starving man places more value on his next meal than does a honeymooning couple aboard an all-you-can-eat pleasure cruise, and a picture of Grandma will always be more valuable to you than to anyone attending your garage sale. In the same way, a private backyard has inherent value, but the exact level of value that backyard holds will be specific to each potential buyer.

Keep in mind that when it comes to real estate property transfer, value is not comprised of trading money alone, rather value is money (and/or other goods of trade) in exchange for real property, *plus terms*.

To arrive at the eventual value, various decisions and concessions are negotiated by principals. Some of their decisions are based in logic, and others are colored by emotion. Some sellers will reject an offer of higher price and financed terms, for one of quick, cash terms, free of contingency. Other sellers will reject quick, cash terms, favoring instead a buyer with a heartwarming story. Likewise, some buyers will place higher value on turn-key properties, ready to move right in. Other buyers will find more value in a rehab project, ready to transform into their own image.

Considering all circumstances, a buyer will find value at—or less than—the highest price (plus terms) he is willing to pay, regardless of what other buyers may be willing to pay for the exact same property. For a seller, value will be at—or higher than—the lowest price (plus terms) she is willing to accept, regardless of what other sellers are willing to accept for comparable properties. In all circumstances, the specific principals of a transaction determine the value of a specific property, based upon a combination of their current, unique needs and desires, at this exact moment in time.

In other words, value is determined each time we trade specific resources/abilities to satisfy our specific needs/desires. For this reason, and this reason alone, value will always be a personal judgement, unique to each individual. 🌳

A residential dwelling is made of many parts and features which, when added together, comprise its overall condition. When that dwelling is FOR SALE, each individual buyer will place a different value on its specific combination of conditions. For example: a cul-de-sac lot will be more valuable to the buyer with bike-riding kids, than to the empty nester. A gourmet kitchen will be more valuable to the buyer with a home-based, catering company, than to the microwave dinner family. And a large, fenced yard will be more valuable to the buyer with big dogs, than to the childless cat-lover. For reasons like these, value is judged by us personally. We look at market behavior to get a sense of what others like us are doing, but individual buyers and sellers ultimately decide how value is defined.

From Where, Oh Where, Does Value Come?

That which is highly valuable to one may be quickly disregarded by another.

A Serious How-to Manual with a Sense of Humor

Value vs. Fair Market Value

The difference between the two is huge, and one that must be understood.

BY NUANCED NELLY

WHEN SPEAKING OF REAL ESTATE transactions, value is the price of a particular piece of real property, plus terms, negotiated between a unique buyer and a unique seller, at a particular moment in time. The value of that particular property can be thought of as an historical event, involving unique characters.[126]

Fair market value (FMV) is when several (or lots) of these historical events are gathered and analyzed to interpret what a future, unknown buyer may rationally pay for a specific property (or for any property within a group of properties—so long as each share specified characteristics).[132] The FMV of a particular property can be thought of as the price an informed consumer *should be* willing to pay, given the current market trend, as it relates to similar sales.

The thing about FMV is that people talk about it like it's a fact. But it's not a fact—it's an opinion. The specific statistics analyzed, and how those statistics are interpreted, affect the resulting "FMV." The point is: FMV is not an absolute, it's a guess. And whether or not that guess is a good one, depends upon the guesser.[150]

Since value is derived from an agreement of price plus terms, and since agreements are private, we (the guessers of FMV) are privy to only select bits of data. The public record and MLS data are the least bits we can see without direct information fed to us from parties to a particular agreement. From the information readily available, we may be able to ascertain whether or not financing was obtained (and what type), the number of days the property was on the market before an offer was accepted (days on market, DOM), the duration of the contract term (the number of days from contract signing to transaction closing), seller-paid closing costs (dollar amount), the listed price, and the sales price. Because we cannot ascertain unknown, valuable concessions or terms of an agreement, we are left with questions, like: did the seller provide a home warranty? Did the seller paint or make repairs as part of the agreement? Were there other unknown contingencies? What was the seller's loan payoff? Because we don't know these answers, we can only guess at the actual net-sale. Should any of these questions matter? Or, does the sales price alone tell the whole story, thereby establishing another comparable for FMV?

Through public record research, we may see if a seller had an outstanding loan on the property and guess at the payoff amount. This information may nudge us closer to understanding a net-to-seller figure for a given transaction,[135] but does that number really matter when considering value? It may, when one seller has hundreds of thousands of dollars in equity, while a comparable seller has only a few hundred. However, when considering FMV, the net-to-seller figure is irrelevant because while net-to-seller may influence a seller's bargaining position, it does not change the subjects's condition, and therefore has nothing to do with FMV.

It's in the seller's best interest to get the highest possible net income when selling her property. Therefore, should she care what the actual sales price is, so long as she receives her desired net-to-seller? Comparable property sales often times have dramatically different net-to-seller figures. One seller may only sell if she nets $100K, or more. Another seller may sell, so long as her *loss* is no more than $100K. What one seller considers to be good value can be very different from another. For this reason, a seller's potential net income should not be a considering factor of FMV.

The unique buyers and sellers of specific transactions *determine* value. The most anyone else may ever do is *interpret* FMV.[342] 🌳

Everything Sells for Its Value

Everything, that is—not just some things.

BY NORA THE KNOWER

IMAGINE ANY GIVEN PROPERTY. There are hundreds, if not thousands, of people out there who would purchase your imagined property right now, at this very moment.

For the vast majority of these potential buyers, the top price they're willing to pay right now is far below FMV. However, there are still many people out there willing to pay a price within the range of FMV. Best yet, a few people are willing to pay at the top end of the FMV range, if not a bit more. This is because each property is unique, and some buyers will place a higher value on its particular peculiarities than will most other buyers. The trick to finding these selective buyers is to get most, if not all, current buyers to visit the property.[153]

Because value is personal and unique to each buyer and seller, every transaction is *at value*. Otherwise, the buyer and/or seller wouldn't make the trade. Even when you hear a principal cry-out, complaining that their transaction hurts—*given their current circumstances*—they must have believed that making a trade at this time, at this price, is better than not. In other words, they see value in doing so.

Condition Is Everything That Price Is Not

For all listed property, price and condition are inseparable.

BY CAPTAIN OBVIOUS

OFTEN TIMES WE THINK of a property's condition being only its cleanliness, the materials used in its construction, the functionality of those materials, its style, its size, and its age. However, a property's condition is comprised of more—much more than may be listed here.

The three main conditional categories of real estate are generally defined as:

Hard conditions—those that cannot be changed, or whose change would require significant labor and expense.

Soft conditions—those that supplement hard conditions, whose individual change is not of significant expense.

Peripheral conditions—those that cannot be directly controlled by the owner, primarily due to the economic and ecological environments.[132] To robustly explore the conditional aspects of a subject property, ask yourself questions like these:

Regarding the physical features of the structure and the building lot: Does the lot slope level or steep? Can it support a garden? How sunny is the lot? How much sunlight comes inside? Can children comfortably play soccer in the yard? Where does the lot reside (in a cul-de-sac, on a main street)? What is the lot size? What is the parking situation (garage, on-street, in the yard)? Is the driveway steep, or extremely short? Does the structure sit above, below, or at street level? How does rainwater flow on/around the property? Is there an out-building? Does it have permanent utilities (if so, what type)? Does the lot front a golf course, lake, or other feature? What is the view? Does the structure support an addition? How close are the neighboring properties? Is there privacy in the backyard, or can the neighbors see you barbecuing? What cardinal direction does the structure face?

Regarding the neighborhood: What does the air smell like? What sounds can you hear (airplanes, gunshots, children playing, construction, traffic)? Are there sex offenders living nearby? Where is the school bus stop? Is there a home owner's association (HOA)? If so, what are the expenses/benefits/restrictions? Does the garbage man come once a week, or are there cans in the street most days? Does the neighborhood have old-growth trees, or is it clear-cut? Do neighboring properties share the same style, or is there randomness? Are you allowed to park a semi truck in the driveway? Better yet, may your neighbor park a semi truck in his driveway?

Regarding expenses and utilities: What are the costs of taxes, insurance, maintenance, and utilities? Is it on septic or sewer? Municipal or well water? Natural gas, electricity, on-site propane? Choice of internet/TV providers? How is cell phone reception for your brand?

Regarding access to financing: Are there any financing vehicles made unavailable by the property's condition? If so, which ones? What portion of buyers depend upon this restricted financing? In other words, does the restriction of financing significantly alter demand?

Regarding the proximity to other things (and the quality of those things): How close are shopping, schools, transportation routes, playgrounds, parks, recreation? How likely is surrounding zoning to change? Are there any nearby planned developments in shopping, schools, recreation, housing?

Regarding the buyer: Does the property possess features that are in- or out-of-fashion?

When compared to otherwise-comparable properties, the subject property may possess a single, conditional feature that significantly affects its value (whether up or down).[160] Therefore, when interpreting FMV, consider *all things* that comprise condition, and you'll be better able to pick a reasonable price to accompany it.[154] 🌳

YOU CAN'T SMELL PICTURES

...so go see the competition with your own eyeballs. Each property is unique, with a particular combination of light & setting, fixtures & floor plan, wear & disrepair, designs & smells. Pictures rarely tell the full story: omitting moisture, rot, odor, and neglect. The price may accurately reflect the condition—or it may not. The only way to know for sure is to see it for yourself. So, visit every listing. Doing so will improve your valuation skills. Because, soon you will have been INSIDE EVERY SOLD LISTING in your niche market. And with first-hand knowledge of each one, you will begin to develop a nose for price.

A Serious How-to Manual with a Sense of Humor

Crime & Other Conditions

*Factored together,
all of these things determine
a property's condition.*

Hard Conditions

property type (ranch/two-story/condo)
style (traditional/modern/Victorian)
actual age (year of construction)

living (heated & cooled) square footage
deck/patio/unfinished square footage
total square footage

number of and type of rooms
(bedrooms/bathrooms/specialty)
room sizes/shapes and floorplan

types of storage
storage capacity
storage allocation

lot size and setting
topography (lot slope/grade)
on-site outdoor amenities

parking type and capacity:
garage (de/attached), driveway,
street, overflow, off-site

front elevation

views/sounds/smells

utilities (plumbing/electric/gas):
type, functionality, expense,
sources of supply, efficiency

How many residents was the
property build to occupy?

Were post-construction
add-ons permitted?

The value of properties, pulsating
from the immediate neighbors...
to the entire neighborhood...
to a one-mile radius...
to a three-mile radius,..

Soft Conditions

effective age (the combined effect
of latest updates to fixtures, systems,
and other conditional features)

type of construction materials used
quality of craftsmanship
fixture material and quality

cleanliness (including smells)
staging efforts
curb appeal

appliances (HVAC/water heater/kitchen):
type, style, functionality,
efficiency, and effective age

use of outdoor spaces:
functionality, fixtures, design
How clean is the yard?

basement/attic/extra spaces:
Are extra spaces finished or not?

style and design:
Is it consistent or hodgepodge?
Do interior and exterior match?

physical condition:
Is the property turn-key?
or does it need repairs?

Is the property water-tight?
or does it leak a little bit?

...and the use of those properties
(residential/retail/industrial/farm)
are all part of a subject property's
condition.

Peripheral Conditions

school districts (elem/middle/high)
home owners association (HOA):
restrictive covenants and bylaws

tax and crime rates
insurance rates and restrictions
available financing options

amenities (type and quality):
off-site, in-neighborhood,
within walking distance

regulations/ordinances
!! the neighbor's condition !!
proximity to things, like:

city center, shopping, recreation, transit,
schools, sex offenders, worship sites,
highways, fire hydrants, emergency services,..

A Serious How-to Manual with a Sense of Humor

Effort Meter

You're Gonna Need:

Potential Fixture
Questions
Assumptions
Clarification

tips

Discernment between fixtures
and personal property is
vital when interpreting
a property's value.

Address fixtures before they
become a mess. Disputes can
be avoided by educating clients.
A listing agent should point-
out any fixtures that her seller
may wish to remove and take
along to the new property. In
doing so, the seller should
replace removed fixtures with
similarly-functioning fixtures,
and repair any damage caused
by removal—all prior to the
property being listed FOR SALE.

Many fights have been spawned
by heirloom chandeliers. To
avoid it happening to you, as
Buyer's agent, explain fixtures
to Buyer and seek clarification
with Seller on any fixtures that
may lead to dispute—all prior
to making a purchase offer.
Then, define these questionable
fixtures in the purchase offer.

As Seller's agent, include a list
of transferring fixtures in your
listing's marketing package.[234]

Σ Fixtures are real property,
meaning they are conveyed to
the buyer at time of ownership
transfer, and are therefore part
of a property's condition.

How-to
Conduct the Fixture Test

A fixture is real property that was at one time personal property. The
nails and two-by-fours that were bought at a building-supply store,
and brought onto a construction site via pick-up truck are personal
property, but once made into the walls of a house, these materials
become real property (fixtures). That part is easy to understand, but
what about things that aren't nailed-down, like keys, remote controls,
curtains, mirrors, appliances, prefab storage buildings, landscaping
ornaments, and the koi fish in a pond? While fixture exclusion may
be part of a negotiated agreement, the sale of fixtures are assumed to
be a seller's intent. To know for sure, ask yourself these questions:

1 Method of Attachment

Is the item bonded to the property? Would removal
leave a scar? Would removal require labor? If YES to any of
these questions, then the item is a fixture. Examples:
- Cement, nails, screws, plaster, gunk, and glue attach personal
  property to the land permanently, creating fixtures.
- Roots anchor vegetation to the land.
- Decals, stuck to mirrors or walls are fixtures.
- A mirror glued to a wall is a fixture. A mirror hung by hook
  is not a fixture (unless made so by customization; see
  STEP 2), but the hook used to hang that mirror is a fixture.
- Gravity can be a method of attachment if the item is
  extremely heavy and requires special equipment to
  move, like large landscaping boulders or prefab sheds.

2 Adaptation/Customization

Has the item been adapted to fit another part of the property?
Customized to fit the property? Has the property been customized
to fit the item? Is it unique to this property? Would transfer of this
item to another property require disassembly or re-tooling of the
new property? If YES, you're looking at a fixture. Examples are:
- Drapes or Venetian blinds that are cut to the dimensions of a
  window are fixtures (even more so when these window dressings
  are made custom for multiple windows of the property).
- Keys designed to fit specific locks, remote controls to ceiling fans,
  garage doors, and wall-mounted TVs are customized fixtures.
- A free-standing tanning bed is not a fixture, but if a closet is built
  around it, requiring disassembly to remove, it becomes a fixture.

3 Intention

Does removal of the item render another item
inoperable? If YES, it's a fixture. Examples being:
- Batteries in smoke detectors and installed light bulbs are fixtures.
- Non-attached shelving boards are fixtures because their removal
  would leave only mounted brackets, not storage spaces.
- Koi ponds with their koi fish removed are no longer
  koi ponds. Therefore, the fish are fixtures.

How-to
Calculate Net-to-Seller

Net-to-seller and *net-sale* are similar but not the same. Sellers use net-to-seller estimations when deciding whether or not to list and when comparing offers. Buyers *and* sellers use net-sale figures when making offers and counter-offers (especially when buyers are competing for best-offer status).[259] Before you calculate, know the terms:

Net-to-Seller—denotes all the money that is leftover after a transaction has occurred, going into the seller's pocket (or *from* the seller's pocket, as is sometimes the case).

Net-Sale—see *Seller Earnings Before Lean & Loan Payoff*

Seller Earnings Before Lean & Loan Payoff (SEBLLP)—while a seller's lean and loan payoff amounts have an affect on her own, personal assessment of value, net-to-seller is of no concern to buyers. Therefore, the inclusion of SEBLLP deductions should be reserved for seller information only; otherwise, when comparing comps,[140] or when Buyer is composing an offer,[252] the seller's-net figure should be considered equal to SEBLLP (AKA **net-sale**).

Sales Price—the dollar amount on the P&S contract.

Seller Expenses—taxes, commissions, closing costs, and improvements to condition that were completed and paid-for prior to listing.

Seller Concessions—commissions, closing costs, and improvements to condition that were completed and paid-for as part of the P&S contract.

Closing Costs (CC)—the collective title given to expenses associated with closing a transaction. Buyer and Seller each have associated costs to close: those associated with the seller are **seller expenses** and any portion of buyer-associated CC paid by the seller are **seller concessions**. The following list of potential closing costs is extensive, but not exhaustive:
- **Stand-alone CC** (associated with buyers and/or sellers): property taxes, transfer tax, insurance (owner's title, hazard), document recording fees, attorney/escrow fees, inspections (general, termite, survey), HOA transfer fees & premiums, courier fees, governmental assessments/disclosure report fees, notary fees, proration of shared expenses (utility bills, alarm monitoring, pest-control maintenance),..
- **Loan-specific CC**: application fee, origination fee, processing fee, credit report fee, underwriting fee, discount points, insurance (lender's title, PMI/MIP,) pre-paid interest, appraisal, title search,..

1 From: Sales Price → Net-to-Seller
Begin with a sales price in-mind. Then *subtract* all seller expenses, seller concessions, and lean & loan payoffs. The resulting figure is net-to-seller. Demonstrated at right: (fig. 3.1).

2 From: Net-to-Seller → Sales Price
Begin with a net-to-seller figure in-mind. Then *add* all lean & loan payoffs, seller concessions, and seller expenses. The resulting figure is the sales price. Demonstrated at right: (fig. 3.2).

Effort Meter

You're Gonna Need:
Paper
Pencil
Calculator
Expense Tallies

tips

Encourage your sellers to find *all* lean & loan payoff figures; don't forget about second mortgages and home equity lines of credit (HELOC).

For great service, run a net-to-seller sheet at time of listing, and as each offer comes in.

Depending upon market forces, sellers may (or may not) be expected to pay a buyer's closing costs.

Σ Net-to-seller figures help sellers when deciding whether or not to list and when comparing offers; considering the net-sale figure helps buyers negotiate.

(fig. 3.1) PRICE → NET

	Sales Price
−	Seller Expenses
−	Seller Concessions
=	Net-Sale (SEBLLP)
−	Lean & Loan Payoff
=	Net-to-Seller

(fig. 3.2) NET → PRICE

	Net-to-Seller
+	Lean & Loan Payoff
=	Net-Sale (SEBLLP)
+	Seller Expenses
+	Seller Concessions
=	Sales Price

Principles of Value

When evaluating real property, one must consider the highest and best use of that property.

BY VALERIE THE VALUATOR

SINCE EACH INDIVIDUAL PIECE of real property is completely unique, interpreting the fair market value (FMV) for a specific property can become challenging. Aside from the technical wrangling used to calculate FMV,[150] the fact remains that where one may find value, another may not.[126] While the individual opinions of buyers in the market surely matter, FMV should defer to the highest and best use of each individual property. This means that FMV will encompass all the things that give a particular property its value, and not just the average price per square foot of its comparables.

An example: property A and property B sit across the street from each other, comparable in all ways except one—*different school districts*. Property A resides in a district with a much higher school rating than does B, which is acknowledged by the local population. Regardless of whether a particular buyer has school-aged children (or plans to conceive), the value of A will remain higher than B, because the highest use of A includes the better school, whether or not this utility is consumed by its owner. Therefore, when picking properties to compare to the subject,[138] be sure to consider these principles:

Supply & Demand
Relative to willing buyers: an increase in the quantity of listings will decrease their value, and vice versa.[144]

Inelastic Price
It takes a large change in a listing's price to affect its demand.[144]

Substitution
When several comparable properties are FOR SALE, the one with the lowest price will have the most demand.

Externalities
The things that surround a property affect its value.

Conformity
Demand for a specific property is highest when located amidst properties that share similar age, size, and style.

Progression
A lesser property, located amidst greater properties, will have a higher value than its comparable counterparts, located amidst conforming properties.

Regression
A greater property, located amidst lesser properties, will have a lower value than its comparable counterparts, located amidst conforming properties.

Balance
Demand is higher for properties in close proximity to amenities (schools, shopping, work, transportation routes, recreation, entertainment,..).

Anticipation
A buyer's future benefits, including enjoyment of the property and potential profit from its eventual sale, influence a property's current value.

Dearest You,
Always remember that we are each different from all others, no matter how similar we may seem.

That makes each property an absolute, Unique Beauty!

Effort Meter

You're Gonna Need:

Listing Data
Sorting Barrel
Critical Eye
to Think like a Buyer

How-to
Pick Apples (Comparable Properties)

Just like real property, fruit comes in many classifications (apples, oranges, pears, cherries,..) and each class has several varieties. While each piece of fruit is comparable to all others within its class, it shares the most resemblance to fruit within its variety. Now pretend your subject property is an apple. To interpret its fair market value (FMV),[342] you must compare your apple to apples of all varieties (Granny Smith, Red Delicious & Pink Lady), but never to pears or cherries (each of which sometimes look like apples). Also, to avoid confirmation bias (the natural tendency to select properties that confirm a pre-formed opinion), ignore prices when picking apples and narrow your search by the following steps:

tips

Comparable properties (AKA comparables or comps) are those that are similar to a subject property.

Choosing comparable properties is mostly science with a bit or art tossed in—with practice, you'll get better at it. For example: within three months is *usually* considered recent history, but depending on how quickly the market is trending,[149] "recent" activity may be defined as anywhere between one and six months.

Approximately ten to twenty apples per status is an ideal basket full. Can't find enough apples? Widen your search criteria. Got too many? Narrow the criteria.

Generally speaking, properties with basements do not compare to those without.

The best way to accurately assess all potential comparables is to visit each in-person. The second best way is to study the hell outta pictures and MLS data.

Always consider the source of square footage data (ideally all comps should share the same source).

Choose wisely—your comps will be used to create CMA[140] and interpret FMV.[150]

Σ   The collection of accurate comparables is the first step to interpreting FMV.

1 Evaluate the Subject Property
With a discerning eye, critique your apple and record its precise condition.[130] Your honest and thorough evaluation of the subject is the foundation for choosing accurate comparables.

2 Define the Shopping Zone (Location)
Identify regions on the map that naturally divide buyer preferences. These shopping zones are the geographic markets that segregate comparables and are defined by the boundaries of school districts, county lines, zip codes, MLS areas, high-traffic lanes, or a side of the tracks. Limit your apple search to those in the same shopping zone as the subject.

3 Limit by Age & Type
Considering only these conspicuous characteristics, select all apples that were built within ten years of the subject, and are of the same type (detached one-story, detached two-story, condo, townhouse,..).

4 Limit by Size & Function
For a quick measure of a property's size, count the number of bedrooms and bathrooms in its original construction; these factors reveal the number of people the property was designed to accommodate. While all apples have a kitchen and living room, some apples have more than one. As well, most have additional spaces for specialty use (basement, attic, bonus room, workshop, storage room, out-building,..). A property's overall size is the number of and type of rooms (spaces) it has, as related to its square footage. Therefore, as is the subject, choose all apples with the same quantity of bedrooms, bathrooms, and type of specialty rooms—all within 25% of the subject's square footage.

5 Consider Listing Status
A prime aspect of interpreting FMV is observing the recent fate of comparable listings. To do so, your basket of chosen apples should include listings that have *recently*-SOLD, *recently*-EXPIRED, are currently-PENDING sale, and those that are ACTIVE (currently FOR SALE).

When searching for comparable properties, think about the subject property, and then think about its eventual buyer. Forget all about price for a minute and pretend this buyer has just purchased the subject property.

Looking at condition alone, ask yourself: *Which other properties would this buyer have considered purchasing?* Select all recently-sold, recently-expired/withdrawn, currently pending sale, and actively-listed properties that match-up to your thought experiment.

When you properly channel this imaginary buyer's needs/wants, these selected properties will be your comparable apples.

YORK IMPERIAL

Barrel Ahead with a Buyer in mind

A Serious How-to Manual with a Sense of Humor

Effort Meter

tips

CMA is short for comparable market analysis.

The more apples you have to choose from, the more accurate your FMV guess will be.[342]

In a marco CMA, hard condition should be nearly the same for each property. Square footage may vary up to 25% from the subject.

In each micro CMA, soft condition should be nearly the same for each property.

If your macro CMA has too many apples (more than twenty per status), then uniformly tighten your "recent activity" time frame.[146]

Your macro CMA should be full of similar properties, from the same shopping zone.[148]

Because micro markets are A, B, or C GRADE, some macro markets may be overly heavy in one and slim in another.

caveat

Using only subdivision comps to price a listing is like watching a movie with your face pressed against the screen—you're never gonna see the full picture.

Σ A macro CMA is a zoomed-out view of a subject property's marketplace, and a micro CMA is the zoomed-in view.

How-to
Generate *One* Macro CMA

A comparable market analysis (CMA) is the formal comparison of all your picked apples.[138] Regardless of the fact that today's buyer is unlikely to purchase one of the SOLD, PENDING, or EXPIRED listings, your report should include every status (to compare status fate). In this way, a CMA includes all the apples that a given, *rational* apple buyer would consider, before choosing *one* to make a purchase offer.

1 Create Spreadsheets
Spreadsheets will make your calculations simple and your presentation pretty. Create one for each listing status: SOLD, PENDING, EXPIRED, and ACTIVE. Fill the rows with each apple's address and fill the columns as shown in the sample on the facing page (fig. 3.3). Your MLS probably supplies CMA-making software. If this application fails to allow for customized categories, then it's no good to you, and any old spreadsheet software should be used instead.

2 Import Data
Carefully insert HARD CONDITION and MARKET DATA for each apple in your barrel. By looking at MLS data and photographs, score SOFT CONDITION entries on a scale of 1-10, with ten being a perfect score. *Example:* an old, unrenovated apple gets an effective age score of zero.

3 Evaluate Hard Condition
Each apple should share similar HARD CONDITION (exception: front elevation may vary). Apples with hard conditions that vary too much from the subject are either pears or cherries (not comparable), so toss them from your CMA.

How-to
Generate *Three* Micro CMA

Each piece of real property is unique, so an exact match does not exist. However, just like apples, those of the same variety are the most similar. Therefore, if a macro CMA compares apples to apples, a micro CMA compares Pink Lady to Pink Lady, and no longer considers Granny Smith or Red Delicious (because Granny Smith and Red Delicious get their own micro CMA).

1 Reorganize by Soft Condition
Considering only SOFT CONDITION scores, use your judgement to divide your apples into three varieties: top, middle, and bottom conditions (A, B & C GRADES). Create a new set of spreadsheets for each grade (fig 3.4 at right). These are your micro CMA:
- Apples with high soft condition scores are A GRADE (Red Delicious).
- Apples with average soft condition scores are B GRADE (Pink Lady).
- Apples with low soft condition scores are C GRADE (Granny Smith).

Macro & Micro CMA Charts

(fig 3.3) MACRO CMA

(fig 3.4) MICRO CMA

STATUS	HARD CONDITION						SOFT CONDITION (ranked 1-10)				Date SOLD/PEND/EXPIRY/LIST	MARKET DATA					
	# Bedrooms/#Baths	# Extra Spaces	Extra Space Type	Square Feet (SQFT)	Age (or year built)	Front Elevation	Effective Age	Cleanliness	Materials Quality	Craftsmanship		Listed Price (LP)	LP/SQFT	DOM	Sales Price (SP)	SP/SQFT	SP/LP
Subject	3/2	1	basement	1500	1956	brick	3	8	5	7	●	●	●	●	●	●	●
SOLD																	
Apple #1																	
Apple #2																	
Apple #3																	
AVERAGES	●	●	●	●	●	●	●	●	●	●							
PENDING																	
Apple #21															●	●	●
Apple #22															●	●	●
Apple #23															●	●	●
AVERAGES	●	●	●	●	●	●	●	●	●	●					●	●	●
EXPIRED																	
Apple #31															●	●	●
Apple #32															●	●	●
Apple #33															●	●	●
AVERAGES	●	●	●	●	●	●	●	●	●	●					●	●	●
ACTIVE																	
Apple #41															●	●	●
Apple #42															●	●	●
Apple #43															●	●	●
AVERAGES	●	●	●	●	●	●	●	●	●	●					●	●	●

One macro CMA is comprised of *three* micro CMA (A, B & C GRADES). ●=N/A

1 TYPE
The more closely a property's style, construction materials, floor plan, and front elevation match the subject property, the more comparable it becomes.

2 SIZE
Regardless of square footage, properties with the same type and number of usable spaces (bedrooms, bathrooms, bonus spaces, basement,..) as the subject property are more comparable than those with more or less spaces.

GETTING COMPS IN CONCERT

3 LOCALE
The closer a comparable property is located to the subject property, the more comparable it becomes.

4 TIME
The closer to today that a comparable sale was made, the more comparable it becomes. The same goes for EXPIRED and WITHDRAWN dates.

Supply and Demand

The number of sellers and buyers in the market effect values.

BY EGON THE EGGHEAD

THERE IS AN INVERSE RELATIONSHIP between the average price of listings and the quantity of listings demanded by the market. This means that, when all other things remain unchanged, an increase in market prices will lead to a decrease in the market's desire to purchase those listings, and a decrease in prices will lead to an increase in buyer demand.

[Quick sidebar: generally speaking, this demand for real estate is considered to be *inelastic*—meaning that it takes a large change in prices to significantly change the number of buyers willing to purchase. Such inelasticity comes from the fact that each listing is completely unique, durable, immovable, and its sale has a high transaction cost.]

Each market is comprised of buyers who compete with each other for listings, and sellers who compete with each other for buyers. Because sellers exercise choice over the price of their own particular listings, and because buyers exercise choice over which particular listings they actually buy, the total number of buyers and the total number of sellers in a marketplace will dictate each particular listing's FMV, which in turn, collectively equals that market's FMV. This concept may be better understood through graphic explanation:

A *buyer line* (demand curve) can be plotted on a graph, and is simplistically demonstrated with a straight line on the facing page (fig. 3.5). This line (B) represents all the buyers in a given marketplace. As the total number of buyers in the market changes, the position of the buyer line will shift left or right on the graph. When the overall number of buyers in the market increases, the line moves right (B+1), and when buyers decrease in numbers, the line moves left (B-1). Many factors, working together, will cause an increase or decrease in buyers at any given time. Some of these factors are:

income/wealth (I)
market size (population) (M)
expectation of future price (X)
price of renting (or living with Mom) (P_r)
cost of ownership(taxes, maintenance,..)(P_o)
the prices of current listings (P_c)
availability (and cost) of credit (C_r)
governmental/regulatory forces (G)
consumer preferences (K)
crime rate (Q)

Because these factors influence the position of the buyer line, it can be said that the number of buyers in the market is a function of these factors, notated as:

$f(I,M,X,P_r,P_o,P_c,C_r,G,K,Q)$ = number of buyers

A *seller line* (supply curve) can also be plotted on a graph (fig. 3.6). This line (S) represents all the sellers in a given marketplace. As the number of sellers in the market changes, the position of this line will shift left or right on the graph. As additional sellers add listings FOR SALE, the line moves right (S+1), and when the number of sellers adding listings shrinks, the line moves left (S-1). Many factors (some the same as above) will cause an increase or decrease of the number of sellers (listings) in a given marketplace, at a given time. Some of the important ones:

the prices of current listings (P_c)
expectation of future price (X)
availability (and cost) of credit (C_r)
foreclosure rate (F)
builder/investor activity (N)
crime rate (Q)

Because these factors influence the position of the seller line, it can be said that the number of listings in the market is a function of these factors, notated as:

$f(P_c,X,C_r,F,N,Q)$ = number of listings

In each market, the place where the seller line meets the buyer line is the point of equilibrium—the point where the average price of a listings conjures a buyer for each one, AKA fair market value. This point moves around the graph, depending upon how the seller and buyer lines move (fig. 3.7). If the seller line moves right, and the buyer line stays put,

FMV will go down. Conversely, if the buyer line moves right, and the seller line stays put, FMV will go up.

Because transactions are occurring all the time, we can figure the FMV of a given market, and then look for the presence of a Buyer's Market (one in which prices and the quantity demanded have led to a surplus of listings), or a Seller's Market (one in which prices and quantity demanded have led to a shortage of listings) (fig. 3.8). Unless the seller or buyer lines shift first, overtime, the prices in these markets will slowly move toward FMV.

Of all the factors influencing supply and/ or demand shift, *the expectation of future prices* (the x-factor) generally exerts the most force. When people think that prices will rise, demand may also rise as additional buyers buy now, fearful of paying more later. At the same time, supply may shrink because some sellers will choose to *not* list now, waiting instead for higher, future price. The combined effect may hasten a rise in value.

When prices are expected to fall, supply often increases because some sellers will list now, fearful of a lesser price later. At the same time, demand may shrink because some buyers will grow greedy and wait for a lower, future price. The combined effect may hasten a drop in value.

Generally, when demand for purchased housing rises, FMV will rise. This usually causes more properties to become FOR SALE. When it does, the increased supply tends to curb rising prices, but when it does not, FMV rises faster and faster.

To see supply and demand in action, you must study your niche marketplace on a monthly basis. To do so, utilize such tools as market activity,[146] absorption,[147] and trend analysis[149] reports to create a market-place dashboard.[345] When created/updated monthly, this dashboard will acquaint you with the market as is moves, allowing you to forecast the near future;[150] it may also aid in the formation of pricing strategies,[154] and with pre-qualification of seller-prospects.[189]

Fair market value may be a moving target of complex calculation, but it often moves slowly, so we can predict its moves—until forces build, swinging it rapidly and wildly. 🌳

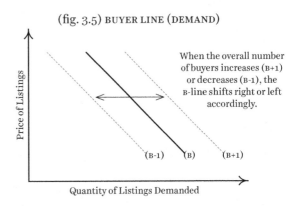

(fig. 3.5) BUYER LINE (DEMAND)

When the overall number of buyers increases (B+1) or decreases (B-1), the B-line shifts right or left accordingly.

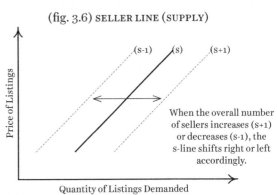

(fig. 3.6) SELLER LINE (SUPPLY)

When the overall number of sellers increases (S+1) or decreases (S-1), the S-line shifts right or left accordingly.

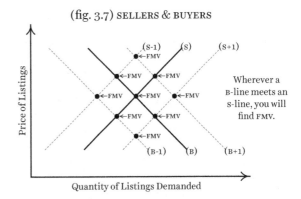

(fig. 3.7) SELLERS & BUYERS

Wherever a B-line meets an S-line, you will find FMV.

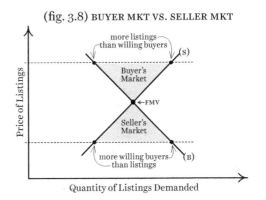

(fig. 3.8) BUYER MKT VS. SELLER MKT

Effort Meter

You're Gonna Need:

Events
Rows & Columns
Thinking Cap
Contemplation

tips

When you track market activity from month-to-month, you'll be able to notice trends and thereby predict the future with accuracy (such as the number of new listings coming next month, and the number of sales in the next thirty days). Armed with this information, you'll be able to forecast the activity you'll get on your listings.[150]

To save time, and to increase your awareness, create a market activity report at the end of each month, to serve the entire month approaching.

Notice: a market activity report shows the number of ACTIVE and PENDING listings at the beginning and at the end of each period. Intra-period activity is shown between those times.

questions about data

How do the figures between markets compare to each other? Is the average price of new listings higher or lower than the average price of all listings? How do the figures from this report compare to previous reports? Are the average days on market (AVG. DOM) getting longer or shorter? How do the prices of your listings compare to the average ACTIVE, EXPIRED, and SOLD prices?

Σ   A market activity report is a glance at the behaviors of current buyers and sellers.

How-to
Observe Market Activity

A market activity report shows the current marketplace as a snapshot, and is part of an agent's *Monthly Marketplace Dashboard*.[342] Therefore, your report should be of statistics over the previous thirty days, showing all the relevant happenings in the market. This report may be created for a single macro market, several macro markets, an agent's super macro marketplace (entire niche), or for an aggregate, metropolitan market.

1 Compile and Arrange Data

Your MLS may already generate market activity reports; if so, learn to use their tools. Otherwise, you may be able to purchase data from a vendor. However, the good ol' fashioned way is to hand-select data from the MLS (to do so, see *How-to Pick Apples*).[138] Regardless of where you mine the data, compile the following statistics to be part of your report:

- Beginning inventory totals include the number of ACTIVE and PENDING listings on the first day of the month.
- The number of new listings during the period, the average price of those new listings, and the average price of all ACTIVE listings (all existing listings plus new listings).
- The number of listings that were WITHDRAWN and EXPIRED during the period, and the average price at the time of expiry/withdrawal.
- The number of total sales during the period, and of those sales: AVG. SALES PRICE, AVG. DOM, AVG. SP/LP.
- Ending inventory totals include the number of listings that are currently ACTIVE and PENDING sale.

(fig 3.9) MARKET ACTIVITY REPORT

MARKET	Period Beginning		ACTIVE			EXPIRED/WITHDRAWN			SOLD				Period Ending	
	# ACTIVE	# PENDING	# NEWLY ACTIVE	AVG. LP (NEW)	AVG. LP (ALL)	# WITHDRAWN	# EXPIRED	AVG. LP	# SALES	AVG. SP	AVG. SP/LP	AVG. DOM	# ACTIVE	# PENDING
Macro #1														
Macro #2														
Super Macro														
Metro														

2 Observe Data

This report is full of 'big picture' data and is meant to give you an idea of the marketplace. In this way, macro markets may be easily compared to each other and to reports from months previous. *Example:* how do EXPIRED and SOLD prices compare? (more in the column)

How-to
Generate & Analyze an Absorption Report

While some listings will remain FOR SALE for many months (or even years), most sellers will eventually succumb to market forces and either sell or remove their listing from the market within a certain time frame. With this in mind, absorption analysis is meant to gauge the rate at which listing inventory changes, turns over, or is otherwise *absorbed* by the market.

Effort Meter

1 Gather Data
Absorption rates are usually calculated for macro markets; therefore, you may use the same data as defined by a macro CMA.[140] For accuracy (to smooth-out any volatile months), add-up the total number sold from the *last twelve months*. Then, add-up all the current listings.

2 Calculate Data
For each market you wish to study, make calculations in the following order, as demonstrated by the chart below (fig 3.10):
1. Divide total number SOLD by the number of MONTHS within which those sales occurred, which equals AVG. SALES PER MONTH.
2. Divide the total number of ACTIVE listings (inventory) by AVG. SALES PER MONTH, which equals MONTHS OF INVENTORY.
3. Divide ONE by MONTHS OF INVENTORY, which equals the ABSORPTION RATE of that market, during those months.

(fig 3.10) ABSORPTION REPORT

# SOLD / # MONTHS	# ACTIVES / AVERAGE SALES PER MONTH	1 / MONTHS OF INVENTORY	ABSORPTION RATE

3 Analyze Data
Verbalize your findings by saying things like:
- The forecast calls for (quote AVG. SALES/MONTH) this month.
- Assuming no additional properties become listed FOR SALE, at the current rate of absorption, it will take about (quote the MONTHS OF INVENTORY) months for all current listings to sell.
- Approximately (quote ABSORPTION RATE) percent of the current listings will sell within the next thirty days.

Generally speaking:
- less than 4 MONTHS OF INVENTORY = Seller's Market (because when ABSORPTION RATE is higher than 25%, prices may begin to rise)
- more than 5 MONTHS OF INVENTORY = Buyer's Market (because when ABSORPTION RATE is lower than 20%, prices may begin to fall)

You're Gonna Need:
Sold Comps
Active Listings
Calculator
Thinking Cap

tips
Your ability to decipher whether markets favor buyers or sellers makes you valuable to investors, since you know which markets have high transaction volume, coupled with low inventory. The same information may be used to determine where to prospect for FSBO and EXPIRED listings.

An absorption report allows you to forecast the future.

Calculate and keep absorption reports on your niche and metro markets. Revise them monthly,[342] and (eventually) you will know absorption rates by heart.

Once you generate absorption reports for three months in a row, a trend will totally emerge, dude.

caveats
Absorption analysis may be inaccurate when SOLD and ACTIVE listing totals are small numbers.

Three months of inventory (33% absorption rate) is a perfectly balanced market. However, the market is imperfect, because some listings will never sell. Therefore, a fudge of the numbers is necessary to find a realistic balance. For this reason, between four and five months of inventory is said to be balanced.

Σ   Absorption rate analysis exposes listing shortages or surpluses in the current market.

HIT THE BULLS EYE

The ongoing valuation of a particular market is like trying to hit a moving target. Therefore, to be accurate in your assessments of value, study the marketplace on a monthly basis.[342] When doing so, be sure to consider the proper data.

Shopping Zone: the geographic boundaries by which most buyers shop.

Price Zone: the range of list prices by which buyers generally shop.

Macro Market: all properties that share the same shopping zone and the same price zone.

Super Macro Market: all the macro markets in an agent's niche.

Metro Market: all macro markets in town.

Macro CMA: all properties in the same shopping zone that have the same hard conditions as a subject property.

Micro CMA: all properties in a macro CMA that have the same soft conditions as a subject property.

How-to
Chart a Market Trend

When pricing a listing,[154] it's helpful to know which way the market is moving and the rate at which it rolls. So that you may observe a trending market, plot it properly on paper.

Effort Meter

1 Gather Data

When charting a market trend with a subject property in-mind, be sure to choose data points that are comparable to the subject, but of the widest scope possible (so that you may plot lots of data). When you're charting a trend as part of your Monthly Market Update,[342] use macro market apples.[148] Because trends are best observed over a long period of time, collect at least a year's worth of data.

2 Plot Some Dots

Draw straight lines on paper, marking TIME along the x-axis, and PRICE along the y-axis. Go slow to ensure accurate placement and spacing of TIME and PRICE. For each SOLD property, place a dot on the graph where its SOLD PRICE matches its SOLD DATE. Give your chart a title (and date it, too) so that you may refer to it later. Depending upon the way your trend develops, you may wish to zoom-in or zoom-out of the twelve-month trend chart. Making multiple charts is encouraged; just be sure to attach the proper titles.

3 Draw Best-Fit Line

Individual dots do not matter as much as the entirety of all the dots. So, lay your straightedge on the page, positioned so that approximately half the dots are hidden from view. Strike a line across the straightedge, exposing the market's trend. *Important:* small fluctuations make a trend not. You want the line to remain straight; no bumping around.

4 Calculate Trend Rate

Trend rate (TR) is the market's average monthly gain or loss in value. When the trend rate is expressed in SP/SQFT (instead of a percentage), it can be a useful pricing tool:[343]

$$\text{TREND RATE} = \frac{\text{AVG. SP/SQFT now} - \text{AVG. SP/SQFT then}}{\text{\# months between now \& then}}$$

You're Gonna Need:

Sold Comps
Pencil & Paper
Straightedge
Squinty Eye

tips

A line that slopes upward, from left to right, denotes a trend of increasing values. A line sloping downward denotes a trend of decreasing values. Don't try to fit a sloped line where it doesn't belong—sometimes the market trends flat.

Use the macro market's trend rate to calculate the *Right Price*, and its trend chart as a graphical tool to explain your pricing strategy to sellers.[154]

If the market has shifted course over the time frame of your chart, you may need to draw two lines, connected at a single angle.

To create a powerful pricing tool, plot your dots and label the best-fit line: SOLD. Then, (using a different color) plot dots and draw best-fit lines for ACTIVE and EXPIRED listings, too.

Σ   Trends tend to continue along the same trajectory until news breaks, inciting a change of fear to greed, or vice versa.[144]

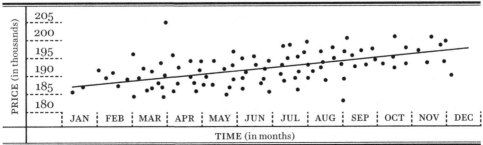

(fig 3.11) MARKET TREND

PRICE (in thousands): 205, 200, 195, 190, 185, 180

JAN | FEB | MAR | APR | MAY | JUN | JUL | AUG | SEP | OCT | NOV | DEC

TIME (in months)

Effort Meter

You're Gonna Need:

Macro & Micro CMA
Absorption Report
Market Trend
Mkt. Activity Report

tips

Remember, price is best measured when comparing listings by price/SQFT.

For very accurate calculations of SP/SQFT, first subtract the known seller concessions from sales price.

Looking at the macro CMA, how does DOM correspond to SP/SQFT?

When AVG. SP/LP is less than one, most sellers in the market are negotiating their price down. When AVG. SP/LP is more than one, most sellers are negotiating their price up.

Look closely at your CMA.[140] When soft condition is similar, does a large difference in the style of front elevation alter SP/SQFT? If YES, create a macro CMA whereby all apples share a similar front elevation.

When you create absorption,[147] market activity,[146] and trend reports,[149] all you're really doing is rearranging micro and macro CMA data.

Ask yourself: is the subject property in a Buyer's or Seller's market? Is a seasonal change in demand on the horizon? How do these factors influence the potential FMV in the near future?

Σ The study of market data allows you to interpret the FMV of yesterday, today, and (the near) tomorrow.

How-to
Interpret the Market and Find FMV

Prospective sellers want to know your opinion of fair market value (FMV).[128] They also want to know future FMV and how conditional improvements may change their current FMV. Using the tools and methods outlined in this chapter, you should be able to satisfy each curiosity.

1 Interpret the Subject's Macro Market[140]

If your subject property is in the bottom or middle micro market, then conditional improvements should yield a shift into a higher micro market. By studying the soft condition of higher micro markets, decide which specific improvements would warrant a micro market shift. Does the AVG. SP/SQFT of the upgraded micro market justify the expense of those improvements? Which micro market has the most sales? Which micro market has the most PENDING sales? Which has the most ACTIVE listings? The micro CMA with the highest absorption rate[147] is the hottest micro in the macro.

Within each micro CMA, rank the SOLD listings by SP/SQFT (soft condition should improve as SP/SQFT increases). Notice the relationship between SP/SQFT and SP/LP amongst each listing. This shows the impact LP has on resulting SP.

2 Interpret the Subject's FMV

Begin by identifying which micro market the subject belongs. For each micro and macro CMA: FMV = AVG. SP/SQFT. Otherwise, FMV of each micro (or macro) CMA may be quoted as a range: from the apple with the lowest SP/SQFT to the apple with the highest SP/SQFT.

FMV of subject property = AVG. SP/SQFT of its micro CMA
(or AVG. SP/SQFT of its three closest comparables)

3 Forecast the Subject's Future

There will always be more potential buyers (shoppers, lookers), than actual buyers (those who close) in the marketplace. You want at least half of these shoppers to visit your listing within the first ten days it's listed. To know if they all show, do some simple math. For the sake of an educated guesstimation of the *macro* market, assume:

current SHOPPERS = total macro SALES in last 90 days

ESTIMATED SALES in next 30 days = ABSORPTION RATE × ACTIVE listings

To guess at which *micro* ACTIVES will go PENDING in the next thirty days, arrange them by LP/SQFT. Those with a similar LP/SQFT as currently-PENDING and recently-SOLD listings are the most likely to become the next round of PENDINGS.

NOTE: see this page in flow chart format: *Valuation Flow Chart*.[342]

How-to
Valuate Investment Property

When a buyer intends to occupy the property he purchases, his notion of value comes from the sales price, plus terms, plus his imagined future joys and benefits of owning that specific property. An investor derives his notion of value the exact same way, except the investor *quantifies* his future joys and benefits. This distinction causes the investor to find value of a specific property not by price, plus terms, near its fair market value (FMV), but by price, plus terms, near its net present value (NPV). By calculating value this way, an investor may compare several properties, choosing the one(s) that yield the highest return per dollar spent. To begin, an investor must know (or estimate) two of the following three factors:

- **Net Operating Income** (NOI) is an annual figure, calculated by adding all the income from rent (for a year), then subtracting all the expenses during that year. Expenses include (but are not limited to) taxes, insurance, management fees, maintenance fees, repairs, HOA dues, and utilities. Interest payments on promissory notes are not considered an expense. Annual rent minus annual expense equals NOI.

$$NOI = NPV \times R$$

- **Rate of Return** (R) (AKA Capitalization Rate/Cap. Rate) is the percentage of today's outlay of money (NPV) that is returned every year (NOI). The exact rate of return desired will vary from market to market and investor to investor, but in residential real estate, a generally accepted rate of return is between five and eight percent. *Examples:* a five percent rate of return will pay-back NPV in twenty years; an eight percent rate returns NPV in twelve and a half years.

$$R = \frac{NOI}{NPV}$$

- **Net Present Value** (NPV) is the value of a specific property today (plus the expense to acquire it), that will return a specific annual income at a known rate of return. In other words, NPV is today's value of tomorrow's return.

$$NPV = \frac{NOI}{R}$$

1 By Comparison

When investors compete with owner-occupants for the same properties, investors will be forced to pay near FMV, not the NPV that matches their preferred rate of return. However, by plugging FMV in place of NPV, investors may compare properties by the rate each returns.

2 For Marketing

When selling investment property, include NPV math in your marketing package,[234] delineating the monthly income and expense statements. This effort will allow potential buyers to understand your NPV price, thereby encouraging them (with logic) to pay that price.

Effort Meter

You're Gonna Need:
Subject Property
Calculator
Income & Rate or
FMV & Income

tips
Investment property refers to any real property whereby the owner draws income from another's use of their property.

In residential realty sales, small, multi-family properties (duplex, triplex, quadruplex) are typically valued using the NPV method.

While a generalized rate of return is acceptable to most investors within certain markets, the exact rate will be subjective to each investor.

Unless otherwise adjusted-for, NPV assumes continued, steady rental-income at a fixed, annual dollar amount.

When FMV is greater than NPV, an investor purchasing property must accept a lower-than-desired rate of return.

caveat
Many HOA and condo associations have a cap on the total number of rental units allowed at a given time. Because of this, ensure the subject property can be used as intended, otherwise a new owner (investor) may find himself at the bottom of a to-be-rented waitlist.

Σ   Net present value (NPV) is used by investors to valuate and compare investment properties.

The Conditional Function

Price dictates not only the number of offers a listing receives, but also the timeliness and quality of those offers.

BY THE PRICEMAN

FOR EACH GIVEN SUBJECT PROPERTY, there exists a set of prices, each of which (within reasonable time) will attract one or more reasonable purchase offers. This set of prices is known as the conditional function of a property's salability. In other words, a property's salability (its ability to attact reasonable, timely offers) is a function of its price/condition combo. To understand this concept, consider that the conditional state of H_2O is a function of its temperature, notated as:

$$f(temperature) = state \ of \ H_2O$$

There are only three conditional states of H_2O: steam, water, and ice. The state of H_2O is dependent upon the application of a temperature, from a set of independent temperatures. These sets are notated as:

steam {temperature : $\geq 100°C$}

water {temperature : $> 0°C$ and $< 100°C$}

ice {temperature : $\leq 0°C$}

This means that for H_2O to be water, its temperature must be within the set of temperatures that are more than zero degrees and less than one-hundred degrees, Celsius ($> 0°C$ and $< 100°C$). When the temperature is higher than this set, H_2O boils away as steam, and when the temperature is lower than this set, H_2O freezes to ice. In other words, water only exists when its temperature falls within a specified set of temperatures. When H_2O is any temperature other than the set for water, the function of its temperature cannot yield water.

In the same way, a subject property becomes salable only when its price falls within a specified set of prices. This salability is the number of offers a listing receives, given the combination of its price, its condition, and its exposure to the marketplace; also known as *The Sales Formula*, its equation is notated as:

$$price + condition + exposure = salability$$

The conditional state of a listing's salability is a function of its price, notated as:

$$f(price) = salability$$

This notation may be restated as: the salability of a listing is a function of a set of prices to a range of offers, notated as:

$$f: price \rightarrow offers$$

In this way, the number of offers a listing receives is dependent upon its price. More than one price will generate offers, but only reasonable offers will make a listing salable. To find a salable set of prices, three factors must be known about the subject property: its FMV, its salability differential (SD), and its trend allowance (TA). The formulas for these pricing factors are included in *How-to Price a Listing*[154] and the *Valuation Flow Chart*.[343]

Like H_2O, there are three conditional states of a listing: not-salable, salable, and offer-overload. The salability of a listing is dependent upon the application of a price (as determined by its pricing factors), from a set of independent prices. These sets are notated as:

not-salable {price : too HIGH}

salable {price : just RIGHT}

offer-overload {price : too LOW}

This means that for a listing to be salable, its price must be a number that falls within the set of prices between too high and too low.

While the set of temperatures that make water are fixed, the set of prices that make a listing salable are governed by that listing's condition.[130] Therefore (pricing psychology aside),[156] there are many prices that will generate at least one reasonable offer, within reasonable time. This salable grouping of prices is the functional range of a listing's condition. As price approaches the top end of this range, buyer interest and offers decrease. As price approaches the bottom end of this range, buyer interest and offers increase.

Assuming market exposure is optimized,[236] when a listing does not generate at least one reasonable offer within reasonable time, its price is to blame—*without exception.* ♣

Buyers Are Like Moths

Attracting buyers is easy when you set your light to bright.

BY SOME DIMMER-WIT

BUYERS ARE ATTRACTED TO LISTINGS, the same way moths are attracted to light. While an average light will attract some moths, a really bright light will attract every moth in town (small ones, big ones, fat ones, skinny ones, spotted ones, smooth ones, and fuzzy ones, too), for two reasons: 1) bright light over-powers the glow of neighboring bulbs and 2) bright light can be seen from far-off distances, attracting moths from many miles around.

Light bulbs come in all shapes, sizes, and styles. Most are simple, round, and incandescent, some are fluorescent and totally tubular, and others are glowing diodes. Regardless of their design, all bulbs serve the same function: the emission of light. Likewise, real property comes in all shapes, sizes, and styles. Some are simple, petite, and adorable. Some are immense and utterly elaborate, while others smell super funky. Regardless of their condition, all residences serve the same function: shelter from the elements.

When a residence is placed on the market FOR SALE, a price is attached to its condition (whatever that condition may be),[130] and its brightness is thereby determined by this price, as a function of its condition.[152] If a listing's condition is a light bulb, then *price is its dimmer switch.*

Setting a listing's price much higher than its perceived fair market value (FMV)[128] is like setting the switch to dim. The result will be few (if any) moths coming to visit (or calling with inquiries of interest, for that matter).

Setting a listing's price at (or near) its perceived FMV is like setting the switch to average brightness. The result will be several moths touring the property, and an offer (or perhaps two) will come in average time.

Setting a listing's price lower than its perceived FMV is like setting the switch to blindingly bright. The result will be every moth in the market coming to visit and many of them making an offer, including moths from adjacent markets (those who were not previously considering property of comparable condition, but because of the blindingly-bright price, cannot pass-up an "incredible opportunity"). The sheer abundance of these offers often creates a bidding war, generating offers of higher price than would a dim or modestly-bright bulb.

Conventional, customary strategy calls for the pricing of a listing at a price higher than perceived FMV, then negotiating the eventual sales price downwardly. This strategy assumes that only one buyer will ever be interested in purchasing a given property, and it's therefore flawed in two ways: 1) buyers are attracted to price, as it relates to condition (whereby a bright price = more lookers, more lookers = more offers, more offers = more options) and 2) sellers don't have to negotiate down on price. This tactic is only necessary when dealing with a single moth. When multiple moths compete, price can be negotiated up! And when asked, most competing moths will tell you that they're more than happy to pay a bit more because now that they've toured the property and made an offer, they're hooked—they want *this one.*

For sellers, the best possible value comes from lots of lookers and several offers. This way, a seller can compare competing bids and pick the best one—the *fattest* moth. For buyers, the best possible value comes from few (if any) buyers even noticing a property is FOR SALE, and then becoming the only buyer making an offer. This way, the seller has nothing to compare, and must pick the only buyer bidding—*assuming* he's the fattest moth.

If you were a seller, would you prefer to make your decision to sell after hearing from all possible purchasers? Or would you rather be left to guess at whether or not there is someone else out there willing to pay more?

If you want to attract lots of buyers, then brighten the price of your listing, and stand back as buyers bang-down your door. 🏠

Effort Meter

You're Gonna Need:

Fair Market Value
Salability Differential
Trend Rate
Calculator

How-to
Price a Listing

The fate of a listing depends mostly on how many shoppers stop-in and smell it for themselves. Since price (as a function of condition)[152] is what lures buyers, even a hole in the ground full of toxic sludge will sell quickly—*at top price*—when marketed with *The Right Price*.

1 Calculate Pricing Factors

First, do some simple math to find the pricing factors you need:

(fig. 3.12) PRICING FACTORS

FMV	fair market value = (subject SQFT) × (AVG. SP/SQFT *of micro* CMA)
SD	salability differential = (FMV) × (1 - AVG. SP/LP *of micro* CMA)
TA	trend allowance = (subject SQFT) × (trend rate *of macro* MKT)[149]

NOTE: When AVG. SP < AVG. LP, then SD is a positive number.
              When AVG. SP > AVG. LP, then SD is a negative number.
              When AVG. SP = AVG. LP, then SD is zero.

2 Calculate Price Ranges

Next, apply the pricing factors to find high and low price ranges:

(fig. 3.13) PRICE RANGES

If SD is (+) number:	high range =	all prices higher than (FMV + TA + SD)
	low range =	all prices lower than (FMV + TA)
If SD is (-) number:	high range =	all prices higher than (FMV + TA)
	low range =	all prices lower than (FMV + TA + SD)

3 Choose *The Right Price*

The Right Price is one that generates at least one reasonable offer within the average days on market (AVG. DOM):

PRICE AND ITS EFFECT ON THE LIKELY FATE OF A LISTING

HIGH	will expire or sell at low SP/SQFT, in longer than AVG. DOM
BETWEEN	sells at average SP/SQFT, within average DOM
LOW	generates multiple offers, sells at high SP/SQFT, short DOM

Best practice is to choose a list price that falls on the cusp of a typical buyer's search criteria; *example:* $225K is a better price than $224K or $226K. *Top price* is typically achieved when more than one buyer knowingly competes to purchase the same property. A half-dozen offers will give the seller ultimate leverage, causing at least one of those offers to surpass AVG. SP/SQFT of the subject's micro market.

WARNING: Because it is unlawful for an agent to price a listing at less than he knows his seller will take, best practice is to not know the seller's bottom line price. Instead, agree on a specific list price as a tool[270] to get a *likely* sales price. This detail is important because a seller's bottom line may change once offers come, and a seller who keeps her bottom line private will not lose face by changing her mind.

tips

The salability differential (SD) measures the difference between a micro market's average list (AVG. LP) and SOLD (AVG. SP) prices, then applies that metric to the subject property's square footage. This factor is important to pricing because it takes into account the expectations and behaviors of most buyers and sellers in a micro market.

The trend allowance (TA) compensates for the moving market, and is an especially important pricing factor when FMV is rapidly decreasing.

Some sellers expect to be FOR SALE for several months before accepting an offer, but waiting is unnecessary. In fact, listings that receive the highest SP/SQFT usually go PENDING within the first two weeks.

Price it correctly now, and you won't have to reduce it later.[202]

For a pricing example, see the *Valuation Flow Chart.*[343]

Be sure to show your calculations, but if a seller-prospect asks you to leave your homework, politely refuse their request. These are the tools of your trade. Would a plumber be expected to leave behind a wrench?

Σ   The calculations of this article will be most-accurate when your opinion of FMV matches that of the average buyer.

PRICE CURES ALL DEFECTS

A Serious How-to Manual with a Sense of Humor

The Psychology of Value

*The presentation of property is part of its
condition, and therefore influences its value.*

BY SIGMUND FLOYD

A PROPERTY'S CURRENT USE OF ITS SPACE, as presented to buyers via furnishings (or the lack thereof), will be interpreted by most buyers in a similar manner. If, due to its presentation alone, the majority of buyers feel a property does not meet their needs and/or wants, then its value will be diminished. This short-sightedness of buyers is inherent in most humans and cannot be avoided.

In other words, most buyers will deem a bedroom without a bed as another type of room. When a bedroom contains only a desk, it becomes an office. When a bedroom contains only clothing, it becomes a closet, and when a bedroom contains only scissors and glue, it becomes a craft room. Likewise, a dining room containing only toys becomes a play room, a basement containing only tools becomes a workshop, and a garage containing only junk becomes a question of rodents.

On the other hand, the addition of furnishings may influence value positively. When a kitchen contains a table, it becomes an eat-in kitchen. When an entryway contains a bench and shoe rack, it becomes a mudroom, and when a patio contains a fire pit, it becomes an outdoor living room.

When rooms and spaces are congested, their apparent use is dwindled. A bedroom with a huge bed dwarfs the actual size of its space. The same interpretation befalls a dining room with an oversized table, and closets stuffed with stuff. The color of walls, floors, and ceilings may have a similar effect on the appearance of size (as may lighting).

None of these situations suggest to buyers that the current furnishings will stay after closing, or that walls cannot be painted, rather these features help buyers to visualize possibilities—or take them away, altogether.

Due to these conditional effects on buyer psychology, at times, vacant property will be presented more favorably than would a seller's chosen motif.

For these reasons, a property that displays its use of space prudently increases its own value—perhaps by virtue of increased competition from buyers (if nothing else).

Elusive Value

When facing a valuation dilemma, consider a crafty strategy.

BY CLEVER TREVOR

SOME PROPERTIES ARE EXTREMELY unique, which creates a valuation challenge, due to few, if any, comparable sales. Other times, prospective sellers will take extraordinary exception to your opinion of FMV. Either way, you're likely to lose your listing opportunity over valuation, unless you do one of the following: 1) pick a price and see what happens, or 2) get an appraisal. The pick-a-price strategy will probably lead to frustration and lost opportunity, but a pre-listing appraisal rarely disappoints.

Whether or not its coupled with a home inspection (and subsequent repair of the discovered, dysfunctional conditions), an already-completed appraisal becomes an effective tool when presented to shoppers; buyers will become encouraged to make offers at (or near) the appraised value (with few contingencies, to-boot).

The brilliance of this strategy comes by removing any questions of doubt regarding condition and its accompanied value, thereby giving buyers offer confidence.

1 Practice

The best way to get better at valuation is to perform valuation on lots and lots of properties. Test your skills by doing CMA on properties listed by other agents. Then, based on the list price, condition, pictures, and marketing efforts, hypothesize the sales price and under-contract date. Chart your results by days on market (DOM) and sales price to listed price ratio (SP/LP). Soon you will begin to notice your skills improve.

2 Systematize

Formally study market forces (sales activity, absorption rates, and market trends) at the end of each month. Create forms to quickly generate CMA and checklists, ensuring you collect and consider all available data.

3 Enterprise

Sell your FMV homework to other agents. When your work is good, some will gladly pay for the service. If your work is bad, then you need more practice.

Ways to Sharpen Your Skills 3

A Serious How-to Manual with a Sense of Humor

THE ACCOUNTANT

Slinging knowledge of numbers impresses people.

"**P**INT OF PALE ALE, PLEASE," I belted out, with my belly to the bar. Happy hour on a random Tuesday always brings me a smile; the discounted booze seems to taste better, and people seem even more chatty in response. My favorite part of this twilight tradition is the chance at killing an entire flock of birds with one stone. At the same time, I can drink beer, prospect for clients, drink some more beer, prospect for a date, and drink beer.

"Happy to be off-duty?" I asked the well-dressed fella to my left. He smirked and raised an eyebrow, giving a half-glance in my direction while suckling the ice from an empty gin and tonic. "What's your profession?" I tried again, with the determination to not be ignored.

"I'm an accountant."

"Yeah? I heard you put those debits on the left like a champ!"

As he turned to face me, his smirk morphed into a full-on grin, and he gave a look like I may just understand his plight. Then, he surprised me with a tone of provocation when he asked, "What do you know of it?"

"I once had a steady job, counting items for the mob," I said, looking down, clenching my beer with both hands. After a dramatic pause, and with the slightest shake of head to sell my case, I added, "It's a shame those boys couldn't be more copacetic."

He laughed, knowing I was full of malarkey. "I'm Tom," the accountant volunteered, extending his hand. "What's your profession?"

"I'm a real estate agent."

"Oh, yeah? How's the market?"

"Why do you ask?" I questioned his question with a question.

"Just curious," Tom replied. "I'm always interested in how things work."

"You want the numbers?" I teased, raising an eyebrow of my own. His face told me that he did. "There were three-thousand five-hundred twenty-five detached residential sales in the metro market last month, which is a three percent gain over the month previous. Those properties sold in an average of seventy-five days and received ninety-five percent of their listed price, with the average sale being about one-hundred seventy-eight thousand dollars. The county numbers were similar, with eight-hundred twenty-five detached residential sales, which was a five percent bump, with the average sales price being one-hundred ninety-six thousand dollars."

Tom's eyes were wide. "Interesting," was the only word he said, sitting, thinking, then, "How many houses are currently for sale?"

That question sparked an hour-long conversation about real estate statistics, the definition of value, and the psychology of markets. When our chat was finished, Tom paid our tab, and we walked to the parking lot together, stopping at the curb's edge to shake hands, exchange farewells, and other cordial niceties.

"So, which car is yours?" Tom asked. "Do you drive this luxury car or the silver sporty one over there?"

"Neither one," I said. "I drive this here compact car."   (continued)→

A Tale of Two Listings

A pricing strategy classic, comes to the small page.

BY RHYMING RALPH

*I*T WAS THE BEST OF LISTINGS, it was the worst of listings. Twin homes, standing side-by-side for ten years, were occupied by twin brothers and their twin wives. Their furnishings were perfectly alike: each had the same wallpaper and mounted, walleyed pike. Even their fittings were akin, as each owned the exact same mahogany, rolling pin.

The brothers met weekly, on Wednesdays, to buffet at the Cabaret Risqué, following an arousing match of croquet, with the café's carefree valet. And everything was groovy until one day, whilst preparing for their usual bout of lawn ballet, the one called Ray declared a new place to stay. "Hey," said Ray, "Let's pack our stuff, and move today!"

Since the twin owners of the twin abodes conducted their lives in total twin harmony, the brother named Jay piped-in to say, "But if you go away, I'll miss you like the dickens. My hair will surely grow gray, as I sit solemnly and slowly go cra-zay. Dear brother Ray, be that as it may, we must follow your play." So, the very next day, Chez Ray and Chez Jay were FOR SALE and on display, in the cul-de-sac of Ray Jay Way.

Then a very strange thing occurred: the twin brothers listed their twin homes at differing prices, to their much-befuddled agent's bewildered dismay. Because Brother Ray intended to convey without delay, his desire was reflected by the market prices he chose to obey, and his house sold at record price, the very next day.[154]

In stark contrast, and led astray by his own, silly survey, Brother Jay picked a price certain to keep all lookers at bay. Often he was overheard to purvey the obscured, old cliché, "I'm not about to just give it away!" And so his listing grew stale, like a sappy sideman's sad toupee. Due to Jay's preposterous price alone, his property was properly passed-over, like a perniciously-pureed, pork parfait, served within the remains and decay of a pre-owned, homemade ashtray.

Soon Jay questioned his agent's very forte, when even an open house soiree,[240] replete with apple pie bouquet and wooden floors of parquet, failed to sway an offer, per se. And so it went that Jay's house never sold because despite his sassy sashay, Jay's house was priced right out of this Milky Way. Before long, slayed-Jay resented Ray for selling and moving away, and their relationship frayed, like a sink basin built of papier-mâché.

The moral of the story is that remembering this cheesy prose about the pricing woes of identical bros should keep you on your toes. To put it another way: realistic pricing saves the day. Just ask Brother Ray. Hey! Hey! 🌳

"There's no way a guy like you,.. a guy who speaks real estate statistics like you,.. There's no way you drive a compact," Tom insisted. "C'mon, now. Where's your car?"

My insistence of ownership fell on deaf ears. Even as I started the motor and drove away, Tom stood in disbelief.

This barroom encounter taught me two extremely-valuable lessons: 1) drunken accountants are boisterous people, willing to trade drinks for conversation about numbers, and 2) knowledge and articulation of the numbers surrounding my business made me seem super smart and successful.

 TRUE STORY

None Such Thing as Hard-to-Sell Property

Dear Andy,
I'm a buyer, and my agent keeps telling me to avoid certain listings because they will be difficult for me to resell. Sometimes he says, "No-one will ever want to buy this place." What do you think of his assertion?
—*Betty the Buyer*

Dear Betty,
    You are not alone. Your agent (like many others) touts this line because he has (previously) listed similar properties, and he (presuming you'll hire him when it comes time to resell) doesn't wanna list "hard-to-sell" properties. Your agent's misgiving is glaring him in the face (and is the basis of his reasoning), but he just doesn't see it.
    First off, your agent should not dissuade you from pursuing a property that's caught your eye. However, your agent should suggest an offer price based upon: 1) the condition of the property you desire,[132] and 2) your needs and wants.[174] At times, a buyer may wish to make offer on property that does not meet their declared needs/wants. When this happens, their agent should (and rightly so), highlight the discrepancies between the buyer's plans and the buyer's actions—but, I don't think that's what's happening here.
    What your agent is really telling you is that, based upon his experience, the subject property has an unchangeable feature of its condition (or a changeable feature that is so expensive to repair, it has been rendered practically-unchangeable), that is unappealing to most buyers. This feature may be extreme lack of privacy, constantly-loud road noise, uninviting views, chaotic floor plan, ugly exterior, or difficult topography. This unappealing feature, whatever it may be, has rendered its property less valuable than its otherwise perfectly-comparable comparables.[136] No big deal: runt properties trade at a discount to their well-developed siblings and cousins; it's the size of that discount that worries most agents.

    I'm willing to bet that these so-called "hard-to-sell properties" are actually just over-priced. You (and plenty of other buyers) have been lured to view these properties because their runt features are not obvious from their advertised photographs. Once viewed with live eyeballs, the runt feature becomes pronounced to some, but others will not take as much notice. This is where your agent comes in—he doesn't want you to over-pay.
    It's also likely that your agent has been conditioned to avoid making "low-ball" offers. Low-ball is written here in quotes because a near-FMV offer on an over-priced listing is not really a "low-ball" offer. But, to over-priced sellers (and often times, their agents), a near-FMV offer will always appear to be insultingly-low when it is compared to their grossly-inflated asking price, causing a reasonable offer to become mislabeled as a "low-ball" offer.[257]
    As a result, agents receiving "low-ball" offers will typically heap a shovel-full of grief upon anyone who dares to submit one. This listing agent-guilt trip is typically spawned from either one or both: an unwillingness to seriously discuss listed price with their seller,[215] or their complete ignorance of FMV to begin with.[150] Your agent's reluctance to engage is a shame, because making FMV offers on over-priced listings is actually a kind service to over-priced sellers. Whether or not a seller sells is due to their response of market forces. Your FMV offer may be the third such "low-ball" offer they've received, and you might be the one who finally convinces them to sell at a reasonable price.
    Therefore, if you don't mind the runt feature of a property, then by all means, pursue its purchase. Just make sure you pay a fair price, because that runt feature is likely to still be there when you resell. This means that a runt property will always trade for a discount, compared to otherwise-comparable properties that don't have a runt feature. Remember, runt features do not make property hard-to-sell, but being over-priced always will.[152]

Dear Andy,
I convinced my seller to reduce his listed price, but buyer activity has not changed. On the rare occasion of a showing, I call the buyer's agent for feedback. They always say it's a beautiful property, but their buyers don't make offers. How do I get this place sold?
—Flummoxed by Forecast

Dear Flummoxed,
Your challenge is one that many agents face. You and your seller each acknowledge the fact that your previous price was too high for the market, and have made an adjustment. That's the good news, because some agents and their sellers refuse to acknowledge market forces altogether. Instead, many dig-in their heels, and blame "stupid buyers" for being unable to see the true value of their property.

When showing-agents tell you the property is beautiful, then you should believe them, as they're undoubtedly telling the truth. Due to their politeness, however, they're not telling you the entire truth (not with their words, at least). While everyone can see the inherent, unique beauty of your listing, what they cannot see is paying a price that is higher than their perception of that beauty's value. Your listed price is either beyond their feather-ruffling comfort-zone,[257] or they perceive your price to signify an unreasonable seller (one who is unlikely to ever negotiate a FMV price). In other words, your price isn't worth their time.

There are a range of prices that surround the FMV of a listing, each of which encourage buyers to make fair offers.[152] The prices at the extreme edges of this range are usually five percent or greater than FMV (typically whatever the difference in the average listed price versus the average sales price, of properties that have recently SOLD). This force of the market leads to the fact that a small change in price (one percent or less) will not change buyer behavior.

For example, when a list price of $250,000 does not inspire lookers, a reduction of $5000 is unlikely to change things, and a $1000 reduction is laughable. Therefore, depending upon how over-priced a listing is to begin with, a reduction of several thousand dollars (while being a big chunk of money) may not be a large enough percentage of change to place its price within the FMV window.[144]

Typically speaking, when a listing gets zero to few showings, it means you're grossly over-priced. When a listing gets showings, but no offers, it means your price is close, but remains too high for most buyers to bother with.

The lesson to be learned here is, assuming you've optimized a listing's exposure to the market,[236] a price reduction that doesn't affect buyer response is too small of a reduction. The market is telling you (with its deafening silence) to get real and try again.[154]

✳✳✳

Dear Andy,
The appraisal for my listing is lower than the sales price of our contract. I feel like the sales price is in-line with FMV. How do I fix this blunder?
—Agitated by Appraisals

Dear Agitated,
An appraiser's interpretation of FMV is an unbiased, emotion-free opinion—meaning, his opinion may be swayed by the presentation of previously-unseen market factors. For this reason, you should bundle your homework,[150] and send it to the appraiser, with an invitation to consider the opinion of value held by the buyer and seller. If your opinion is well-established, and free of confirmation bias, the appraisal value should change. If the appraiser's opinion remains unchanged, the buyer and seller may re-negotiate their price, or the buyer may pay the difference in cash, or both.

Because the opinions of appraisers are tied to loans, when a buyer requires a loan, it is not just the buyer and seller who establish value of a specific property, at that moment in time.[129] Rather, the seller, the buyer, and the buyer's lender establish value.   -AA

Whand interpreting the value of real property, few will hit the nail square-on-the-head every time. That's because every transaction is a unique combination of price and terms, mixing together, creating the *actual value* to its buyer and seller.[126] However, when the price of listed property is within the window of its perceived value,[152] buyers will make reasonable offers—guaranteed! For this reason, it is necessary to spend adequate time contemplating value, but not to obsess over its perfection. In this way, pricing a listing is like horseshoes, hand grenades, and curling stones—close is close enough. Close doesn't mean you should just toss-out any number and see what happens. To earn the listings of serious sellers, you must show your homework and explain the facts of the matter.[150]

The research is not complicated. All you have to do is:

1) Accurately assess the subject property's condition.[130]
2) Find recently-SOLD properties of similar condition.[140] Then,
3) do some math.[154]

Stand confidently with your number, and hold firm to any challenge (unless presented with over-riding information). So long as you're a good estimator, sellers who go-fer your spiel are likely to actually sell. If instead, you're far too often far-off from value, then you're a bad apple-picker.[138] Develop a discerning eye and rest assured: when it comes to value, the market will tell you when you're close enough.[161]

Close is Close Enough!

A Serious How-to Manual with a Sense of Humor

Chapter 3 Quiz

Who *determines* the value of real property?

1
   a) buyers
   b) sellers
   c) appraisers/agents
   d) a unique buyer and seller combo

Who *interprets* the value of real property?

2
   a) buyers
   b) sellers
   c) appraisers/agents
   d) all of the above

How does the calculation of net present value benefit investors?

3
   a) it allows for comparison of properties
   b) it determines value
   c) it estimates the number of sales
   d) it estimates the value of rent

What makes a listing hard to sell?

4
   a) its price
   b) its condition
   c) its smells
   d) its location

What does absorption rate measure?

5
   a) percentage of listings that sell per month
   b) number of shoppers per month
   c) months of inventory
   d) all of the above

Which conditional features should you compare with a macro CMA?

6
   a) hard condition
   b) soft condition
   c) front elevation
   d) all of the above

Which conditional features should you compare with a micro CMA?

7
   a) hard condition
   b) soft condition
   c) front elevation
   d) all of the above

When choosing comparables, which of the following should be ignored?

8
   a) size
   b) style
   c) price
   d) none of the above

Which pricing factor accounts for the expectations of current buyers/sellers?

9
   a) salability differential
   b) front-end differential
   c) net present value
   d) fair market value

Are the batteries in a garage door opener fixtures?

10
   a) hell no, they pop right out
   b) yes, by adaptation
   c) sometimes, but not always
   d) what's a fixture?

Find the best answers throughout this chapter and on page 323.

Logic Puzzle
The Right Agent for the Job

So that she may play Canasta whenever she likes, Ms. Loutfire has decided to sell her house and move to an old-fogies home. After interviewing five real estate agents for the job of listing her home FOR SALE, *Ms. Loutfire has decided to hire the agent who agreed to advertise in the newspaper.* However, she cannot remember which agent that was. Now she ironically calls upon you, her real estate agent/neighbor of ten years, to help solve the problem.

Oddly, Ms. Loutfire remembers the names of all the agents and the various times of day when their visits occurred. She also recalls each agent's wardrobe and their preferred marketing methods, but for some reason, she cannot remember how all these assorted bits match-up.

Ms. Loutfire says to you:
1. The agent wearing the pant suit kept talking about how she would book my house on her face, and said it was called social media.
2. Harper was not wearing a plaid jacket nor a golf shirt, and does not participate in social media.
3. Jaime didn't come by in the morning and wasn't wearing a plaid jacket either, but did promise to host an open house every weekend until the house sells.
4. Ducky wasn't wearing a name badge, and did not come in the morning nor while I was eating dinner.
5. The agent who came in the morning wasn't wearing a name badge either, and refused my newspaper advertisement request.
6. Cookie rang the bell while I was watching Judge Moody, and then also refused my newspaper ad request.
7. The agent with the billboard ads stopped by after lunch.
8. I remember now, the agent who was wearing the plaid jacket interrupted my dinner.

		Morning	After Lunch	Noon	During Judge Moody	During Dinner	Plaid Jacket	Pant Suit	Name Badge	Golf Shirt	Flip Flops	Open House	Billboard Ad	Social Media	Yard Sign	Newspaper Ad
Agent	Ducky															
	Pat															
	Harper															
	Cookie															
	Jaime															
Strategy	Open House															
	Billboard Ad															
	Social Media															
	Yard Sign															
	Newspaper Ad															
Attire	Plaid Jacket															
	Pant Suit															
	Name Badge															
	Golf Shirt															
	Flip Flops															

Knowing *all the details*, which agent should Ms. Loutfire hire?

Answer on page 322.

For all the hard work that goes into prospecting, the result is merely an opportunity to deliver a presentation that further demonstrates your value. A half-assed display of "I'm great, now sign here," squanders your ability to separate earnest clients from the scores of tire-kickers who are a guaranteed waste of time; it's also likely to scare-off the ones who carefully consider more than one agent for the job.

This chapter is meant to show the reader how to treat presentations as a way to mutually discover whether or not each potential agent/client combo has a chance of success. Because, while you may not politely pick your nose in public, you may certainly pick your clients.

CHAPTER FOUR
PRESENTATIONS

Your Presentations Set Future Expectations

Look into my eyes: your time is wasted on those with erroneous presumptions; charm them with the truth, or doom may follow.

BY FANNY THE FORTUNE TELLER

IT DOESN'T TAKE A PROPHECY to foresee that you and your client will together set-out on adventure.[344] While you may be a well-worn traveller, your client is likely a tenderfoot, equipped with a layman's notion of the path ahead. When their expectations are matched to your own—*and to reality*—the outlook is good. So, before becoming bound by agency, whereby you undertake the role of shaman on their excursion, insist upon a formal gathering.

Getting a prospect to sit for a reading is certainly an accomplishment,[186] but by no means does it guarantee they'll become a client. Your presentation will be their deciding factor, and it should be yours, also. For this reason, your pre-agency conversation is as much an interview of them as it is of you.

Don't become their agent just because they're willing to sign their name. Only do so once a unified front is established, complete with a chartered list of each party's duties, a developed strategy with coherent, defined goals, and mutual expectation of events to occur. An agent-client relationship works best as an alliance, so cast your spell for harmony before any field work begins.

An effective presentation is like a magic wand. At once, it will project pure professionalism and competence,[214] while simultaneously preparing them for the journey ahead. To wave your wand with efficiency, *focus on learning about them.* Your value will become apparent through well-placed questions and comments.

Begin by preparing yourself for the meeting, well ahead of its scheduled time. Collect needed tools, and practice your scripts.[050] Convene at a quiet place of comfort, whereby you may control the environment,[171] at a time when all parties are fully engaged. When distractions flourish, focus will be lost and the overall effectiveness of your meeting will be diminished. You've brought them this far, so don't lose them by being boring.[195]

Channel their needs and wants,[174] and fully explore the hidden meanings behind their words. Conjure their desires and abate their fears. Outline the process of buying/selling real property,[176] and resolve any concerns. Discuss your fee and justify its rate.[181] And above all else, *tell the truth* of every matter, regardless of what they want to hear.[006]

It does no one good to go into the field with mere assumptions of success, so when you discover a prospect is harboring expectations that don't match the realm of possibilities, show them the tea leaves and get their consensus. Turn away those with hazy qualifications.[169] You may think they'll become redeemed in the field, but my sources say NO.

Just like you cannot cast a spell without an eye of newt, you and clients cannot become a coalition without full discussion of where they are, where they're going, and how they'll get there. As a requirement of agency, you should sign only well-tuned prospects who want to travel by your side; when your presentations are properly performed, prospects will jump at that chance.[204]

When I look into my crystal ball, I see two agents: one delivers thorough presentations, and the other goes at it half-assed. The first agent finds fortune for his clients, while the second wanders like a gypsy in the dark.

The greatest danger a client may face is being unprepared, so don't be their blind companion. Before doing that real estate voodoo that you do so well, sit with them for an hour. Reading their present will surely shed light on their future. After all, you're a real estate agent, not a clairvoyant. ♣

A BUYER'S FORTUNE

Saturn is in the house of pre-qualification.

You are extremely persuasive when you want to be. Your words can be commanding without being combative. Don't write people off without giving them a fair chance, but do walk away from those who don't share your sense of earnestness. You tend to attract people who test your mettle, but this is not a day to give-in to their refusals. You will see buyers everywhere you look. Be receptive to their hesitations. Then, focus on what is best for them: your system. Steady your resolve, or you may find the tides mounting against your effort. Slow before you show. First, insist they flash their bankroll. Be true to this and your star will be on the rise.

A Serious How-to Manual with a Sense of Humor

Effort Meter

You're Gonna Need:

Buyer Prospect
Script
Telephone
Loan Officer

tips

In the lending world, pre-qualification means Buyer is assumed to possess the ability to borrow, based upon cursory inquiry into the facts, and pre-approval means that Buyer has proven his case and is cleared to close the transaction.

Working with people you already know and trust will usually make transactions less troublesome for you and clients alike. So, whenever a prospect is already pre-qualified at the time you meet, urge him to pre-qualify with your posse, too.[79] Who knows?—your mortgage gal may just find a better-fitting loan product.

If your buyer prospect does not financially pre-qualify at this time, introduce him to a posse member who can coach him through credit rehabilitation.

caveat

Giving buyers a choice of multiple mortgage officers may cause them to become overwhelmed, resulting in buyer inaction. As a consultant to the buyer, recommend *one* mortgage officer, but stress the fact that Buyer may choose to borrow from anyone.

Σ   A buyer willing to show you proof of pre-qualification is demonstrating an ability *and an earnest intent* to purchase.

How-to
Pre-Qualify a Buyer

"Buyers" lacking an ability to pony-up cash aren't buyers at all. Therefore the sake of logic and reason, insist upon finding-out for yourself. Because when you take them at their word—that they're good for it—more than just valuable time may be wasted.

1 Ask About Other Agents

Always begin with: *Are you already working with an agent?*
- If NO, go to STEP 2.
- If YES, ask: *Have you **signed exclusive-agency** with that agent?*
- If NO, go to STEP 2.
- If YES, abort. You may not lawfully (nor in good conscience) interfere with existing agreements of any kind, so proceeding further with intent of pre-qualification is unnecessary. However, Buyer may have real property to *sell*, but has yet to decide upon a listing agent. Therefore, be sure to ask: *Do you have real property that needs a-selling?*
  - If YES, pre-qualify this prospect as a seller.[189]
  - If NO, bid farewell to Buyer with a graceful high-five.

2 Ask About the Money

Typically, a buyer will either pay with all cash or borrow money. Ask: *Do you plan to borrow money from a bank, or will you be writing a check for the purchase?*
- If Buyer is paying cash, go to STEP 3.
- If Buyer plans to borrow money,
  - and claims to be already pre-qualified, go to STEP 3.
  - but is not pre-qualified, ask: *Would you be offended if I shared your phone number with my favorite mortgage gal, and then she called you?*
    - If NO, call your mortgage gal and make an introduction.
    - If YES, ask: *Why do you take offensive to that?*

3 Get Proof

For cash-paying buyers, get written proof by means of either an official letter from their bank's manager or an account statement with their security data redacted. For borrowers, get written proof from their mortgage officer in the form of a letter on official letterhead; be sure it includes the date, buyer's name, pre-qualified dollar amount, interest rate Buyer is expected to pay, and the loan type.

Then, speak directly with the lender and ask the following questions:
1. Does this loan have any restrictions to the types of properties Buyer may purchase? Is there a limit on seller-paid concessions?
2. Once Buyer signs a P&S contract, how long will the mortgage process take to close?
3. What is the minimum down payment required (percentage-wise)?
4. As Buyer's agent, what else should I know about this loan?

How-to
Lure a Buyer to Your Lair

Effort Meter

Before you spend time showing properties to Buyer, you should first spend some time getting to know each other.[174] You want to know: *Does Buyer's budget match his expectation? Is he aware of how current market forces will influence his purchase? Is he sure he knows what he's really looking for? Does he plan to buy something, or is he just kicking tires? Do you provide the service he requires? Will you get along together? Are you worth each other's time? Is he willing to pay your fee?*

A face-to-face discussion in a controlled environment is recommended for your inquiry, and the only way to get them there is for you to ask:

1 Ask Buyer to Meet

Say something like: *In my experience, it's best when we meet before looking at any properties. During our meeting, we'll discuss your needs and wants,[174] specific strategies to acquire property,[219] finance options, and other details that are related to your success. This discussion will leave you informed of the current market, and of options available to you—some of which you may not yet be aware. When our chat is done, we will mutually decide whether or not to work together. At the very least, you'll leave our meeting feeling confident about the purchase process. So, whatdaya say?*

- If YES, go to STEP 2.
- If NO, confront the buyer's intent: *No offense taken, and none implied when saying that I only work with informed, serious buyers. That's because informed, serious buyers move with intent, and are not just "kicking tires." They're choosy with their time, and are particular about the property they purchase. Informed, serious buyers select a single, competent agent, giving them an edge over their competition. I provide a premium service, with a system that helps buyers acquire property smoothly—without hassle. Meeting at my location, to discuss your goals and obstacles, is the first step in this system. Remember this: any monkey with a lock box key can be a cab driver, but only a skilled agent can guide you through the jungle of a transaction. Meeting first is good for you, and it's good for me. So, tell me: are you an informed, serious buyer?*
- If YES, go to STEP 2.
- If NO, try another script, or let them go.[119] You'll never be able to convert every buyer to your system, so don't lose sleep over it—and don't pander to those who refuse your good intentions.

2 Make Appointment

Suggest the first two meeting times that best-fit your schedule.[064] Make your request in a leading manner: *Would you like to meet today at (insert time) or would you prefer tomorrow at (insert another time)?*

If the prospect rejects your suggested meeting times, or acts reluctantly, ask them to pick a time. Those who continue to rebuff your advances are not yet convinced of their need to meet with you. Go back to STEP 1.

You're Gonna Need:

Buyer Prospect
Lair
Script
Conviction

---

tips

Your lair is any distraction-free location, with a cleared-off tabletop and chairs—where you can control the environment.

Prepare your lair. Get there at least fifteen minutes early. Arrange your presentation materials, entertainment for children, and refreshments for all.

Before luring a buyer to your lair, make sure they're not already contractually engaged in agency with another agent.[170]

Some buyers will flake-out, and leave you stood-up.[096] If they dodge your call to ask *Why?* then, try calling upon them again every few days or weeks. Sometimes a little time away from you and your wacky conventions are just what a prospect needs to be convinced of working with an agent who utilizes a robust system.

You get to decide whether or not your systems are created and followed.

Your suggestion of meeting, and your logical reasoning to do so, is all it takes for most prospects to comply.

Σ Meeting buyers in a controlled environment sets a tone of professionalism, competence, and efficiency.

Effort Meter

You're Gonna Need:

Self-Regard
Brochure
Script
Two Minutes

tips

When you're new to real estate sales, focus upon the skills you've gleaned from life and from past careers.

When you explain exactly what you do, potential clients are better able to decide if you're right for them.

Think of selling your services as an elevator pitch. It shouldn't take any longer to describe your usefulness than it takes to ride an elevator from the penthouse to the lobby. If you cannot convey your value concisely, then you cannot expect them to indulge your inclinations.

Instead of the usual jibber-jabber, consider placing your service brochure on the *About Me* page of your website.

Once you are able to effectively and efficiently sell your services, fewer prospects will object to (or challenge) your fee.[181]

Your agent statistics are a measurable aspect of the service you provide. Tell prospects about your stats: AVG. DOM, AVG. SP/LP, CTR.

Σ The purpose of selling your services during presentations is to put prospects at ease about you; it also helps them to understand your role in their goal.

How-to
Sell Your Services

Real estate agents are not created equal.[035] There exist vast differences between agents based upon niche (or lack thereof), experience, and wherewithal (the ability to diagnose and solve problems). So that potential clients may more easily differentiate between you and all others, properly define how you (and your unique set of skills) will benefit them and their goals. Define your promised service, then present it in a way they can easily digest.

1 Niche[042]
In one or two sentences, explain the exact concentrations and limitations of your real estate services.

2 References and Testimonials[314]
Always have the good words of others handy to do some bragging for you; otherwise, you may say: *My clients love me because...* Declaratory statements like these will serve to illustrate your value by specific examples. Don't shy away from presenting your expertise in a way that highlights the benefits of being represented by you.

3 Posse[179]
Show them your team. Hand-over a list of all vendors and/ or support personnel whom you rely upon to amplify your excellent services. Recommending only one vendor (instead of three) is okay, so long as you formally disclose the reasoning and (possible) remuneration behind your endorsements. The single vendor you propose is the same person you would hire, if in the same situation as your prospect/client/customer.

4 Expectations
Tell them exactly what to expect from you and what you expect from them. Include time lines and plans of action. Agree upon the means of communication and how often you will communicate.

5 Put It in Writing
When you formally commit to a level of service, prospective clients will feel confident in their choice to hire you, rather than any one of the hundreds (or thousands) of other real estate agents in the marketplace. Present your written commitment in the form of a brochure at the time of initial presentation.[186]

6 Say It in Two Minutes
Create a script that is focused upon exactly what you do, for whom you do it, and why it benefits those people. Pick-out specific features of your service that benefit clients, then explain why. Put your brochure into words and they'll listen-up.

Don't turn your soliloquy into a brag-fest. Instead, focus on the client, their needs, their goals, and their comfort.

How-to
Create an Agency Checklist

Effort Meter

Some buyers will outright object to signing an exclusive agency agreement.[184] Their reasons are numerous, but mostly stem from their ignorance of the fiduciary relationship that accompanies exclusive agency.[212] A well-crafted checklist will highlight these benefits and force buyers to formally decide upon the type of relationship they want with an agent.

You're Gonna Need:
Fiduciary Contemplation
Earnestness
Compelling Questions
a Line in the Sand

1 Think of Your Services

To begin, consider the answers to these questions:
• What are the basic services you provide to all buyers?
• What services do you provide to buyers who sign exclusive agency agreements (clients)?
• What services do you provide to buyers who do not sign exclusive agency agreements (customers)?

2 Concoct Questions

Compose questions about your services in a brief manner, with somewhat-sensational overtones. Highlight your most-compelling, fiduciary services that will invoke strong YES/NO responses. Craft your questions so that YES answers correspond to affirmation of exclusive agency.

3 Create the Document

Fit your entire checklist onto one side of a printed page; approximately ten to twenty questions will suffice. Lead-in with some simple direction at the top of the document, and make a place for Buyer to add their name and the date.

Whether or not they realize it, buyers who answer YES to *all* questions are requesting an exclusive agency relationship with you. Buyers who answer NO to *any* questions are requesting a non-exclusive agency or a customer relationship with you.

tips

Some states require all agency and/or customer relationships to be in writing. This means that agents who provide agency services without a written agreement to do so may be breaking the law.[184]

Consider making an agency checklist for sellers too, added to your pre-listing package.[193] A seller agency checklist may be used to showcase the sheer volume of services you provide.

Σ   Clearly defining exactly what exclusive agency is (and what it is not) will allow you to easily overcome the most-common objections that buyers have to signing agency agreements.

(fig. 4.1) Buyer Agency Checklist

YES	NO	Please answer each question: *Would you like for me to...*
		...help you develop a negotiation strategy based upon market conditions and your needs?
		...tell you if I think a particular property is over-priced?
		...give advice on which clauses and contingencies to add to your purchase agreement?
		...suggest financing alternatives that might be in your best interest?
		...provide my opinion of fair market value (FMV)?
		...represent *only you* in your transaction?
		...keep your needs and wants confidential?
		...investigate and report all information about sellers to you?
		...give my opinions and insights regarding real estate customs as they affect you?
		...notify you first, before all others, when new properties of interest come onto the market?
		...search-out any and all non-listed and FSBO properties that match your desires?

Effort Meter

You're Gonna Need:

Buyer
Curiosity
Pen & Paper
Onion Peeler

tips

Often times, buyers are not fully-informed of all the conditional options that properties in the current market offer. Help them to discover what they need to know before picking a property to purchase.

Always fully discuss and examine budget, location, size, style, age, and condition.

If Buyer desires property in multiple locations (*i.e.* three sections of town that are separated by many miles), ask Buyer to rank the locations. Discuss the virtues of one location over another, and attempt to limit the search to one at a time.

If Buyer has few needs and/or zero wants, probe with an exercise. Say something like: *Close your eyes. Imagine you are walking up to and throughout the property you're gonna purchase. Describe what you see and include all the details.*

Buyers feel much more confident and ready-to-purchase after completing a proper needs analysis.

Do your part to keep buyers outta the weeds and in the tall heather: conduct a needs analysis today.

Spotlight your onion-peeling ability when prospecting.

STEP 3 ain't over until every onion is peeled.

How-to Conduct a Needs Analysis

A willy-nilly approach to property search leaves some buyers feeling uncertain and prone to impulsive decisions, while a logical, disciplined approach always uncovers the *best-fitting* property. Therefore, looking for property before clearly distinguishing between what he actually needs and what he merely wants may leave a buyer bathed in disgruntlement, set adrift an endless sea of "possible" properties to purchase. Rigorously prioritizing his needs/wants (and comparing them to reality) narrows this sea of possibilities, and also serves to fizzle any future feelings of frustration.

Therefore, it is your job to sort through the buyer's list and systematically identify each bit of criteria. You must then label it, analyze it, rank it, and record it for future use in the field and in discussions. Sit with your buyer, face-to-face, with pen in-hand, to get what *he needs* to avoid selection paralysis and/or buyer's remorse.[188]

1 Prepare the Page

Select a single sheet of paper. Draw a line down the middle of the page, creating two columns. Label one column NEEDS and the other WANTS. Additional pages will be needed for list revision.

2 Fill the Page

Needs are defined as *absolute-must-haves*. These are the things a buyer cannot live without, which often include budget, size, and location. Wants are defined as *would-be-really-niceta-haves*. These are the things that may be compromised (depending upon each specific property), which often include soft and peripheral conditions, as related to each buyer's lifestyle and aesthetic proclivities.[132]

Ask Buyer to list his every need and want, as he dreams them to be. Record each bit in its respective column. Be comprehensive and don't judge; just dig until you up-turn all his desires.

3 Probe the Page

Probing questions about list items may uncover hidden needs/wants. This occurs because sometimes buyers and agents use different words to describe the same thing, and sometimes buyers speak in generalized terms. To best understand what a buyer really needs and wants, ask question after question, peeling layer after layer from the onion that is each need/want—exposing the true, stripped-down essence of that particular need/want.

At times, these questions may seem silly, because you'll assume the answer to be glaringly obvious; however, your assumptions will sometimes be supplanted. Besides, your goal is to prevent future frustrations, so keep making progressively-pervasive probes into each need/want until all pertinent details are pinpointed. As Buyer supplies answers, take notes, add newfound needs/wants, and strike now-defunct needs/wants from the list.

To peel an onion, begin by selecting a single need/want:
1. Ask the buyer why this item is so important.
2. Ask a follow-up question, composed to expose the significance of the previous answer.
3. Keep asking questions until the need/want is fully-explored.
4. Along the way, suggest alternative (or re-defined) needs/wants and ask questions that pit the importance of potentially-conflicting needs/wants.

Onion Peeling Excerpt

« Why is a five-bedroom house a *need* for you? »

« Our current home has four bedrooms: three bedrooms for people to sleep, and one for me to do my hobby crafts. I want our new house to have a proper guest room. »

« So what you are really looking for is a four bedroom house and an area to do your hobby crafts. Is that correct? »

« Yes, I suppose so. »

« What if your new house has four bedrooms, but also has a designated place for you to get crafty? Suppose a basement, or a bonus room, or a loft area, or an out-building with heat and air conditioning? »

« That would work for me! »

« How big is the ideal craft room? Does a guest room include an on-suite bathroom? If budget becomes a limiting constraint, precluding one space or the other, which would you rather live without? »

4 Refine the Page

Due to the invasive nature of the proceeding conversation, most buyers will be inspired to shuffle their list. To assist in refinement, ask Buyer to rank each item in order of importance. Place the top three, four, or five ranked items in the NEEDS column, and encourage Buyer to move all other list items to the WANTS column. Based upon your understanding of the marketplace (as defined by Buyer's needs/wants), discuss the possibility of list items clashing with each other, and contingency plans for such occurrences. Once the buyer's bona fide needs/wants are established, make a new page, with list items clearly labeled, defined, categorized, and ranked.

5 Initial the Page

With final draft in-hand, ask: *If we find a property that matches all your needs and your top (five) wants, will you purchase that property?*
- If YES, say: *That's wonderful! Please show your commitment by initialing the page. Your initial does not obligate you to purchase the property described, but rather is an expression of our mutual understanding. We will use this page as a guide to select properties that meet your specific needs and wants, and we will revisit this list in the field. Based upon our field experience, we may again edit this page, until we zero-in on the best-fitting property for you.*
- If NO, say: *Do you believe this needs/wants list accurately describes and prioritizes the property features you desire?*
  - If NO: Go to STEP 1.
  - If YES: Ask why, and then have a frank discussion about it.

Once Buyer initials the page, add your initials, the date, and time.

tips

All buyers come equipped with a list of needs and wants. For many buyers, this list is jumbled-up and un-examined. Act like an investigative journalist by asking probing questions and getting to the bottom of Buyer's story.

Sometimes buyers come to the meeting with specific properties in mind (or on paper). After the needs analysis, you may compare their selected properties with their *new* needs/wants list.

Remember, every buyer is unique, and therefore his list will be unique. That which one considers a need, another will find a want.

Consider creating a checklist which includes every possible room type and conditional feature available in the marketplace. Then, use this checklist as a guide, to ensure all possibilities are explored during onion peeling.

caveats

To fully analyze needs and wants, it is helpful to know if a buyer has children (so that the children's needs/wants are also considered). Directly asking a buyer if he has children is unlawful (discriminatory practice by federal fair housing regulations). However, if your buyer volunteers the information, you are in-the-clear to discuss. To beg his voluntary data, ask the names of the people who will be living in the property. If your buyer is a parent, he will likely tell you much more than just his children's names.

When Buyer initials the page, he is committing to the process with you, so don't skip this step.

For many buyers, budget will be the constraint on needs/wants that forces compromise of all other list items.

Σ A well-developed needs/wants lists saves time in the field and mitigates buyer anxiety.

Effort Meter

You're Gonna Need:

Topical Knowledge
Scripts
Five Minutes
Attentive Ear

How-to
Explain the
Home-Buying Process

An agent's best friend is an informed client and a client's best friend is a dutiful agent. Therefore, when you point out the proper procedures of property procurement everyone becomes best friends.

1 Searches & Showings

Explain your process for searching property with your client's specific needs/wants in-mind.[174] Then, outline your procedure for showing property and choosing the best-fit one.[216]

2 Earnest Money

Define its use,[255] and suggest an estimated dollar figure to match the current market. Prepared buyers bring a checkbook to all showings.

tips

Develop a spiel (to explain the home-buying process) that may be delivered in a consistent manner, from one presentation to the next. Even if they know you've rehearsed it, they'll still appreciate it.

Provide a list (and detailed description) of all potential vendors, services, warranties, insurances, options, and outside helpers that a buyer or seller might want to utilize when making transaction decisions. Clients who discover needed services and/or warranties post-closing might blame you for failure to mention all options pre-close. When your omissions hurt your clients, bad things follow.

For buyers who borrow money: stress the importance of submitting all requested loan documentation ASAP, and of remaining diligent to not negatively alter creditworthiness until after closing.

A script to accompany:
Because it is so complex, serious buyers hire a single, competent agent to guide them through the real estate purchase process.

Σ   Buyers who know what to expect are likely to act with confidence, and not intimidation.

3 Offer & Contract

The legal aspects of a transaction are the most unsettling to buyers. To mitigate their fears, show them sample contract forms and explain all the parts, including possible addenda and contingencies.[252] Briefly discuss contract basics,[250] counter-offers,[256] multiple offer scenarios,[259] and offer strategy (which is dependent upon market conditions). Review the seller's disclosures together.

4 Inspection

Explain the cost of inspections and how a generalist inspector will define the subject property and its systems, highlighting its features, maintenance, deficiencies, and ideas/suggestions of improvement. Invite Buyer to further investigate deficiencies with specialty inspectors for roof, HVAC, pool, structural issues, pest, mold, radon gas, lead paint, or other potentially-hazardous conditions. At the same time, buyer should conduct due diligence.[220]

5 Re-Negotiation

With appropriate contingencies, Buyer may re-negotiate his purchase contract to reflect previously unknown conditions. This re-negotiation may include a price reduction, change in contract terms, repair requests, and/or inclusion or removal of contingencies.

6 Appraisal

Tell Buyer all about the appraisal. Explain when it's ordered, how it's ordered, its cost, what will happen if appraisal is low,[161] and how you will protect Buyer within the purchase contract.[252]

7 Walk-Thru & Closing Table/Escrow

Explain the procedure of contract follow-through.[221] Discuss a final walk-thru,[222] warranty and insurance procurement, and the closing ritual. Whew!

PRACTICE!

Practice your presentation on friends and fellow agents. Request constructive feedback, then contemplate that criticism with an open mind. Practice your presentation before a mirror. Record your voice and gestures, then play it back for your education. Carefully eliminate robot voice and st...st...stutters of speech, for these awkward idiosyncrasies distract from your message. Break your presentation into parts, and practice those parts as acts in your performance. This logical flow will keep you on-point during recital—even when prospects inevitably veer you off-course with tangential conversation. Practice your presentation until it flows naturally, but never, never, never practice your presentation on live prospects. Doing so shows a lack of respect for them and of yourself. Show some pride by being prepared. After all, your rehearsed presentation will appear professional to prospects, and a pitch delivered in a make-shift manner will feel choppy and disorganized. Since the whole affair is essentially a job interview, the way you lay-out a strategy (or lack thereof) is a demonstration of the service you are likely to dispense later. So, act appropriately.

A Serious How-to Manual with a Sense of Humor

Locksmith

Photographer

Pool
Guy

Insurance
Agent

Mortgage
Gal

Home
Inspector

Stager

Coach

Part of your value is knowing the right vendor for the job at-hand.[090] To do so, seek-out the experts of various real estate-related fields, then make-nice with the ones who deliver excellent customer service. These people are an extension of your service, so endorse them by connecting your clients and your posse via email, website, paper flyer, and with your mouth.

HOW TO PRESENT YOUR POSSE

Landscaper

Appraiser

Handyman

Exterminator

Closing Attorney

Your Broker

Painter

Mentor

Cleaning Lady

It is not necessary to refer three mortgage officers or three home inspectors. Once you knowingly affirm a vendor as on-the-level (deemed them a true expert of unparalleled service), it becomes okay to refer that person alone. Disclose with a caveat: *This is the vendor whom I would hire, should I find myself in your particular situation.*

A Serious How-to Manual with a Sense of Humor

Effort Meter

You're Gonna Need:

Cogitation
Scripts
Forms
Time

tips

If you question whether or not to disclose something, then you probably should. Ask a subject matter expert before disclosing (potentially-harmful) unnecessary information about your clients.

Your disclosure is dictated by federal and state statutes/regulations, local ordinances, your broker's policies, and local customs.

Material facts are those that a reasonable person would rely upon when deciding to buy, sell, or negotiate terms—and should always be disclosed to your clients.

The best practice of disclosure is complete, clearly-described, and in writing.

Whenever a client/customer signs something, leave them with a copy of the signed document. If your plan is to send an electronic copy, then do so before you part company.

It's your job to know which disclosures should be made, to whom they should be made, and the precise time at which they should be made.

Always disclose your license status when acting as a principal.

Σ Disclosure is the best way to protect yourself and your clients, while simultaneously treating everyone fairly.

How-to
Disclose Your Ass Off

Real estate agents are required by law, compelled by decency, and ingratiated by virtue to make particular disclosures during the course of business. To learn what these disclosures are, and to whom you ought disclose, consult your broker—then validate it yourself. For best-practice, put all disclosure in writing, then get the disclosee to sign-off, in acknowledgement of receipt.

1 To Your Clients

It's important for your clients to understand exactly where you stand in relationship to them. For this reason, insist upon putting all agency relationships in writing.[184] Include disclosure of all the ways you and/or your broker may be possibly compensated by the actions of clients. From the agents/brokers you consort, the real estate principals you engage, and the vendors you recommend: disclose whether or not you receive (or share) compensation, in any form—whether it be money, equipment, advertisement, marketing, referrals, shared office space, and/or favors.

2 On Behalf of Your Clients

Do not disclose any information about your client (or their property), unless you are required by law or you have your client's written permission. Nonetheless, what you disclose, how you disclose, and when you disclose may be of strategic importance. Sometimes telling the other side a few juicy details will be in your client's interest. This is because disclosure of pertinent information may be interpreted as either openness or rationale to persuade the other side to act in a manner that is beneficial to your client. Other times, releasing that same bit of info will be detrimental. If the law requires your client to disclose, then encourage them to disclose fully and in good faith; otherwise, disclose with only strategy in-mind.

When representing a seller—*whether or not your client is willing*—the law requires you to disclose all property conditions (of which you are aware, and a rational buyer would want to know) that may not be discovered by routine inspection. These latent conditions (material facts) are those that are potentially-hazardous to the property's ecosystem or structural integrity, such as the remnants of previous flooding, un-permitted construction, or bodies buried in the yard.

3 To All Others

Whenever you and your client share a material relationship (familial, business-related, or romantic in nature—from the past or present), disclose this fact to all who care to listen. Non-disclosure of these relationships may cause ill feelings if discovered later, and it's this exact perception you wish to avoid.

The Discloser's Razor: when you question whether or not to disclose something, then you probably should. At the least, consult your broker.

How-to
Hustle Harmony with a Commission Schedule

Effort Meter

Before discussing agency with anyone, you should decide how much you're gonna charge clients and exactly what they will get in return. Go so far as to write it all down on paper, then present your fee schedule to all comers, with honor in your heart and a smile on your face.

Prospects will claim that other agents charge less. However, the question should not be an agent's rate, rather the result of their work (measured in time and net-to-seller dollars). In this way, many prospects are willing to pay a premium rate for premium results. The preeminent justification (your persuasive argument) for a premium rate is found in your personal statistics (AVG. DOM, AVG. SP/LP, CTR).

1 Normal Fee

Build the structure of your schedule by considering niche and outta-niche transactions. You might also mix and match the fees you charge, depending on each client's situation and/or goals. Common structural elements include fees based upon: percentage of the sales price; percentage of net-to-seller; flat fee; minimum rate/fee; maximum rate/fee; and sliding scale, whereby fees are paid à la carte for specific services. Regardless of the structure you choose, consider a minimum fee (which will allow you to financially provide full, quality service, no matter the sales price),[299] an unrepresented buyer fee (bonus paid by seller-client when you attract the buyer yourself),[295] and a termination fee (which guarantees the recuperation of costs if/when you get fired).[311]

2 Multiple Transaction Fee

Some prospects come with the promise of multiple transactions. Whether they want to buy one/sell one, or buy/sell several times over, consider offering a discount to repeat clients. Because events may go awry on back-to-back deals, the smart play is to charge the full, normal fee on the first, then apply discounts to the second closing.

3 Rebates & Retainers

Commission rebates may be used to attract prospects and incite referrals. Typical buyer rebate: any extra commissions earned above a pre-determined fee are rebated to Buyer at closing, or discounted from the sales price. Typical seller rebate: fees are subtracted in pre-determined increments for each seller-provided referral during their listing period (a limit may be warranted).

Meant to offset the fixed expenses of client-provided services, retainer fees may be charged upfront, before agency begins. Often applied at times of prospect overflow or when representing a hesitant client, these fees are either kept by the agent, or rebated in the form of a commission discount at closing.

You're Gonna Need:

Preconception
Justification
Conviction
Persuasion

tips

There are many more ways to organize a commission structure than can be listed here.

Always attach your fee schedule to agency agreements.

Embrace the fact that buyers pay commissions.[262] Tell this truth, then justify your fee.

You have to negotiate for yourself before you can negotiate for a client. Arguing your fee shows your ability to advocate.

Your fee should not be determined by how many hours you work, but by the result of that work.

When you routinely offer a discount, you may be referred to others based solely upon this discount—which may or may not be a good thing.

Always check laws, regulations, and with your broker before making any agreement to rebate commissions.

Confucius Sez:
Weigh the services you provide, your skill level, the number of waiting prospects, and the competition's commission rate. Your fee is in this balance.

Σ Establish your compensation at the beginning of each client relationship, then (because you're covered) forget all about it.

GIVE...
ME...
A...
B-U-Y-
E-R
What's That Spell?

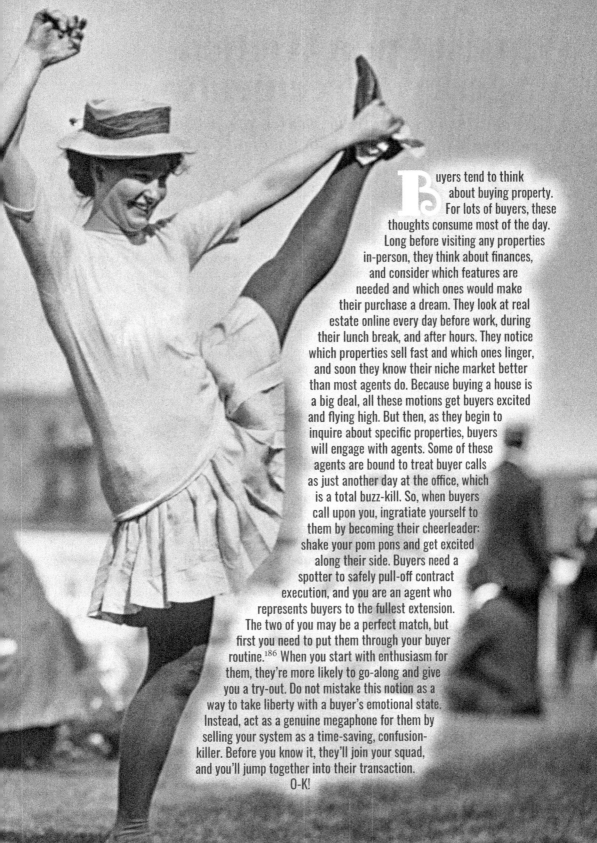

Buyers tend to think about buying property. For lots of buyers, these thoughts consume most of the day. Long before visiting any properties in-person, they think about finances, and consider which features are needed and which ones would make their purchase a dream. They look at real estate online every day before work, during their lunch break, and after hours. They notice which properties sell fast and which ones linger, and soon they know their niche market better than most agents do. Because buying a house is a big deal, all these motions get buyers excited and flying high. But then, as they begin to inquire about specific properties, buyers will engage with agents. Some of these agents are bound to treat buyer calls as just another day at the office, which is a total buzz-kill. So, when buyers call upon you, ingratiate yourself to them by becoming their cheerleader: shake your pom pons and get excited along their side. Buyers need a spotter to safely pull-off contract execution, and you are an agent who represents buyers to the fullest extension. The two of you may be a perfect match, but first you need to put them through your buyer routine.[186] When you start with enthusiasm for them, they're more likely to go-along and give you a try-out. Do not mistake this notion as a way to take liberty with a buyer's emotional state. Instead, act as a genuine megaphone for them by selling your system as a time-saving, confusion-killer. Before you know it, they'll join your squad, and you'll jump together into their transaction. O-K!

Insist Upon Written Agency Agreements

If your clients' goals are the focus of your business, then adherence to your system is in their best interest.

BY DEBBIE THE DENTIST

HAVE YOU EVER TELEPHONED a random dentist, requested a buff job of your gnarly gnashers—*to be conducted in someone else's suburban driveway, no less*—and expected it to all go down within the hour? Her rational reply to your absurd appeal would likely be a sensible script like, "While I would be thrilled to earn a new client, my business simply does not operate that way. I require all new patients to make an in-office appointment, whereby I fully inspect the mouth, teeth, and gums, take x-rays, and *then* clean your teeth. After polishing your pearlies, I provide oral hygiene advice based upon your unique condition. This system allows me to maintain a standard for all clients, while imparting the finest care to you as an individual. I have available appointments today at 3PM or tomorrow at noon. Which time is better for you?"

Most professionals are likely to respond in similar fashion, but not so for the average real estate agent. When her phone rings with requests of impromptu listing tours, she is likely to drop her scheduled tasks, and run toward the caller with arms out-stretched, lock box key in-hand. Since this practice is so prevalent in the real estate sales industry, buyers have been trained to expect it.

As a result, the market is full of buyers who just wanna shop for property and skip all advancing agents, using them to open doors and little else. In this way, buyers engage with agents in a transactional manner until they bump into the one they eventually hire (which is usually the one who seems knowledgeable, resourceful, and is insistent upon following a bone fide property acquisition system).[176] Working with yet-to-be-qualified and/or unsigned lookers sends the message that your system is not bone fide, but it may be worse than that.

Depending upon your state's laws and your broker's policies, your relationship with buyers may take one of several forms, each of which comprises a different set of duties. Whether you engage a buyer through sub-agency, designated agency, dual agency, exclusive agency, non-exclusive agency, or as a customer, your duties should be clearly explained through conversation and written agreement. At the same time, your fee—*in exchange for services provided*—should be discussed and agreed.[181] It makes no sense to work with a buyer, unless you are guaranteed payment at the time they accomplish their property acquisition goal. Agency is not free, so don't give your eye teeth without a promise in return.[173]

Further, a buyer may fancy himself a good negotiator, but a house isn't a fondue pot at a garage sale, or even a new car—it's far more complicated. Those who realize this fact are unlikely to hire an agent who seems unable to negotiate for herself. Therefore, you should demonstrate your bartering value by only showing property to two types of buyers: those who want to see your listings (customers) and those who sign exclusive agency (clients).[186]

Besides, exclusive agency is in a buyer's best interest,[212] and the guarantee of a paid fee will incentivize his agent to work diligently, forever searching-out matching properties, regardless of listed status.

Just as you should avoid dentists who meet in parking lots, buyers should avoid agents who work without agency agreements. Remember, you set the stage and strike the tone for the path your relationships take;[168] prospects do the same thing. When you insist but they refuse, then you should walk away because, just like prospects in the sea, there will always be more teeth to clean.

Some buyers would rather sit for a root canal than sign an agency agreement with you. Others feel the same way about merely sitting-down for your presentation. Don't take it personally; they won't behave as you desire because they don't trust you yet. Yank hard (with scripts) on those who rebuff your advances. Show them your nerve by walking away if they won't bite.

PULLING TEETH

Have the wisdom to know when your words are on the cusp of impacting a prospect's actions, and when your scripts are wasted like tooth decay.

A Serious How-to Manual with a Sense of Humor

Effort Meter

You're Gonna Need:

Macro CMA
Agency Checklist
Scripts
Agency Agreement

tips

If one of your listings attracts a buyer, then stop after STEP 1, and represent your seller, treating the buyer as a customer. If Buyer rejects your listing, proceed to STEP 2.

Memorize several different scripts for asking Buyer to sign, and for justification of your commission. You're gonna need them!

Always get your commission into the agreement.[067] Otherwise, you're potentially cheating yourself, your broker, and your family.

When you show buyers what the current marketplace looks like, they will be prepared to tackle that market head-on. When buyers are unsure of the environment, they are more timid and less-likely to trust your words.

Agents possessing exclusive agency agreements without commission clauses may be forced to represent clients for free.

You could skip to the end by asking Buyer to sign the agency agreement upfront. This works sometimes, but by putting Buyer through these steps, you ensure that you understand each other, and that Buyer is best-educated about the process—making your job of representation more-rewarding and less time-consuming.

How-to
Sign an Exclusive-Buyer Agency Agreement

Working without a signed agency agreement is foolhardy at best,[184] especially when most buyers are more-than-willing to sign with the right agent. Not to mention, most states forbid agents from providing services to buyers (or sellers) otherwise. So, if you're gonna get buyers to sign an agency agreement, then it might as well be an exclusive one. Follow these simple steps to keep you legal, protected, and paid:

1 Pre-Qualify Your Prospect[170]
First, become certain Buyer has the means to actually buy; for there's no point proceeding further if he can't muster the cash. Ideally, this step should be done prior to meeting, but if not: call your favorite mortgage officer, make a quick introduction, then hand the phone to Buyer.

2 Lure Buyer to Your Lair[171]
Use home-field advantage to your advantage. Get there at least fifteen minutes early and set-up space in a distraction-free room. Ensure all presentation materials and needed supplies are in the room and don't forget to provide entertainment for children of all ages. When the kids are cool, parents can get into the scene.

3 Present Agency Checklist[173]
Once Buyer has completed the agency checklist, take it from him and set it face-down on the table, next to your seat.

4 Conduct Needs Analysis[174]
Buyers with unreasonable expectations will be a future hassle for all involved.[168] So, if you believe a buyer's needs/wants cannot be matched to his budget, now is the time to say so; together, make revisions until the two jibe. Because going into the field unprepared usually results in wasted time and effort, you should consider referring unreasonable buyers to another agent;[112] otherwise, once Buyer's needs/wants are pinpointed, he will feel prepared and you will be able to find best-matching properties.

5 Discuss Market Conditions[146]
Your marketplace chat will educate Buyer and demonstrate your value at the same time. Draft a macro CMA that corresponds with the market Buyer is about to enter.[140] Show and discuss whether the current market is trending in favor of buyers or sellers.[147] Show him the current number of ACTIVE listings, the average number of transactions closed in recent months, and the number of new listings expected within the next thirty days.[150] Then, show Buyer photos of recently-SOLD (and PENDING) listings that match his needs/wants. Once Buyer confirms liking the images, show and discuss the sales price, SP/LP, DOM, and seller-paid concessions, for each. This step helps Buyer set realistic expectations.

6 Explain Home-Buying Process[176]

Talk about how you'll go-about finding matching properties, as well as the buyer's involvement. Tell how you'll arrange showings and what Buyer should do to prepare. Share your system for analyzing each showing[216] and a brief summation of offer and acceptance (demonstrated with sample contract forms).[256] Talk about inspection,[220] appraisal, and settlement procedures. If Buyer plans to acquire foreclosure, HUD, short-sale, or other specialty properties, explain those specific transaction procedures now. This step further demonstrates your value, while educating and setting expectations for the buyer.

7 Discuss Agency Checklist[173]

Bust-out the checklist that Buyer filled-out in STEP 3. Explain what agency is and is not. Tell Buyer that you're all-in for your clients,[212] and that you provide every service on the checklist— whether or not he likes it. You are exclusive with your clients and you expect your clients to be exclusive too, which means that you're each willing to sign an agreement proclaiming such.[184] For buyers who refuse your logical advances, consider a referral to another agent[112] (but not before laying some powerful scripts on them first).[051]

8 Define Your Value[172]

If he's not yet sure of your worth, tell Buyer what separates you from all the other agents in town.

9 Talk About Your Fee[181]

Be upfront: you are not interested in working for free. You own and operate a business, not a charity, so develop several scripts to logically justify your monetary value,[048] then lay them down smoothly. Once your commission rate is agreed, explain all aspects of the agency agreement, including any special verbiage added by you/your broker.

10 Use a Closing Script

If you've executed STEPS 1-9 properly, most buyers will eagerly sign an exclusive agency agreement. To facilitate their scrawl of approval, begin with a simple request: *Sign here at we'll get started.* If Buyer objects to signing, ask: *Why will you not join me in finding the property you desire?* Depending upon his answer, apply the appropriate script you've practiced so many times.[051]

Once Buyer has signed the exclusive agency agreement, distribute and/or acquire Buyer's signatures on all other relevant documents and disclosures required by your brokerage and/or regulatory bodies.

Note: regardless of the law (but with regard to your broker's permission), you should only work with buyers who sign exclusive agency agreements. Buyers who sit through your presentation, but refuse to be exclusive are likely to cheat you later (whereby you get paid *nothing*). When you do not insist upon exclusivity, it's as though you're telling buyers that you do not respect your business, nor your time. As far as they see it, if you (so obviously) don't give two spits about yourself, then why should they?

---

tips

The purpose of exclusive agency is to trade your promise of diligent, fiduciary effort for a guaranteed payment of those efforts. If you're not willing to give diligent effort to buyers, then do not insist upon exclusivity. And if you do sign exclusively, but fail to deliver diligent effort, you have breached that agreement, and should forgo your fee (or reduce it proportionately).

When making a case for agency, don't say things that aren't true, such as: *My representation is free to you because the seller pays my commission.* OR *You can cancel this agency agreement at any time, without penalty.* OR *I don't really mind if we don't sign this thing, but my broker insists upon it.* Instead, make honest and direct statements like: *The seller has exclusive, expert representation, and so should you.* OR *I only work with serious buyers, and in my experience, serious buyers commit to a single agent.* OR *I'll bust my ass for you, earning every penny of my commission.*

A flip chart may be used to present ideas more clearly, and to keep you on-track.

A perfect prospect-to-exclusive-buyer conversion rate is elusive for even the best agents. For no matter what you say or do, some buyers will refuse exclusivity, outright. Agents with strong prospecting skills will refer these perfidious purchasers to another agent, and choose to work instead with the next buyer waiting in line.

Tis better to have presented and lost, than to have never presented at all.

Use a closing script.[198]

Σ Buyers are happy to sign exclusive agency agreements with agents who clearly demonstrate a valuable role in acquiring property.

Effort Meter

You're Gonna Need:

a Buyer
Needs Analysis
Foresight
Jelly Beans

tips

Undoing a transaction due to buyer's remorse is a stressful chore for all involved.

Skipping a discussion about buyer's remorse could lead to disaster.

At times, it will be helpful to remind your buyer that his property selection has been made carefully. *All systems are a-go, so don't chicken-out now.*

To keep buyer's remorse at bay, reiterate and refocus your buyer's attention toward pertinent details throughout the transaction, and not dwelling in the mire of second-guesses.

Buyer's remorse is an unavoidable sensation for some. For most, it may be stymied by a prepared agent, willing to guide clients through all the transaction's hurdles.

Σ Comfort is the perfect prescription to mitigate remorseful symptoms.

How-to Prevent (or at least Mitigate) Buyer's Remorse

Whether it's new shoes or a new house, buyer's remorse will inevitably drum its pulse of panic on the hearts of select buyers. Its beat begins slowly, then steadily quickens in pace until—if left unabated—conjures enough anguish to cause purchaser paralysis. While the shoe salesman performs a snappy exchange within hours or days, the real property purveyor usually faces his buyer's affliction weeks after its throbbing palpitations began.

Instead of ensnaring yourself an the avoidable, sticky wicket that is the unwinding of a perfectly-good transaction, be proactive of pending possibilities, and write your buyers a prescription:

1 Address It Head-On

The first time you meet, mention the possibility of buyer's remorse—the brain's apprehension to change. Remind your buyer that his decision to purchase a specific property is one that will be made over several days or weeks. Together, you will prepare extensively, by analyzing and scrutinizing each property and the purchase process. He will be fully aware of all his options and ample consideration will be given to his eventual choice. Therefore, while it may feel real, there is no reason to give any credence to buyer's remorse. It's a natural feeling, but not necessarily the right feeling (kinda like wedding-day jitters).

2 Arm Your Buyer with Education

When Buyer feels informed and prepared, he is less likely to feel the pangs of buyer's remorse. If, by chance, this informed, prepared buyer does sense the beat of doom, he may quickly reason his trembles away as positive excitement. To supply your buyer with a sense of ease, perform a thorough presentation,[186] which will familiarize him with the purchase process[176] and instill confidence in his needs/wants.[174]

3 Use Humor

Just after signing an agency agreement,[186] give Buyer a bag of jelly beans. Put on your favorite smile and say to him: *These are magical, buyer beans. When you feel excited about buying a house, eat a green one; it will elate you. When you feel the pangs of buyer's remorse, eat a yellow one; it will calm you. When you get the feeling that I have done something awesome, eat an orange one; it will make you wanna tell a friend.* Later, you can ask Buyer: *How many jelly beans have you eaten today?*

This script pokes fun at buyer's remorse while simultaneously and subtly demonstrating that you have the foresight and experience to duly deal with all aspects of the pending purchase.

How-to
Pre-Qualify a Seller

The in-depth analysis of a subject property,[150] followed by a full-blown listing presentation,[196] requires several hours of work. Before dedicating yourself to these laborious tasks, spend some time speaking with the property's owner. During your chat, gather intel for valuation, gauge the seller's motivation and explain your strategy for selling property. Because your choice of listings greatly impacts your success rate, your pre-qualification goal is to determine whether or not Seller is willing and able to actually sell.

Effort Meter

You're Gonna Need:
Homework
Questions
Ears
Patience

1 Investigate Seller
Gather all public and MLS data you can find on the subject property. Drive-by (or look at satellite images) to see the property's setting. Compare this gathered information to your *Monthly Marketplace Dashboard* and estimate a high and low range of the subject's value.[342]

2 Interview Seller
Some sellers are motivated to sell and some are not. Most are willing to tell you all about their exact plans, goals, and reasoning, if you just allow them some space to let it all out. So, get them talking and when they stop, ask another question, encouraging them to wax lyrically about the type of client they'll be.

Why are you selling? Who lives there now (you, a renter, or is it vacant)? Once you sell, where are you going? Do you have a selling deadline? Have you already purchased another property? Will this sale determine the purchase of another? Are you a first-time seller? What have previous listing experiences been like? What did you like/dislike about those experiences? What would you like to see done differently this time? What if I find a cash buyer tomorrow who wants you out in ten days? Would you comply? If EXPIRED:[100] *Why do you think it didn't sell the last time?* Validate the data gathered in STEP 1, then ask: *What do you like about your current home? Why did you buy it? Which feature is your favorite? Least favorite? Why do you say that? What makes it different than others? Is the attic/basement finished? Do you know of any nearby, planned development? Tell me more.*

3 Discuss Marketing Strategy[229]
Explain how price attracts or repels buyers,[153] and seek their agreement to price according to the market.[154] Ask: *Do you have a price in-mind? How did you figure that?* If their price does not jibe with the range from STEP 1, ask them to justify their reasoning.

4 Ask About the Competition
Don't hide from the fact that sellers tend to weigh their options.[201] Ask: *Are you interviewing other agents or am I the only contender? When will you make a decision on which agent to hire? What factors will determine your choice? What is your list date deadline?*

tips

Begin your chat with this script: *I believe people make the best decisions when they have the most accurate info. Therefore, may I have your permission to always tell you the truth, no matter what it is.*

End your chat with this script: *Are there any questions I didn't ask? What else should I know? When I arrive, I'll show you the homework that proves my selling strategy, and I will tell you the best price to attract buyers. If what I show and tell you makes sense, will you sign an agency agreement with me at the conclusion of my presentation?*

Don't rely upon someone else to relay your conceptions; request all decision makers to be present at the time of your presentation.

Don't bother marking-up a full CMA until the seller is pre-qualified.[140]

Use your pre-qualification conversation to set expectations of the listing presentation. Get the seller ready to say YES to you.

Σ Probing questions that identify which sellers are mentally-prepared and fiscally-able to sell will save you time and hassle, because it never pays to work with duds.

A Client Isn't a Commission Check

Don't count your birds as in-hand before they hatch, especially when you've still got the bush to contend.

BY AXEL TAGRIND

FIRST THINGS FIRST: not all that glitters is gold, only fools rush in, and the road to hell is paved with good intentions. That notwithstanding, it sure feels good when someone says YES to your advances of agency. However, you have a system and a reputation to uphold. So, you cannot sign-up just anyone, because as ye sow, so shall ye reap.[345]

A common malfunction of hopeful sellers is the tendency to choose the agent quoting the highest price; it's hard to blame them for wanting to get every penny in trade for their property. But by signing an agency agreement, you are (in essence) telling a seller that you can sell her property at the listed price; when you believe otherwise, your fiduciary bond is immediately broken. Therefore, amassing a stockpile of over-priced listings, used to re-direct would-be buyers to competing listings, ain't your cup of tea. In fact, this shameless practice is the opposite of seller agency. If your thing is collecting trophies, then try hoarding belt buckles or snow domes and leave sellers alone. Your clients trust you will treat them right, so don't be a listing slut to them.[191]

For certainty, an agent can catch more listings with a sweet-sounding price, but that doesn't mean he can sell them.[159] No listing is an island—it has to compete with other listings. Therefore, a listing worth taking is worth pricing right,[154] because when you price it right, *they* will come.[153] Convincing sellers of this conception can be a challenging task, but well worth the effort. You have tools and logic to make your case, so put them to clever use.[125] A competent agent who speaks the truth is worth more than one who is not and does not. So, demonstrate to sellers that paying peanuts attracts monkey agents.

Listing property should be a two-way street, whereby seller and agent first agree on a marketing strategy.[229] An acceptable strategy may be for seller and agent to plan on starting with a high price, and then adjust that price according to the market's reaction. An unacceptable strategy would be for an agent to misrepresent a high price as the perfect one, while secretly planning a price-reduction presentation in the near future.[202]

The purpose of your listing presentation is not to sign-up every willing seller, rather to discover whether or not a seller's goals match your abilities. Sellers list because they want to sell property, but those who disobey the market seldom succeed. When you lie with these dogs, you wake-up with expired listings. Plus, hell hath no fury like a seller scorned, so it's best to avoid those with market misgivings.

Of course, some listings are worthy of an over-priced gamble, but not each one you meet. Because, when you put all your eggs in the same basket, others are watching. Buyers, sellers, neighbors, and other agents see every listing you take, and they're judging you on the results. You are known by the company you keep, so limit yourself to earnest sellers.

If your listing presentation fails to get them singing your song, then let your actions speak louder than your words, and walk away—they will respect you for it. After all, you can't make an omelette without breaking a few eggs, but first impressions are the most lasting, so stick to your guns and don't burn any bridges on your way out the door. Instead, leave them with a script: *Would you be offended if I called you when your listing expires? We can re-visit my system at that time.*

Absence makes the heart grow fonder, and Rome wasn't built in a day, but sellers have been known to change their spots, so be a squeaky wheel after each expiry.[100] For when you play your cards right, you'll get the grease, but when you don't, they're liable to shoot the messenger. Fortune favors the brave. 🌳

Nobody Really Likes a Listing Slut

So Keep Your Scruples Together.

There are agents who always say "YES" to every seller:
YES! I'll list at any price.
YES! I'll hope you reduce it later.
YES! I'll say whatever you wanna hear.
YES! I'll take any listing, under any condition.
YES! I'll mow your lawn. Just sign here, please!

A Serious How-To Manual with a Sense of Humor

Effort Meter

You're Gonna Need:

Topical Knowledge
Rehearsal
Props
Audience

tips

Do not assume experienced sellers already know the drill. Your explanation may provide insight which was previously unseen by them.

Develop a spiel (to explain the home-selling process) that may be delivered in a consistent manner, from one presentation to the next. Even if they know you've rehearsed it, they'll still appreciate it.

Show your prospects all the documents and materials used in the preparation and execution of selling real property. The sheer volume of your paraphernalia is sure to impress them somewhat.

If the seller is planning to buy/sell or sell/buy, in a back-to-back transaction, discuss a strategy that safeguards the seller without alienating potential buyers.

Σ Showing-off your real estate aptitude, while teaching prospects a thing or two, can put everyone at ease.

How-to
Explain the
Home-Selling Process

Selling real property can be a stressful undertaking, but a reasonable understanding of coming events tends to lessen anxiety. Therefore, it's a good idea to show your prospects the ropes. Use your explanation of the home-selling process to pull double duty: educate the seller, while simultaneously demonstrating your expertise on the topic. You'll lose listeners when you delve too deep, so keep your commentary brief and on the surface—unless your audience requests details, of course.

1 Evaluate the Subject Property

Begin with a thorough assessment of the subject property's condition,[130] then compare it to the marketplace.[140] Make any desired repairs and/or upgrades,[200] then re-assess the subject and its current market. Establish an interpretation of value.[150]

2 Implement & Monitor a Market Strategy [229]

Select a price for the subject,[154] upload it to the MLS,[236] and tell the entire world about it.[239] Create promotional materials, conduct showings and host an open house.[240] Elicit feedback [242] and adjust the price as the market commands.[202] Show prospects samples of your marketing package,[234] web displays, flyers,[233] MLS datasheets, and the breadth of your listings' syndication.

3 Negotiate Offers and Sign P&S Contract [249]

When the price is right, offers will come.[153] Knowledge of the rules, customs,[036] recent (comparable) sales,[138] and a system to qualify candidates[170] allows a seller to negotiate a purchase & sale contract that is both fair and likely to close. Explain how, throughout the purchase agreement term, you continue to invite offers (all the way 'til closing day),[274] giving your sellers leverage during contingency periods (which also serve as contingency plans, should the current contract not close).

4 Manage Contingencies

As contingencies dictate,[252] purchase agreement re-negotiation may re-occur until closing. Therefore, it's in a seller's interest to stay actively involved in the inspection, appraisal, and financial aspects of the home-*buying* process.[176] Entrusting the other side of a transaction to execute time-sensitive contractual obligations may lead to NO SALE.[221] Explain your methods to handle repair requests,[268] low appraisals,[161] and finance issues.

5 Close the Transaction & Move-Out

Show samples of closing documents and give a quick description of the corresponding ceremony. Explain that move-out may occur either before or after closing, as negotiated between the parties.

How-to WOW with a PRE-LISTING PACKAGE

Don't pass on this opportunity to demonstrate your marketing abilities. Frame your argument with style, then deliver it with pizzazz, and you'll be a step ahead before you ring their bell.

Pick a theme, and a noticeable container to match (toolbox, picnic basket, hat, mop bucket,..). Creatively carry this theme to the content inside: list of your services,[172] testimonials,[314] copy of agency agreement, disclosure statements,[180] sales process,[192] and case studies for starting with the right price. Send this bundle the day before your scheduled presentation, then check to ensure delivery. You could send it in an email, but it wouldn't have the same WOW factor. Besides, you're showing off here, so don't be so stodgy.

Send it to their place of employment, and when co-workers ask who it's from, your prospect is apt to declare, "From *my* agent." Nice.

A Serious How-to Manual with a Sense of Humor

Opening

(Choose one or more of these)

Tell a Quick Story Outline two realities, comparing a real-life buyer/seller who failed to buy/sell with one who succeeded.

Share a Shocking Statistic Did you know that __% of sellers don't sell in their first listing period?

Pose a Question Do you want to be a buyer/seller who wins or one who loses?

Offer Your Solution My plan for buying/selling is a winning strategy. Here it is: __

Words

Conjure emotional response, but don't be overly sensational. Limit jargon. Use adjectives to your advantage. Give enough details to color their understanding, but not enough to bore. Set cadence to a marching beat. Maintain appropriate volume. Avoid rambling and tangential topics. Abandon robot voice.[205]

Thru~out

Be calm. Recite memorized lines. Look them in the eye. Ask rhetorical questions. Repeat your main point. Sprinkle humor where appropriate. Stay focused.

Closing

Your presentation must have an ending whereby you ask them to make a decision: *Will you hire me or not?* Ask for their hand in business in a hard-to-say-no kinda way.[198] For those who need time to mull it over, ask for a decision deadline.

Props

Show statistics, photos, testimonials in simple-to-digest formats. Then take them away after use or your props may become a distraction.

Attention Getters

Keep their interest, or you're just wasting time.

Effort Meter

You're Gonna Need:

Seller Prospect
Statistical Analysis
Rehearsed Scripts
Agency Agreement

tips

Being on-time (or *slightly* early) to your listing appointment shows the seller that you respect her time and are serious about representing her interest.

Before meeting with prospects, look professional and put on your game face.[025]

Earn bonus points by bringing a pop-up table and chairs to vacant listing presentations. Your make-shift conference room shows foresight and attention to detail.

During your presentation, use assumable words like we, us, and them, that seemingly place you and the seller on the same team.

Make it clear to seller-prospects that you always follow a client's lawful commands, but not before they clearly hear your informed opinion.

Presentation Variation #1
Conduct STEPS 1-3 at a single meeting, then go away and do all your market research and interpretation at your office. Meet the seller a second time to conduct STEPS 4-9.

Presentation Variation #2
Conduct STEP 1, after which the prospect emails pictures of the subject property to you. After your market research is complete, conduct STEPS 3-9 via telephone or web presentation.

How-to
Deliver a Slam-Dunk Listing Presentation

Because the mutual pursuit of reasonable goals favors a successful relationship, the best listing presentation is one that explores the compatibility of seller and agent. To encourage their union, state your case, then seek their accord.

1 Pre-Qualify the Seller[189]

Begin with a simple script that sets the tone: *I believe people make the best decisions when they have the most accurate information. Therefore, may I have your permission to always tell you the truth as I see it, regardless of what it might be?* Then, if you think Seller is motivated to sell, conduct market research and interpret the subject's FMV.[342]

2 Take the Tour, then Sit-Down

Knock on the subject's door and build rapport as you strut-thru the property together, as though you and seller are home inspectors.[222] Jot notes regarding the effective ages and types of: features, appliances, systems, utilities, construction materials, as well the quality of craftsmanship. Make a list of all the repairs required to return the subject property to turn-key status. Once the tour ends, your presentation begins. So, lead your prospect to a table and chairs that promote alertness; the kitchen table is most suitable for boardroom-like presentations, followed by dining room or patio tables. The living room couch is preferred seating for sellers if your presentation is a stage show.

3 Explain the Home-Selling Process[192]

Briefly outline the steps of successful property selling. Use a flip chart, laptop, tablet, or other visual device to ease communication.

4 Define the Subject Property's Condition[130]

Summarizing your notes from STEP 2, rank the subject property's soft condition as either top, middle, or bottom tier.[150] Explain which (in any) repairs/updates would bump the property up a tier or two. If nothing else, strive for the seller's agreement regarding the property's current tier because, if you disagree on its condition, you will likely disagree on its value, too.

5 Present the Current Apple Market[150]

Show all relevant statistical reports from CHAPTER 3: macro and micro CMA,[140] absorption & trend analyses,[147] buyer forecast and activity reports.[146] Then, present a single-page, dashboard report, displaying just the highlights from each of these long-forms.[342] In other words, show your homework and then your answers, by declaring your guesstimations of value for each tier (top, middle, bottom) of the subject property's CMA.[141]

6 Discuss Pricing Strategy[154]

Explain how there exists a buyer for every property, but that buyer wants to see a fair asking price, otherwise he will skip to another listing. Then calculate net-to-seller[135] for three potential sales prices, based on the salability differential,[152] and offer each as list price options:

- The High Price: few lookers & low-ball offers, slowly or never sold.
- The Low Price: many lookers & *many* offers, sold fast.[153]
- The Right Price: several lookers & fair offers, sold within AVG. DOM.

Question the seller: *Which result would you like?* Depending on the answer, quote a list price that corresponds. If the seller agrees, *Whoopee! You found a golden egg*. If the seller disagrees, begin a scripted dialogue to logically and/or emotionally argue your opinion. If/when your painstaking attempts to persuade the prospect on price flop in your face, go to STEP 7, then repeat your argument from STEP 6 with a fresh script. If the seller remains unconvinced, abandon ship.[119]

7 Describe Your Service[172]

Show your personal market statistics: AVG. DOM, SP/LP, CTR. Show the results of marketing strategies you have deployed in the past, with MLS datasheets of your previously SOLD & EXPIRED listings. Discuss why these past clients got the results they did, by displaying the number of inquiries, showings, and offers each received.

Next, show sample material you use to sell property, including pictures,[230] ad copy,[232] scope of MLS syndication, online classified ads, social media, and a sample marketing package.[234] Tell how you will spotlight features,[227] stage the property,[226] make showings easy, host open house(s),[240] and report honest feedback.[243] Lastly, establish your availability and a mutually-agreed upon method of communication.

8 Discuss Your Fee[181]

The sellers reaction to your commission schedule will be in response to your performance of STEP 7. If the seller rebuffs, use clever scripts to argue for your normal rate. There is nothing wrong with negotiating your fee, but you should only agree to list when you feel your compensation is just. Otherwise, you may become susceptible to providing lackluster service.

9 Utilize a Closing Script[198]

End your presentation with a series of questions. Begin with: *Are there questions that I did not ask, or aspects that need clarification?* Next, recite a closing script,[198] which asks the seller to sign on the dotted line. Fill-in the price on your listing agreement (that you have previously prepared), and present it to the seller. Once signed, commence with disclosures and all the necessary data forms.

If Seller's response is hesitation based on interviewing other agents, or a desire to mull it over, then seek a decision deadline. If her response is hesitation based on anything else, then fully extract her objection(s) and handle with care.[052]

Effort Meter

You're Gonna Need:

Scripts
Creativity
Tenacity
Scripts

How–to
Utilize a Closing Script

It's uncool to leave your audience hanging, so be sure to ask for their hand in business at the end of each presentation. There's no wrong way to ask them to sign-up, but you should limit yourself to those likely to sell.[190]

Ask Three Questions

1. *Are you serious about selling your property* by the stated deadline?
2. *Are you willing to help yourself* achieve that goal by setting a list price that is fair and reasonable to both you and buyers alike?
3. Have I demonstrated my value *and* my ability to help you achieve your real estate goal of selling quickly, at top dollar?

Once you hear YES to each of these, hand-over a pen, and say: *Great! Sign here, please.* Otherwise, handle their objections with style:

tips

Sometimes the first script will not work, regardless of its quality and delivery. Some people will hold-out on you, just to see how well you can justify your position. Keep trying without becoming frustrated. This is one of the fun parts of the job.

Use parables, analogies, and real life examples to illustrate your perspective.

Help them understand why their price is important to selling.[153] Also, your commission rate reflects your level of service. No one else (that they're likely to meet) will do it like you do.

If they don't sign at the time of your presentation, consider sending a handwritten note immediately after you get back to the office. Thank them for the opportunity to discuss their goals and express (once again) your desire to help.

There will always be competing agents willing to work for less commission, or list at a higher price. Don't be afraid to address the other choices that Seller may be considering.

3 questions for buyers
Are you serious about buying?
Are you willing to pay a fair price?
Have I demonstrated my value?

Σ   If you don't expressly ask for their business, many sellers won't give it to you.

1 If the Objection is Your Commission Rate

Begin by justifying your rate with logic and reason: *A good agent does more than take pictures and upload data to the MLS. If that's all you need, there are brokerages that provide marketing services for a flat fee of a few hundred dollars. I'm worth my commission because I will lend advice on preparing the property, devising a pricing strategy based upon the current market, interpret and negotiate offers, qualify buyers, maintain purchase agreement obligations, coordinate closing procedures, and lead you through obstacles that are sure to pop-up en route to closing.*

2 If the Objection is Suggested List Price

Once again, use reason and insight: *If you think my interpretation of your property's condition and corresponding FMV are wrong, and that your pricing strategy is better than mine, then you should list with another agent. However, you should only agree to hire them if they agree to a specific stipulation:* **they'll pay you cash for all requested price reductions.** *You see, I suspect any agent who lists at that price falls into one of two categories: they either don't know their quoted price is too high to attract buyers, or they do know the price is too high, but their plan is to lie to you now so you'll hire them. They're betting that a few weeks or months of inactivity will wise-you-up to reality, and you'll finally relent to their persistent insistence to reduce your price. A cash-for-reductions stipulation will expose all charlatans and amateurs, leaving only the miracle worker you're gonna need to get that price.* When Seller asks if you will make the same cash-for-reductions guarantee, say: *No, because I'm not quoting a crazy price. Whatever our price may be, the market will show its approval or disapproval. Here is what I will guarantee: if our price is too low, the market will respond with multiple buyers, bidding for top price.*[153]

3 If the Objection is YOU!

You can't win 'em all, but you can learn from fails. So, ask 'em why.

uyers and sellers are like old, divorced couples. They may be able to share a room, but, given enough time together, are prone to become annoyed and/or bicker over the dumbest things. Since these dumb things may ruin a transaction before it even gets started, buyers and sellers are best separated at all times—until closing day.

Your seller is best represented by you, and not by their tendency to follow lookers around the house, pointing at things, and telling boring stories about why the drapes hang the way they do. You want visiting buyers to feel comfortable and to stay for as long as they want, because the longer a buyer lingers, the more likely he is to make an offer of purchase. But buyer comfort is fleeting when a seller is hogging the kitchen, making dinner smells, or children are splayed across the living room floor, playing video games, or Granny's zonked-out in the guest room, taking a late-afternoon nap. When a buyer's view of a property is encumbered by its occupants, the showing may be dashed and considered *not in the running*.

Some sellers get-it and get-lost, unseen at every showing, with no problems whatsoever. However, these same sellers routinely leave a family member locked in a cage, or sequestered behind a door with a DO NOT ENTER sign attached. The hammering howls of a mangy mutt and/or denied entry to any space on the property are each a disservice to your listing. For this reason, the pooch should take a hike, too. Simply tell your sellers to: *Get lost, and take your tail-wagger with you.*

Some will argue: *But, this is still our home, and our lives should not be so disrupted.* Perhaps so, but smart sellers tend to realize their plight is one of transition. Besides, showing their property in its best light is more conducive to receiving top price, and is therefore worthy of temporary discomfort.

The best plan is for all occupants to be absent during showings and inspections. The dog should either go with the seller, stay with family/friends, or join doggy day-care during the listing period. Mongrel removal is a hassle and an inconvenient expense. So, use this fact to fetch a better list price.[154]

How-To
SEND SELLERS
AND THEIR DOGS
DOWN THE LINE DURING SHOWINGS

A Serious How-to Manual with a Sense of Humor

Effort Meter

You're Gonna Need:
Property Evaluation
Note pad
Two Micro CMA
Calculator

tips

Unless its a ramshackle mess to begin with, de-cluttering and deep cleaning a property provides the greatest value bang for the repair buck. Fresh paint and basic functionality runs a close second.

Consider conducting professional inspections and appraisals prior to listing in MLS. When coupled with a corresponding price, these documents will inspire buyers to make offers with confidence and few contingencies.[156]

Σ   The primary repair rule is to keep expense under its resulting jump in value.

How-to
Suggest Repairs

Property will sell in any condition. However, many sellers desire a price higher than their current condition will bear. When you meet one of these, explain that while sellers should expect increased value from conditional repairs and upgrades, there is a limit. The highest values go to turn-key properties with contemporary, stylistically-neutral updates. Some sellers will want to go all the way—full update. Others will be modest in their efforts or will have a limited budget for repairs. When left to their own devices, these sellers are prone to over-spend on things that add little value, or modify with a personal style that is outta-whack with the current market. Your job is to help them decide how much to spend and what to spend it on.

1 Evaluate Current Condition
Walk-thru the property together and discuss functionally-defective items, aesthetics, curb appeal, and systems upgrades.[222] Make a list.

2 Calculate Repair Expense
Together, decide which jobs will be conducted by the seller and which jobs need professional attention. Help seller enlist contractor bids and determine the time needed to complete. Make a list of expenses for each potential repair item.

3 Numerate Value Added
Create two micro CMA:[140] one to reflect current condition and another to forecast the after-repair value. Overlay the itemized expense list from STEP 2. With their budget in-mind, use your judgement to determine which repairs will command the highest return on expense. Prepare two net-to-seller worksheets to illustrate your work.[135]

How-to
List *Before* Repairs Begin

You will meet sellers who wish to complete all desired repairs prior to signing with an agent. If you provide guidance to these sellers throughout the repair process, your failure to secure written agency is likely unlawful, as well as risky to your pocketbook. After all, your unsecured, free work now may be paving the way for another agent to list a turn-key property with a great price.

1 Sign Agency Agreement Now
Insist on an official, professional relationship, which begins with a written agreement. Attach a target list price and a stipulation that the property will not be displayed in the MLS or otherwise marketed until a target date is reached. As events unfold, amend this agreement as needed, such as if/when: repairs take more or less time than expected, the market value changes in the meantime, or the resulting repairs are insufficient to support the target list price.

Effort Meter

You're Gonna Need:
Agency Agreement
Special Stipulation
Plan of Action
Logical Argument

Σ   You should neither work for free, nor squander listing opportunities.

THE AGENT

When a seller interviews multiple agents, go first.

IT SEEMS TO BE STANDARD PRACTICE for experienced agents to ask a seller-prospect if they are interviewing multiple agents for a listing opportunity. It also seems standard for those same agents to request the last position, when the afore mentioned inquiry is answered with YES! The strategy here is that once the seller speaks with each competing agent, the last agent to speak has a distinct advantage of winning the listing by comparison, and by having left the freshest presentation in the prospect's mind.

I once implemented this strategy on a routine basis with great success, until an average, autumn afternoon. On that fateful day, I realized how risky it is to be the last agent interviewed. The day previous, I had secured the last position to interview with a seller whose listing was freshly EXPIRED. His intention was to meet with nine listing agents that day, beginning at 9 AM; my appointment was set for 6 PM.

As I was preparing statistical analysis of listing price, I received a phone call from an agent whom I knew. He told me not to bother

meeting with his new client that evening, for he had secured an exclusive right to sell.

I asked my friendly foe which position he had in the lineup. "First!" he proudly declared, "I always ask to go first. I then present a convincing listing strategy based on intensive statistical analysis, and I speak of it with such conviction that I am able to win not only the mind, but also the heart of my prospect. I then use a strong closing argument.

"My closing script today was, 'Mr. Seller, I know you have appointments scheduled with multiple agents today. I also know it's a gorgeous fall afternoon, and there are not many days like this left in the season. You should spend the rest of today outside, with your family. You and I both know that I am the right agent to sell your house quickly, for top dollar. So, let's not waste a moment of this beautiful day. Sign this listing agreement with me now, and my first service to you will be to call the agents you have appointments with and cancel them for you.'"

It worked for him. And it has worked for me too, ever since that crisp fall afternoon.

—◉ TRUE STORY ◉—

My Fave'rit Listings

Bright, gourmet kitchens and beds made of chiffon,
Sellers with reasons to split-town and move-on,
Fine, friendly neighbors with no misgivings:
These are a few of my fave'rit listings.

Counters and cupboards bereft of all clutter,
Stowed little doggies who give not a mutter,
Pre-qual'fied buyers come out ev'ry Spring:
These are a few of my fave'rit listings.

Rich, pro-shot pictures and warm, glowing colors,
Sellers referring me to their own mothers,
Full-price on offers with no continge'cies:
These are a few of my fave'rit listings.

When the deal busts;
When my glee sinks;
When I'm feeling plowed:
I quickly recall my most fave'rit listings,
And then I don't squeal so loud.

Effort Meter

You're Gonna Need:
Statistical Analysis
Target Price
Scripts
Courage

How–to
Provoke a Price Reduction

Some agents think a price change of any amount will cause activity on MLS hot sheets and syndicated websites. However, buyers and their agents have seen your listing ten or more times before; they weren't attracted by your price then, so a minute shift won't fool them now. The only responses such cheap efforts will inspire are under-the-breath chuckles, because they find your veiled attempt to address a major beauty flaw laughable.

If your listed price is not attracting offers, its reduction should be drastic and not wimpy because small price drops will not change buyer behavior.[144] However, price cuts sink sellers' hearts. So, to avoid seller gloom, set sail with the right price from the start.[154] If you missed that boat, then grab your homework,[150] and float your reduction by one of these three ways:

1 Automatically
Planning ahead prepares sellers for price-paring possibilities, so insert a price-reduction schedule into your listing agreements: after a pre-determined number of days pass without an acceptable offer, the price drops by a specified percentage or dollar amount. This way, an otherwise tough conversation is just another turning-point in your marketing strategy, and not a mishandling of your services.

2 Reasonably
Make an appointment to speak with the seller. Once you convene, redo STEPS 4-6 from your listing presentation.[196] In your discussion, include feedback from buyers and their agents.[242] Strongly advocate for the price you think will generate offers. Combine detailed market research with your best scripts and convince Seller to see the light.[153] Implement weekly updates to acclimatize sellers to market realities.[243]

3 Analytically
Sellers contemplating price changes have lots of questions:
« If I drop the price, won't the offers be at a lower price, too? »
« We don't have offers now. »
« Won't we look desperate to the market? »
« No, you will look like a reasonable seller. »
« What if the property still doesn't sell at the reduced price? »
« Then the price reduction was not big enough. »

If you haven't noticed by now, this book makes a big deal about putting the right price on listings.[154] This is because *price is the thing* that attracts buyers. All listings have competitors in the market. For the most part, each of these competitors share the same generalized features and are fighting with each other for buyer attention. Since the competitors are so comparable with each other, price becomes their differentiating factor. So, do your clients a huge favor and learn ways to convince them of this fact, as it will undoubtedly help them sell their property.

tips
Talking about a possible price reduction during your listing appointment will soften the blow when its time comes.

Get your scripts out. Acquiring a price reduction is a tough conversation.[215]

Once you reduce the price, call on previous inquiries and/or visiting buyers and announce your news; one of them may jump at it.

Provoking a price reduction sucks butt, so get it right this time. You don't wanna pucker-up for a second round with the same seller.

The market is like Goldilocks. It decides if the price is too hot, too cold, or just right.

yer seller sez:
I hate changing my price. I would rather price it right from the get-go. Whenever I see my agent coming, I always think she's gonna say: *Let's reduce.* Now, I hate her face!

Σ Listings that do not attract reasonable offers are not reasonably priced.

How-to
Exhort a Listing Extension

Three things will prevent property from selling during its first listing period: either the listing period was too short, no one noticed it was FOR SALE, or it was over-priced. If your listing period was for at least double the AVG. DOM, and it was listed in the MLS, then price was—*for certainty*—the culprit. Regardless of why it expired, you have lost time, money, and reputation to its cause. Before allowing exhaustion or embarrassment to silence your voice, gather your wits, and show the seller why you are worthy of another try.

You're Gonna Need:

Proof of Effort
Market Research
Change of Strategy
Self-Assuredness

1 Show Your Work

Call the seller at least a week ahead of expiry, and make an appointment to meet in-person. Once you arrive on the scene, show proof that you have been working diligently by giving to them:
- the names of every person who inquired about the property during the listing period. Indicate whether the caller was a buyer, agent, or nosy neighbor, and the number of times you spoke. Include phone numbers, email, and any other bit of relevant information.
- the total number of inquiries, categorized by how they were alerted to the property (MLS, yard sign, online ad,..)
- the total number of showings, and which ones were repeats.
- all marketing efforts, including internet analytics, MLS click rates, print-outs of internet ads, and the number of marketing package downloads.[234]
- sign-in sheets from open houses.[240]
- written feedback from buyers and their agents.[242]

2 Discuss a New Strategy

If you repeat the same stuff that you did last time, then your listing will probably expire again. Therefore, you need a new marketing strategy, which begins with a price reduction.[202] Use your trusty valuation skills to draft fresh market research,[150] and present it to the seller with care. In addition to a new price, discuss adding some new market exposure, such as new photographs (especially if the season has changed).[231]

Your listing agreement should contain a clause with similar verbiage: *If, within _____ days after listing expiry, Seller makes contract to sell Property to any person made aware of Property during Broker's listing period, then Seller will pay commission to Broker, so long as Broker remits names of all inquiring persons to Seller prior to listing expiry...*

If this is your case, then you should provide that list of names to your seller at the time you discuss listing extension. The best play is to explain this clause to sellers before they sign the listing agreement. Don't worry; most think the clause is fair. Plus, when they know its there ahead of time, sellers will not feel ambushed when you mention it at expiration (or anytime thereafter).

tips

Your expiry meeting is a good time to revisit any past offers that were turned-down. Suggest re-opening dialogue with those buyers, addressing the issues that stalled previous negotiations.

If Seller will not improve the price, maybe she will improve the condition.[200] Suggest simple fix-ups like staging, minor repairs, and generalized clean-up.[226]

During your expiry meeting, show Seller the statistics for *your* average listing. Include the average number of inquiries, showings, and offers that you typically receive. The comparison may motivate your client to try a different strategy this time.

Because a new listing gets a new listing number in the database, some say that when you extend a listing, you should also re-list it from scratch with the MLS. However, this effort is wasted without a new price to match.

Agency agreements that expire while your client is under a P&S contract automatically extend through closing. But should that P&S contract suddenly terminate, then so does agency.

If the seller refuses your change of strategy, consider walking away after the listing expires.

Σ   Second chances are given to those who earn them.

THE PROSPECT

When said with conviction, an austere argument will garnish an agent a higher-than-average prospect-to-client conversion ratio.

WHEN I WAS NEW to real estate sales, real property appreciation was climbing at record rates. It seemed everyone was an agent, and houses were selling fast. So, I decided upon a prospecting method that was largely under-utilized: direct mail of postcards to out-of-state owners.

My postcards were homemade, large, yellow cardstock with bold font and a clear message: *Real estate values have surged dramatically in the last decade, with an average of 10% growth per year, over the last three years. Call me today for a free valuation of your property.*

For every one-hundred postcards mailed, I received five to ten phone calls. After fielding the initial call, gathering contact information, property features, and address, I would schedule a return call upon conclusion of my homework. Preparing for the return phone call included a full, detailed market analysis through MLS data and public record search, and a drive past the subject property to get a better idea of topography, condition, and the surrounding neighborhood.

Although I had a well-formed opinion of the market through studied statistics, as well as several sales in my first few months, I was still a bit uncertain of my skills. This uncertainty was obviously apparent in my dialogue with astute prospects, because the average phone chat went something like this:

"Hi, Mr. Prospect. *Um*...I'm calling you back. After doing my homework on your property...I think its worth is about, *uh*... one-hundred fifty-three thousand, or *uh*...

maybe as much as...*um*...one-hundred fifty-five thousand dollars. So, *um*...what do you think of that?"

The average response to my hesitancy was, "Thanks for your work. I'll let you know."

My conversion ratio of calling prospects to actual listings was about one in twenty, which was about one listing per month. Worse yet, shortly after our phone chat, many of my prospects listed with another agent. Those were to be my listings! I had made those sellers aware of the market, I had informed those sellers of their values, I had put forth the effort, but I was not reaping the commissions.

I quickly realized that these outta-state prospects did not have allegiance to any particular real estate agent, instead they were listing with the agent who commanded the most esteem and confidence. My dialogue was not delivered with certainty; it was rather quivered, with hesitation and timidity. Not only so, but I was failing to incite action on the part of my prospects. I decided to change my approach: from now forward, I was to speak with authority and always ask for the sale.

The leap was a natural one: my opinion of value was founded upon known principles, and my efforts were thorough. I needed to explain my work in a non-apologetic manner, standing by my assessment of value and my method for converting that value into dollars.

The very next prospect was my guinea pig, and I delivered the news to him with confidence, "Mr. Prospect, I have concluded my work on the value of your property.

(continued)→

"In doing so, I have visited the property and seen its setting. My opinion is based upon comparison of similar properties that have SOLD in the last sixty days. The value of your property is approximately one-hundred forty-five thousand dollars. Based upon the current, average days on market and the average SP/LP ratio, a listed price of one-hundred fifty thousand should fetch you the previously-quoted sales price of one-hundred forty-five thousand dollars within thirty days of listing. You should know that my clients love me because I work hard and communicate often. I charge seven percent commission and I'm worth every penny. Share your fax number with me and I'll have the listing paperwork sent to you within an hour."

There was silence on the line, which felt to last for days. Suddenly, the prospect said, "Well, okay. That sounds fine with me. My fax number is..."

From that day on, my conversion ratio increased from one listing per month to four or five, and the only thing that had changed was the way I spoke my words. We all have opinions, but some are more valid than others; so long as your opinion comes from a place of diligent research, you should state that opinion with conviction, and say it like you mean it. Your pocketbook will thank you.

❧ TRUE STORY ❧

THE ROBOT

Keep the robot on the dance floor, and away from your presentations.

WHEN I WAS FIRST LEARNING to deliver scripts, I memorized all seller objections and all possible responses. At the time, I was concentrating on FSBO listings, which require heavy script work.

Many FSBO prospects told me that I seemed to have an answer for everything, but they didn't feel comfortable with me. I even had a script for this brush-off: "You should seek comfort when picking-out a new sofa; when picking an agent, you should seek an aggressive salesman who will bring you top price for your real estate." —OR—"Few people are comfortable around a bulldog like me, but all people are happy when that same bulldog is on their team."

While these scripts earned me adoration, I was still not earning their signatures on agency agreements. So, I performed my entire listing presentation (replete with objections) for a friend. She had the same response as most of my prospects: "You obviously know what you're talking about and you seem highly capable of performing the job, but something is *off*," my friend explained. Then, she added something new, "Say it all again, but this time, pretend you're making it up as you go along, as though the thoughts are coming to you for the very first time."

She was right: I was a cold robot. Once I slowed-down and warmed-up, my listing intake increased dramatically.

TRUE STORY

Mr. Seller, You have Five Options

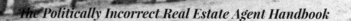

For reasons financial and/
or emotional, the occasional
seller will dawdle with
indecision, wrestling with
the notion of alternative
choices in his to-list
or not-to-list dilemma.
Ease his impasse by
explaining that all
owners have the same
five options:

1 Live There

Your home provides shelter from storms and a place
to clean your body; use it for its intended utility.

2 Sell for Value

Match price to condition and it will sell quickly;
it works every time.[154]

3 Rent for Value

Match the monthly ask to condition and it
will rent quickly; it works every time.

4 Foreclosure

If you've stopped paying the mortgage, taxes, and
insurance, and cease to maintain the condition, someone
is likely to take it away from you. When the pressure's on
and you choose to not decide, you still have made a choice.
Believe me, your sofa isn't gonna look good on the front lawn.

5 Burn it Down

Strike a match and watch your troubles chase your
memories, as each are engulfed in flames of despair.
Supposing you have insurance (and avoid fraud charges),
the structure will be rebuilt, and these five options will be
again staring you in the face, begging your decision.

Chapter 4 Quiz

Before showing property to a buyer, what first must that buyer show you?

1
- a) presentation
- b) pretext
- c) pre-qualification
- d) pre-approval

Why should you conduct buyer presentations in your lair?

2
- a) because you can control the environment
- b) because it sets the tone
- c) because that's where you store your toys
- d) all of the above

What is the primary purpose of conducting a needs analysis?

3
- a) to thoroughly define a buyer's property search
- b) it convinces a buyer to sign an exclusive agency agreement
- c) to seek a buyer's commitment
- d) none of the above

What is the preferred method of disclosure?

4
- a) some things must be written, but other things can be verbal
- b) complete, clearly-described, in written format
- c) it depends on who you represent in the transaction
- d) any of these will work

Why should you pre-qualify a seller?

5
- a) to discover how much money the seller has
- b) to see if the seller will pay your fee
- c) to get the seller started on the paperwork
- d) not one of these are right

Why should you present your posse to prospects?

6
- a) because they are paying you to do so
- b) because they are an extension of your service
- c) because they are good at their jobs
- d) all of these reasons are right

Which gets sellers most excited about a forthcoming listing appointment?

7
- a) your agency checklist
- b) your pre-listing package
- c) your commission schedule
- d) your jelly bean prescription

Why should you firmly argue for your normal commission fee?

8
- a) because you're worthy of the fee you charge
- b) because you ain't no jive turkey
- c) because it demonstrates your ability to advocate
- d) each of these are correct

What is the primary reason sellers (and dogs) should stay away from buyers?

9
- a) they sometimes make bad smells
- b) they sometimes make bad noises
- c) they sometimes make buyers feel uncomfortable
- d) none of these seem right

When should you walk away from presentations, electing to not sign?

10
- a) whenever their goals do not match your abilities
- b) whenever you cannot agree on your fee
- c) whenever they seem like a giant pain in the ass
- d) all of these are a good cause

Find the best answers throughout this chapter and on page 323.

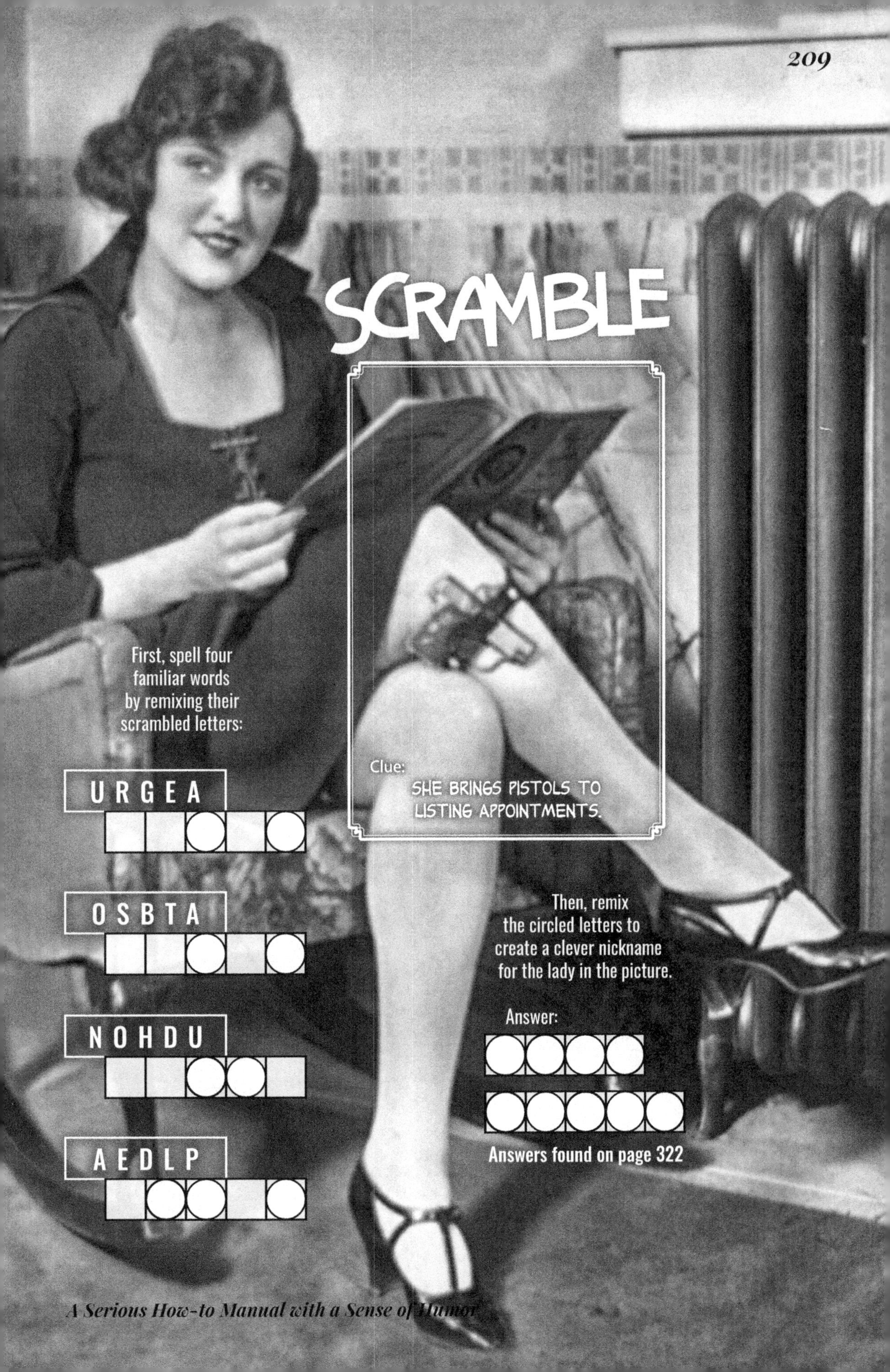

SCRAMBLE

First, spell four familiar words by remixing their scrambled letters:

URGEA

OSBTA

NOHDU

AEDLP

Clue:
SHE BRINGS PISTOLS TO LISTING APPOINTMENTS.

Then, remix the circled letters to create a clever nickname for the lady in the picture.

Answer:

Answers found on page 322

A Serious How-to Manual with a Sense of Humor

Undoubtedly, people hire agents because they need someone to help them buy and/or sell real property; they think the agent they've hired knows what they're doing, so when it's your turn, be the advocate they need by going outta your way to fulfill your promises.

To foster advocacy, this chapter is meant to show the reader how to represent clients with earnestness and gusto.

CHAPTER FIVE
AGENCY

Your Client Comes First

Once you engage in agency, your needs come second.

BY FARRAH THE FIDUCIARY

AGENCY BEGINS AT THE SIGNING of an agreement and ends by one of the following events: fulfillment of the agreement (typically, the successful closing of a transaction), expiration of the agreement, breach of the agreement, mutual termination of the agreement, death of the broker or client, insolvency or bankruptcy of the client, the broker's loss of license, or (for listings) destruction of the subject property. Before and after the term of agency, you may treat future/past clients as anyone else in the world. But during agency, real estate agents are legally-required to provide clients special duties, collectively called fiduciary care.

While the particulars of these special duties vary by state statutes and court decisions, a common definition runs throughout: *while acting as a fiduciary, an agent must place her clients' needs above all others, including her very own.* To be more specific, fiduciary care is generally composed of six duties: disclosure, skilled care, loyalty, confidentiality, obedience, and accountability.

Disclosure: an agent must provide all information that may affect her client's ability to make reasonable decisions. This duty includes giving advice on value[150] and price,[154] explaining customary practices,[036] obtaining public records, and recommending third-party counsel for advice outside the scope of a real estate agent's expertise.[042]

An agent's duty to disclose to clients is far greater than an agent's duty to disclose to all others.[180] To do so, discuss with clients the pros/cons of each pending decision, until they understand the ramifications that each choice may bring. As well, be sure all contract parties are aware of who represents whom and the duties owed by each, to each.

Skilled Care: an agent must perform the basic tasks of her job with competence. Incompetent agents should only engage in agency with the assistance of tutelage[043] and/ or her client's written disclosure.

Loyalty: an agent must not engage in secret profits or otherwise act in ways to profit from client dealings, except as disclosed prior to the agency relationship. In this way, a fiduciary cannot represent buyer and seller at the same time (AKA dual agency), nor act as purchaser nor seller, nor be related to any of these parties, unless the client is fully briefed and agrees in writing. In other words, no other relationship may supercede a client's interest.

Confidentiality: an agent must not divulge information that may jeopardize a client's ability to bargain. This means a listing agent should not tell others that she thinks her listing is over-priced,[266] nor should a buyer's agent apologize when presenting a low-ball offer.[257] In some states, the duty of confidentiality never ends.[036]

Obedience: an agent must obey all lawful instructions given by her client. This does not preclude an agent from arguing with her client, but once heard, she must obey.

Accountability: an agent must account for all client funds in her trust and keep her client informed throughout the relationship.[243] Further, agents must present all offers,[256] regardless of format or timing, and must not discourage offers at any time before or after her client enters PENDING status (unless, once again, her client gives written instruction to not present).

The provision of fiduciary care is a big responsibility and one worth being paid to undertake. Therefore, before entering into an agency relationship, an agent is wise to first explain to her potential client all mandated and elective duties being offered, and then secure equitable compensation in exchange. Because once agency (and its mandated duties) begins, an agent may not seek to further enrich herself. Although fiduciary care is required by law and carries penalties for those who neglect clients, a commission guaranteed at closing provides agents the greatest impetus to uphold their duties. 🌳

How-to Clean-UP in Real Estate

The prospect of financial freedom is a major attraction of hopeful agents. Their goal is achieved by converting clients into closings, over & over again.

The hardest part of this equation is prospecting for new clients. To shortcut the system, a smart agent re-uses the same clients, over & over again. However, a client will not allow himself to be re-used if the agent is a crappy one. For this reason, agents who get the job done properly, who go outta their way to provide *the greatest* possible service, who forever act as a true fiduciary, who exhale advocacy with every breath, and who do the things they say they'll do, have clients who not only **insist** on being re-used, but often and freely give glowing referrals. And you can sweep that to the bank.

Effort Meter

You're Gonna Need:

Informed Opinions

Scripts

Genuineness

Respect

tips

You serve your client, not the other way around. However, you are not a servant, so don't speak like one.

If you believe a client wants to act in a manner detrimental to their interest, ask them to sign a document that states you advised against their action. This practice covers your ass, while illustrating your strong objection. Always discuss these situations with your broker.

Scripts allow you to present information in a direct, clear, and complete manner, making for effective and efficient communication.

caveats

As a human, you will make mistakes, but don't let that hold you back. So long as your opinion is informed and earnest, you will do well by clients.

Make sure clients know that you'll never act in unlawful or unethical ways, regardless of whomever it may benefit.

Don't be silenced or intimidated by those who speak with an authoritative tone. If your client actually knows better than you, then why did he hire you?

Σ Make sure your clients understand that you will always follow their direction, but only after stating your well-informed opinion.

How-to
Speak with Clients

If you say the right things, at the right times, you will summon grateful clients and a high client turnover rate.[063] Always remember: its not just what you say, but how you say it.[008]

1 Set the Tone

Establish your role, your client's role, and the guidelines for mutual communication at the first meeting.[168] Define your hours of operation, protocol, and likely events to come. This step lends clients comfort, by removing some of the uncertainty that accompanies a new relationship.

2 Have an Opinion

At every turn of the sales process, you should have an opinion on how to proceed next. When facing a decision, supply clients with *all* available choices and the pros/cons of each choice. Then, state your case (your opinion of best choice): make it clear, concise, and easy to understand.

That being said: form your opinions from facts,[038] but stick to your role. Do not make definitive statements that supercede your real estate sales license. Defer questions that fall outside your expertise to actual experts—even if you were that expert in a past career.

3 Be Respectful of Their Opinions

At times, your client will have an opinion—*on an important matter*—that differs from your own. Handle their objections by method.[052] When you disagree, don't say: *You're wrong.* Instead say: *I disagree, and here's why...*

You and your client may not always be simpatico to have a successful relationship, but you must always consort on how to proceed next. To further your accord, mutually agree on which information to disclose in the MLS and during discussions with buyers/sellers/agents. Seek Seller approval of all your marketing efforts (listing copy, etc,..).[234]

4 Use Scripts[046]

Once ironed-out, your presentations should be the same, every time. This consistency affords you a standardized level of service and will prevent you from forgetting any details or pros/cons. Always be comprehensive, and give them your best effort.

5 Skip the Sugar-Coating

Your client deserves to know the truth of *every* matter. Therefore, convey messages from outside parties accurately. Find the right words to precisely tell them the happenings surrounding their transaction, but don't spare their feelings just to be a nice guy. Yes-men are ugly creatures, so speak with conviction, and when you mess-up, fess-up. You're not trying to make a friend; you've been hired to do a job. Note: STEP 5 advocates neither cold nor callous attitudes or actions, rather transparent conduct, handled with graceful certitude.[310]

How-to Have Tough Conversations

S ome of your most challenging chats will be with clients, and some will be on behalf of clients. Either way, there will be tough conversations ahead. Ignoring a thorny issue will only cause it to fester, potentially putting you and/or your client in a nasty headlock later. Therefore, it's best to not shy away from arduous encounters, but to grapple with them right away, before moving forward. Of course, you don't want to needlessly ruffle feathers, so following some guidelines will hopefully minimize their emotional response. To start with, keep a hold on *your* emotions. Speak in a direct manner, and be nice about it. If you're at fault, then come forward honestly, but don't apologize for things that are beyond your control. Be prepared for the discussion, and remain focused throughout. Bring a proposed resolution to the issue, and present it with reason. An example: suppose you're newest listing reeks of cat pee. The stench obviously has a negative impact on the property's value, so you have to discuss it. Broaching the subject according to the above guidelines, you might say, "You're hiring an agent to represent you, which sometimes entails telling you things that you might not like to hear. The fact is, all homes have a smell. Since a *good* smell is subjective, neutral smell has more value than non-neutral smell. That said, my nose tells me that a cat lives here, and buyers will notice, too. To maximize our value, we need either a neutral smell or a list price that matches the cat." Then together, wrestle with options for each course.

A Serious How-to Manual with a Sense of Humor

Effort Meter

You're Gonna Need:

Lock Box Key
Needs/Wants List
MLS Datasheets
Pen or Pencil

tip
There becomes no chance of locking a house key in its property if that key never enters the property. Leave the house key outside (best practice being to put the key back into the lock box before entering the property). Leaving the key outside will prevent you from standing in the yard, dialing a locksmith, looking like a buffoon, while your clients look-on with disdain. After all, if you lock a key in the house, what other kind of bone-headed mistakes might you make during the transaction?

caveats
Before showing unlisted property, get written permission from its owner.

If you discover someone sleeping, showering, or otherwise occupying the property without knowledge of your presence, get outta there immediately. Don't create a potentially hazardous environment by startling a property's occupants.

Keep your personal bias at bay. The buyer's specific needs/wants rule the day. Voice your opinion as their advocate, not as though you're the buyer.

How-to
Show Real Property

To the outside observer, a buyer's agent is little more than a cab driver with house keys. While this may be true of some, a good buyer's agent is a curator of listed homes. Follow these steps to do it right:

1 Preview[223]

When you show property that doesn't match your buyer's needs/wants,[174] you look mighty silly. Plus, pictures never tell the entire story (nor do they come in scratch 'n sniff).[131] Therefore, previewing each property before showing it is the best practice for mitigating surprises and for maximizing your buyer's time; it's great service.

2 Let Them Finish

If the property is being shown when you arrive, then wait your turn outside. A buyer and their agent should enjoy privacy during a showing, so they may speak openly about the property, and their strategy to acquire it. You should expect the same privacy during your showings. For this reason, when you're showing property, and a buyer/agent/owner/neighbor or any other person arrives on-scene, politely ask them to wait outside until you have finished.

For safety and security, modern, electronic lock boxes are designed to capture an accessing key-holder's information. Should there later be an issue of theft or vandalism, you don't want to be the only agent on-record as having accessed the lock box that day. Therefore, always lock all doors/windows, then place the house key back inside the lock box after showing—even when another agent is waiting to show. Explain your reasoning as security; only dubious agents will complain. If the waiting looker is a lone buyer, tell them they need an agent (or the owner) to go inside; it's a conflict of interest for you to show the property to another party (especially if your buyer is interested).

3 Announce Yourself

Even when you believe the property is vacant, first knock on the door *and* ring the bell, *then* open the lock box. Once you open the door, announce yourself by yelling: *Real Estate! Here we come!* or *Open Sesame!*

Your declaration of entry will prevent potential occupants from being taken by surprise. Startled people are apt to act abruptly, creating potential danger for you and your clients. To mitigate the likelihood of catching someone with their metaphoric pants down, call every listing agent before you show their listing—even for properties marketed as VACANT, SHOW ANYTIME.

4 Dress the Property

So that your buyer may see the property in its best light, turn on the lights, open the blinds, and close the toilet seat lids. Before leaving, make certain to return everything as found.

Lock all doors and windows. If you arrive to find the property unsecured *in any way*, call the listing agent and report your findings. If the returned instructions are to leave the property unsecured, request written instructions, via text message or email, delivered to you before leaving the property. This precaution may prevent you from being blamed later for theft or vandalism.

5 Tour It
Walk through the property, pointing-out its features, and answering Buyer's questions.

6 Review It
Once Buyer has sufficiently toured the property, convene on-site (in a comfortable setting) for a formal review. Turn the property's MLS datasheet over, exposing its blank backside, and record the date/time. Ask Buyer if the property meets his needs/wants. Record his answer beside the date.

Go through each need/want and validate its presence or absence within the property. Take note of any discrepancies between Buyer's words and the actual property condition. Next, ask Buyer to list specific pros and cons of the property's features (conditional aspects). Ask which features he likes the most and which features he likes the least. Point-out any features that Buyer fails to mention, ensuring all aspects of the property are reviewed.

7 Nickname It
With Buyer's help, choose a nickname that will distinguish this property from all others and record it on the back of the MLS datasheet. This nickname will be forever spoken when discussing this property in the future, so be deliberate in your choice. Be creative, selecting a name that is both obvious and unique to the property. Don't use the street or neighborhood name because such monikers are not specific enough; they're easily forgettable.

Property nicknaming is a fun practice which makes future conversations simple. When it's done right, you and your buyer will be able to recall this specific property months (or even years) from now. Remember to keep the nickname unique to the property. It won't serve its purpose if another (shown) property shares the same "unique" identifier.

Examples: if the property sports a prominent decor, then *Butterfly Cottage* or *Henhouse* or *Party Pad*. If the property possess a memorable feature, then *Swing Set* or *Birdbath* or *Chef's Dream*. If the property boasts a landmark view, then *Big Oak* or *Garden Lot* or *Water Tower*.

8 Rank It
Once Buyer has seen three properties, pull-out the MLS datasheets/reviews. Ask Buyer to rank each property: 1, 2, 3. Record the rankings on each corresponding MLS datasheet. From then on, after each subsequent showing, ask Buyer to rank the freshly-toured property. Always keep the 'top three' in a lofty position, for comparison.

Effort Meter

You're Gonna Need:

Ears

Eyes

Acute Observation

Intuition

tips

Listen-up for not only what Buyer is saying, but also *the way* Buyer is saying it.

Often times, buyers will have difficulty deciding between two or more properties. In these cases, your acknowledgement of their inadvertent buying signals may serve helpful.

Ultimately, buyers decide which properties to buy, but there's nothing wrong with pointing-out their obvious interest.

Some buyers will linger at all showings. This is usually a sign that they either are not picky, or are generally indecisive. They probably need a nudge and some direction.[219]

Some buyers will do their best to deliberately squelch buying signals. This is usually a sign that they don't trust you.[294]

Σ   Buying signals are the natural (and often unconscious) result of a person being really, really stoked about the thought of purchasing a specific property.

How-to # Recognize Buying Signals

Some buyers will not be forthcoming with their thoughts; however, your on-site observations may reveal the truth they conceal. To pick-up what they're putting down, watch for the way they:

1 Ask Questions

Everyone expects buyers to ask questions about properties and the purchasing process, in general. However, a buyer is showing specific interest when he suddenly asks lots of questions, in detail, about a specific property, its FMV,[128] amenities, neighborhood specifics, financing specifications, and/or about the offer process.[252] Often times, Buyer will ask you to repeat previous answers. All of these are buying signals.

2 Linger

Buyers who spend a long time at a property, or sit-down on a couch to look-about, are conveying buying signals. Same goes for when Buyer has a change in attitude/mood from normal to anxious/excited, or shows increased energy. Long pauses in conversation, as Buyer looks around, are sure signs that Buyer is thinking carefully and specifically about this specific property. For an average-sized property, more than fifteen minutes stay is a typical sign of interest.

3 Choose Their Words

When buyers speak as though they have already purchased the property, it's a strong buying signal. Buyers will speak about promising properties by identifying the purpose of rooms, arrangement of furniture, repairs they would make, how they'll spend their time, and otherwise "measuring for drapes." When a buyer really likes a specific property, these statements will increase in scope and frequency. Their voice may rise in volume and quicken in speed as they become excited.

When your buyers are coupled, listen to the way they speak with each other. Listen for agreement or disagreement over specific features. Listen-up for when one begins to make an argument of strong advocacy. Don't take sides, but definitely take notes.

4 Seek Validation

When a buyer likes a property, he will often wish to seek validation. He may ask if you like it (over and over again). He may want for his influencers to visit, such as a spouse, parents, children, or trusted friends.

5 Return Visit

It may seem obvious that buyers wishing to return to a property are showing interest. However, sometimes a buyer will want to return so that he may directly compare it with another property. Use these opportunities to help your buyer decide.[219]

How-to
Help Your Buyer Decide

Purchasing real property is a big deal for most buyers. As a result, some will second-guess themselves and others will seek reassurance in the form of external validation (to confirm their thinking is right). Regardless of his ability to carefully choose, present a decision-making system to your buyer—you'll each siphon a sense of ease from it.

1 Discuss Strategy

Before visiting any property, have a chat about what might happen in the field. Ask things like:
- *What if you absolutely love the first one we see? Will you make an offer that day or will you feel like you need to see more?*
- *If there are multiple offers on the property you like, are you willing to make your initial offer a competitive one? Are you willing to pay more than list price, if necessary?*
- *What is the absolute latest date you can close? What if we don't find a property that meets your exact needs/ wants by that deadline? Will you choose to not purchase or will you choose to edit your needs/wants?*

2 Acknowledge Buying Signals[218]

When in the field, don't shy away from pointing at doting buyers, and saying things like: *I can tell you* (love/hate) *this one. Now tell me why.* Open and on-going dialogue will allow them to deliberate aloud, fostering either confirmation or modification of their needs/wants.[174]

3 Keep a Top 3 List

After visiting ten-plus properties that adequately match his needs/ wants, ask Buyer to choose between the top three.[216] Encourage him to make an offer on his favorite one. If he balks at your notion, suggesting instead to keep looking at more properties, ask: *At what price is this "the one"?* Then propose an offer at that price. If Buyer bristles again, don't push the issue. Buyers who respond to this type of nudging are usually ready to decide, but just need a bit of encouragement.

4 Make a Suggestion

Based upon all you know about your buyer, from the essence of his needs/wants, to his buying signals in the field, and through analytical discussion of each visited property, select the one you think best-fits the buyer. State your case with confidence, then invite your buyer's reaction. When you take a stand, your buyer will (usually) either agree with you or select another property as his favorite, then vigorously argue its merits. The result is typically one whereby Buyer makes a decision.

When all else has failed, and Buyer continues to languish in decision mire, present a "lucky" coin to flip and suggest fate be dictated by the flick of his thumb.

Effort Meter

You're Gonna Need:
Needs/Wants List
Top 3 List
Vigilant Observance
Strategery

tips

Once he has visited several properties, it may sometimes be revealed that your buyer's stated needs/wants do not match his reaction to the realities of the market. When this occurs, either adjust the properties you select to show as you go, or formally sit together and revise his needs/wants list.[174]

If Buyer suggests visiting properties that do not match his needs/wants, remind him of this fact. If he insists, then show a few, and if the result is wasted time, remind him of *this fact* the next time.

When you find yourself saddled with a buyer who won't decide after dozens of showings, consider a referral to another agent.[341] Sometimes buyers need the personality of another agent to elicit an offer and sometimes they'll never decide. It's up to you to know when to say when.

Before deeming a buyer flaky, consider the preparation and guidance you've offered.[294]

If you only want to pay a significant discount from list price, then we'll have to limit our search to only significantly over-priced properties.

Σ The purpose of showing multiple properties is to systematically narrow the choice to one.

Effort Meter

You're Gonna Need:

Subject Property
Inspectors/Contractors
Internet Connection
Investigative Eye

tips

People sometimes make mistakes, so verify all information supplied by the seller and listing agent. Whenever possible, go to the source for accuracy.[038]

Determine your level of participation in clients' due diligence, then supply a checklist to buyers, outlining their responsibilities.

Through written disclosure,[180] recommend inspections and surveys, and make buyers aware of warranties. Further, your buyers should attest to not rely upon your due diligence assistance, but to instead verify your efforts.

Seek and fully examine disclosures and utility expenses from Seller. Ask questions to clarify concerns.

Regardless of separate loan contingencies, smart buyers satisfy all lender requests during due diligence.

Prior to making an offer, estimate the expense of expected repairs and write your offer with these blemishes in-mind. During due diligence, compile bids from contractors for accurate planning.

Σ   While Buyer is ultimately responsible for performing due diligence, his agent may assist by gathering documents and recommending vendors/resources.

How-to
Do Due Diligence

Buyers sign P&S contracts with assumptions in-mind. With embedded contingencies meant for the examination of these assumptions,[252] the due diligence contingency stands as the catch-all, standard-bearer. During its reign, the discovery of negative changes in value may allow a buyer to re-negotiate or cancel his purchase altogether. Aid your clients' investigations by showing them where to look.

1 Haunt the Subject Property
Tell your buyer to walk the neighborhood a few times, alternating weekdays, weekends, and time of day. Does the air smell bad? Do dogs bark? Is there a flight path overhead? Are the neighbors noisy? Drive the area, inspecting shopping choices. How is the commute to work?

2 Perform Inspections
Encourage buyers to hire a home inspector for identification of generalized blemishes, like roof leaks, HVAC and appliance malfunctions, and structural weaknesses. Then, encourage specialist inspectors to further investigate found issues, to scrutinize unpermitted structural additions and code violations, and to search for the presence of termites/bugs, lead paint, radon gas, asbestos, and other hazardous conditions.

Buyer and Agent should attend the last thirty minutes of the primary home inspection for a 'show & tell' with the inspector. Buyer should bring a list of questions, and record any complicated answers. When their plans include repairs, buyers should now draft that plan on paper, complete with contractor bids/reviews, deadlines, and expenses.

3 Investigate the Home Owners Association
Provide the service of gathering documents regarding the home owners association (HOA), including all written covenants and restrictions. Speak directly with HOA representatives, and attempt to answer the following questions: what amenities are provided? Is there an initiation fee? How much are dues and when are they collected? Are special assessments coming soon? Is the HOA managed professionally or by the owners? How solvent is the organization? Are the subject property's fees in arrears?

4 Examine Online Records
Learn to use the county's web services, as lots of due diligence may be performed there. Gather an information package, including the sources of your findings, and instruct Buyer to verify your work. Include in your report: flood and school district maps, recorded surveys, tax reports, current zoning (plus proposed changes), easements or other encumbrances, and the proximity of any sex offenders. Depending upon your buyer's need, answer land use restrictions, like: may owners operate a business on the property? raise animals? grow food? store large equipment? use hazardous materials? What is the adjacent land use now, and its potential future use?

How-to
Take a Buyer from Contract-to-Closing

Effort Meter

You have helped your buyer locate the right property[219] and secure it by contract.[260] Now, your job is to get him safely to the closing table. To do so, create checklists from the STEPS below, then execute each task as prescribed by time.

1 Organize Activities

Begin by reviewing the P&S contract.[260] Create (and then email to all parties) a timeline of its events, with expiry dates/times for each contingency. Update the timeline and re-send it if/when the P&S contract is amended; this practice will mitigate future disputes.

Other first-day activities include your oversight regarding: earnest money deposit, MLS status change to PENDING, and scheduling the closing date/time with closing attorney or escrow company. Then, ensure the buyer has scheduled inspections and surveys in a timely fashion.

2 Strive for Loan Approval

Email the purchase agreement to Lender and request weekly updates. It is not uncommon for lenders to request additional reports throughout the transaction term. Some of these items will be borrower-specific and others will be property-specific. Encourage Buyer to remit requested documents quickly, as his loan acquisition is arguably the most important aspect of a successful closing. Hold yourself to the same account regarding property-specific requests.

3 Mind Contingencies

Do not wait until near-deadline to address contingency matters. Instead, schedule all research and inspections with plenty of time to contemplate and/or re-negotiate the P&S contract (if necessary).[266] Help your client complete his due diligence,[220] order the appraisal with its contingency deadline in-mind, and ensure that contractual repairs are completed on time.[268]

4 Recommend Insurance

Through written disclosure, encourage your buyers to acquire hazard and title insurance policies and a warranty on the home's systems. Houses have been known to burn-down during closing ceremonies, so buyers are wise to insure themselves prior to settlement.

5 Go-to Closing

On the day of (or just prior to) closing, visit the property, and with client in-hand, strut-thru a walk-thru.[222] Then, procure the settlement statement and review it together. Answer Buyer's questions and instruct him to bring photo identification to the signing ceremony; arrive early and confirm the settlement documents have not changed.

tips

When you represent the seller, check with the buyer's agent to confirm timeliness of the tasks on this page. When the buyer is unrepresented, you should become heavily involved in this process.

Remind Buyer to notify friends, family, and the postman of his changing address.

During this time, Buyer should change the account holder with current utility companies, and/or choose new ones.

Create two, different checklists—one for you and Buyer, each. Include required and elective tasks that you both must undertake to ready yourselves for closing.

If you decide to outsource contract-to-close work,[286] you are still responsible for its proper achievement. Create a checklist that will remind you to check-in at important deadlines.

Make certain Buyer has been briefed by Lender and Closer on the precise funds required to close and the form those funds should take (certified check/wire-transfer), but do not involve yourself with the transfer of funds.

Σ Feeling halfway home, your buyers-under-contract rely upon you to get them there.

Effort Meter

You're Gonna Need:
Your Buyer
P&S Contract
Inspection Report
Seller Disclosures

tips

It's a good idea for the seller and/ or the seller's representative to be present during the walk-thru. This way, found issues may be addressed immediately.

Before your walk-thru, ask the seller's agent to confirm Seller has officially changed her address.

If the P&S contract has a survival clause, then a failed final walk-thru inspection should not dissuade the buyer from closing. In this case, Seller is obligated to correct contractually-bound condition issues, whether before or after closing. A buyer who holds-out closing until repairs are made may himself be in default.[268]

STEPS 1 & 2 are a guide to checking-out any property prior to making an offer.

Σ Buyers who make a final, last-minute inspection of their soon-to-be home arrive at the closing table with confidence.

How-to
Strut-Thru a Walk-Thru

The purpose of a final walk-thru is to ensure the property is delivered in its agreed-to condition. Failure to offer this important service may be detrimental to your buyer. So, the day before (or hours before) the transaction is finalized, go to the subject property with your buyer and take a walkabout.

1 Walk the Property

Ensure the house is still standing and that (if the P&S contract dictates) it's broom-clean—meaning the property is clean, but not sterilized. All the seller's personal belongings should be gone from the dwelling and grounds, unless otherwise stated in the P&S contract. Likewise, check that all fixtures remain, and have not been down-graded or replaced.[134] Look for an empty mailbox, freshly-mowed lawn, clean gutters, and fresh paint.

Small defects in condition, like chipped countertops, broken cabinet drawers/doors, and general cleanliness are more noticeable in vacant properties. For comparison, when you find an issue, check with the inspection report to determine the condition at that time.

2 Check Its Systems

Boiler plate P&S contracts state that the subject property must be delivered in the exact same condition as when the P&S contract was signed. Therefore, you should make certain this is the case, as sometimes systems will break just before closing.

• Flush all the toilets and run the hot water to ensure the water is on and the water heater is heating water.
• Run the dishwasher.
• Light the stove/oven.
• Check the air conditioner, furnace, radiators.
• Check windows for cracks, and make sure they open/close properly.
• Open and close doors for proper latch and lock.
• Check lighting.
• Check plumbing for leaks, and that all interior/ exterior spigots are functioning.
• Check all appliances for functionality.

3 Check Contractual Repairs

If Seller agreed to make repairs, then ensure those repairs are completed exactly as outlined in the P&S contract. If the seller is obligated to provide receipts of the repaired work, then secure those receipts at this time.[268]

4 Resolve Found Issues

If the walk-thru uncovers a defect, missing fixture, incomplete (agreed-to) repairs, or Seller has left personal property, take pictures and detailed notes. Then, report issues to seller's agent immediately.

SEVEN REASONS TO PREVIEW PROPERTY

223

Earn your keep: before taking buyers to look at properties, go take a look by yourself. Because you just never know what you might find there.

1 It's great service. 245
2 You can't smell pictures. 131
3 To eliminate non-matching properties. 174
4 Chatty sellers divulge stuff. 199
5 It saves your clients' time. 070
6 It's your job. 060
7 Because you're always prepared. 223

A Serious How-to Manual with a Sense of Humor

Listing Agents Sell Listings

Sellers pay listing agents big bucks to sell their properties. In exchange, these clients deserve more than a half-assed attempt.

BY TRUSTEE TRUDY

AGENTS REPRESENTING SELLERS are typically called listing agents, and agents representing buyers are often called *selling agents*. These somewhat-confusing monikers are leftovers from the days of sub-agency, when buyers were unrepresented by their escorting agents. At that time, selling agents represented listing agents and—by extension—the seller's interest. In this way, agents bringing buyers assisted listing agents with the selling of listings.

The residual sentiment of these titles/roles has left some thinking that modern-day buyer agents do the selling, when the opposite should be true. These days, buyer agents represent buyers, and in doing so, do not care which property a buyer buys. Instead, their intent is for their buyer to get the best price/terms possible. This reality (and the mandated, fiduciary duty of skilled care)[212] leaves the responsibility of selling completely to the listing agent. But don't fret; the successful selling of a listing is simple: just make it easy to find and hard to look away.

To make your listing easy to find, advertise it through every reasonable channel that buyers (and the influencers of buyers) may look. These channels include online portals, such as the MLS, web syndication, classified ad websites, and social media; signage, in the form of posted flyers,[233] FOR SALE/directional signs, and printed media; and word of mouth, by speaking with neighbors, agents, and prospects. Make it hard to look away from your listing by providing overwhelming evidence to justify its price. This can be done by advertising a rational price/condition ratio,[154] cogently-supported by fantastic photos,[230] compelling copy,[232] and a comprehensive marketing package.[234]

For the sake of effectiveness and efficiency, begin with lots of research and get to know the subject property well.[138] Discover its best features, then prepare it for market.[226] Utilize these features to advertise it far and wide,[239] and advocate for its sale at top price.[236] If an unrelated person, organization, or website wants to advertise your listing, then you should let them do so. So long as the price and condition are accurately portrayed, their efforts are essentially free advertising and you should encourage that.

Stay involved throughout the selling process by tracking all market activity and feedback from lookers.[242] Because a key aspect of selling at top price is to encourage and invite all offers,[153] manage your sellers' expectations with consistent updates,[243] and adjust their listed price as needed.[202]

Despite your best efforts, a listing's top-paying buyer is likely to come through another agent. However, when a listing agent is proactive, he may find *the buyer* himself. To these ends, some listing agents are incentivized by double commission to find an unrepresented buyer. While there is nothing wrong with the lure of bonus commission to urge hustle, your fee schedule should not place payout over client needs. To retain your loyalty,[212] think-through and negotiate all possible scenarios before agency begins, then do everything you can to find the top-paying buyer, regardless of the commission schedule payout.[181] Further, since you already represent the seller, avoid dual agency when attracting an unrepresented buyer. Instead, explain agency and offer an agent referral.[341] If the buyer chooses to forego an agent, get him to sign a customer acknowledgement disclosure.[180]

The bare minimum in selling effort is to pick any old price, post a sign in the yard, and some pictures in the MLS, then kick-back and wait for a "selling" agent to do the rest. Providing the bare minimum is okay when your client agrees in writing, but be warned: when mixed with hope and prayer,[237] the bare minimum often leads to expiry and an agent holding his hat in hand.[203] ❧

How-to Market a Tacky Listing

1 Price it Right
A price that matches the condition is always the first and foremost important part of any listing. So, lead with your price,[154] and let the pictures follow.

2 Spotlight the Tacky
Instead of trying to hide its funky features from photos, embrace the chintzy decor. Bring it front and center; it is what it is.

3 Give it a Nickname
Without being rude about it, derive a name from the mood the property exudes. Utilize this namesake in your marketing efforts; make it a thing.

Don't fret the client sporting a lil' bit o'flair or pizzazz. And don't be the goofball who disparages his inventory, either. Instead, make it fun while helping your spunky seller off-load those righteous digs. Betcha!

A Serious How-to Manual with a Sense of Humor

Effort Meter

You're Gonna Need:

Checklist
Discerning Eye
Deadline
Willing Seller

How-to
Prepare Real Property for the Marketplace

When it comes to preparing a listing's condition for market, the seller bares most responsibility. So, provide your clients a list of chores and insist the list be completed prior to going to market. Attention and care in the following areas will put your best listing-face forward:

1 Declutter
A closet stuffed to the gills looks small. Cluttered countertops give the illusion of not enough storage. Excessive knickknacks are distracting to the eye. Rearrange furniture to give rooms better flow and appear more spacious. The property is on display, not its contents.

2 Remove Personal Items
When a house is personalized, buyers feel like they're intruding into another's den. Instead, mimic a model home. Pictures of the wedding, fridge magnets from the Jamaican honeymoon, and the thousand frames of Junior's grin gotta go. Put the personalized stuff into storage, including religious and political artifacts.

3 Pack Away Seasonal Items
When it's cold outside, pack-away tank tops and swim trunks. In the summertime, box-up bulky sweaters and heavy coats. If your seller is short on space, neatly-stacked boxes in the basement or garage are an acceptable look. If your seller protests, remind her that she will be moving soon, so she might as well pack now.

4 Clean
Give everything a deep cleaning. Pay special attention to bathrooms, windows, and the kitchen. Degrease the kitchen, as cooking oils will build on every surface, including vent hoods and baseboards. Steam the carpets. Return the smell to neutral.

5 Enhance Curb Appeal
The façade is the first thing buyers see in pictures and in-person. So, give lookers a reason to get outta the car and into the house. Mow the lawn and trim the edges. Pressure wash the house, driveway, and walking paths. Clean the gutters and plant some flowers. If necessary, repaint or replace the mailbox, and make sure it's standing straight.

6 Quick Fixes
Sticky doors, loose drawers, and wobbly toilet handles are symptomatic of an unattended property. The presence of these blemishes cause buyers to wonder what might lurk behind the walls. Stop ill feelings before they start by ensuring proper functionality of all fixtures. And, if they're feeling froggy, fresh paint is an inexpensive, do-it-yourself fix that can go a long way towards neutralizing visual and aromatic conditions.

tips

Property preparation is your job to oversee, not to execute. So, get your seller's commitment to a deadline, but don't pick-up a broom.

Unless a listed home is vacant, bedrooms should have beds and dining rooms should have a table. Otherwise, buyers may view these spaces as offices or playrooms.[156]

If your seller is *decoration*ally-challenged, hiring a professional stager may be to their advantage.

Create a standardized "property prep" checklist for repeated use. Customize this list for each client, so you can give them a homework cheat sheet (pun intended).

If your seller protests such changes, remind her that it's temporary and that she's moving-out anyway. Property preparation is for the buyer's benefit, which is the same as the seller's.

Before each showing: open interior doors and window shades. Turn on lights. Lock-up or remove valuables.

Often overlooked, sellers should also spend this time notifying their lender of a potential sale and clearing-up any title issues.[273]

Σ   Putting makeup on the face of your listing—*before the big date*—will increase its value in the eyes of buyers.

How-to
Spotlight Property Features

Effort Meter

Each and every property has peak features. Even a cinder-block shack with mud floors might boast a hot tub hideaway, just beyond a backyard grove. Since you cannot rely on other agents to know exactly what your listing offers, you must advocate its perks. Ensure all lookers leave with a full understanding of what they just saw; otherwise, if you don't point it out, it may go unnoticed.

Now imagine a buyer, standing in the living room of your latest listing, checking-out the merchandise. He, and all others at his side, are a captive audience. More than likely, all they know of your listing are its price and its online photographs. Use their presence and their curiosity to your advantage by enlightening these buyers in one of two ways:

1 Be There for Every Showing

Some listings are so special that they require a personalized, guided tour by the listing agent. When you get one like this, leave-off the lock box and make the showing by appointment only. Arrive early and walk-thru the property with the buyer (and their agent, if they have one), declaring every nook, cranny, and facet of fancy.

2 Hang Postcard Snippets

Type-up and print-onto postcards the characteristics of your listing. Include descriptions of prominent features, not-so-prominent features, and some catchy phrases. Then stick your notes to walls, mirrors, cabinets, appliances, windows, and inside drawers and closets. To catch their eye, use a postcard color in stark contrast with the surface attached.

Additionally, set-up an agent station somewhere on the first floor. In this space, display the flyer,[233] marketing package,[234] and a greeting (or instructions, if necessary).

The use of humor will have lookers scanning every inch of the place, searching for the next note, becoming familiar with the property in the process; see, it's working.

Sample Postcard Snippets

- **Kitchen:** Gas range is a chef's dream; Big enough for ten cooks; Want appliances from this century? Put it in your offer.
- **Basement/Cellar:** Notice that smell? Me neither. Dryer than The Sahara in here!; Two living rooms? Are you kidding me?
- **On Windows:** Double-paned glass saves you money; You could play football in this yard; Look! You can see (landmark) from here.
- **Bathroom:** Has everything on your list; This closet is big enough for all your skeletons; (on the mirror) This place looks great on you!
- **Random:** Gas logs warm your bones; (on thermostat) Zoned heating & cooling; Breathe easy. Ducts cleaned (give date); New lighting fixtures; Think of the memories you'll make here.

You're Gonna Need:
Peak Features
Postcards
Catchy Phrases
Charm

tips

Anticipate the questions buyers may ask and questions buyers might not think to ask. Then answer those questions.

When a buyer feels informed, that buyer is more-likely to draft an informed offer, which is more-likely to pass contingency periods and close on-time.

All houses have blemishes; don't try to hide them, as blemishes will surely be discovered eventually. Instead, repair blemishes, accentuate them, or spin them in a positive light. Buyers appreciate honestly and prefer to buy from honest people.

Don't forget to spotlight the property's grounds, neighborhood amenities, and nearby attractions.

The very presence of your person, or of postcards in your stead, make a visit to your listing a memorable one.

When drafting its postcards, assume buyers know nothing of your listing.

When done properly, buyers and their agents will be sure to comment that your postcards are a big help.

Σ   To effectively advocate a listing's sale, become an omnipresent voice within its walls.

1 Price

The right price is the first step to being an attractive listing.[154] Think of a property's price-to-condition ratio as a hotness knob.[153] The hottest listings are realistic in their assessment of value, promoting the appearance of a hassle-free closing. Without the right price, pictures and posture mean nearly nothing. Buyers are judging you on price first, so put your best number forward.

2 Pictures

Take pictures of your beauty like its the Taj Mahal. Capture high resolution images at great angles;[230] find all its unique details and tell its story.[231] Don't try to hide a property's condition with missing or misleading photos. Instead, pick the right price, and then show them what they get for their money.

3 Posture

Take your price and your pictures, and broadcast them to anyone with eyes and ears.[236] Get complete and accurate information into the MLS, because this data is the likely source for thousands of third-party websites, drawing details for display on their sites.[239] Buyers flock to these syndicated places, so don't leave out any specifics.

Real Estate Beauty Contest

Price, pictures, and posturing sell properties. Look your best in just three simple steps.

A Serious How-to Manual with a Sense of Humor

Effort Meter

You're Gonna Need:
Camera
Tripod, Lights & Level
Photo-Editing Software
Time

How-to
Put Forth Perfect Pictures

Always remember that most realty shoppers are looking online for their *future home*. Therefore, images that provoke an emotional response will get the most clicks. This means your picture-posting prowess will inspire more butts through the door when it stirs buyers' wanton desires.

1 Get the Right Equipment

You do not need an expensive camera, but you do need to know how to use it properly, so study-up on its particulars. Acquire a wide-angle lens to fit more in, a tripod to steady your hand, a bubble level to even the scenes, and lights on stands to avoid dark images.

2 Set the Stage

Instruct your seller to thoroughly clean, de-clutter, and stage the house,[226] including windows, mirrors, counters, and refrigerator tops. Put away sink items like soap and sponges, and add a focal point with color, like fruit bowls and flowers. Put-down toilet lids and add fresh towels. Make the place look good.

Unless you list in Alaska, execute your photoshoot during daylight hours, at times of great weather. Reserve nighttime photos for showcasing dramatic exteriors. To do so, turn on all interior and exterior lights, then shoot at dusk (you may have to add interior lighting for balance). Take front elevation shots early or late in the day, whichever has the most sun facing the front door.

3 Compose & Capture

Turn-on all interior lights, turn-off your flashbulb, and use the extra light you brought, which should always be thrown at an angle, never head-on. Set your camera to low-light and activate high dynamic range (HDR). Then, turn on grid lines, and practice the *rule of thirds*, which states that images are more interesting when a focal point is positioned at these grid line intersections. Remove furniture from foregrounds to create the illusion of more space. Keep vertical lines (door frames, windows, corners) vertical. Zoom with your feet, not the camera, and try to capture a sense of depth.

Regardless of lighting conditions, the human brain automatically adjusts to see white color, but cameras cannot perform this trick. To avoid color clash in your snapshots, scroll through the camera's white balance settings until white objects appear as white on your screen. Then, take 100+ pictures, with multiple shots of each room/feature, from various angles and perspectives.[231]

4 Edit for Excellence

Find some simple software to finish your work. Adjust contrast, color balance, and then crop to MLS dimensions, but never edit your images in misleading ways. Appropriately tag each, identifying the image subject and the subject property. Then, caption and sequentially-number the best ones for MLS upload.

tips

Quality photographs are the result of staging, composing, and lighting.

When seasons change, update your pictures.

Your cell phone camera probably takes acceptable photographs, but lacks wide-angle capability.

Your MLS may limit listings to images of real property only. Therefore, your pictures of surrounding views or local attractions should go into online galleries and your marketing package.[234]

Use drone or satellite images to show setting and topography.

In vacant listings, stage kitchens and bathrooms with towels and flowers.

There's no shame in hiring professional help to get great pics.

listing photo no-nos
• Selfie by reflection or shadow
• Flash from mirrors & windows
• Portrait-orientation images
• Fisheye lens distortion
• Time stamps
• Dark pictures
• Clutter & Blur

Σ Buyers drool over quality photographs of interesting subject matter, so lure them into your listings with some superior snapshot skills.

How-to Tell a Picture Story

Narrate your listing through
the logical sequencing of MLS photographs.
Begin with the front elevation,
then proceed through the front door...

Indoors

Show off rooms from floor to ceiling, but not too much floor/ceiling. Avoid pictures that show just a bed, or just wall corners by a window. Feature some close-up shots of interesting faucets, hinges, door knobs, stained glass, ceiling fans, lighting fixtures, moldings, windows, and countertop/flooring textures. Demonstrate functionality through the display of organized spaces like closets, cabinets, pantries, storage rooms, and pull-down stairs.

Angles & Perspectives

Draw viewers in with dynamic shots of your prized listings. Get the good stuff by taking most pictures at belt-buckle height. Small rooms are best captured from high or low corners, while overlooks from balconies, staircases, and decks add character. Squat in the corners of backyards to capture outdoor glory.

Outdoors

Finish your slideshow with exterior highlights. Show patios/decks, gardens, birdbaths, out-buildings, firepits, outdoor living and cooking areas, playgrounds, and tree house fixtures. Avoid cars, garbage cans, and neighboring properties.

Tidbits

The MLS imposes a picture limit on listings, so to fit more in, splice two or more corresponding images into a single collage. Floor plans and lot surveys get buyers swooning. Avoid holiday decor, unless you plan to reshoot your listing when the season changes.

A Serious How-to Manual with a Sense of Humor

Effort Meter

You're Gonna Need:

Subject Property
Objectivity
Creativity
Thesaurus

How-to
Write Listing Copy

Most real estate buyers are not shopping for a house—they're searching for a new place to live. So, sell them with a story that includes the facts, but *not just the facts* alone. Instead, strive to evoke emotion and invoke action. Because when you bore your audience with arid drivel, their reaction is likely to snore.

1 Think Unique

What makes the subject property like no other? What are its standout features? Take notes, but do not simply repeat what the pictures already show. Instead, tell the things that pictures cannot, like how the ventilation system has been recently cleaned or a new roof was added yesterday.

2 Be Truthful

Do not exaggerate your claims. Be sure all advertised data is complete and accurately represents your listing. Spotlight the good, but do not try to hide the ugly parts, as buyers will see your listing in all its glory once they arrive to view it in-person. The wrong foot is not a springboard to earnest offers, so if your listing has some really ugly parts, mention a reflection in price. This way, buyers will not feel bamboozled by your portrayal.

3 Write a Headline

Address your audience. Ask a question or answer one.
*Knock, knock: Dream home calling!—*OR*—Looking for sweat equity? You've found it!—*OR*—Impressive finishes will wow your guests.*

Twinkle, twinkle, little home—It only needs your garden gnome.

Know, know, know this quote: This home is bright and clean. Breathlessly, Beautifully, Truthfully, Certainly... Its price will make you scream!

4 Use Sizzle Words

Adjectives and adverbs are your copy-writing friends. Your skillful use of words will cause your listing to leap into life. To do so, place the reader inside the property with terms of depiction.

Large spaces are grandiose, colossal, jumbo; small spaces are humble, quaint, modest; and lots of storage is abundant, expansive, generous. Talk about copious cabinetry, bountiful basements, and cavernous closets. A second sitting room is a parlor. A tiny lawn is mitigated maintenance. A private setting is an oasis amidst the pines. A big bathroom is a retreat from life to recharge the soul.

5 Provoke Action

Mention a promotion, like special financing and/or a link to your marketing package.[234] Otherwise, invite your readers to see your listing in living color. Prod them from their couches with *Now Showing! All Offers Welcome!* and/or *Priced to Sell!*

tips
The goal of listing copy is to stand-out from the crowd, so break-out that old thesaurus and blow-off its dust.

There are plenty of books and websites dedicated to real estate headlines and advertising copy. Creatively-challenged agents are encouraged to seek these resources.

Write your listing copy once, then use it for the MLS, website syndication, online yard sales, flyers, and marketing package.

caveats
Hyperbole is fair game, but do not overstate reality.

In the old days, character space was limited, so real estate ads became notorious for featuring hard-to-understand abbreviations. The internet age affords agents more space, so spell-out all words to avoid buyer confusion.

DO NOT WRITE LISTING COPY IN ALL CAPS!

Only advertise real property, as your state may require an additional license when brokering personal property.

Σ A listing with an honest, emotional appeal will garner more interest than one spouting a mere checklist of attributes.

How-to
Concoct a Listing Flyer

Buyers often engage in whirlwind days of house shopping, seeing up to a dozen, one after another. For some, this experience causes property details to morph and blend together. So, to keep your listing in-mind and in-contention, provide its lookers a reminder of their visit with an old-fashioned, low-tech handbill.

1 Paper & Design

The flyer size in common usage is a full sheet (8½×11 inches). A half sheet (5½×8½ inches) is a novelty, costing half as much. Printing on both sides of a quarter sheet (4¼×5½ inches) is offbeat and costs half as much, again. Whether it be landscape, portrait, or square, choose the shape and size of your creation. Block-out sections for page elements (images, copy, contact info), and include *white space* to let these elements breathe, bestowing order and readability.

Choose no more than two typefaces: one for the headline (a legible matching of the subject property's personality) and the other for copy (being a serif or sans serif that complements the headline typeface).

2 Images

For quality print jobs, convert each picture to 300 pixels per inch (PPI), then resize its dimensions to match the page (for times when the camera image is 10×8 inches, but the flyer image is 5×4 inches—or vice versa). Place borders around your cropped pictures to avoid the appearance of pictures floating on the page. Then select a few more (or not) as supplemental images. Depending on your design, images may comprise the entire flyer, bleeding off its page, or arranged in a geometric pattern.

3 Copy

Condense the listing copy you've already written into a bulleted list of highlights.[232] Grab attention with a bold headline and a call-to-action. Include the property address and the words FOR SALE, OPEN HOUSE, or something similar. Altogether, your listing copy should consume no more than a quarter of the page.

To include the price, or not to include the price? That is the question agents love to debate. The argument against price inclusion is one of buyer curiosity, whereby serious contenders are compelled to call the listing agent. However, to many, price exclusion may appear as either a design goof, or to suggest that the price is too expensive to mention. If you decide to forgo the list price from your flyers, then address the issue head-on with words like: *Current price quote when you call.*

4 Contact Info

In the bottom-right corner, stack just the essentials: your name, your brokerage name, phone numbers, email, and a (clearly marked) shortened URL or QR code that links to the property's marketing package.[234]

Effort Meter
(Lil' Bit, Some, Lots, Helluva Lot)

You're Gonna Need:
Desktop Publishing Software
Listing Copy
Perfect Pictures
Marketing Package

tips
To shortcut your time involved, use one of the many flyer templates from the internet. When you do so, choose one that follows the guidelines on this page.

For printing, use CMYK color scheme at 300 PPI and save your work as a PDF. For web publishing, use RGB color scheme at 72 PPI and save your work as a JPG.

Paper weights and finishes vary, so seek samples from your printer.

Photographs tend to look better on glossy paper, but a matte finish can be sharp, too.

caveats
As with all content you disseminate, proof read for typos, punctuation, grammar, and omissions. Be sure to follow state-mandated guidelines for real property advertisement.

Add a disclaimer to your flyers: *All of this information is believed accurate. However, it was compiled by humans and is therefore subject to error, so it cannot be warranted.*

You can share flyer expenses with your posse,[179] but if you include finance options, be sure to follow Regulation Z, from the Truth in Lending Act of 1968.

Σ An attractive handbill is a perfect way to leave the memory of your listing, long after its lookers have walked away.

Effort Meter

You're Gonna Need:
Digital Dexterity
Valuation Homework
Internet Cloud Access
Research Skills

tips

Think of your marketing package as the first volley in the purchase negotiation sequence yet to come.

Place a copy of your marketing package for permanent display at the agent station inside your listing. Include a note with words like: PLEASE DO NOT REMOVE *Full copy of this marketing package is available online. Take a flyer for details.*

Mention and link to your marketing package on the MLS, and on flyers with words like: *for disclosures, reports, and more,* CLICK HERE.

Once your listing sells or expires, remove its marketing package from the internet. Continuing to display its details may violate your agency agreement and/or license law.

Top three ways to expose your listing to the marketplace: 1) MLS listing (datasheet), 2) marketing package, 3) MLS listing syndication.

Incorporate a running footer with the property address, your name, brokerage, and phone numbers. This way, your work is branded to direct communication back to you.

Σ When you remove their doubt, buyers become encouraged to make offers.

How-to
Fashion a First-Class Marketing Package

You are the most-qualified person to speak for your listings. Since you cannot be present for every relevant conversation, a digital mouthpiece may be leveraged in your stead. To remove uncertainty (thereby encouraging offers), gather all the evidence buyers need to make an informed decision, then give it away for free.

1 Amass & Arrange

Compile and convert all pertinent documents to PDF format. Next, arrange your assertions into a logical succession of pages. Your preparation may include sensitive documents, so do not use a web-based tool to sort your work. Instead, download a PDF tool that will extract, merge, and re-order pages on your desktop. Then, save as a single PDF. Grant latitude to the following themes:

1. Introduction: Use your flyer as an overview of the subject property.
2. Table of Contents: This classy option will organize your structure.
3. MLS Datasheet: Show driving directions and property details.
4. Photos: Limit pictures to a few, with a prominently-displayed hyperlink to a photo file containing a hundred more.
5. Public Records: Include county statements of square footage, sales history, tax assessments, and a legal description of the subject.
6. Maps: Make your diagrams large and easy to read. Include one zoomed-in (to show lot dimensions) and another zoomed-out (to show the surrounding area). Also consider topography maps, satellite images, surveys, floor plans, and blueprints.
7. Other: Add school district info, nearby attractions/shopping options, amenities, and HOA bylaws/covenants/restrictions.
8. Disclosure Statements: Insert all relevant disclosure by Seller.[180]
9. Valuation Reports: Provide a quick explanation of value, with the inclusion of inspections, appraisals, CMA,[140] marketplace statistics, and finance options. Your goal is not to give an abundance of data, but rather a justification for the listed price. For investment properties, include historical rental rates, proforma income statements, and NPV analysis.[151]
10. Biography: Information about you and your brokerage should go last in the stack.

2 Upload & Link

You can easily share your marketing package with everyone in the world by uploading it to the internet. Choose a cloud-service website to host your file, then save its (very long) URL to your listing's private records. Next, visit specialty websites to shorten the URL and generate a quick response (QR) code. Save these links to your private records, too. This step makes it simple to post, email, and track your clicks.

Spread your links everywhere buyers and their agents may look: the MLS, flyers, your email signature, yard sign, social media websites,..

Why do so many people fancy themselves real estate
experts? What makes them so real estate savvy? Is it
because they are (or are about to become) property owners?
Most of these same people own a car. So, do they stand over
their mechanic, telling him how to turn the wrench?
Is it because these buttinskies have bought
or sold real property once or twice in
the past? I'm sure they've had plenty of haircuts. After
giving style directions, do they tell the barber how to hold
the scissors? Is it because real estate sales is so prevalent on TV and
in print? International politics frequents the news
feed. Do these folks feel qualified to
negotiate as special envoy on foreign concerns?
Is it because they mow the lawn, change air filters,
and clean the drapes, and in the process become
intimately familiar with their property and all its nooks and
crannies? The same is probably true of their underwear,
too. So does that make them qualified to lecture at the
semi-annual tighty-whitey waist band convention?
Would they tell a surgeon where to cut, a dentist
what to drill, or a garbage man when to
compress his haul? No, because they
trust that most people know
how to do their job. Their
real estate apprehension probably
has something to do with the horror stories
that circulate about **bad real estate
agents**, which have
resulted in the industry routinely
topping the list of least-respected
professions (along with lawyers and
car salesmen). The fear that
drives some to an
overbearing nature may
have something to do with the
average agent using average
skill to perform a task of
utmost importance to the
principals involved. So, instead of
hiring your college roommate's cousin,
or your boss's kid to sell your house,
carefully consider the agent you hire: choose one who
knows what the hell they're doing. The most successful clients are
the ones who align themselves with a great agent, then turn
that agent loose to do the job well.
But, what do I know? I'm just
a guy with happy clients.

the
Random
Rantings
of an
Angry
Agent

Effort Meter

You're Gonna Need:
Benevolence
Promotion
Persuasion
Fortitude

How-to
Sell Your Listings

Remember, Price + Condition + Exposure = Salability.[152] At this point, the subject property has a price and a condition.[154] To sell it, you must now expose that price/condition to the marketplace, *fully and widely.*

1 Annotate

Gather and record all the informative and interesting aspects of your listing, including warranties and public record documents. Then create a marketing package,[234] with its highlights upfront and an overwhelming amount of data to follow. Take great photographs,[230] and compose a visually-appealing flyer.[233] Use sizzle words in descriptive copy,[232] and develop a catchy phrase, unique to each of your listings.

2 Advertise

You never know from where buyers will come, so tell the world, in multiple ways, that your listings are FOR SALE.[239] Since a yard sign and MLS posting are just a base layer of exposure, make certain your listings are in wide syndication across the internet. Then create additional postings via yard sale websites, online videos, email blasts, social media outlets, digital photo galleries, and your agent website(s). Without the assumption that buyers will automatically find your content, place hyperlinks to these postings *everywhere.*

Post flyers in all places that seem appropriate and install directional signs at traffic intersections, guiding passersby to the subject property.

3 Advocate

It's hard to sell real estate from a desk, so be assertive with your actions. Start spreading the news and don't stop laying it on thick until the transaction is complete. Talk, talk, talk about your listing and promote it to whomever is willing to listen. Always sell your listings with a campaign of advocacy:

- On the first day of a new listing, darken at least five doors on either side and ten across the street. Pass-out flyers and open house invitations.[240] Dare your audience to choose your forthcoming buyer through their own personal referral.[108]
- Pick-up the phone and place calls to people you know, and to those who may be interested. Speak to fellow real estate agents, vendors, investors, and the seller's friends and co-workers. Seek targeted buyers for unique or special interest properties.
- Assume inquiring callers have no knowledge of your listing, and push your marketing-package download on each one.[234]
- Do what you can to get buyers inside the property, then to make an offer. Whenever someone shows interest in your listing, continue a dialogue until the day they say they are no longer interested.
- Vigorously pre-qualify buyers before your client becomes contractually-tied to one,[260] and then
- Continue to allow showings and entertain offers until the day of closing.[274]

tips

Expose your listings to the marketplace with extreme prejudice.

Track the results of each advertising channel. Spend more time and money on the worthwhile ones, and drop the duds.

When posting your listing to the MLS, fill all available data points with accurate info. Provide excellent driving directions. Never post to the MLS without pictures.

Be the catalyst that gets the job done, but remember that assertive action is not the same as annoying pester.

Within your marketing package, include every bit of data you have on your listing, leaving nothing to the imagination. Answer the questions they forgot to ask or didn't even know they had.

Make your flyers eye-catching with only pertinent details, plus a link to your marketing package. Post these flyers in your office window, at the seller's place of business, restaurant bulletin boards, and other public places.

Having a robust marketing package to share is a great reason for callers to share their email in return.

Σ   You (and only you) are the driving force behind the sale of your listings.

How-to
Bury a Statuette

Saint Joseph is the patron saint of home buyers and sellers. Some say that a statuette of Saint Joseph buried in the yard will quicken the sale of that home. If you wish to participate, follow these instructions:

1 Acquisition

The statuette you desire may be procured from the local MLS or Christian bookstore. The internet offers discounts on bulk purchases. Go with pewter if you're classy; plastic makes an economical statement.

2 Excavation & Internment

Using a shovel or garden trowel, dig a six-inch hole near the FOR SALE sign. For yards with grass, carve a divot, as you don't wanna muss the curb appeal. Stand Saint Joe on his head in the hole and face him towards the house. Replace the dirt and divot patch. Then, pat the ground with the back of the shovel, signifying to onlookers that you have finished the chore.

3 Prayer

Get on your knees before the burial site (you should already be in this position). Close your eyes and interlace your fingers. Depending upon your denomination, say one of the following prayers:

- Catholics: *O Blessed Saint Joseph, I have placed you in the darkness of ground, a place you will not enjoy. I pray that your discomfort will encourage your support for a quick sale of our humble home. Your internment is temporary, as upon the sale, with God as my witness, I promise to position you in a place of honor within our new home. Amen.*
- Protestants: *Dear God, please ask Saint Joe to encourage offers on our over-priced listing. Amen.*
- Agnostics: *Gawd, I hope this works. Aww... man.*

4 Reclamation

It is said that once the property sells, it will continue to change hands forever, so long as Saint Joseph remains in the ground. Since this would be rude to the buyer, retrieve your shovel on closing day. Go to the burial site (near the FOR SALE sign). Unearth the statuette and wash-off the dirt. Then, place the statuette on the mantle of the seller's new home and say a prayer of thanks.

5 Burial for Buyers

Buyers may try a variation. After presenting a purchase offer, go to the subject property and complete STEP 2. Then say one of these:

- Catholics: *O Blessed Saint Joseph, I have placed you in the darkness of ground, in prayer of the seller accepting our offer to purchase this humble home. Amen.*
- Protestants: *Dear God, please ask Saint Joe to make these sellers accept my low-ball offer. Amen.*
- Agnostics: *Gawd, I hope they don't arrest me for this. Aww... man!*

Effort Meter

You're Gonna Need:

Statuette
Shovel
Prayer
Hope

tips

This practice also works on condos and other dwellings without a front yard. Simply bury Saint Joe in a flower pot, placed by the front door.

Alloy-cast statuettes may be reclaimed by metal detector. Plastic ones may be harder to find.

If months pass without a sale, then Saint Joseph has let you down. Replace him with a statuette of Saint Jude (the patron saint of lost causes).

Instead of burying a statue, try pricing the property congruent with comparable sales.[154] It works every time! Plus, it will save you ten bucks and time on your knees.

Σ Sometimes a seller needs some inspiration and sometimes a seller needs a price reduction.

SPREAD EVERY LISTING...

Through the mandated, fiduciary duty of skilled care, an agent is required to attempt to sell her listings at top price, in the shortest time possible. To achieve this task, a competent agent insists upon a price that matches the property's condition, then she exposes that price/condition to as many eyeballs as possible.

FAR & WIDE

Statistically, the top-paying buyer is attracted when every potential buyer is alerted.[153] And since lots of buyers look online when shopping, your listings should appear on as many websites as is feasible, especially when doing so requires little time and money. *At the very least*, a listing should appear in the same places as its competition. In this way, listing in the MLS and its push-thru syndication to thousand of websites are—*by far*—the most effective and efficient ways to expose REAL PROPERTY FOR SALE to the largest audience.

However, the desire for privacy may induce some sellers to quietly market their property sans syndication, as a pocket listing or with a COMING SOON sign in the yard. If—*for whatever reason*—an agent's marketing strategy does not include listing in the MLS and/or web syndication, that agent is compelled (duty-bound) to disclose the effect that limited exposure will have on achieving top price in the shortest time possible.[236] Therefore, for the protection of client and agent alike, a limited-exposure strategy should only be implemented after an in-depth, pros/cons conversation, and written disclosure to follow.[180]

A Serious How-To Manual with a Sense of Humor

Effort Meter

You're Gonna Need:
Listing w/ Right Price
Advertisement
Sign-in Sheet
Enthusiasm

How-to
Throw a Kick-Ass Open House

The purpose of an open house is not just to allow potential buyers access to your listing, but also an opportunity to speak with them directly—so that *you* can do the selling of its features. Never forget: even if an individual looker is not interested, they may identify your listing as ideal for another, so seek their referrals.

Throwing a kick-ass open house may also provide several additional benefits, whereby you may: meet unrepresented buyers, meet future sellers that have yet to select a listing agent (who are now impressed with your open house prowess), add new members to your database, and have fun!

tips
Every kick-ass open house begins with the *Right Price.*[154]

Open houses fail for one or more of three reasons: 1) the price is too high; 2) the event is not properly advertised; and/or 3) the house is not open for enough hours.

Expand the customary two-hour open house time frame. Try noon til 6pm on weekends or on weekdays after working hours.

With a pen/pencil, write your name, phone number, and email at the top of each sign-in sheet. Your example will encourage subsequent signers to provide full details, too.

To assure a record of your day, say to all lookers, "Please sign-in for me, so I can show my seller that I was working today, instead of playing hooky."

Before your event begins, lock-away all valuables, medicines, and weapons.

The primary purpose of an open house is to get even more people aware of and talking about your listing. So, if you're gonna do it, do it right and make it count.

Σ When properly performed, an open house fosters a listing's sale and more (offers).

1 The Bare Minimum
Begin with the *Right Price.*[154] Next, make certain everyone knows you're throwing a party. Advertise on the internet, through the MLS, and with an email blast. You don't have to serve food, but you do need a sign-in sheet, lots of pens/pencils, an open house sign, and directional signs placed at nearby traffic intersections. To be eye-catching, attach balloons, strobe lights, or other moving object to your signs.

2 The Ol' College Try
Commandeer a large sign, electronic marquee on wheels, or other audacious landmark that will draw attention. Emblazon the words OPEN HOUSE onto this monstrosity and place it in the front yard of your listing. Then, beckon their entry by lining the driveway/pathway with pendant flags, all the way to the door.

Then, strap on your walking shoes. Knock on neighboring doors, granting everyone an invite and a plus-one. Hang flyers[233] and post directional signs on the eve of your event.

3 No Holds Barred
Being different is sure to garnish their notice. Increase attendance by including an attraction other than the subject property itself, then advertise your dual event with a fittingly-witty tagline. Ideas include, but are not limited to:
- Erect a bouncy-house in the front yard (with liability release forms) to lure people with kids.
- Employ a bartender or juggler to entertain guests (no clowns).
- Patronize the local art community and dress-up your vacant listings with wall hangings and/or sculptures.
- Host a continuing education (CE) class to get agents in the door.
- Hire a band to play the offer-writing theme song.
- Emcee a charity fund-raiser.
- Throw a wine and cheese party.
- Pay someone to cook hotdogs in the driveway (because everyone else serves cookies).

In the most flagrant of fashions, complacent agents can be overheard everywhere, espousing the myth that open houses don't work. Believing the practice a waste of time, they preach their phony notion to anyone willing to listen, including buyers, sellers, and the public at large. Their spiel is somewhat similar to "If you want an agent to spend her Sunday on your couch, watching TV, and serving fresh-baked cookies to your nosy neighbors, then call a blue-haired agent of yore." Hogwash! If you allow people to eat your lunch on a regular basis, then I can see why you would feel this way. Duh. It's human nature to be interested in the happenings of one's neighborhood, therefore neighbors will always attend open houses. However, when *only* neighbors attend, it's a sure sign the hosting agent screwed-up long before flying that first balloon. The fact is: an open door, widely advertised with *The Right Price*, will bring people in droves. But, without *The Right Price*, an open house in nothing more than thumb-twiddling downtime, interspersed by forced conversations with people seemingly astonished by the novelty of a floor plan slightly different than their own. Ha!

the Random Rantings of an Angry Agent

I love nosy neighbors and all the silly things they say. When you think of it, the neighbors are just people. If you look closely, you will notice that people usually know other people, and some of the people they know also know of other people whom the first people might want as neighbors. So, instead of shuttering in panic at the thought of yet another snooper darkening your latest listing, go and knock on their door a few days before the big event: your warm invite and a plus-one permit just might sell this sucker. Remember, you never know who knows whom, and from where your buyer may come. But then again, what do I know? I'm just the guy with a hundred people at his open house.

Effort Meter

You're Gonna Need:

Feedback System
Customized Questions
Earnest Request
Reciprocal Action

How-to
Get Constructive Feedback from Buyer Agents

The collective opinions of buyers rule the marketplace.[144] Reliable feedback from these buyers is helpful when tweaking a lackluster pricing strategy,[202] but to get your hands on their opinions, you must go through their agents. Be warned: some agents think giving feedback harms their buyer's ability to negotiate,[266] and other agents are too lazy to participate; however, plenty more are happy to oblige, so long as you make the task simple.

1 Create a Feedback Form

Some agents are turned-off by automated emails, so customize your questions to show personal involvement. You don't need to ask about price because offers (or the lack thereof) will answer that question. If you make their involvement too labor-intensive, you may get bupkis. Instead, ask only three questions, then invite further comments:

1. Does the property's condition match the buyer's needs/wants?
2. Which (one) property feature does the buyer like most?
3. Which (one) property feature does the buyer like least?

Remember that just like buyers, agents see lots of listings, so include a listing picture (or two) to remind them of you.

2 Systematize Requests

Automated feedback systems may be offered in your market through lock box/key providers, the MLS, and/or showing services. Choose one that allows your customized questions from STEP 1 and generates a statistical report of received answers. Feedback phone calls also work, but may be disruptive to buyer agents. Since they probably don't remember your listing, ask if you can text a link to your form. If you go with the telephone, be quick about it; you want fresh thoughts, but you should also let them finish with the day's showings first.

How-to
Give Constructive Feedback to Listing Agents

If you wish to receive, then you should also contribute. Regardless of your feelings otherwise, always report to listing agents hazardous or troublesome conditions like unlocked doors, vandalism, and water leaks.

1 Record On-Site Reviews[216]

At the conclusion of each showing, quickly discuss the property's condition with your buyer. Create a pros and cons list from which you may report feedback, but be careful to not compromise your buyer's bargaining position on listings still in contention.[266]

How-to
Keep Your Sellers Updated

Effort Meter

Your clients are entitled to know the happenings of their listings—*and they know it*. As a result, when they feel outta-the-loop, some sellers will become hypersensitive, calling you to hyperventilate each time a competing listing goes PENDING or a passing motorist slows to throw a glance in their direction. In the opposite extreme, other sellers will silently fume over your lack of communication, imaging you sitting on your hands or dedicating your time to other, more-favorable clients.

To keep everyone calm and well-informed, tell your clients of evolving market conditions[150] and of your efforts to sell.[236] To be effective and efficient about it, establish an update system and explain it to sellers as a feature of your service.[172] Otherwise, your clients will undoubtedly be uninformed, causing unnecessary stress and/or heartache to fester.

1 Commit to a Routine
Make seller updates a weekly task of your business.[064] Select a day to compile data and an hour to convey your findings. Monday mornings are preferred because weekends typically engulf the majority of a week's activities. Whichever day/time you choose, be sure your sellers know when to expect your communiqué.

2 Create a Report
Create a form to systematize the seller-update task.[070] For each listing, fill-in the form, draft a market activity report,[146] and attach other pertinent records. Make yours pithy and easy-to-understand with charts, graphs, and/or tables. Your update should include:

1. Subject Property Activity
   - Tally the number of showings, phone inquiries, web clicks, and open house attendees for the week and for listing-to-date.
2. Comparable Properties Activity
   - Show all properties newly listed (ACTIVE), PENDING, and SOLD.
3. Your Efforts to Sell
   - Report a timeline of everything you've done to expose/advocate the listing. Include your marketing efforts and conversations.
   - Show buyer feedback forms and corresponding statistics,[242] such as: 80% of lookers say the driveway is too steep, 60% say they like the large bedrooms best, 10% say the yard is too small.

3 Conduct a Briefing
Compose a quick *State of the Listing* speech. Then, either upload your seller-update to a web server or attach it to an email and send it to Seller the night before your oral briefing. The next day, telephone the seller and read your speech. Answer Seller's questions and discuss the coming week.

Regularly-updated sellers become accustom to market realities. So, until a listing attracts its eventual buyer, discuss a price strategy revision every third or fourth week.[202] Then, once under contract to sell, continue to update your seller on happenings until closing.

You're Gonna Need:
Listing Clients
Feedback Forms
Daily Log
Market Activity Report

tips
Preparing a weekly update is quick and comprehensive when you log your daily activities.

Weekly market research is a breeze when all your listings belong to the same niche.[042]

When your listing is not generating offers, use market reports and gathered feedback to alter your selling strategy.[154]

When the same objection is raised repeatedly, the seller is wise to address it with either a conditional improvement or a change in price.

Buyer feedback can be used to draft a reverse offer.[263]

caveats
Caution sellers to not place too much emphasis on a single opinion, but rather to take recurring objections to heart.

As the messenger of negative feedback, some clients may be gunning for you. Remind them that you are on their team and that all feedback/activity should be considered without emotion.[310]

Σ Sellers who sense transparency from their agent are more likely to trust that agent.

1 Knowledge

Know what you're talking about; keep learning and stay curious. Sometimes you won't have an answer, but you should always have the ability to quickly discover the correct way to proceed.[038]

2 Preparation

Keep clients ready for events and occurrences before those events and occurrences occur. Use your systems[070] to anticipate their next step. Make it easy for them with forms and other premeditated content.[073]

3 Strategy

Offer a customized strategy to buyers and sellers, based upon their unique needs. One size doesn't always fit all, so listen intently, then design a plan to get them exactly what they want and need.[174]

4 Honesty

Regardless of all other arguments, considerations, and circumstances, your transparency, frankness, and sheer sincerity builds trust with clients.[212]

5 Availability

Answer your phone, return emails, and be your client's Johnny-on-the-spot; show them that you care. If you cannot be available, provide someone who can. You cannot be expected to work twenty-four hours a day, but it should appear to your client that you are there for them at every step and during every freak-out.

6 Disclosure

Always provide disclosure to your clients so they understand (exactly) your role, as well as the pros and cons of each decision they face. Also, help your clients disclose relevant information to those they owe it. Disclosure is not just great service; it keeps everyone outta hot water![180]

6 steps to Sustain Superior Service

Chapter 5 Quiz

In reality, which gives an agent the greatest impetus to put clients first?

1
    a)   pride
    b)   the ethical code
    c)   love of the job
    d)   commission guaranteed at closing

When showing property to a buyer, what should you never bring inside?

2
    a)   MLS datasheets
    b)   the house key
    c)   children
    d)   all of these are safe to enter

Which of the following is the best way to help a buyer decide?

3
    a)   scold their indecision
    b)   only show properties that you like
    c)   keep a top-three list
    d)   flip a coin

Ultimately, who is responsible for a buyer's due diligence?

4
    a)   the buyer
    b)   his agent
    c)   the seller
    d)   all of these people

Which of the following is not a typical listing agent duty?

5
    a)   pre-qualification of buyers
    b)   struting-thru a final walk-thru
    c)   spotlighting property features
    d)   having tough conversations with clients/customers/agents

Which of the following is an acceptible listing photo format?

6
    a)   dark pictures
    b)   time-stamped images
    c)   blurry snapshots
    d)   none of these

Why should the neighbors be invited to your open houses?

7
    a)   because they know people
    b)   because they might teach you something about the property
    c)   both of these are good reasons
    d)   neither of these are worthy of entertaining nosy neighbors

Which is the best way to promote your marketing package?

8
    a)   a printed copy on the kitchen counter
    b)   uploaded to the MLS
    c)   via hyperlink on listing flyers
    d)   the best way is comprised of each of these

Why do some sellers know more about selling their property than you do?

9
    a)   because they've occupied the subject property
    b)   because they've sold real property previously
    c)   because they think real estate agents suck at their job
    d)   because they've watched too many real estate TV shows

Which is the best way to sell a listing?

10
    a)   match price to condition, then widely expose it to the market
    b)   wait for buyer agents to do the selling
    c)   bury a statuette
    d)   all of these are correct

Find the best answers throughout this chapter and on page 323.

Crossword | Keepin' It Real Estate

Answers on page 323.

...for the most part, anyway. This puzzle boasts 17 real estate specific answers.

Across

1 Talk, incessantly
5 Kiss
8 Exclusive claim, for short
10 Senior Smurf
11 Precedes a junta, often
12 Encumbrance
14 Party you can't crash
15 Bullets, for short
16 Terminate
18 Legal documentation of ownership
19 Buyer's decision
21 Pluralizing suffix for words ending: -ch
23 Yonder
25 Huffing it gives a high voice: Abbr.
27 Easter entrée
30 Hall of mirrors?
31 Vatican City, e.g.
34 Killer whale
36 Opposite of rent
37 Square footage measure
38 House without steps
40 Formerly
43 Goof
44 College deg.
45 Fish food?
47 Neptunium symbol
49 Story that may hold secrets
51 Spanish dwelling
53 Plunk or plop opener
55 Knight wear
56 The open version is sought by some buyers
59 A sailor's greeting
60 Cat call
61 Creek peak
62 Symbol for tin
63 Hyperbolic sine (trigonometry)
64 Ordeal

Down

1 Property valuation by agent, Abbr.
2 Pin place
3 With the stroke of __
4 Butch Cassidy was one
5 Old French coin
6 Hired goons
7 Chest thumper
8 Fractional ownership
9 Repeated response to, "Who wants ice cream?"
11 Pass along ownership, formally
12 Fill with cargo
13 Skull salute?
17 Beer sign brightener
20 Protection in battle
22 Viking carpenter?
24 Wells of science fiction fame
26 Second to last word of fairy tale
28 Mideast native
29 Fast food estate?
31 Listlessness
32 A note to follow so
33 Rake in, rightly
35 Tummy muscle
39 Crammer's concern
41 Real estate account
42 Canadian interjection
45 Taken the wrong way?
46 Quill companion
48 Balanced
50 Bermuda or Maui Waui
51 Property valuation by agent, Abbr. (not same as 1 down)
52 Refreshing reactions
54 Ultimatum ender
56 Ad coax: "__ __ __, call 1-800...": Abbr.
57 Buyers outcry at seeing "the view"
58 Singer __ King Cole

By its very nature, the offer and contract process is adversarial. This fact does not portend a contentious affair, nor does it signify that one party must score a knockout to be successful—it just means that its parties have differing goals. Because you (and your clients) will be entangled in your contracts for weeks or months at a time, the best negotiation strategy is always one that anticipates future likelihoods. Planning-for and then implementing such contingencies requires training, time in the ring, and (at times) some fancy footwork.

With these realities in-mind, this chapter presents offer and contract as a fluid process, showing the reader when to pull his punches, and when to take his gloves off.

Chapter Six
Offer &
Contract

Contracts 101

Plain and simple: a contract is whatever its parties want it to be.

BY THE STUFFY PROFESSOR

FOR STARTERS, the words contract and agreement are interchangeable terms, as each have the exact same meaning: the *mutual* promise of performance. A contract may be in writing, of verbal construct, or a combination of the two. It may contain as many terms, stipulations, and contingencies as its parties want.[252] It may be amended in any way,[260] as many times as its parties wish, and it may be destroyed, if its parties so desire.[276] In fact, a contract is whatever its parties want it to be.

The creation of a contract occurs only when one party makes an offer to another party, who, in-turn, accepts that offer without change.[260] In this way, a contract is the mirror image of the offer that created it, which is why this requirement is called the mirror image rule. Further, the parties must each have a full, *mutual* understanding of their agreement. Because this *meeting of the minds* must transpire, one cannot be tricked into buying or selling under misunderstood terms—the whole thing must be completely voluntary. Therefore, the conditions required to create a contract are nothing more than the mirror image acceptance of an offer between cognizant minds.

However, this basic contract is not good enough for your clients, so your job is to help them create *enforceable* contracts (ones with the force to legally hold its parties accountable), which come with additional, legal requirements. For the purchase/sale of real property, these requirements are:

1) The contract must be completely written and no parts may be verbal. 2) Its parties must be of competent mind when it was created and it must have a lawful purpose, free of fraud and misrepresentation. To further outline a meeting of the minds, real estate contracts include the seller's disclosure of known property defects and a declaration of marketable title (one that is free of burden/encumbrance and is otherwise free to sell). 3) The contract must explicitly identify: the property by a legal description beyond reproach (fixture list, metes & bounds, lot & block), and its parties by name and title (being buyer(s) and seller(s), collectively called principals). 4) It must clearly describe *mutual* consideration (something of value, traded for something else of value). In this case, consideration is real property traded for real property, personal property (money), or a combination of the two. 5) It must also contain a date of consummation (the closing date) and 6) the signatures of its parties.

When a contract contains each of these enforceable elements, its parties are said to be bound by it. In other words, a party to a binding contract is one who may be forced by a court to perform specific contract duties, including purchase or sale. To avoid the hassle of court at times of breach or non-performance, the parties of enforceable contracts often settle on the forfeiture of money. *Important note: earnest money (held by whomever the parties agree) is **not** an element of enforceability.*[255]

Because the exchange of property does not occur immediately, its agreement to do so is called an *executory* contract (one in which its parties have agreed to perform tasks and duties before closing). Only once each of these tasks and duties are fully performed and ownership changes hands, is a contract *executed*—not before. In the time between contract creation and closing (the executory period), the seller gets her consideration ready for exchange (title and conditional improvements), while the buyer performs due diligence,[220] and gets his consideration ready (financing). Throughout, the parties may continue to negotiate and amend their agreement as many times as desired, but neither party is forced to do so.

Because a contract is whatever its parties want it to be, whenever someone asks: *Is this allowed?* consult the contract first, as the answer is usually found within its pages. 🌳

Assuming a contract is composed in plain English, for lawful purpose, and the parties are of sound mental capacity...

Offer & Acceptance

A written offer, containing all of the elements listed below, must be overtly accepted by Offeree via communication to Offeror.

Party Names

All buyers and all sellers must be named.

Legal Description

The property must be described in unequivocal terms.

Consideration

Valuable goods given in exchange for Property must be described.

Closing Date

Calendar date, or means to calculate the day of exchange, must be stated.

Signatures

Only the parties who sign are officially bound to the terms of an agreement, so be sure all involved principals are signers.

Elements of Enforceability

Contracts and amendments must include these elements to be enforceable (bind its parties).

Effort Meter

You're Gonna Need:

Contract Forms
Offeror & Offeree
Attention to Details
to Consider Everything

tips

Any and all commission agreements between brokers should be made prior to their clients entering purchase/sale negotiations.

Before sending an offer, double and triple check its numbers and dates, and ensure all exhibits are referenced and attached.

If you are not yet a competent agent, ask for expert help.

Always leave a copy of signed documents with clients and customers.

Avoid writing your own stipulations. Instead, select from an attorney-drafted list or seek an attorney to draft fresh ones.

If you must write your own stipulations, omit pronouns from offers because pronouns create ambiguity.

Give your offer an edge over others with supporting documents that express worthiness and/or validation of offer terms, such as a cover letter, proof of funds/pre-qualification letter, copy of earnest money check, CMA,[141] and/or a Dear Seller Letter.[269]

Σ   A contract is the mirror image of the offer from which is was born.

How-to
Draft an Offer

Utilize fill-in-the-blank contract forms. Leave no blanks nor ambiguity.

1 Construction
Acquire and attach the proper legal description and the proper names of all involved parties.[251] Add exhibits (AKA addenda) in the form of disclosure statements, fixture lists,[134] surveys, floor plans, and/or lot plans. Title each exhibit with sequential lettering and reference these pages within the primary contract form, officially tying the documents together.

2 Consideration
Choose a price and a form of payment (cash, loan, real property, or a combination of these). In addition to filling-in the numbers, be sure to spell-out the price with words, just as when writing a check.

3 Contingency
Contingencies are conditions that must be met before a transaction can be completed and closed. *Exercising* a contingency allows either Buyer or Seller to cancel their agreement. Common contingencies include:

Inspection—obligates Seller to repair dysfunctional property systems; Buyer may cancel over their refusal.

Finance—specifies loan type, interest rate, and deadline for Buyer approval; non-approval prior to deadline allows Buyer to cancel.

Appraisal—states that appraisal must be within a specific deviation from price and if not, re-negotiation occurs or Buyer may cancel.

Due Diligence/Option-Out—period of time that allows Buyer to closely inspect *all aspects* of the purchase,[220] giving him the ability to cancel for any reason, without penalty. For a competitive offer, all previously-mentioned contingencies could be omitted and satisfied within this one, shorter contingency period.

Secondary Sale—Buyer and/or Seller name another property that must first either close or go under contract, prior to closing this contract.

Kick-Out—allows Seller to kick Buyer out of the contract, unless Buyer removes *Secondary Sale Contingency* (triggered by subsequent offer).

4 Concession
Add a date/time for Buyer to take possession and earnest money details.[255] Include repairs, warranties, closing costs,[268] or any other stipulation that requires Seller's time, labor, and/or money.

5 Time Limit
Add an expiration date/time to the offer. With strategy in mind, choose one that is as short as is comfortable to the offeror.[254]

6 Signature
Add your broker's name as the offeror's representative, then sign your name. Finally, secure the offeror's signature, too.

Yard signs, MLS listings, and internet ad postings are not seller-extended offers. Such overtures are merely tickets to a seat at the negotiating table. Invitees (potential buyers) accept these invitations to bargain in several ways, such as by touring the property, inquiring about specifics, and/or by making an offer. To attract lots of guests, invitations are usually decorated to be as welcoming as possible, often including a written description, photographs, and/or a price tag.

Because it alone does not constitute an offer, a seller cannot be forced to sell at the price quoted on an invitation to bargain. Instead, just like any offeree, a seller may say NO to any offer,[256] even offers submitted at or above the listed price. For this reason, a listing's price tag is a tool used to attract offers,[270] not an offer than may be "accepted" by any passing buyer.

Please Accept My Invitation to Bargain

A Serious How-to Manual with a Sense of Humor

Offer Window Should Be Short and Custom

Dear Andy,
How long should an offer be left open for acceptance?
—*Twisting in Time*

Dear Twisting,

When it comes to negotiating the purchase of real property, the time limit placed on an offer is of strategic importance. If this expiration window is too short, an offeree may not have enough time to respond, find it overtly aggressive, or elect to ignore. If it is too long, an offeree has time to consider agreements with alternative parties (whether that offeree is a seller, receiving subsequent offers of purchase, or a buyer, discovering new listings, fresh on the market).

At times, a listing agent will suggest to you an extended offer window, claiming reasons such as an outta-town client, a scheduled open house, or a client who wants to wait until the weekend is over (which almost certainly means they're shopping for a competing offer). However, by the time a property is listed FOR SALE, its seller has had plenty of time to contemplate potential terms of sale. Because of this reality, offers made before 3PM should reasonably expect a same-day answer. For offers made after dinner hours, a response before noon the next day is plenty of time for consideration.

Long or missing time limits can complicate active buyers and sellers. Eager buyers have, at times, unintentionally agreed to purchase two, different properties. Even worse, sellers sometimes accidentally contract to sell a single property to two, different buyers. To avoid nightmare scenarios like these, your clients are wise to extend no more than one offer at time. Before making an offer to a second party, wait until the first offer either expires, is counter-offered,[256] or is officially rescinded.

Best practice is to suggest to clients an offer window that is as short as is comfortable, given their circumstances. When their strategy is to remain nimble, a short time frame will provide flexibility and a two-hour offer window may be long enough; at other times, however, two days will be strategically appropriate.

Dear Andy,
Which is better: a cash offer or a financed one?
—*Curious about Coinage*

Dear Curious,

At the closing table, money is money, regardless of how the buyer acquires it. So, instead of fretting over the source of a buyer's funds, a seller should consider the likelihood of the buyer and his money showing-up to the closing ceremony.

Because a loan requires third party approval, financed money is less certain than cash. Also, cash offers typically contain fewer/shorter contingencies, fewer (if any) seller concessions, and a faster closing date. However, in exchange for these seller-friendly terms, cash offers are typically for less price.

After considering all significant terms of an offer (price, contingencies, seller concessions, form of payment, earnest money, and closing date) some sellers would prefer the certainty of less money, now. For others, the risk and hassle of inspection, finance, and appraisal contingencies are worth waiting on extra price. So, to answer your question succinctly: it depends upon the other terms of offer and the unique circumstance of a particular seller.[126]

***

Dear Andy,
Can I trust the validity of electronic signatures?
—*Leery of Legitimacy*

Dear Leery,

U.S. courts first acknowledged and upheld the validity of electronic signatures (e-sigs) in 1869 for contracts via telegraph. Since then, laws have been written for use via computer. To protect yourself and clients alike, review these laws. Then, adopt three e-sig practices: 1) acquire the parties' written agreement to accept e-sigs, 2) only utilize e-sigs through reputable, law-compliant service providers, and 3) electronically store all e-signed documents (and their encrypted affidavits of authenticity), in a place where all parties have access.   -AA

A defaulting buyer is said to damage his seller in immeasurable ways because time wasted with a defaulting buyer could have been spent with a closing buyer and because it is difficult to measure that lost opportunity. For this stated reason, sellers customarily expect buyers to post earnest money (EM). In other words, a buyer puts his cash on the ledge as a seller's hedge; should the buyer default, his money blows away. However, a seller would much rather sell her property than to collect EM, and therefore EM is most often used as a whip to suppress buyer default, rather than as a reward to offset monetary loses caused by default.

On the other hand, a defaulting seller damages a buyer in ways that can be measured. Money lost to inspection and appraisal fees may total in the thousands. Not to mention the opportunity lost in buying another property, or (in the case of an expired, lower interest rate) the loss of thousands of dollars spent on higher payments over the life of a subsequent loan. At times, sellers prone to default will make themselves known by insisting upon long-winded, strange, or complicated contract terms. Another red flag may be a sale contingent upon the seller's purchase of another property; depending upon the terms of this other transaction, your buyer may be at risk of losing his purchase.

When you encounter sellers who seems likely to default, ask them to match the buyers EM. Provide thoughtful reasoning for your request, then don't act too surprised when they oblige or waive the buyer's earnest money altogether.

The Importance of Being Earnest Money

A twist in this old custom puts sellers on the ledge.

You're Gonna Need:

an Offer
a Client
Deliberation
Strategy

tips

You must present all offers to your clients, regardless of price, terms, date, or format. Oral, written, partially-written, low-ball, and high-ball offers must be presented. *No exceptions.* Even when your seller is already under-contract to sell to another, all offers must be presented—even if you're sitting at the closing table! It's the law, dude.[212]

Offerors give offers and offerees receive offers.[285]

The counter-offer process may technically go back-and-forth between parties forever.

The courts have ruled that a "reasonable amount of time" shall be inserted into offers that are lacking an expiration date. To avoid trouble later, include a time limit on all offers (same goes for counter-offers).[254]

Once an offer is countered, it cannot later be accepted.

If the parties wish to negotiate verbally, then oblige them with the (written) understanding that only written agreements are enforceable.[250]

Be sure to keep clients fully updated throughout the offer/counter-offer process.

Σ   Offerees have four choices, each of which result in offer obliteration.

How–to
Receive an Offer

Remind clients of the fact that offerees have exactly four choices:

1 Accept

An offer is accepted when it is signed, without changes, and notice of acceptance is delivered to the offeror.[262] Once an offer is accepted, it is converted into a contract,[260] just like a caterpillar transforming into a butterfly. In this way, the offer (caterpillar) no longer exists.

2 Reject

An offer is rejected by sending notice of: NO. Once an offer is rejected, it no longer exists. It's like squashing a caterpillar dead.

3 Counter-Offer

A counter-offer is the simultaneous rejection of an offer and the formation of a new, different offer, which is completely unique to this world. Once an offer is countered, it no longer exists. It's like squashing a caterpillar dead, then replacing it with another caterpillar.

4 Ignore

When an offer is ignored, it will eventually expire. Once an offer expires, it no longer exists. It's like starving a caterpillar to death.

Just as a dead caterpillar can never become a butterfly, an offer that has been rejected, counter-offered, or ignored to expiration cannot come back to life and be retroactively accepted. So, choose wisely.

How–to
Counter an Offer

So the acceptance of your counter-offer may result in an enforceable agreement, employ one of these three, written methods:

1 Counter-Offer Form

Generally, contracts negotiated with fill-in-the-blank, counter-offer forms will be comprised of the original offer, *plus the last counter-offer*. For this reason, be sure to include incrementally-agreed terms on each subsequent counter-offer form, until complete agreement is reached.

2 Scratch 'n' Sniff

Counter-offers are sometimes made by the parties passing the original offer back and forth, striking-through and handwriting changes. To be valid, each change must be initialed and dated by the offeror. Acceptance comes when the offeree initials and dates all the same places.

3 New Draft

Often used when the scratch 'n' sniff method becomes a confusing mess, or after the parties reach a verbal agreement, this counter-offer begins with a fresh, new set of contract forms.

The Low-Ball Offer

Get the ball rolling from the:

Buyer's Perspective: Target listings with high days on market (DOM). Write a clean offer, with few (if any) contingencies and/or concessions. Justify your price with detailed analysis. Send over more than just a list of comps. Attach a Dear Seller Letter.[269] If negotiations fail, or the seller ignores you, resubmit your offer every few weeks. This repetition shows earnestness, so keep trying until they give-in, sell to another, or file a restraining order against you. **Seller's Perspective:** An offer is an offer. This is business, so don't attach emotions and don't ignore their offer, either. Before responding, think about your situation. If you're new on the market and full of hope, then counter at/or above list price. This volley may spur their reasonable response. If you've been FOR SALE more than double the average DOM and received zero offers, then you're over-priced. If so, that supposed low-ball offer may be more modest than first thought. Counter at your best take-it-or-leave-it price. Then counter their counters with this counter every time thereafter— it's the best you'll do.

Seller Side

When all the balls are in a seller's court, the advantage is clear. For this reason, sellers should invite all-comers, while remaining careful not to intimidate or scare offers away. Therefore, before returning anyone's serve, a seller is wise to assess all offers and contemplate their situation: How long has the property been FOR SALE? How many offers are there now? Are more offers likely to arrive within a day or two? Are most or all of the offers similar? Or is one offer much better than the others? As part of a strategy, the number of current offers and/or competitive offer details may be disclosed to one or more offerors, or may be kept secret from all. Remember, as with all choices, pros and cons exist, and circumstance will dictate the best play. With a grip on the situation, a seller may:

1—Reject them all. 2—Choose one to accept, and reject the rest. 3—Counter one, and reject the rest.
4—Putting all others on hold, counter one. If agreement is not reached, counter a second one.
5—Tell all offerors of multi-offer situation, allowing each to re-submit a "highest and best" offer by a deadline (AKA a bidding war).

The Multiple Offer Racket

Buyer Side

Most of the time, buyers will be alerted to multiple offers, but not always. Therefore, buyers are wise to ask, and then take a competitive swing, putting forth their best offer. Perhaps the seller will favor an offering which allows them stay, post-sale, or one that proposes a quick closing. Maybe the seller has a deep emotional connection to the property or maybe they're mostly concerned with a buyer's ability to purchase. Gathering information on the seller, the property, and the other offers, allows for a customized offer that matches a seller's hang-ups. A buyer can stick-out with a personalized Dear Seller Letter,[269] pre-qualification documentation,[170] increased earnest money,[255] minimized seller concessions,[135] minimized/shortened contingencies,[252] and/or a larger down-payment. Regardless of offer construction, establish a baseline that is not to be crossed and take an attitude that if rejected, another property or a back-up position may be sought.[274] Walking away altogether is also an option, but buyers really have nothing to lose by participating.

Multiple offers usually occur for new listings with excellent price/condition ratios.[154] However, some properties have an *offer-in-waiting* that triggers the situation as soon as a second offer is made. Regardless of how multiple offers come to be, the way they're served is always the seller's choice (given state laws and regulations on the topic).[036]

A Serious How-to Manual with a Sense of Humor

Effort Meter

You're Gonna Need:

Offer
Acceptance
Offeree's Signature
Notice of Acceptance

tips

The words *contract* and *agreement* are interchangeable terms; each means the same thing.

The acceptance of an offer creates an agreement.

Before creating an agreement, make sure there is a *meeting of the minds*, whereby everyone is on the same page, so to speak. Do not insert surprises nor gotchas, otherwise contract voidance may be in your future.[276]

For conflicting passages in a contract, the scrivener's hierarchy rules by the following order: handwritten words override typewritten words, which override pre-printed words.

If requested by one party or the other, some pre-printed contract forms compel its parties to sign a conformed copy.

Whenever the parties to a contract wish to alter the price, move the closing date, add an exhibit, or make any other change, an amendment is required.

Amendments may be numbered or lettered, but not both. Whichever you choose, keep the system consistent, and in sequential order of creation.

Σ   A contract is the mirror image of the offer(s) from which is was born.

How-to
Create an Contract

The creation of a contract is as simple as offer and acceptance.

1 Offer

First, an offer must be made by one party to another.[252] To create an enforceable agreement, the offer must be written and include the parties' names, a legal description, mutual consideration, a closing date, and the offeror's signature.[251]

Sometimes lengthy negotiations will erode, from written to verbal format. Once a verbal contract is made, quickly construct a written offer, containing the verbally-agreed terms and the aforementioned elements of enforceability. Then, submit it for acceptance.

2 Acceptance

To accept the offer, the offeree cannot make any changes, except to sign the document. Then, prior to offer expiration, the offeree's acceptance must be communicated to the offeror by means of official notice.[262]

3 Draft a Conformed Copy

If the newly-minted agreement is a result of numerous, written counter-offers or fierce scratch 'n' sniff sessions,[256] a conformed copy may be created. Also called a *clean copy* or a *working copy*, this document should contain a bold stamp identifying it as: CONFORMED COPY. With the official copy hidden from view, the conformed copy is given to mortgage officers, closing attorneys, title companies, or any other relevant party, for easy, un-cluttered reference.

How-to
Amend an Contract

The parties of a contract may change the terms at any time, for any reason—so long as all parties agree to do so. However, changing a contract requires an amendment; to amend, the offer process must begin again.

1 Offer

First, an amendment offer must be made by one party to the other. To create an enforceable change to the agreement, the amendment offer must be written and include the parties' names, a legal description, mutual consideration, and the offeror's signature.

2 Acceptance

To accept the offer, the offeree cannot make any changes, except to sign the document. Then, prior to offer expiration, the offeree's acceptance must be communicated to the offeror by means of official notice.[262]

Don't Be Just Any Monkey

Customary practice often dictates that the buyer's agent act as architect of a purchase agreement's conformed copy.[260] This chore (as some find it to be) is super-important: the creation of a transaction's guiding document. A task of such substance should be performed by an agent of competency—not just any monkey.

The two, most-complex aspects of real estate sales are valuation and contacts. You provide the finest, fiduciary service to clients, so neither of these aspects should be left to the whims of custom. In fact, you would be a monkey's uncle to kick such responsibilities to the other guy's agent.

Your competent involvement in the creation of contracts will prevent your transactions from going bananas. Start by learning all about the contract forms you use and then stay updated. Become competent, and then insist on becoming the drafting party, regardless of custom. Whenever you are not the drafting agent, check their work closely. To do so: ensure all dates match and that all special terms, contingencies, exhibits, and elements of enforceability are included.[251] If you are still a monkey, get broker support or pay an expert to review your pages.

Buyers Pay for Everything

Otherwise, sellers would never sell.

BY THE BUBBLE-BUSTER

BEFORE LISTING, MOST SELLERS invest time, money, and labor on improving the condition of their property. With the intention of coaxing every last bit of value from a sale, these efforts are meant to become competitive in the marketplace. Then, with the property's perceived fair market value in-hand and an estimated NET-TO-SELLER figure in-mind,[135] the seller chooses a list price.[154] After listing, but before *the offer* comes, sellers usually continue to invest time, money, and labor into maintaining the improved condition. If nothing else, by keeping the property in a show-ready state, their quiet enjoyment is disturbed.

Once *the offer* comes, a seller negotiates an agreement based upon the payoff of their total investment (whether that payoff yields gain or loss). Their calculation is:

$$\begin{array}{r} \text{PROPERTY ACQUISITION COST} \\ -\text{ COST TO SELL} \\ +\text{ SALES PRICE} \\ \hline =\text{ NET-TO-SELLER} \end{array}$$

A seller's COST TO SELL includes pre-list, conditional improvements, listing maintenance, and P&S contract concessions. These seller concessions include all buyer contingencies (the type and terms of each), sales commissions, the payment of closing costs, conditional improvements (repairs), and any other stipulation that requires the seller's time, money, and/or labor.

Similarly, the price paid for a package of peanuts covers the total expense of growing, harvesting, roasting, packaging, distributing, advertising, and selling that package of nuts. This price also includes an agreeable profit to be gained, otherwise the seller would not be in the business of selling peanuts. Likewise, the seller of real property only makes a trade when an agreeable profit or loss is to be had.[129]

Therefore, because the SALES PRICE offsets all seller expenses related to a transaction, *everything* related to that transaction is included in the SALES PRICE—and the buyer pays for it all. 🌳

Focus on Notice

Observe the official communique of offers and contracts.

BY THE TOWN CRIER

THE PASSING OF INFORMATION between the parties of offers and contracts is known as notice. The form of notice (usually, in writing), the delivery channels of notice (usually personal delivery, postage-paid mail, email, and/or facsimile), and the terms by which notice is deemed received are each negotiated and defined within the language of an offer/contract. Notice that is sent in defiance of these rules is deemed *not sent*.

Often times, these rules state that once notice is sent to an agent it is simultaneously deemed as sent to their client. Therefore, once notice comes your way, pass it along immediately and keep proof of all notice sent/received.

Sometimes, a co-operating agent will ask you to send notice elsewhere, for the sake of their convenience. In these cases, do so as a professional courtesy, but also simultaneously send the notice through the defined, official channels. To protect against future disputes, follow-up phone conversations with an official email, summarizing the chat.

From time to time, a client will wish to withdraw an offer. When given such direction, your job will be to quickly deliver word of rescission, by the rules and through official notice channels, before the offeree accepts. Whenever notice delivery is super-important, *send it through **all** defined channels.* 🌳

Sometimes a particular listing will be in serious contention with several different buyers in a row, but not one of them makes an offer. Usually caused by excess inventory, this happenstance can become frustrating to sellers. The next time your seller feels like jumping off the deep end, initiate an in-depth chat with an interested buyer('s agent). Ask about financing, desired concessions, and a shopping deadline. Seek their specific LIKES and DONT LIKES about the property. Then, help your seller compose an offer that addresses the buyer's unique concerns. ¶ Not expecting the seller to open negotiations, buyers are typically shocked, at-first. Next, they feel flattered to have received an offer that has their interests at heart. Due to this *humanizing effect*, the Reverse Offer boasts a high success rate. Its detractors claim the procedure conveys seller desperation. However, a seller spring-boarding her own transaction is generally preferred to one suffering an expired-listing belly flop.

THE REVERSE OFFER MAKES A *Splash*

Americans Hate to Negotiate

Style clashes kill their deals; it's up to us to help them.

BY YANKEE DOODLE AGENT

SOME PLACES IN THIS WORLD are full of people who haggle, dicker, and barter over the price of food, clothing, and other stuff on a daily basis. Markets in the United States are quite different. Here, we like to acquire things by shopping in a store, with products on shelves, and a price tag on each. We like to examine our choices, and then select the one that best fits our needs, *at a fair price*. With a quick stop at the cashier, where an on-the-spot contract is executed, we walk away owning a new thing; with barely a word spoken, it's just the way we like it.

Of course, there are those amongst us who enjoy negotiating, or at the least, do not cower from it. But most of us dislike the practice, especially since it's not part of our daily lives. We accept that big ticket items come with some negotiating, but we would prefer to just pay a fair sticker price. Not knowing how to act otherwise, we adopt one of these five roles:

Deal Seekers like to challenge opponents. They are known to display authority as an attempt to intimidate, and they crave small wins throughout negotiations. Their competitive attitude can be hostile, which often kills their deals. They do not seek a high/low price because of a financial need to do so, but rather for the sport of it.

Stone Walls think of themselves as fair-minded people. However, they tend to draw a line at list price (or initial offer price), then refuse to budge, regardless of market activity. Their take-it-or-leave-it attitude is the deal seeker's worst nightmare.

Perfunctory Players would rather be doing anything else than negotiate. They are easy-going, accommodating types who usually take the suggestion or advice given to them.

Straight Arrows do not like to play games. These people say what they mean and follow-through on ultimatums. They are reasonable collaborators, who like information and logic.

Fickle Fawns are emotional, mind-changing worry warts. These types need reassurance and will often include others in their drawn-out, decision-making process. Along with perfunctory players, fickle fawns are susceptible to buyer's remorse.[188]

When these style types square-off against each other, otherwise agreeable deals can sometimes turn to mush. Instead of blindly relaying your client's default style, you should help them to assess exactly what they have and want, and what their opponent has and wants in exchange.[266] Learn to trust your instincts, and overcome your sense of fear.[056] Then, give clients sensible advice on how to achieve their stated goals.

Whether a negotiation sequence results in a deal or no deal, turn it into a learning moment with clients. Together, review everyone's role in the process: how did attitudes and expectations effect the result? How might things go differently next time? Remember, your job isn't to negotiate with your client, but on behalf of your client. When adjustments to strategy and tactic are warranted, lend logical advice in a way they can understand.

I once had a seller client, who had endured recent, emotional hardship over the property she was now selling. She had already bought and moved-into a new property, and we were in the final stages of negotiating the sale of her old house. The buyer had been nit-picking the entire deal; the whole deal hinged on a squabble of $300. The seller, irritated by the clash of styles, refused to negotiate further. She was extremely stressed-out with concerns of hosting a full house during the holiday season. Instead of empathizing or negotiating with my client, I asked her a reasonable question. "Which is worth more to you: three hundred bucks or a good night's sleep?" With perspective, she quickly accepted the buyer's offer.

Now, that's a feather worthy of any cap. 🐾

INTRODUCE YOUR CLIENTS AS TROPHIES

Americans may hate to negotiate, but we love to compete. If there's a prize to be had, we want it, and we relish the opportunity to vie for it. Whenever a real estate trophy is within grasp, people tend to get caught-up in drama, which often leads to them paying more or taking less than they otherwise would. Therefore, when you replace your opponent's negotiation mind-set with one of competition, he is likely to become more generous with his offer. ¶ Turn your clients into trophies by making them more attractive than other would-be trophies. Then, create a sense of urgency in your negotiating opponents by declaring your client's alternative choices (other buyers or other listings). Once an opponent knows he's competing for a prize, you have gained advantage. Beware: some people hate competition so much, these tactics will cause their avoidance; luckily, they are few in ranks. ¶ To make buyers compete for your listings, pick the right price.[154] List it with lots of sexy photos[230] and a complete marketing package.[234] Give wide distribution,[239] and keep track of all activity; then tell all inquirers of the flurry that surrounds. To make sellers compete for your buyers, prove their financial strength through documentation and down payment.[170] Show their sincerity with a larger-than-customary earnest money check.[255] Compose a clean offer (one without lots of special terms), and include a *Dear Seller Letter*.[269] Then, be sure the seller knows all about *that other property* your buyer likes (almost) just as much. Your buyer is a trophy when he is seen as low-risk, with a high probability of closing.

4294967295

Effort Meter

You're Gonna Need:

Homework on Subject
Homework on Opponent
Strategy & Tactic
Confidence

tips

An accurate CMA is required to negotiate with confidence.[140]

When sending offers to and fro, have chats with your agent opponent. Ask: *So, what do you think of it?* This question often leads to all kinds of info about their client. The more you know, the better your bargaining nimbleness becomes. Ask follow-up questions to their responses. Stay curious, not interview-y.

Regardless of your client's offer, never feel bad about it or apologize for it when presenting it to your opponent. It's just an offer, not the measles. On the other hand, don't allow a single client to waste your time with fifty offers that don't stand a chance.

Remember, representations made by an agent are treated as though they were made by their principal.

Never underestimate your opponent.

Whenever you draft or receive an offer, also draft a net-sale or net-to-seller form.[135] This calculation allows for informed, no-surprises-later negotiations.

Read books/blogs and attend classes/workshops to refine your bargaining powers throughout your career.

It certainly sounds cliché, but *know when to walk away.* You're not here to just sit on the pot.

How–to
Negotiate Like a Champ

The strongest bargaining position is having the choice of alternative negotiating opponents (other buyers/listings). This situation allows you to walk away from negotiating with any one of them, without the risk of not finding a deal with at least one of them. The weakest bargaining position is being desperate to trade due to a lack of alternative opponents, coupled with an approaching deadline (whether self-imposed by financial limitations, or by divorce, foreclosure,..). Technically, anyone can walk away (even desperate dealers), but emotion prevents many from doing so.

1 Count the Chips on the Table

Before you can effectively negotiate (trade chips for chips), you must survey the bargaining table and the people seated around it. Each principal's assets *and circumstances* are their bargaining chips. Count your client's stack, and then investigate what their opponent has. Start with the subject property: what is FMV? How long has it been FOR SALE? What's the AVG. DOM? Current absorption rate?[147] Are other buyers interested? Any title encumbrances?

Learn about your opponent and keep gathering intel until closing (because it ain't over 'til it's over). Engage them in chat: *Why are you buying/selling? Do you need to buy/sell another property to make this deal work? -or- Do you need this deal to work before you can buy/sell another property? Do you have a deadline? Are you financially able to trade? Owner juggling two mortgages? How many decision-makers sit on your side of the table? Have you been negotiating with others? What was the cause of no deal, previously? What is your hot button: is it price? closing date? seller concessions? closing cost help?* When asked outright, these questions are often rebuffed. However, ways exist to extract such data via conversation.[oo8]

2 Build Trust

The way things begin are a strong indication of the way things will end. When either side comes to the table seemingly unhappy to be there, unready to deal, or with something to hide, trust is immediately eroded. For sellers, clarity of disclosure and general courtesy of showing are trust builders. For buyers, a display of financial ability and an overt acknowledgement of property admiration build trust. Ease of communication and earnest attitudes are also trustworthy traits.

3 Strategize

When price/terms balance for each principal, a deal is made. Although all terms are a debit against price, most tend to focus on price alone, and under-valuate other terms. To avoid this mistake, monetize every part of the deal. Write down the obvious ones, like closing costs and other concessions that can be purchased. Then consider the value of closing date, contingencies, stipulations, and earnest money. Considering all the chips on the table (including the table's location in the marketplace), establish a target price (ideal terms), an offer price (better than ideal terms), and a walk-away price (minimum terms).

4 Employ Tactics

It's all about what you say, how you say it, and to whom you say it.[008] You speak for your client, so present a unified front. It's okay to justify a position, but never apologize for it. Sometimes their tactic will be to put a time crunch on you, or otherwise ruffle your feathers. Opponents often yield to calmness, so remain stoic at times of heated conflict. Expect to push and pull, give and get. The back and forth of many counter-offers will emotionally-commit some people to a deal, but others will be driven away by the hassle. With confidence, overcome stalls by:

- giving them the choice of two offers, whereby price/terms zero-out.
- remembering that rounded prices seem arbitrary ($125,000), but specific prices seem to embody careful consideration ($124,682).
- giving them an ultimatum: *Take it or leave it.* Once you take a stand, your opponent may continue to make counter-offers. Sometimes after you walk away, they will come back—a week or more later.
- reminding them of their circumstances, by saying things like: *You're not gonna find a better deal than this!*
- mentioning your options (alternative buyers/listings).
- re-starting deliberations with a concession, presenting a new offer that highlights their interest.
- slowing things down with: *We're gonna weigh our options.* If your opponent is emotionally committed, this tactic will bring them back to the table with renewed earnestness.

5 Don't Over-Play Your Hand

It's okay to be hypocritical in tactic, but be careful doing so. If your maneuvers are sloppy and obvious, your opponent's trust may become eroded. For example, you don't have to provide reasoning for everything in your offer; you just have to ask for it. On the flip side, ask them to rationalize their position; sometimes their response will be a concession. Also, feel free to ignore their ultimatums (just because you can), but don't give-in on yours. Put a time crunch on them, but don't take their crunch too seriously. Play these tactics sparingly, when opportune.

Puffery is an expected part of negotiations, but it's never okay to lie. Instead, re-phrase: *I cannot afford to pay more/ take less,* becomes *I do not want to pay more/take less.*

Enter the contract with a smile, because negotiations do not end until closing. Successful amendment is usually made of logical reasoning, and not due to whim. Therefore, once a contract is created, it seems like bad faith to negotiate further, unless a good reason exists. When a contract is made by over-playing your hand, your opponent becomes less willing to later amend at your request.

Do not hide any parts of the negotiation sequence from your client. Sometimes they will have difficulty understanding specific aspects of a deal (and potential pitfalls of decisions); keep explaining until they do.

caveats

If no deal is made, then be nice at departure; leave room to revisit them later.

When repeated negotiations with several different opponents each result in no deal, it's time to revisit strategy and tactics with your client.

Put your ego to the side when speaking on behalf of clients. In other words, don't be the thing that ruins their deal.

Beware: whenever personal property becomes part of a real property deal, any and all lenders involved must be made aware. Otherwise, you may become party to mortgage fraud.[292]

Do not negotiate your commission as part of the principals' purchase/sale negotiation. Your value was established before they met.[181]

Your actions are a reflection upon your client and co-op agents will remember you, so remain professional; when you lose your cool, you also lose their respect.[310]

Except when feigned for the sake of puffery, your emotions should remain packed-away when negotiating on behalf of others.

Negotiation is half what's on paper, and half what is said betwixt offers. Because of this, it's easy to slip into verbal negotiations. Keep each offer in the black and white of paper, but continue to color it in with your spoken words. Use conversation to better understand them and to reinforce you.

Negotiations are not always reasonable events. But remember, people won't agree unless they want to. Even if they complain about it, the deal they signed was preferred over no deal. Otherwise, they would have chosen no deal. Duh.[129]

Σ One never gets screwed in negotiations, rather he gets exactly what he has negotiated.

Make Failure to Repair Hurt, Really Bad

Dear Andy,
Today is closing day, and the seller has performed only one of three repairs—which was done horribly. Now, my buyer says he won't come to closing until all the work is done. What should I do?
—*Reeling in Repairs*

Dear Reeling,
First, check the agreement for a survival clause, which states that seller obligations to perform conditional improvements "survive the closing." This statement compels a seller to complete repairs *after* closing, if need be. Under such clause, any buyer refusing to close due to incomplete repairs may be the one defaulting on the agreement, not the seller. If the buyer agreed to a survival clause, explain it to him now. Talk to the seller's agent about the situation, and seek a post-closing repair schedule, to reaffirm their commitment. Then, get your buyer to closing, and help him hold the seller to repairs later.

Relying on the survival clause can cause a rotten hassle, because sellers tend to lose repair-making motivation after a transaction is completed. Once paid, a seller's reward for overseeing quality repairs vanishes. Further, should the seller never complete all repairs, the buyer's only remaining remedies will be to make the repairs himself and attempt to collect payment from the seller, and/or legal action. If your buyer rebuffs closing for reasons like these, recruit help from your broker.

Next time, try this instead: add a stipulation that requires the completion of repairs a few days before closing. Go further, requiring the seller to employ licensed contractors, with receipts as proof. Then, go to the extreme, triggering either cancellation or an automatic reduction in sales price if the seller fails to meet repair deadlines; more than anything else, a potential loss of proceeds will motivate lazy sellers.

While this tactic is sure to encourage timely repairs, a price reduction may ultimately fail to help cash-poor buyers (who otherwise cannot afford repairs), or those with loans that require a pre-closing completion of repairs.

Dear Andy,
My seller refuses to pay the buyer's closing costs because she paid her own when purchasing the same house. How might I overcome her objection?
—*Cramped by Closing Costs*

Dear Cramped,
When a seller pays lender-based closing costs (CC), the buyer is essentially financing those costs, amortized over the term of his loan. Had he negotiated to pay the CC in cash, the buyer would have likely also negotiated a lower sales price,[254] because during negotiations, whenever one gives something of value, they expect something of value in return.

In essence, Buyer and Seller are bargaining over a net-sale figure,[135] which is price minus concessions. With this in mind, a seller paying CC is acting like a seller who provides a home warranty or one who repaints walls.

While the expense of closing costs may be higher than other concessions, it should not be categorized differently. Instead, a seller should negotiate an acceptable net-sale figure. Once this number is agreed upon, any push on concessions will cause a push on price.

✳✳✳

Dear Andy,
I'm in love with a listing. If the seller discovers my excitement, I might pay too much. How can I ensure offer acceptance, while keeping my enthrallment a secret?
—*Flushed by my Crush*

Dear Flushed,
Expressing your adoration to the seller may be more help than hindrance in your efforts to secure purchase. Sellers usually harbor an emotional connection to their property, and would love for it to go to a good home, so to speak.

To protect your pockets during negotiations, avoid putting property on a pedestal. Instead, establish a price at which you will walk away, and then do so, if need be. Remember, while seeking top-paying buyers, sellers can only take advantage of your passion if you allow it so. -AA

Dear Seller,

Your home is just perfect for all the things our family does. We can picture the children playing ball in the yard and practicing piano in the parlor. While you're probably entertaining many offers, please give ours special consideration, as we just love the place.

sincerely,
The Smiths

The Dear Seller Letter

Buyers may endear themselves with a cover letter on an initial offer. Likely to warm any seller's heart, this letter is meant to open negotiations pleasantly. For maximum effect, include emotion, a desire to acquire, and planned usage of specific rooms/features.

Sellers Are Kings & Queens

Because they own the castle until closing, sellers rule their deals.

BY THE ROYAL AUTHORITY

EACH PARCEL OF REAL PROPERTY is unique onto itself and comes with an equally unique owner.[126] Therefore, to acquire a particular property, a buyer must deal with its particular seller. Because the seller must be convinced to relinquish ownership, the price/terms of a particular property deal will (always and forever) be *whatever satisfies the seller*. Even sellers under financial pressure to sell cannot be absolutely forced to do so. However, a buyer is forced to endure a seller's attitudes, stipulations, and quirks; otherwise, no deal. Of course, if the seller is too much of an unreasonable nutter, the buyer may walk away from negotiations, or terminate their contract through contingency. There will always be similar properties FOR SALE, but (at least for right now) *this property* is owned by *this guy*.

Buyers usually negotiate several contract contingencies, with the assumption that the seller will reasonably amend their agreement later, as circumstances dictate. However, regardless of how amiable a seller behaves at the time of contract formation, time and events transpire between deal making and contingency expirations. A seller who was once open for business may now be closed to further amendment.[260]

While acting reasonably (as other, similarly-informed people would probably act) is more likely than not to result in a fair trade in a timely manner, a seller does not have to be reasonable. For this reason, buyers should enter contracts knowing that while their understanding of value (or their ability to close on-time) may change, the contract they currently hold may be as good as it gets. ♣

Price Is Just a Tool

A listing's price is always the first volley in negotiations.

BY THE PRICE MASTER

USED TO EITHER ATTRACT OR REPEL buyers, list price is a seller's tool. In negotiating terms, it's called an anchor, because price is seen by potential negotiating opponents as being hard to move. This anchor sets not only buyers' expectations, but those of sellers, too (which is why buyers tend to avoid over-priced listings).[159]

Everyone expects list price to go up or down, at least somewhat, because few properties sell for their exact list price. Sure, the listed price may become the contract price, but most sellers make at least a single concession, which lowers the net-sale.[135]

Because so much of negotiation is puffery and posturing, when an opponent takes your client's offer straight away, their tendency is to think, "Oh, no! I've paid too much/not gotten enough." While this reaction may or

may not be valid, remind them, "If you were happy to make the offer, you should be happy with it as a contract. Don't second-guess yourself; perhaps you made the perfect offer."

On the other hand, you may sometimes think your client is paying too much, or selling for too cheap, but that's not your choice to make. If the deal is of value to them, then it's of value to them; each of us are different.[129] Advise your clients as you will, then respect the decisions they make.

Learn to recognize a good deal when you see it: paying full price (or more) is not a bad thing if value is there. Besides, price is an arbitrary starting point and a "deal" is when both sides are happy. Always remember, when you counter an offer that was a good deal, you run the risk of their answer being outright rejection, and a refusal to continue. ♣

Just like playing poker, you and your negotiating opponents are expected to engage in a certain amount of puffery. Such posturing sometimes leads to an impasse, whereby both sides dig-in their heels, each refusing to blink. To overcome these stalls, begin by making it known that a deal is desired, but not required. When it is known that you will walk away, you gain an advantage, but be careful: overuse may lead to advantage lost. Otherwise, such statements allow you to draw a believable line in the sand. Then, keep your cool, no matter how eager, excited, or irritated the parties become.[310] Keep your client focused on their main goal, not on petty details. When value is hundreds of thousands of dollars, arguing over five hundred is small potatoes. Often times, letting your opponent win something small allows you to win the bigger prize. Parties pushing too hard over pride or "the principle of the matter" may ruin otherwise successful transactions. If a buyer wants to buy and a seller wants to sell, then don't let agents, their egos, or the egos of principals get in the way.

If you feel your message is not being relayed, present it on paper. When rhetoric escalates, consider a face-to-face meeting, or replace yourself with another agent. Whenever someone invokes lawyers, or when your opponent refuses to communicate, a broker-to-broker chat is absolutely, most-definitely warranted.

How-to Win an Ass-Kicking Contest

& How-to Avoid One, Altogether

A Serious How-to Manual with a Sense of Humor

THE PLUMBER

Negotiating for clients requires an ability to negotiate for yourself.

THE CONSUMMATE RESPONSIBILITY of all listing agents is to suggest a price that will generate purchase offers. When a property is priced properly, offers will come quickly. When the price is high, offers take longer. Therefore, the hallmark of a skilled listing agent is choosing the right list price from the start.

One day, I listed a man's home, then received a full-price offer a week later. The seller promptly accepted, only to phone me the next day. "I don't think I should have to pay you the full commission because you didn't have to work very hard to make the sale. Within a few days we had a full-price offer. Seems to me that you under-priced my house. We could have gotten more money with a higher price," the seller impatiently explained.

"I understand your concern," I replied, going on to explain how price affects buyer activity. He quickly understood and agreed, but then restated his case.

"That's all well and good, but I still think you haven't worked very long or hard at this, so you shouldn't get the full commission."

"Would you have rather it taken three months or longer to attract this buyer?" I asked, in a sarcastic tone.

"Oh, no!" he said. "I want this buyer!"

"What is your profession, Mr. Seller?" I asked, already knowing the answer.

"I'm a plumber," the seller said proudly.

"That's wonderful. Tell me, how much do you charge to unclog a drain?"

"One-hundred fifty dollars," he said.

"Great! How long does it usually take you to unclog a drain, and what is the process?"

"Usually about ten minutes or so, but sometimes the clog is somewhere down the pipe a bit, so I must use my drain snake to push the clog and clear the line."

"Does it ever take you longer than ten minutes to finish the job?"

"Sure. Sometimes the clog is farther down the drain than my snake can reach, so I'm forced to go under the house and find a clean-out plug. Then I can put my snake into that hole to clear the drain. Sometimes I'm forced to cut the pipe, snake the drain, then patch the cut," the plumber opined.

"Wow! How long does that take?"

"Sometimes as much as an hour."

"And what do you charge for that, given the extra work?"

"One-hundred fifty dollars," was the response from the plumber/seller, who was beginning to tire of my questions.

"Do you ever have a clog that you clear quickly?" I asked.

"Sure do. You see, most clogs are in the p-trap, located just under the sink. I always start by tapping the pipe with my wrench because that will sometimes clear the clog."

"If that works, what's your charge?"

"One-hundred fifty dollars!" he snapped.

"Why would you charge so much? All you did was tap the pipe," I asked calmly.

"Because I know *exactly where* to tap the pipe!" he snorted, nearly raising his voice.

"Yes, I understand. Just like you, Mr. Seller, I also know where to tap the pipe."

With that, I could hear the seller smiling through the telephone. He then agreed to pay my full commission.

 TRUE STORY

Owner of Record

Title is an ownership claim and a deed is the document that transfers that ownership. As the owner of record changes from one to another, a chain of title is created. When encumbrances, debts, liens, outside ownership claims, or gaps in the record arise, this title chain is said to be broken, or the title clouded. These conditions threaten a title holders ownership, so a grantor (seller) provides their grantee (buyer) a warranty within the deed. Because warranties vary, a value can be affixed, creating a conditional feature over which to bargain. For this reason, the type of deed used to transfer ownership should be clearly stated within the purchase agreement.

Common Deeds:

Warranty/General Warranty Grantor claims full ownership, the right to sell, and further guarantees the property is free of debts, liens, and other claims, pledging to assist in the resolution of any ownership disputes that may arise in the future.

Special/Limited/Specific Grantor claims full ownership and the right to sell, but limits their guarantee to their time of ownership.

Quit Claim Grantor claims no ownership nor right to sell nor makes any warranty whatsoever. It is like saying: *Whatever interest I may or may not have in this property, I grant to you. In doing so, I forever quit my claim and pledge nothing to do with it in the future.*

Back-Up Offer versus Back-Up Contract

Do not conflate these engagements, as they are not the same.

BY THE NIT-PICKER

NO ONE KNOWS WHAT THE FUTURE may hold, and no executory contract is ever a sure thing to close. For these reasons, real property sellers are wise to hedge their bets by soliciting back-up offers. Once accepted, back-up offers become back-up contracts, giving a seller insurance against and leverage over their primary P&S contract.[260]

A seller may create a multitude of back-up contracts—as many as are desired. So, to keep things straight, each subsequent back-up contract is marked by its position in line. [*For the sake of simplicity, the primary purchase contract is notated here as* Kø, *the first back-up contract as* K1, *the second back-up contract as* K2, *and so on.*]

Just like any other negotiation sequence, a back-up offer may be batted back and forth between its parties.[256] The only difference being that any ensuing contract contains contingencies and stipulations that are special to the back-up situation. These terms dictate that if/when Kø dissolves, the seller will give notice to all back-up contracts.[262] At such time, K1 automatically becomes the primary contract (Kø), and all other back-up contracts move-up in line.

To hasten a move-up, back-up buyers should consider the terms of Kø when negotiating (all previous back-ups, as well). When back-up contract terms are similar to Kø, a seller is more likely to stick-with Kø, negotiating contingencies, and proceeding to closing. When back-up contracts have terms that are more favorable than Kø, a seller is more likely to forgo further negotiations with Kø. In this way, back-up contracts may be used by a seller as leverage to encourage Kø to perform, or as impetus to discourage Kø from performing.

It should be noted that a seller cannot kill Kø simply because K1 has better terms. However, a seller may refuse to amend Kø, potentially prompting Kø to terminate via contingency.

To offward the pressure of competing buyers, Kø may include a stipulation that prevents its seller from advertising, or accepting back-up contracts. Because back-ups have value, such stipulation will likely cost a buyer some concession. Even so, such stipulation cannot prevent back-up offers from being presented to a seller, only the prevention of its seller negotiating and creating back-up contracts.

It may seem that positions K2, K3, and K4 are long shots to becoming Kø, but as one cannot know the future, a place in line is better than not. To protect themselves while waiting, buyers are wise to secure a contingency allowing for back-up contract termination upon notice to seller, at any time prior to becoming Kø. Such stipulation gives back-up buyers freedom to continue shopping for substitute properties, without relinquishing their place in the queue.

Back-up contracts pose pros and cons for buyers and sellers alike. Because contracts lock-in price, a fast-trending market may benefit one party over another. Depending upon terms, earnest money may become tied-up, inhibiting its use otherwise. And, because back-up contracts slide into place without re-negotiating, their mere presence may push Kø to quietly sail thru contingences; emboldened to *not lose* what they already have, Kø may peddle faster to win.[265]

Do not mistakenly think that a previously rejected or expired offer will hold a buyer's place in line. Informing a seller of one's interest is nothing more than waiting for a chance to submit a new offer if/when Kø dies, along with everyone else in the world. Such buyers must keep a vigilant watch, knowing that while they wait to negotiate, another buyer may create an actual back-up contract.

A back-up offer is just that—an offer. To secure a place in line, buyer and seller must agree to a *back-up contract*.

Lease/Purchase versus Lease/Option

Depending upon your goals as either buyer or seller, one of these will serve you better than the other.

BY LESTER THE MoLEASER

NUANCE EMBODIES EVERY AGREEMENT, making each one absolutely unique. In contrast, this article embodies an overt generalization of two similar contract types, differentiated by nuance of their own.

Suppose a buyer is either unable to buy now, or unsure whether or not he should buy now. Either way, he wants to buy soon. Now suppose he finds a seller willing to rent now and sell later. This supposed buyer/seller pair has two basic choices of contract construction.

A **Lease/Purchase Agreement** is two *harmonizing* agreements: a lease agreement and a purchase agreement, with an expectation the buyer/tenant will execute each. Think of it as signing a purchase agreement now, which is set to close months into the future—after the buyer first rents the property for those months. The price, closing date, and all other details of the purchase are determined now. Inspections and repairs are conducted upfront, leaving the buyer/tenant responsible for repairs and maintenance throughout the lease term. In this way, the seller is not a landlord in the traditional sense, as he merely collects rent payments.

Typically, lease deposits and earnest monies are abandoned in lieu of a hefty down payment made prior to moving-in. If the buyer/tenant defaults on either agreement, he loses this money. Some sellers agree to rebate a portion of each rent payment at closing. For lease/purchase agreements, the last day on the lease is closing day on the purchase.

A **Lease/Option Agreement** is three *separate* agreements: a lease agreement, a purchase agreement, and an option agreement, with an expectation the buyer/tenant will execute the lease, but not necessarily the purchase. As before, the lease and purchase agreements are negotiated upfront, except this time the closing date is not set by the calendar, rather the buyer/tenant's option.

When a sales price is negotiated today, and the future value is unknown, a buyer may gain value in trade. To offset a seller's potential loss in value from a future sale, the buyer buys an option from the seller. This option gives him the right to execute his purchase agreement anytime before his lease expires. Exercising the option causes the lease to automatically end and the purchase to commence. Some parties agree to discount the purchase price by the cost of the option, but most do not.

Because the tenant may never exercise his right to purchase, the seller acts as a regular landlord during the lease, collecting deposit money and conducting needed repairs.

It should be noted that once the lease/option is agreed and signed, the seller may sell the property to a third party at any time. However, the new owner is obligated to honor the tenant's option. For this reason, a holder is wise to file his option with the county records office; putting all others on notice mitigates the likelihood of future disputes.

It should be also noted that not all option agreements accompany a lease. Some investors buy options hoping to find a buyer willing to pay more than the investor's price, plus the price of the option.

To be succinct: under a lease/purchase, a *buyer* agrees to first rent, then purchase a property. Under a lease/option, a *tenant* agrees to rent a property until either the lease expires or he exercises his option to purchase. 🌳

How-to

Kill Contracts DEAD

Reasons for contract termination vary widely; to name a few: loan denial, repair or price reduction disputes, buyer's remorse, the changing of someone's mind, the occurrence of life events, or simply because a better offer/property came along. Aside from execution/performance, contracts may terminate in one of two ways: *bilaterally* (upon mutual agreement—by amending an agreement to end) or *unilaterally* (upon notice given by one party to the other), of which there are four reasons: 1—Contingency Exercise (AKA, prior agreement) 2—Breach/Default/Expiration 3—Rescission (non-enforceability due to fraud, mistake, misrepresentation, or missing enforceable elements)[292] 4—Impossibility of Performance (loan denial, insolvency, cloudy/broken chain of title). When your client wants to terminate (and has the right to do so unilaterally), use a fill-in-the-blank form, and give written notice of termination through official notice channels.[262] Include a reason to terminate and a citation from the contract as impetus. When your client does not have a unilateral right, attempt to end the contract bilaterally (with some sort of concession).

ecause contracts will cling to life for as long as disputes exist, the parties are wise to mutually agree to go their separate ways and bilaterally end their relationship. As consideration for being released from a contract, a buyer or a seller may have to negotiate payment or concession to the other party. Whether or not contract dissolution is warmly received by its parties, and regardless of the reasons for termination (or the methods employed to do so), the parties will likely be asked (by the earnest money holder) to agree (in writing) over the terms of earnest money disbursement. Obliging this request is warranted and prudent, because any lingering life left in a contract may disrupt the parties' abilities to perform a contract with another, subsequent party.

Therefore, the best way to end it all is for the parties to mutually agree to terminate, and disburse earnest monies; this action will result in a quick divorce and the official death of their once-vibrant contract.

Chapter 6 Quiz

What is a contract?

1
    a)   whatever its parties want it to be
    b)   a written agreement
    c)   an obligation to do something
    d)   a mafia death sentence

Which is not required to make an agreement enforceable?

2
    a)   consideration
    b)   earnest money
    c)   names of the parties
    d)   legal description

Which offers must an agent present to his client?

3
    a)   oral
    b)   written
    c)   all
    d)   all but low-ball

What is the ideal time limit of an offer?

4
    a)   six hours
    b)   twenty-four hours
    c)   as long as the co-operating agent suggests
    d)   as short as is comfortable

Who holds the earnest money?

5
    a)   the broker
    b)   the seller
    c)   the attorney
    d)   whomever the parties want

When co-operating with another agent, who should draft the purchase agreement?

6
    a)   the buyer's agent
    b)   the seller's agent
    c)   the most-competent agent
    d)   the winner of a coin flip

For matters regarding a contract, where should one send notice?

7
    a)   wherever the contract stipulates
    b)   wherever the co-operating agent instructs
    c)   to the co-operating agent's broker
    d)   to your broker

What is meant by "survival of the agreement"?

8
    a)   the contract stipulates the seller has instincts like a woodsman
    b)   contract stipulations must be performed before closing
    c)   contract stipulations must be performed after closing
    d)   contract stipulations must be performed, before or after closing

Which kind of words should never appear in a contract?

9
    a)   proper nouns
    b)   pronouns
    c)   terse words
    d)   curse words

How does one add an exhibit to a contract?

10
    a)   with a stapler
    b)   by amendment
    c)   by addendum
    d)   with letters, not numbers

Find the best answers throughout this chapter and on page 323.

WANTED
TRUE ADVOCATE

SEEKING COMPETENT INDIVIDUALS
WILLING TO TAKE DEADLY AIM AT THE
TECHNICAL, STRATEGIC & PROMOTIONAL
ASPECTS OF REAL ESTATE SALES.
MUST BE ABLE TO ARTFULLY ARGUE
ON BEHALF OF OTHERS &
ALWAYS CHAMPION THEIR CAUSE.
ARMED BY STUDY & TOIL.
MUST DISPLAY FINESSE & ACCURACY
AT HITTING EVER-MOVING TARGETS.
THOSE WITH NOTHING MORE THAN
A YARD SIGN, LOCK BOX KEY &
SELF-RIGHTEOUS INDIGNATION
NEED NOT APPLY.

BIG BUCKS AWAIT THOSE WHO COMPLY
INQUIRE ALL OVER

A Serious How-to Manual with a Sense of Humor

Just when you think the shenanigans of this book are done, there's a chapter that remains. While the previous chapters succinctly explain the real estate agent's job, some bits don't fit neatly into a category, but they are still worthy of mention. Therefore, these last pages are meant to round-out the reader's take-away.

CHAPTER SEVEN
POTPOURRI

Agents Pay for All Services

Brokers charge for all the stuff they provide.
Are you getting your money's worth?

BY THE BARE-NAKED BROKER

THE NUMBER ONE ATTRACTION of agents to my real estate brokerage is the commission split. However, smart agents consider not only what I charge, but also what I provide in return. Their scrutiny is perfectly valid because some of the stuff that brokers hawk is of great use and value, and some of it is antiquated or superfluous crap. Regardless, nothing is free, and so we charge our agents for every last bit of it.

Remember, just like you, I'm in business to make money. My job is to make my agents' jobs easier to manage; because, when I do, they make money, which makes me money. Therefore, I buy helpful products in bulk and negotiate group discounts on supportive services. Then, I sell these tools to my agents at a price less than they would pay individually. I resell some tools for no gain, but others are robust revenue centers for me. After all, I have to pay rent, utilities, and salaries, and still have some money leftover to feed my family. To do so, agents pay me through monthly fees, and/or via commission splits, as stated per independent contractor agreement.[028] Except for à la carte offerings, my agents pay for all the tools I provide, whether they use them or not.

While each broker offers a different mix of tools, most bestow the minimum basics: advice, MLS access and listing syndication, errors & omissions insurance, and a variety pack of some brokerage-branded accessories, such as telephone numbers/voicemail, email addresses, and website domains.

I may become shamed by my fellow brokers for disclosing this fact but,.. *what the hell*: beware of all broker-owned communication tools; after prolonged use, some agents have reported feeling trapped. Owning the basic tools of business gives you some leverage in the relationship with your broker because your ability to quickly walk-away ensures your broker treats you right. Besides, these tools are cheap to acquire anyway, so procure your own phone number, email, and website address. *This passage refers to direct-to-agent communiqué, not state-mandated contact information on marketing materials.*

On the other hand, some broker-provided tools and resources are well-worth the price of admission, like access to shared business machines, meeting spaces, private offices, sales meetings and networking events, listing advertisement, and (through vendor relationships) discounts on products and services. Some brokers roll-out the red carpet and provide concierge services like data entry, training classes, consultation & mentorship programs,[044] and the creation of marketing materials/content that agents may reproduce through blogs,[071] newsletters,[095] and other value-driven vehicles (all meant to save agents' time). Broker-provided prospects are popular with some agents, but can be quite expensive; *it's not that hard to find your own clients.*[078]

The unavoidable issue with bulk-purchased items is that real estate tools vary. As well, the needs of agents vary. Therefore, a single brokerage cannot be suitable to every agent. I'd love to gobble-up every agent in town, and I never want anyone to leave me, but if you are paying for tools that you don't use, or if you need tools that are not provided, it may be time to go broker shopping.[028]

Depending upon your needs and abilities, you will require more or less broker advice and support tools. Therefore, some brokers provide few—*if any*—tools in exchange for a very small commission split/monthly fee. Newcomers are cautioned: these brokerages are best suited to experienced, battle-worn, highly-competent, well-connected agents.

Just remember this: your broker is not in business to give-away signage, websites, and warm vibes. Even the tools that seem free are not; as an independent contractor, you are paying for it all. 🌳

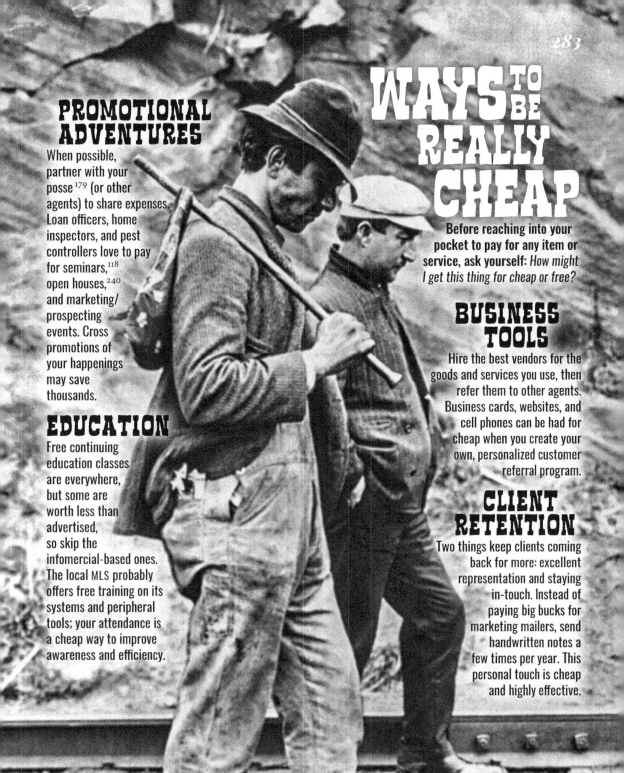

PROMOTIONAL ADVENTURES

When possible, partner with your posse [179] (or other agents) to share expenses. Loan officers, home inspectors, and pest controllers love to pay for seminars,[118] open houses,[240] and marketing/prospecting events. Cross promotions of your happenings may save thousands.

EDUCATION

Free continuing education classes are everywhere, but some are worth less than advertised, so skip the infomercial-based ones. The local MLS probably offers free training on its systems and peripheral tools; your attendance is a cheap way to improve awareness and efficiency.

WAYS TO BE REALLY CHEAP

Before reaching into your pocket to pay for any item or service, ask yourself: *How might I get this thing for cheap or free?*

BUSINESS TOOLS

Hire the best vendors for the goods and services you use, then refer them to other agents. Business cards, websites, and cell phones can be had for cheap when you create your own, personalized customer referral program.

CLIENT RETENTION

Two things keep clients coming back for more: excellent representation and staying in-touch. Instead of paying big bucks for marketing mailers, send handwritten notes a few times per year. This personal touch is cheap and highly effective.

Effort Meter

You're Gonna Need:

Appetite
Invitation
Opinions
A Few Hours Time

tips

Broker open houses are usually scheduled within the first week of a new listing, or after a significant price reduction.

Previewed property tends to stick to the brain.

An appearance of interest is created when lots of agents crowd a listing together. After all, if everyone is talking about it...

The host of a Broker Open is wise to personally invite the listing agents of competing properties, because these agents receive regular calls from buyers in the same pool.

For free adult beverages, attend after-work cocktail parties hosted by industry vendors. These soirees are a great place to network, catch-up, and learn of fresh real estate tidbits.

caveat

Eating a second plate of food may be considered rude; the over-riding factors should be your hunger and the amount of remaining vittles. Line re-entry is expected by those built like toothpicks and linebackers.

Σ Attend broker open houses to feed your belly and your awareness of the marketplace.

How-to
Eat a Free Lunch

They say there is no such thing as a free lunch. *They* also say you should make hay while the sun is shining. But what about making hay while chewing free chow? *They* didn't think of that? Probably because *they* were too busy paying for lunch. Rather than eating at your desk today, you could get paid with food to do your job. Here's the plan:

1 Attend Broker Open Houses

All over your town, agents are holding open houses—*exclusively for agents*. To entice your attendance, Broker Opens often serve food. While free fare usually comes with a price, such events also serve quick previews of your niche market[042] and mingle time with competing agents. Simple small-talk would be a waste. Instead, discuss the subject property's condition, price, value, and marketing. Go along, if for no other reason, than to learn the opinions of other agents.

With a sizable budget, new construction open houses are certain to be catered events, serving quality cuisine. To compete, Broker Open Caravans are created when several hosting-agents bundle their efforts. Depending upon a property's style or the season, an Open may be themed as the Roaring Twenties, an Easter egg hunt, an ice cream parlor, a pool party, or a turkey shoot. Substitutions for food may include raffles, drawings, or door prizes for gas/restaurant gift cards, lottery/sports tickets, or a cash-grab bag.

2 Plan Your Route

To find the feast in your niche, check your email. You will notice the majority of Broker Opens are held on the same weekday, every week. A popular start time is immediately following brokerage sales meetings, but some are held on other days or in the evenings (serving booze). Plan to attend two or three properties within two hours; some Opens advertise a menu and/or giveaways, so prioritize accordingly.

In the spirit of fun and efficiency, consider participating in a carpool caravan with other, touring agents.

3 Eat

Be polite, speak with people, and do not overfill your plate. Sit with agents you've not met and talk about real estate. If you're still hungry, heap-on a second helping, but only after a property tour first. And don't forget: there may some tasty grub waiting at the next stop.

4 Tour the Property

Once you've eaten, you should tour the house and/or community. After all, you have accepted a bribe, so now you must reciprocate. Once the tour is complete, be prepared to offer feedback to the hosting agent. Be direct, sincere, and polite, and you'll be invited back again.

Should there be inadequate room to eat, or if the chow line is too long, you may elect to tour the property before STEP 3.

Don't be confused by real estate titles. Instead, think about young love and its badge of passion. Anyone displaying a neck bruise is a Hickee, and the welt-giver is a Hickor.

The Hickor gives, and the Hickee receives —every single time.

To apply this funny trick, ask yourself: **Which party is the Hickor?** The simple answer will bring a smile. An Offeror gives an offer. A Grantor gives her property. A Lessor gives his house.

Mortgagee/Mortgagor is the exception to the rule, right? Nope. A mortgage is a promise to repay a loan. A borrower gives a mortgage in exchange for money. Therefore, a borrower is a Mortgagor, and his lender is a Mortgagee.

To always remember these titles, think back to your turtleneck-wearing days of high school. Just don't let clients see you puckering-up!

Who makes an offer?
Offeree or Offeror?
Who sells real property?
Grantee or Grantor?
Who is the landlord?
Lessee or Lessor?
Who is the borrower?
Mortgagee or Mortgagor?

WHO IS WHOM?

A Serious How-to Manual with a Sense of Humor

Effort Meter

You're Gonna Need:
Careful Consideration
Pen & Paper
Advertisement
Questions

tips

Because you will need their permission (and to seek their advice), always consult your broker before hiring an assistant.

Start by delegating tasks that are worth a smaller hourly wage than prospecting and agency.

It doesn't make any sense to hire an assistant if the result isn't more income. So, take the task seriously, and don't be so willy-nilly about it.

Hiring employees can become complicated by tax withholdings, overtime pay, and additional paperwork. To make it simple, outsource through a temp agency, or hire a payroll company.

Your state probably has rules regarding an assistant's duties pertaining to licensed/unlicensed and employee/contractor statuses. Read these carefully, and consult legal help before you hire.

To be cheap, share an assistant with an agent or two. Otherwise, find contractors who provide specialty services, like lock box/yard sign install/take-down, contract-to-close,[221] webmaster, marketing creation...

Σ   With just three simultaneous clients, a real estate business may become more work than one person can handle.

How-to
Hire an Assistant

In a nutshell, an agent's job is two-fold: convert prospects into clients and then clients into closings. When administrative and ministerial tasks begin to impede upon either conversion, assistance is needed. You'll know it's time to hire help when paperwork backs-up, calls go unreturned, your service starts slipping,[212] you're riding the roller coaster,[120] and/or your last day-off was months ago.[306]

1 Assess Your Situation

You may use an assistant to simply pick-up your slack, to manage all administrative tasks, or to completely create, document, and implement your systems. Carefully consider, and write-down exactly what your helper(s) will do. *Unlicensed Assistant* jobs: courier, clerk/secretary/bookkeeper, marketing creator/advertiser,[234] database/MLS manager,[089] system creator/manager,[070] photographer,[230] errand runner, message taker, appointment scheduler, webmaster,[071] feedback gatherer.[242] *Licensed Assistants* may: prepare contracts,[260] conduct showings,[216] host open houses,[240] attend closings, obtain signatures, interpret documents, give advice, and negotiate.[266]

Next, consider the amount of control you wish to exercise. Your control over an independent contractor is limited to an agreement defining the quality of specific services, rendered by a deadline. If you own their tools, supervise their actions, dictate their working hours, determine their workplace location, and/or provide training/instruction, then your assistant is an employee. To keep them straight, apply this test: an independent contractor may sub-contract all or parts of his job, but an employee cannot.

2 Estimate Their Value

Your assistant should cost less than the additional income their contribution adds. Ask around, to gauge the market rate for the help you need, and then decide how much, and by what structure, you will make payments. Common choices include salary, hourly, per job, percentage/fee per closing, bonuses, or some creative combination of these. Remember: talented helpers are usually worth the extra expense.

3 Interview Candidates

Your helper should lighten the load, not foster additional worries. So, ask questions that uncover their aptitude, intelligence, and inclination to solve problems. Describe their duties, and get their buy-in. Finding the right assistant takes time, so don't pick the first schmo who answers your advertisement.

4 Give Direction

Avoid training employees by the follow-me method, and do not manage by hover. Instead, give your assistant clear direction of task. Provide training/tools (checklists, scripts, systems), set priorities, and then allow them room to work; evaluate their results regularly.

1 College Kids
Visit art and business departments at the local college. These students will help with logo design, marketing materials, and image/video production. Always looking to pad their portfolio, students are an ample source of cheap labor.

2 Other Agents
Find the ones who are usually standing around the office, with no apparent work to do. These agents are usually happy to help with data entry or contract-to-close management—for a modest fee, of course.[221] Hiring these agents now may lead to their future referrals, too.[112]

3 High School Kids
Plenty of teenaged students are looking for after-school work. Put them to task placing signs in yards, lock boxes on doors, and flyers on counter tops. Send them to run your mundane errands, and you'll find this cheap, go-fer labor is perfect for keeping you on task.

4 Future Para-Legals
While studying to become paralegals, many look for employment in jobs that require paperwork or nuanced attention to detail; real estate is a perfect pseudo-legal environment for their practice. Give them contract-to-close work, and have them catalogue your system while they're at it. Find them by calling paralegal schools; ask about job seekers.

CHEAP LABOR
Once you become needy for help, look to those willing to do a great job for an modest wage.

A Serious How-to Manual with a Sense of Humor

2 SELL LISTING PRESENTATIONS

When you prospect FSBO[101] and EXPIRED listings[100] for several hours every day, you will eventually acquire the skills to book more listing presentations than you can handle. Your extras are valuable to agents who lack the discipline to prospect on their own. So, sell your surplus for a fee, but don't wait to collect once they secure the listing; if you do, your fee will be dependent upon their ability to convert prospects to clients. Boo.

Just to Advertise
Dr BELL'S CELEBRATED
ROOT BEER
COOL & REFRESHING
GOOD FOR YOUNG & OLD
1¢

ROOT BEER 1¢

1 DO CMA FOR AGENTS

Many agents despise delving into market statistics to figure-out the value of their latest listing,[150] so offer them your work for a fee. They will save time, and you increase your market knowledge, all while you practice your skills. When you track the market on a regular basis, CMA generation becomes a quick task.[140] Sweet.

3 OFFER TRANSACTION SERVICE TO FSBOs

Some For Sale by Owner sellers would love to hire you, if only they could afford it. Once you discover their slim situation, make a deal: if they find a buyer, you'll do the paperwork to keep the transaction legit—in exchange for a nominal fee. You represent no one, and answer all questions in the presence of both parties. Nice.

WAYS TO ADD INCOME

REAL ESTATE HOT DOGS RELISH EXTRA CABBAGE

The Perilous Nature of Part-Time Bees

It's hard to make honey when you're away from the hive.

BY THE QUEEN BEE

As the one in charge of this hive, (not really—just go with it) my job is to assist my client (the beekeeper) in the achievement of his goal: the production of honey. However, honey does not happen overnight, rather it comes over time, through the competent completion of multiple tasks. I could do the job all by myself, but I make *gobs of honey*, which requires more time than a single bee can handle. Therefore, I employ a whole colony of bees to help me.

Some of my workers are pollen scouts and others are pollen foragers. Some are career-long comb constructors and others carry water on the weekends. Some guard the hive with their lives and others are my personal assistants. And, because they repeat the same task so often, each of my worker bees quickly become experts at their respective jobs. My system of training and doing has developed their specialty knowledge.

A queen bee who oversees honey production by leveraged labor makes much more honey than most single bees ever could. That being so, most bees dream, with honey pots in their eyes, of one day becoming queen, or at least of flying solo. However, not every bee is competent enough to run her own production, especially not the part-time bees.

Let's forget bees for a moment, and buzz-on-out into the real (property) world. While the basic tenants of real estate sales have remained the same for a hundred years, the rest of it is ever-evolving.[304] This constantly-changing environment is more challenging to navigate for those still learning to fly than for those with years of experience. On top of trying to keep current with changing tides, developing the skills to complete a new, complex task will always come slower to those not fully engrossed in its practice; real estate agents who have another, primary career ongoing also have clients who suffer from it.

Now, think about your clients for a moment. Would you recommend to them a bartender who moonlights as a mortgage broker? What about a home inspector who spends his weekdays crunching numbers in a cubical? Part-time workers are not known for doing both jobs well. Heck! You probably wouldn't even trust a part-time barber with his scissors near your cherished bouffant, so you surely couldn't endorse a part-time real estate agent as anyone's lead representative.

Some agents start their journey with part-time availability. There's nothing is wrong with being a part-time amateur, so long as you don't stay that way.[034] Plan, and then set-out to become a full-time agent, or don't even bother getting involved. Unlike beekeeping, real estate is not a hobby; amateur mistakes may cost clients time, money, and/or opportunity.[212] After all, a butchered haircut will grow-out in a month or two, but a botched real estate transaction may take a decade to recover.

So, before starting a full-time career as a part-time owner, consider an apprenticeship aboard a hive like mine. Doing so will allow you to gain expertise in specific disciplines of production, while sharing your part-time availability with other bees. Begin by learning just one job; no pressure: other bees are helping to carry the load. Once competence is gained, move-onto another role, and then another, becoming full-time in the process. Along the way, you may come to possess enhanced knowledge of the honey-making process, and soon thereafter, desire a swarm of your own. Just remember, lots of bees find value as a hive worker, because 1) they *love* honey, and 2) because making it alone is hard for most to consistently do well.

Alas, a bee who does not produce honey is useless to its keeper. So is one who serves honey from a sticky jar, with bits of bee, dirt, and broken comb suspended throughout. 🐝

YOU SKATE AT THEIR RISK

Before testing your newest program on clients, thoroughly check the ice for any possible thin spots.

Your plan to pull-off a reverse-pivot double-axel quadruple-jump sure sounds great on paper. If you land it, then awesome for you! But if you wipe-out, your client may suffer. Innovative ways may be your signature move, however your clients deserve to know if your methods are tested, or newly conceived. Your client trusts your real estate competency, otherwise they would not have hired you. Reciprocate that trust by spending ample time on research and critical analysis of your plan. Then discuss it with informed people before tossing it into your client's rink.

Your latest theory on pricing/marketing/negotiating may find success, or it may fall flat. Don't experiment on your clients without their consent. Present the pros and cons, and let them decide whether or not it's safe to skate.

Effort Meter

You're Gonna Need:

Open Eyes
Simple Consideration
Backbone
Fortitude

How-to
Avoid Mortgage Fraud

Mortgage fraud is a federal crime. If you commit mortgage fraud (or quietly watch someone else do it) you may end up in the *big boy jail*. Since you find it senseless to participate in fraudulent activities, making yourself aware of its tell-tale signs may stymie the possibility. On the other hand, if you don't heed the advice of this article, you may find yourself doing a nickel upstate.

Avoiding mortgage fraud is easy when you simply keep in-mind that a lender has the right to know all the details of involved real estate transactions. This is because a lender may not prudently decide whether or not to lend money to a particular person, on a particular property, unless that lender has all the facts regarding the person, the property, and the agreement between its principal parties.

☞ The Mortgagor's Razor

When a buyer is obtaining financing, all parts of the transaction must be disclosed to the lender(s).

Continued Explanation

tips
This might sound silly, but if there is no lender involved, then mortgage fraud becomes impossible. You gotta have the possibility of a mortgage before you can commit mortgage fraud.

If a co-op agent insists that an action is not mortgage fraud, but you are certain that it is, politely ask him to call his favorite attorney and present the scenario. Once the co-op speaks with a lawyer, chances are great that he will acquiesce.

Mortgage fraud: just *don't* do it!

caveat
Sometimes, brokers, loan officers, and co-op agents will benevolently suggest mortgage fraud as the correct course of action. These people don't mean harm; they are simply ignorant of their intended crime. At times like these, it's good to be certain your actions are lawful.[036]

Σ   When obtaining financing, all parts of the transaction must be disclosed to the lender(s).

If even a dime is borrowed, the lender of that dime should be given all the facts regarding the transaction, and nothing should be left out, nor placed "on the side."

Ignorance is not an excuse to commit fraud, even if your excuse is that the loan officer told you it was okay. Remember: loan officers rarely lend their own money; most of the time, they work as employees of lending institutions. The decision of whether or not their institution lends money is not their's to make, so just because a loan officer directs you to act in a particular manner does not mean that the prescribed act is free of fraud.

At times, a loan officer will claim: if certain facts are presented to the lender, then the loan will be denied. This is a tell-tale sign that ommission of said facts constitutes mortgage fraud. If this scenario is presented to you, your client must either find a different property, obtain alternative financing, or amend the purchase agreement to remove offending stipulations.

If You Suspect Mortgage Fraud:
1. Tell the parties involved that you suspect mortgage fraud, and that you will not participate.
2. Offer a lawful alternative to the scenario.
3. Tell your broker that you suspect mortgage fraud.

Mortgage Fraud Scenarios:
- Co-op agent suggests that you leave personal property off the purchase agreement, and instead move it to a bill of sale that will be held privately, "on the side."
- Loan officer suggests that you not mention a property defect within the language of the purchase agreement.

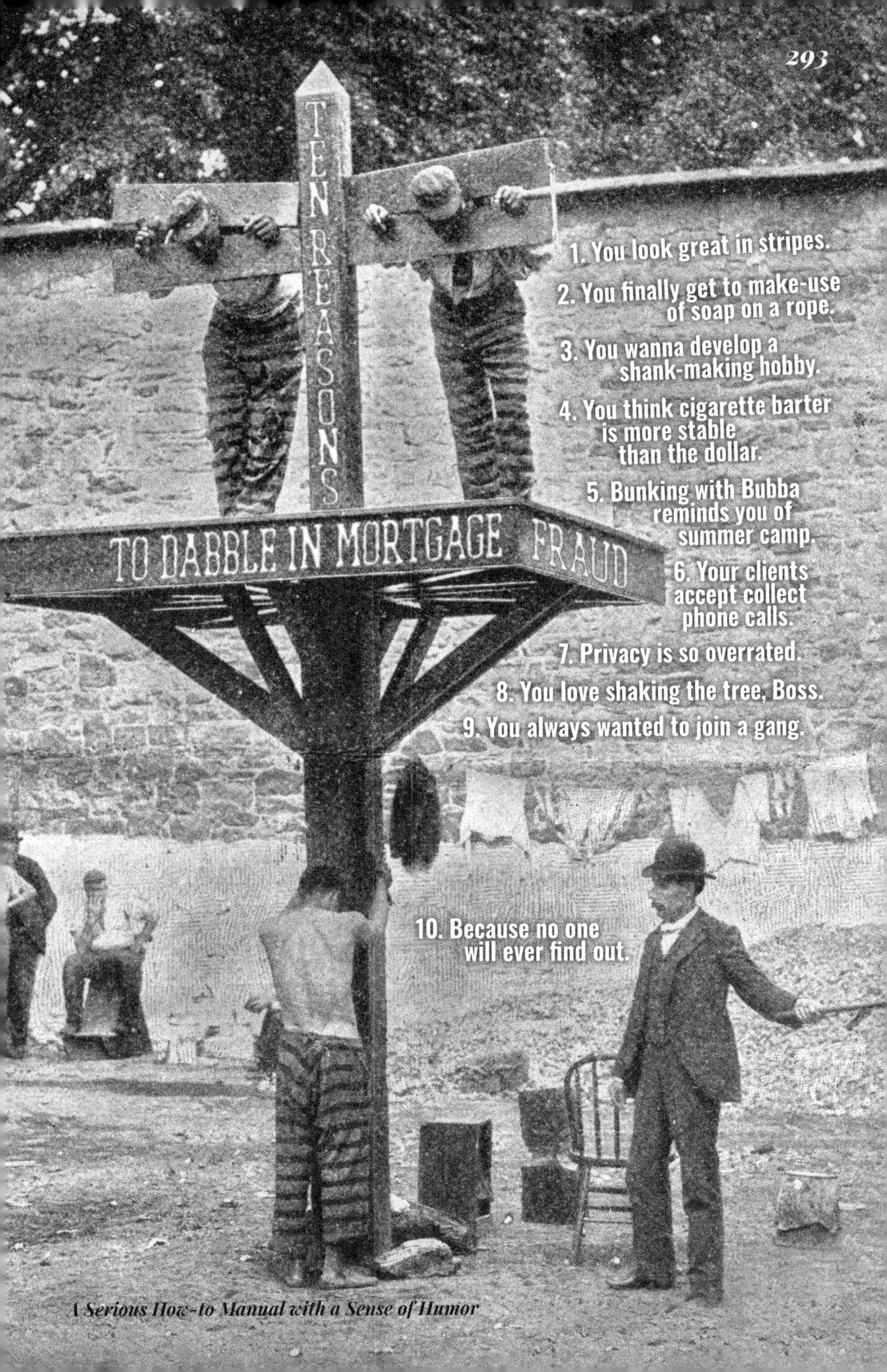

TEN REASONS

TO DABBLE IN MORTGAGE FRAUD

1. You look great in stripes.

2. You finally get to make-use of soap on a rope.

3. You wanna develop a shank-making hobby.

4. You think cigarette barter is more stable than the dollar.

5. Bunking with Bubba reminds you of summer camp.

6. Your clients accept collect phone calls.

7. Privacy is so overrated.

8. You love shaking the tree, Boss.

9. You always wanted to join a gang.

10. Because no one will ever find out.

A Serious How-to Manual with a Sense of Humor

Effort Meter

You're Gonna Need:

Questions

Intuition

Squinty Eyes

Polygraph Machine

How-to
Tell if Your Buyer is a Liar

There is an old saying in the real estate industry: buyers are liars. No one wants to associate with liars, so follow these guidelines to help sort the filthy fibbers from the pernicious perjurers:

1 Ask: *Are You a Liar?*
Start with this simple question.
- If he answers YES: *Bingo!* You've got the truth! Now push that liar to the side.
- If he answers NO: well, isn't that just what a liar would say?

For certainty, assume anyone who answers NO to be a low-down, dirty, rotten liar.

tips

Some people are liars, but this supposed maxim is nothing more than standard-variety hogwash. Its dubious creation was born in the minds of ignorant, excuse-making agents who probably suck at their job.[024]

You may avoid the likelihood of a wishy-washy buyer by conducting a thorough needs analysis,[174] and by establishing clear expectations.[168]

2 Give Your Intuition a Try
Boldly stare your buyer in the eye, and determine just exactly which kinda liar he is.
- Does he possess a brazen look? Bold-faced liar!
- Is he freshly shaven? Bald-faced liar!
- Are his pants on fire? Liar! Liar!

These are important questions; it's hard to argue with sound logic.

3 Hook 'Em Up to a Polygraph Machine
Borrow a lie detector from your local, crime-fighting squad. If the coppers refuse you, make your own:
1. Grab some jumper cables and a car battery.
2. Connect the parts with finesse.
3. Clamp one cable onto your buyer's left index finger and the other to his right ear lobe.
4. Turn up the juice.

If the sensation of electric shock coursing through your buyer's body causes him to cry out in pain, then he is for certain a yella-bellied, horse-thieving, good-for-nothin', lousy-ass liar.

caveats

Do not repeat mythical mantras; doing so leads to bad juju.

Don't make excuses. Instead, arm yourself with the knowledge,[038] systems,[070] and resources[043] to do your job the right way.

Σ   Prospects and clients are not out to waste your time with petty lies.

The Truth About Buyers

Buyers earning the fibber tag are usually not liars; instead, they typically fall into one of the following two categories:
1. they changed their mind, or
2. they withheld information.

Sometimes, a buyer will change his mind; this doesn't make the buyer a liar, it makes him human. Buyers withhold information when they don't trust you. You may avoid closed-off and indecisive buyers by building rapport,[081] demonstrating your value,[090] and by asking the right questions.[174]

Remember, while tossing around an apocryphal anecdote will surely make you sound silly, belief in such phrases may some day cost you commissions. Poopers.

PARACHUTING

is when an agent floats into buyer representation, right before their newfound buyer signs an already-negotiated purchase agreement. It happens when a buyer's licensed-acquaintance learns (at the last minute) of his pending purchase, or when that buyer meets a random agent in a bar the night before. Either way, listing agents hate these plummeting marauders and their commission-slashing ways.

Listing agents incur extra work on behalf of unrepresented buyers, by means of showing the property, helping secure financing, and explaining purchase agreement details. Expecting extra payment for this work, but instead seeing it go to a parachuting agent can be down-right deflating—and rightfully so. However, when these listing agents seethe, it's with misplaced anger. They should instead look to their own commission structure, whereby a seller pays double commission when the buyer is unrepresented; extra pay may be warranted, but double is a bit excessive.[181] Also, prior to negotiating a purchase agreement, a listing agent should disclose agency to an unrepresented buyer—whereby the buyer declares his understanding of unrepresented status, but does not surrender his right to employ representation at a later date. Within this same document, the buyer could contractually release the seller from the custom of paying fees to any potential, future agent.

An agent cannot deny anyone their right to representation. After all, a buyer may hire fifteen agents (if he sees fit), but his decision to do so does not automatically obligate a seller to pay for any of them.

DROP-IN ANYTIME

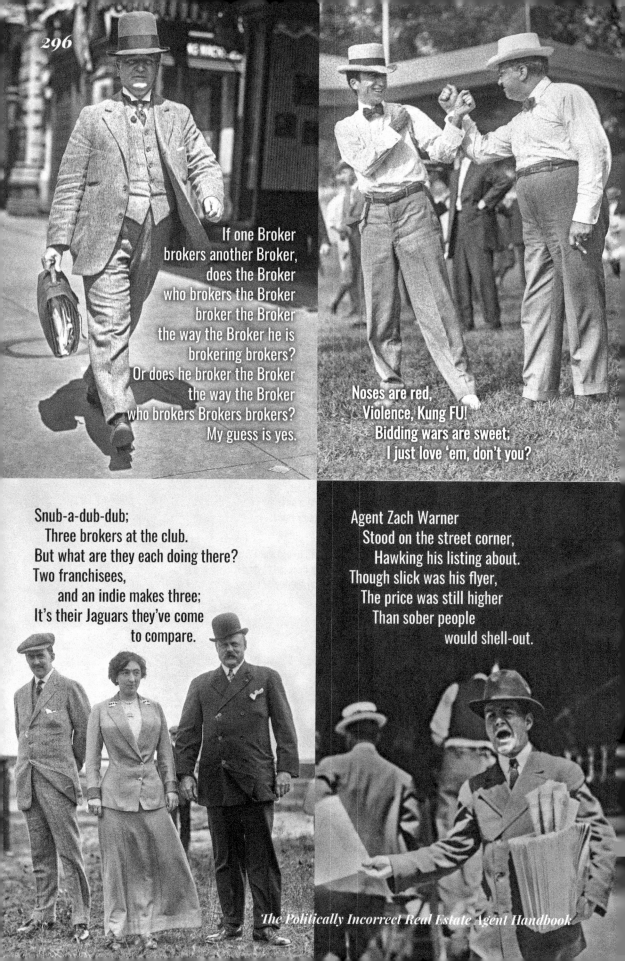

If one Broker
brokers another Broker,
does the Broker
who brokers the Broker
broker the Broker
the way the Broker he is
brokering brokers?
Or does he broker the Broker
the way the Broker
who brokers Brokers brokers?
My guess is yes.

Noses are red,
Violence, Kung FU!
Bidding wars are sweet;
I just love 'em, don't you?

Snub-a-dub-dub;
Three brokers at the club.
But what are they each doing there?
Two franchisees,
and an indie makes three;
It's their Jaguars they've come
to compare.

Agent Zach Warner
Stood on the street corner,
Hawking his listing about.
Though slick was his flyer,
The price was still higher
Than sober people
would shell-out.

The Politically Incorrect Real Estate Agent Handbook

First-Ever Virtual Tour

There once was a house on Nantucket
 Whose owner had wanted to hawk it.
But, little did he know
 That his agent was a schmo,
And the listing shown only from the pocket.

There once was a man with a musket
 Who found that his agent had mucked it.
'Twas a vie for both sides
 That had washed with the tides.
And now *buck shot!*
 His agent can't duck it.

*Unbeknownst to the seller, his house was a pocket listing.

A Serious How-to Manual with a Sense of Humor

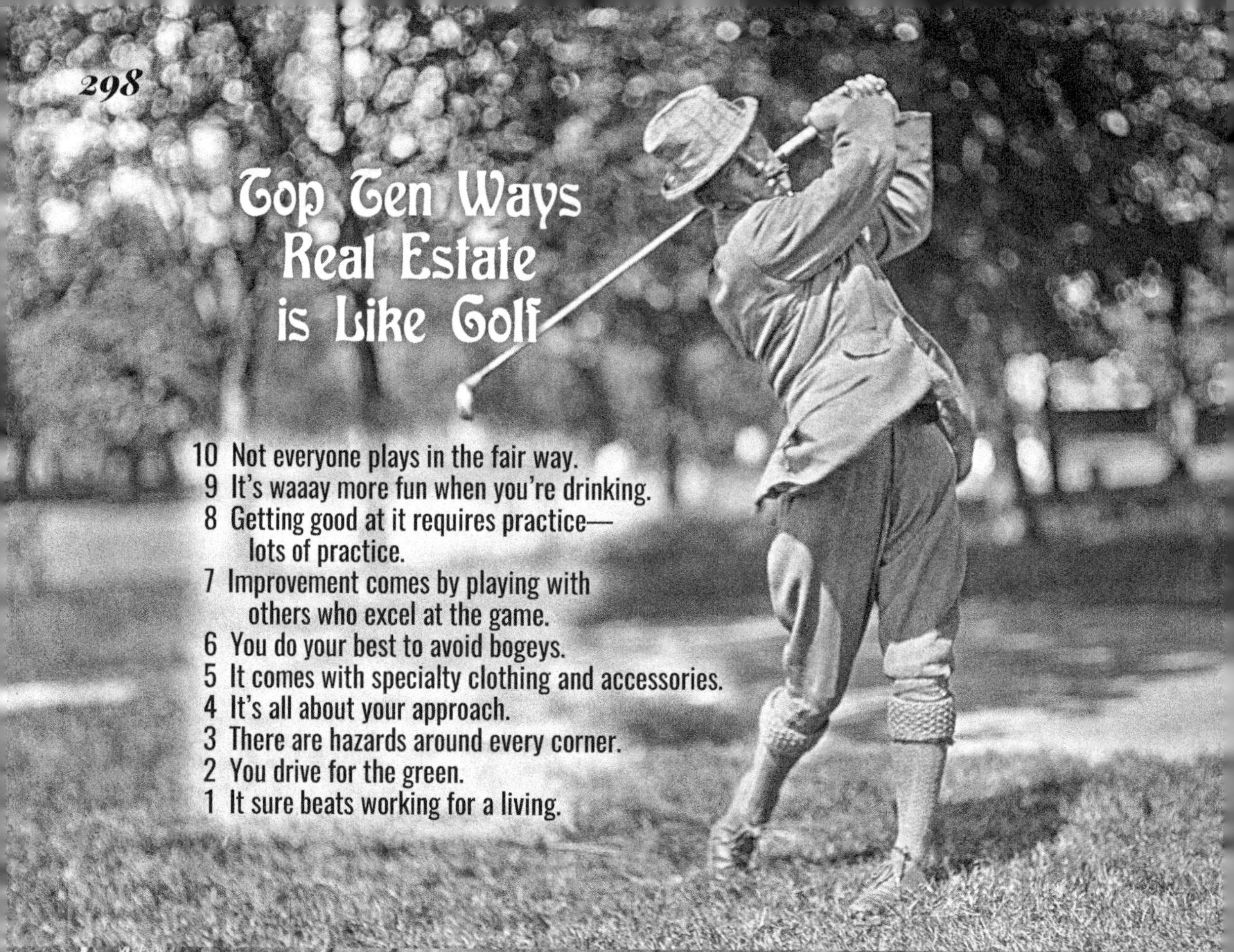

Top Ten Ways Real Estate is Like Golf

10 Not everyone plays in the fair way.
9 It's waaay more fun when you're drinking.
8 Getting good at it requires practice— lots of practice.
7 Improvement comes by playing with others who excel at the game.
6 You do your best to avoid bogeys.
5 It comes with specialty clothing and accessories.
4 It's all about your approach.
3 There are hazards around every corner.
2 You drive for the green.
1 It sure beats working for a living.

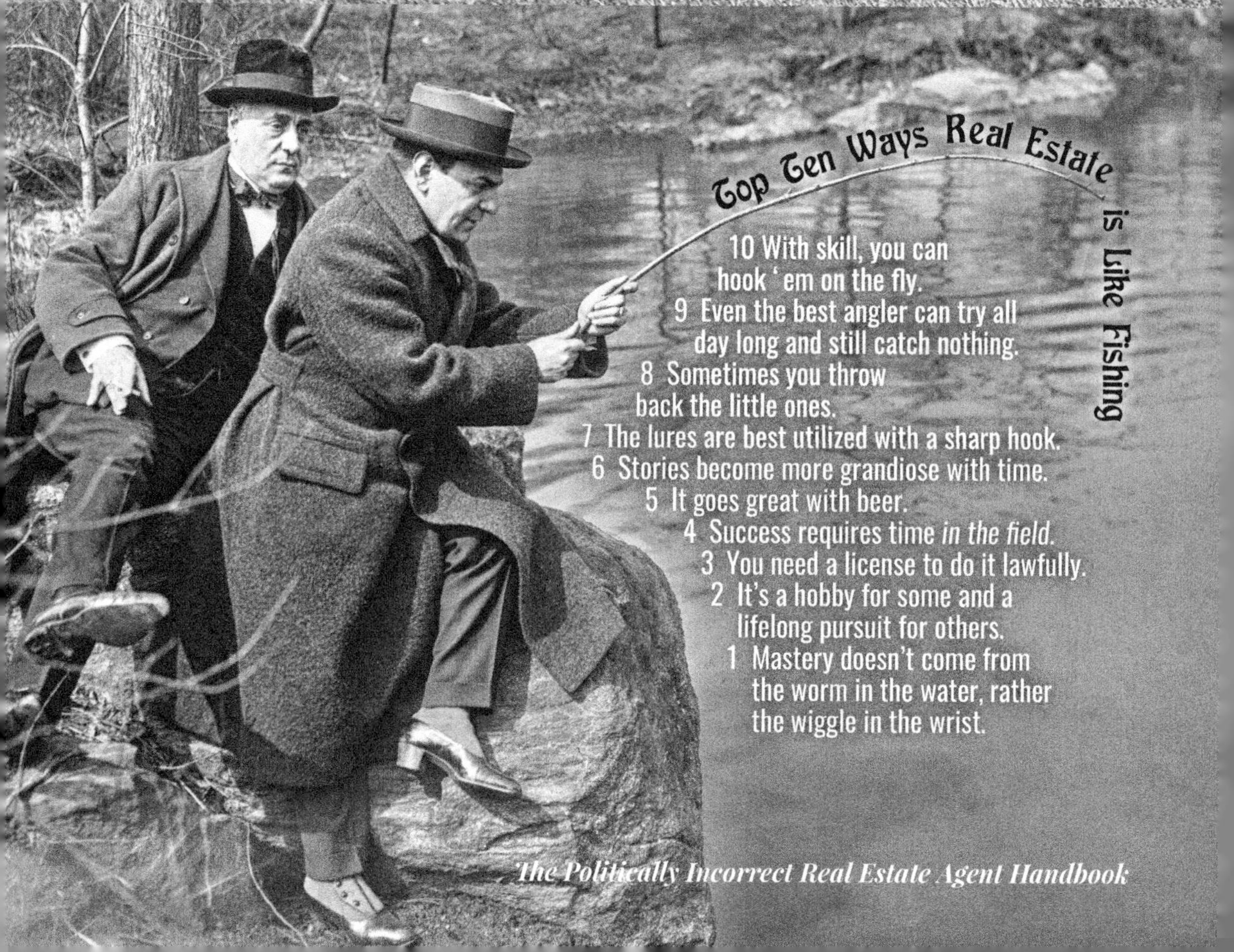

Top Ten Ways Real Estate is Like Fishing

10 With skill, you can hook 'em on the fly.
9 Even the best angler can try all day long and still catch nothing.
8 Sometimes you throw back the little ones.
7 The lures are best utilized with a sharp hook.
6 Stories become more grandiose with time.
5 It goes great with beer.
4 Success requires time *in the field.*
3 You need a license to do it lawfully.
2 It's a hobby for some and a lifelong pursuit for others.
1 Mastery doesn't come from the worm in the water, rather the wiggle in the wrist.

What do you think of my newest listing?
What's that you say? You wouldn't list
this dump of a property? Why do you say
that? Because it's ugly? Because it backs-up
to traffic? Because it will be a "tough
sell"? What is it? Oh, because it's
value is low, and it therefore doesn't pay
enough commission? Is that right? First of all,
**How the hell do you know what
my client has agreed to pay me?**
And for that matter: what defines a "tough
sell" anyway? Are you assuming
my listing is over-priced? Are
you saying it's unlikely that
buyers will want my "dump" of
a listing because it's "low-rent"?

the
Random
Rantings
of an
Angry
Agent

Or do you simply
mean to infer that I
will fail in my attempt
at selling it? Isn't it our
job to bring buyers and sellers
together? Why
should it matter
what the property
looks like? You
do know every
property has a value,
right? Have you, in the
past, made a habit of listing
over-priced property for a small commission,
and then failed at your feeble attempts to sell it? What
makes you think we provide the same level of service to clients?
Did you know distressed sellers are often willing to pay a premium
commission to sell their property? Did you know it's because
they've already hired several agents who couldn't do the job?
Do you realize these sellers just need
someone to honestly assess their property's
condition, and then plainly explain the importance of
price matching that condition? Are you routinely dumbstruck
when your listings get few, if any, showings? When deciding
whether or not to list a property, do you
discriminate based upon
condition alone? Have
you considered discriminating
based upon price instead? You do
realize that's exactly what buyers
do, right? Hey...wait! Where are you
going? Why are you walking away?... Just
so you know, if your original reply had been,
"Because your seller is a jerk," then I might
have agreed with you.

Effort Meter

You're Gonna Need:

Inspiration
Competition
Animation
Fixation

tips

When you find yourself slacking, ask the boss: *How would I react if I were paying an employee to act this way?*

Hire some helpers.[286] Casting the inexpensive, burdensome tasks of your business onto another will free-up time for rest or rededication to the fun parts of realty sales.[346]

Chant your favorite mantra or repeat an affirmation to psyche yourself into a productive mood.

Because a smooth ride is more likely to keep you on the road than a bumpy one, learn from the past, and avoid pitfalls that are bound to recur.

A great attitude will carry you a long way down the path of motivation.[005] When you discover moments of discouragement, simply remember your most-favorite things, and then you won't sob so loud.[201]

Continue to learn and develop your real estate skills. Often times, motivation comes from the discovery of a new "trick."

Σ When you find yourself in times of struggle, and can find no remedy, avoid these words of victims: I concede.

How-to
Stay Motivated

As an independent contractor, a real estate agent is his own boss.[060] Since the boss and employee share the same body, getting fired for excessive fartin'-around is an unlikely occurrence. Still, as boss, you must find ways to keep your employee productive—otherwise, doom. So, before you down-size yourself or seek employment elsewhere, employ these suggestions to keep on truckin'.

1 Stay-Off the Roller Coaster[120]
When you neglect the search for new business in times of busyness, your income will become unsteady. The resulting stress may lead to discouraging thoughts radiating heartache into all aspects of your life. To avoid the nauseating ups and downs of this wavering wage-wobble, cultivate an addiction to prospecting.[078]

2 Abide by a Business Plan[062]
A well-crafted business plan breaks a large goal into bite-sized pieces. When these pieces are digested on a daily/weekly basis, a sense of accomplishment will pervade your being. For best results, convert bite-sized goals into a to-do list. Then keep this list in-hand, and you may be more inclined to stay on-task. After all, when things are going your way, you're likely to keep doing the things needed to keep it going.

3 Commit to a Coach[043]
Coaching shoes are best-filled by a respected non-friend. This person should help you develop a business plan, track your progress, and suggest alterations to your systems and procedures. Some agents find weekly chats with a judgmental coach to be all the motivation needed to stay on-task. This accountability creates an inescapable embarrassment of confessing failure, which drives some to succeed and others to drink.

4 Start a Rivalry
There is nothing like a little competition to spur action. So, find that guy or gal in your office who is producing more sales than you, and develop a friendly rivalry, based upon the completion of weekly goals, improvement of conversion ratios,[063] client intake, transactions closed, and/or total commissions earned. Gamble on the outcomes of your games, but not for money. Instead make wagers that payoff with silly settlements. Once you consistently outperform your rival, find a new one who challenges your abilities. If friendly competition works for you, consider joining a sales club, where you may foster several rivalries at once.

Try some silly wagers to keep you motivated:
- Loser must wash and detail the winner's car (by hand).
- Loser must clean the winner's office (dressed like a French maid).
- Loser must sing a silly song (in a public forum).

5 Ask Yourself: *Why?*

Think about why you work: discover the number one reason (whether it be to feed your family, take luxurious vacations, or acquire more toys). Then, print an image of that thing, and post it in places you frequently look—the bathroom mirror, in your car, at your desk, as your screen saver, and inside cabinet doors. Whenever you feel like goofing-off, taking a long lunch, or leaving work early to play golf, look at the picture. If the image fails to keep you working, ask yourself: *Why?* Then, get a different image.

Example: Take a picture of your children at the dinner table, eating, with forks in-mouth. Now, imagine those forks without food.

6 Reward/Punish Yourself

Celebrate weekly goal accomplishments with small, self-gifts. If chasing a carrot keeps you going, give yourself bigger rewards for closings. On the other hand, if the threat of a stick keeps you moving, censure your goal failures with distasteful environs.

Sample Rewards: ice cream sundae, manicure, movie/ sports ticket, costume jewelry, bottle of liquor.
Sample Punishments: go without TV, dessert, or beer for an extended time; give money to a rival political organization/cause; mow the neighbors' lawns wearing a t-shirt that reads: IF THIS GRASS WERE A BUSINESS TASK, I'D BE SITTING ON MY ASS.

7 Take a Break[306]

Organize your thoughts, your systems, and your methodologies. Exercise, be nourished, and balance your life. Love those around you, and find the will to continue within.

8 Eliminate Distractions

Sometimes all you need to stay on track is to compartmentalize the day. When it's time to do something, get into it whole-heartedly. Sort by priority and then focus solely on the task at-hand.[064]

9 Go Into Debt

Some people are motivated by pending loss. If this describes you, try financing a large-ticket item, with a big down payment, and stressful, monthly payments. If a huge car payment does not scare you, then buy a mansion or a yacht. Like Cortez burning his ships at the shore: there's no turning back, so you might as well keep moving forward.[303]

Ode to the Motivated: *What a Day*

Here you sit,
with no one to complain.
It was you
that we tried to explain
all about
the wax and the wane,
to be found
within realty's domain.

Now you stand,
with business on the brain.
You work hard,
so the family may gain
funds to eat,
and to avoid the distain
that rains down
when your pockets are drained.

So you run,
and you wage your campaigns
with high hopes
all day long—it's mundane.
You push on,
and find ways to sustain.
Shifting gears,
you set pace in the lane.

Now it is,
that no daylight remains.
You've done well.
You steer a gravy train
that drives home
to the old ball and chain,
with the news
that life's goals are obtained!

Here you sit:
retirement attained.
Long has gone
all the stress and the strain.
But you long
for a thrill to be sane.
Close your eyes,
and you'll be there again.

Before a real estate sales business can be placed on cruise control, operator competency must be acquired. This exhaustive task requires about two thousand hours of learning and doing, which an agent can race-thru in six months, or drag-out for six years. Then, to slingshot into the ranks of Great Agent status,[035] another two or three thousand miles of driving lay ahead.

During this ramp-up, hazardous conditions exist: clients suffer from the effects of a rookie road hog, and agent fatigue drives many to burnout. Therefore, the best course to accelerate competency is to keep both hands on the wheel, at all times (all day and all night long), for your first several months. This means you should temporarily disrupt your life until you're up-to-speed. Create more time for your trade. Skip TV and bowling nite for a season. Take-up some constructive habits, and get into the groove. Stay-up late to read about real estate. Go to more classes. Study the market harder. Prospect longer hours. Consort with those sharing your path, and ride the slipstream of their experience.[668]

Along the way, you're sure to skid-out, and cause a fender-bender or two; you may even blow a tire and cause a crash. You are, after all, a human learning how to repeat a complex task. So, make frequent pit stops, but don't waste the opportunity to top-off your knowledge, re-tool your chassis, get motivated, and get going again. The path to real estate glory is a circular one, so jump into the fast lane, and keep-up making laps until each run is as smooth as the last.

BURN SOME RUBBER

Knowledge is your knack
to staying on track; [346]
To increase its flow,
disrupt your status quo.
Then step on the gas,
and get movin' fast.
Because
trophies are never towed,
by those who go slow.

A Serious How-to Manual with a Sense of Humor

Change: The Only Constant

When changing winds are not first recognized,
surging seas may leave you capsized.

BY THE COMMODORE

As the guy hosting this flotilla, allow me welcome you with an omen: everyone is talking about the weather. In fact, the crux of the chatter is the flux of the matter. So, join in, and make yourself comfortable. *But don't get too comfortable,* because time changes the way things are done around here—for the good, the bad, and the sideways.

As you gain your sea legs, you will notice that some changes evolve slowly, over seasons, and others happen quickly, without warning. Some changes are swept-in by the proclivities of a new generation coming of age, and others are blown away by technical or regulatory antiquation. Due to ever-changing tides like these, you are wise to constantly survey the waves, and then go with the flow.

To successfully navigate these waters, you must first acknowledge the exact differences between that which you can control and that which controls you. You are able to control only your ship, crew, and charter by means of your assets (education, tools, helpers), systems (processes, tracking, analysis), and readiness (guidance, forecasting, planning).

You and everyone else adrift these high seas are controlled by the environment, which is comprised of natural (physical and temporal), legal, economic, technological, and societal elements. Changes brought by these elements include: technological advancements in the transmission of voice, image, and data; new products and loan programs; updates to laws, regulations, ordinances, and customs; and buyers' desires, reflected in trends of real property value and fashion (current tastes of particular building materials, finishes, shape/size/functionality of rooms, spaces, accommodations, and amenities).

As skipper, you must always be on the lookout for change. Keep a vigilant watch by becoming submerged in real estate and setting your compass by: reading news, reviews, and forecasts; studying the marketplace;[146] speaking with people actively involved; keeping abreast of ancillary industries;[040] and learning of burgeoning tools and ideas (technological or otherwise).[034] Then, with research in-hand, frequently scan the realm of possibilities, audit your business, adapt to controlling environments, and adopt changes to your ship, crew, and charter which will steady your rudder. A prudent, consistent changing of your ways, ever focused on maintaining an effective and efficient service for clients, will allow you to survive storms great and small.

Complacency (ignoring the environment) and craze daze (hypersensitivity to the environment) are conditions that will weigh anchor to a real estate sales business. By wallowing in either one, you risk running your ship aground because experience alone may not guarantee effectiveness and technology alone does not equal efficiency.

Through it all, you may find solace knowing that the underlying principles of scrupulous salesmanship never change.[010] In fact, the fundamentals of procuring and closing real estate clients of a hundred years ago are the same as today and shall endure a hundred years from now; tools and methods evolve, but not the core theory of it all. Even if the future brings android agents, able to dispense data with deft dexterity, buyers and sellers will remain human. And, when making complex, high-risk (real estate) decisions, humans will forever need the interpretation of information,[150] strategic advice,[154] and transaction management services.[221]

While the principle tenets of realty practice do not change, just about everything else related remains in constant motion. And, while you are forced to adapt to the environment, you get to choose the changes you adopt. In this way, whether faced with smooth sailing or surging storms, an even keel may be kept by agents who know the ropes. 🐾

Some trick Shots

The Reverse Offer

The next time one of your listings gets plenty of showings, but zero offers, select its latest looker; discover his hot buttons, and then craft an offer to match. Buyers are often so flattered by the seller's gesture that a negotiated transaction is the result.[263]

Contingency killer

Buyers enter negotiations with doubt in their minds, which is why their offers contain contingencies. A seller can stymie this doubt by conducting inspections and appraisals prior to listing, then providing these reports, repair receipts, and a matching list price to all lookers. Quick offers at top price will result.

Buyer Hijack

After closing, buyers and sellers go back to being unrepresented prospects. Use this opportunity to add buyers of your listings to your database.[089] Aid in their transition. Then, stay in-touch, and you may, one day, earn their listing.[094]

Effort Meter

You're Gonna Need:

Planned Activity
Clear Mind
Gratefulness
Big Smile

tips

Research shows that people who avoid time away from work are more likely to suffer physical maladies and then die at an earlier age than those who routinely relax.

If you absolutely must work every day (which is against the doctor's orders), then schedule time-off a couple of mornings each week.

When planning your business calendar, insert family events, holidays, vacations, and days-off first; the days that remain are meant for work.[064] This way, work interludes may be planned and anticipated.

Unplug digital devices and avoid shopping. Instead, check event calendars for inexpensive excursions.

Parents should not feel guilty for taking recess while children are in the classroom.

Your body is accustomed to wake at its usual time, so start your day-off early. Go on, get-up, and start relaxing.

Make plans, but don't let the clock dictate a day-off.

Σ   A day without significance allows the brain to reboot.

How-to
Take a Day Off

Self-employed people are prone to work all day, every day. However, all work and no play makes for a rusty, cantankerous real estate agent.[309] When rest is part of your routine, work may become less forced and more enjoyable (more effective and efficient).[012]

1 Pick a Day

Choose a day of the week to consistently skip work. Sundays are a favorite furlough amongst full-timers, but a busy one for buyers. Tuesdays may be best for you, or perhaps a date that alternates; for Pete's sake, never work more than ten days straight without a break.

On your work calendar, pencil-in days-off with ink, and schedule vacations (more than two days in a row) at least two months in advance. When your breathers are anticipated, work may be adjusted to fit.[308]

2 Make Plans

Go to a museum, eat at that new restaurant, or simply lounge by the pool all day long. *Do not* spend your day of liberty running errands or doing chores. If chores pile-up, then hire a maid or an errand boy. Life is too short to mow the lawn or iron clothing when you should be on hiatus from the rat race.

For best results, squeeze more than one fun activity into your leave of absence. Dust-off that long-neglected hobby of woodworking, pottery, fishing, gardening or break dancing. Rediscover that passion for reading, golf, photography, charity, or getting your mahjong on. Try something new like knitting, surfing, glass blowing, archery, or learning to play the glockenspiel.

3 Include Others

While some safaris are to be solo affairs, friends and family should participate in your day-off festivities, too. Bring along loved ones to catch-up and experience life together.

4 Skip the Excuses

People will respect your scheduled R&R, if they know about it. So, tell everyone about your planned days-off, especially clients; otherwise, there may be consternation later. Never apologize for taking your prescribed sabbatical—your business depends upon it.

5 Forget Work

Life is not supposed to be about work, but the fruits derived from your labor. To taste your juicy fruits, cleanse the mind of work-related issues. Because the brain is often resistant to change its routine, this step may be difficult to follow. If you suffer from work-creep, try meditation or taking several deep breaths. If the creeping becomes chronic, consider hypnosis or beer.

Gifting Wisely

A closing gift is by no means obligatory, but clients have grown to expect one. While this may seem like an opportunity to forever remind them of you, gluing your name to a set of steak knives is perhaps a waste of money. Because, no matter how sharp branded gifts may be, they're also likely to be found at the bottom of a box in the basement. Your offering should be a thoughtful gesture, not a token souvenir, a remembrance of the journey, not an excuse to squeeze referrals. So, give them something they'll like, but don't give it at the closing table. Wait a few weeks, until they've settled-in. Then, deliver it in-person, and ask for nothing in exchange. To select the perfect gift, listen to what they say along the way. Your client will probably prompt the perfect giveaway: a dinner party, potted plant, or barbecue rub. A gift card, a nice pen, meat of the month club. A kitchen tool, baked goods, or basket of fruit. The grandest gift is excellent representation, of which there is no substitute.

A Serious How-to Manual with a Sense of Humor

THE LUMBERJACK

When the going gets tough, take a break and sharpen your resolve.

I ONCE ATTENDED A LUMBERJACK festival. Amidst trade booths selling woodcraft, suspenders, and beard conditioners, and hordes of food carts hawking funnel cakes, there were competitive chores draped across an open, timberland plane. Men stood in line to test their mettle; each wanted to know who could climb a tree the quickest and who could saw a log the thinnest, but the top-dog event was a marathon wood chucking contest. Its rules were simple: the man who chops the largest pile of cordwood in six hours is king.

I happened upon the woodchuck stage just as a new head-to-head match-up was being announced. Added to its novelty was an obvious lopsidedness: one competitor was built like a Greek god and the other jack had a physique better suited to the Math Olympics.

A whistle blew, the clock began, and each lumberjack set to chopping and chopping. I stood for awhile, and watched each flanneled man toiled with a chore that my inner-child has long abhorred. Just as my attention was taxed, my belly began growling, so I wandered-off to tackle a hubcap-sized flapjack and to count log-rollers swimming in the pond. Sometime later, I returned to the wood chuck tent, just in time to see Scrawny crowned the winner. Wait... Whuuut? How in the world could this be?

My question was quickly answered as each chopper was interviewed. First, the emcee asked Brawny, "What happened?"

"I ain't too sure 'bout what happened," exhausted the muscle-bound lumberjack, catching his breath between phrases, "I chopped and chopped and chopped...without stopping,.. and every time I turned around...the little guy was sittin' down." With hands on his hips and disbelief in his words, the burly fella stared at his boots, shook his head, and between gasps for air, muttered again, "I don't know what happened."

When the microphone was pointed at the winner, the wee fella exclaimed with a smile, "The big guy is right. I took frequent breaks, but my breaks weren't just for resting; I spent that time sharpening my axe."

SORTA-TRUE STORY

DEEP CUT

All work and no play
Causes rustiness with each new day.
Thusly, swinging a dulled-up blade
Veers best-made plans to be mislaid.

So chop, chop, chop,
And always work hard.
Then take a break,[306]
Or your brain will retard.

Effort Meter

You're Gonna Need:
Patience
Professionalism
Technique
Sanguinity

tips

When you willingly act in their melodrama, an unraveling of opportunity may follow.

Always be truthful with prospects and clients, even when the news is unpleasant. Don't let their potential meltdown prevent you from doing your job.

Your client deserves your consistent professionalism, especially at times when their emotions are running hot.

Bringing bad feelings to work will only invite (and then exacerbate) problems.

emotional pitfalls
getting fired[311]
challenging negotiations[266]
low-ball offers[257]
multiple offers[259]
no offers[161]
parachuters[295]
lying buyers[294]
being over-worked[286]
gossip[315]
rejection[056]
objection[052]
the roller coaster[120]
low appraisals[161]
buyer indecision[219]
buyer's remorse[188]
price reductions[202]
feedback[242]

Σ It is your fiduciary obligation to represent clients with a level head.

How-to
Keep Your Emotions at Bay

If you sell real estate for long enough, your feathers are bound to become ruffled, for one reason or another. Dander is commonly raised through frustration, disappointment, and empathy. When left unchecked, these mind-sets may turn to callousness, petulance, and/or acrimony. Part of client care includes demonstrating to clients that you do in fact care; however, it does not include getting bogged-down in their pain, anxiety, or over-zealousness. Before allowing your emotions to run wild, be warned: bad feelings can wreak havoc upon the success of you and clients, alike.

1 Avoid Emotional No-Nos
Within the course of business, you will encounter agents, prospects, customers, and clients suffering hardships. Depending upon your predilection, more or less of these sad sacks will spur your sympathy—which is perfectly human. However, your empathetic response may trigger defensive protection or a mirroring of emotions, causing foggy brain syndrome: a condition known to cloud judgement and stymie the ability to render rational representation. To always see straight:
- *Do not take offense* to anything, whether directed at you, your brokerage, your listings, or your clients.
- *Do not get pissed-off.* Remain professional, even when doing so challenges your patience.
- *Do not take pity upon others,* especially your clients.

2 Practice Emotional Tolerance
Go into all work situations in a neutral or good mood, and don't allow another's negativity to influence your disposition. Utilize self-control. Be direct, but genteel. When you feel yourself getting emotional, take a step back. Walk away before it's too late to do so. Breathe. Before having the next conversation, look at the facts and write down your thoughts. Run the numbers. Consider another perspective. Ask for help. Don't respond right away.[313]

When a client enters a frenzied state, remain grounded, calm. Allow them room to vent, give them facts, choices, pros/cons, and your opinion. Then, let them decide. When you feel their choices are detrimental to their goals, speak-up. Attempt to chill their fever. If necessary, provide written disclosure to express your apprehension.[180]

3 Consider Your Client
As your client's face, ears, and mouthpiece, always negotiate and advocate on their behalf with conviction, poise, and prudence. Otherwise, your emotional tilt may have the following consequences:
- A good negotiator will recognize manic emotions, and play them to your disadvantage.
- A crabby or languid attitude may dissuade an offer otherwise coming your way.
- Irrational posturing may kill an otherwise closable transaction.

How-to
Get Fired

Agents are fired by clients every day. The reasons for discharge are numerous in scope. Some are legitimate and others are dubious in deduction. Regardless, always remember this: a person can hire and/or fire any number of representatives, for any matter, at any time. However, when a person signs an exclusive-right agency agreement (to pay a fee upon performance by a specified date), simply firing a representative does not automatically nullify an accompanying, written promise to pay upon performance.

This means that if a client fires you, then—*before expiry*—contracts to buy/sell as outlined in your agency agreement, the client owes your fee, even if they hire and pay a subsequent agent. In a nutshell: active representation and an exclusive right to commission are separate issues. This fact gives you leverage in the negotiation that follows your break-up (assuming you have not otherwise breached your duties, as outlined in the agreement).

1 Consider Your Options

Before you see red,[313] think about what you'll do next:

1. *Restore harmony.* Sometimes a frank discussion of circumstance will remedy their reason to reject you. Other times, a quick chat about your leverage will reverse their mind. Periodically, nothing may be said to eradicate your expulsion.
2. *Let them go for free.* Sometimes the best play is to walk away, with bridges left standing, especially when you feel somewhat-culpable of the firing offense. To do so, shake hands and mutually dissolve the agency agreement.
3. *Terminate for a fee.* Explain your leverage, and negotiate something fair, congruent with their reason for booting you. Consider an agency agreement stipulation for such occasions. In doing so, insert a hefty termination fee that will discourage cancellation, but compensate your time and money spent. Beware: a termination fee may give a client incentive to fire you, pay your fee, and then conduct a transaction for higher gain without you.
4. *Wait and see.* If the previous options fail to yield an acceptable resolution, simply refuse to terminate the agency agreement. If expiry comes before they buy/sell, the matter is over and done. If they buy/sell before expiry, approach them again and seek your fee. If they refuse your advances, legal action is your sole remaining option to collect.

2 Consider the Future

Before seeking compensation from those who fire you, consider future relationships, your reputation, and the importance of setting expectations.[168] To protect yourself, document every action you take. Keep a dated record of each property shown to buyers.[216] Catalog marketing efforts/inquiries/showings, and keep sellers updated.[243] Be diligent, do your job, and you will rarely (if ever) get sacked.

Effort Meter

You're Gonna Need:
Broker Buy-in
Preparation
Negotiation Skills
Calmness

tips
Your broker ultimately decides how to handle clients who relinquish their representation.

Setting clear and mutual expectations with clients, then upholding your end of the bargain, is the best safeguard from being fired.

Any third party who tampers with the written agency of your client is committing tortious interference with contract—a legal no-no.

When you're fired due to breach of duties, leverage is shifted to the client.

reasons you'll be fired
• Seller receives an amazing offer from a mystery buyer who wants you gone.
• Buyer finds a FSBO who simply won't deal with agents.
• Client decides to not buy or sell right now.
• Client has changed their mind about you, and *found someone better.*
• You keep nagging them to reduce their listed price.[202]
• You breached the agency agreement.
• You suck at your job.[024]

Σ Agency agreements with commission stipulations give freshly-fired agents leverage to negotiate an equitable divorce.

Shrug It Off

Don't let one bogey ruin your day; shift course and pretend it didn't happen. Don't take their words personally.

Poker Face

Drive a wedge between your emotions and your body language. Keep quiet until the blood fades from your face.

Jot Notes

When you get really mad, put your thoughts on paper. When done, throw it out. Be cool when you re-approach.

Context

When someone is speaking rough, think of their perspective. Perhaps they're not actually out-of-bounds, just frustrated.

Happy Place

Go there. If you don't have one, think of cold beer at the clubhouse. The trick is to let your eyes glaze over. Think only happy, life-fulfilling thoughts and not the pesky negative ones. Your mellow is starting to show.

Walk It Off

Before you take another swing, consider just where your ball lies. A quick putt around the block will settle nerves and refocus your aim.

Laugh

When life gives you divots, make marmalade. Levity offwards the sand traps of your day. Laughter is medicine, so take a double dose.

Ways to Keep Yer Cool

Getting teed-off is bad for business and a hazard to your health. So, chill-out before you give yourself a stroke.

A Serious How-to Manual with a Sense of Humor

Effort Meter

You're Gonna Need:

Willing Fanatic
Video Camera
Script
Merit

tips

Composing a script for your client allows for concise conveyance of your selling features without a long-winded, boring explanation, which may not highlight the proprietary benefits you provided to that particular client.

The best way to get terrific testimonials is to provide a level of service that is so satisfying your clients are compelled to sing your praises.

Most smartphones have the capability of capturing high-quality video, so there is no need for special equipment.

Make your testimonials look professionally produced, with excellent lighting and sound. An internet search will teach you some simple video-recording tricks.

Σ   Pithy video of satisfied clients can propel prospects in your direction.

How-to
Get Terrific Testimonials

Testimonials allow you to talk about yourself without involving your own mouth. The written versions are on-the-outs because, for all we know, typed words may be completely fabricated. Contrasty, video is all the rage! Pithy clips of happy clients, revering the valuable points of your service, are both believable and entertaining.

Craft your testimonials to be specific and brief. Overlay excellent video and you can make prospecting less laborious. Follow these steps to make your directorial debut:

1 Write the Script

Ask your client why they like you. Ask for the reason they would refer your service to another. To build their script, combine their words with statistics from their purchase/sale. Then ask your client to read it on camera.

Remember, you're making a movie here! Scripts are required for maximum impact, so practice with your client until it feels natural. Remember to include your name; otherwise, the testimonial could be about anyone.

Sample script:
Our house was listed for six months, with two different agents, resulting in no sale. Luckily, we then met Agent Andy. He not only found our buyer in twelve days, but got us every penny of our asking price! Now we're able to move-on and purchase our dream home. We just wish we had met Agent Andy sooner!

2 Record the Script

A modest video camera or smartphone will achieve desired results. Use a tripod to avoid a wobbly picture. Make certain the movie star's voice is loud and clearly the primary sound (not wind or traffic).

3 Keep it Short

Your videos should not exceed thirty seconds in duration, with the ideal length being between fifteen and twenty seconds. This brevity keeps your testimonials entertaining and more likely viewed. No worries; lots can be said in a quarter of a minute.

4 Advertise

Post your testimonials everywhere. Include your website/blog,[071] pre-listing package,[193] within the body of mass emails, your monthly newsletter,[095] on social media,[087] in your email signature,[026] within camapigns,[094] and anywhere else prospects may roam.

Sample Clickbait:
- What are sellers saying about Agent Andy?
- Wish we had met him sooner!
- Watch this before you hire another real estate agent!

How-to Blow-Off What They Say About You

Agents can be a catty bunch, especially when the status quo is disrupted. When a change to the norm seems likely to alter their income, claws emerge, and anyone responsible for that change becomes susceptible to spoken stabs. Such behavior is an expected part of the human condition, but this revelation does little to stop it from sucking once you've become the target of their slings and arrows. The trouble is, your successes are bound to rub them wrongly because when you win, they lose—or so it seems to so many of the afflicted.

For example: suppose you begin farming a neighborhood[104] that is already established by an agent or two. Once your listing intake equals theirs, you will be, without-doubt, a ginormous jerk. This goes double if your break-in was due to novelty marketing. Offended agents are unlikely to approach you directly on these matters because you have done nothing wrong, *and they know it.* You are a threat to their income (or they're down-right jealous), so rumors will be concocted and nasty things will be said about you and your business.

What these irritated agents fail to realize is that there remains plenty of business to go around and that the market is constantly changing; agents must adapt to survive.[304] Throughout, you will find some agents championing your successes and others showering you with animosity for years to come. Most won't care either way or will soon settle to accept your placement within the market. So, don't fret over a few wicked words. Fight back by continuing to chase your ideal of upright success. It's not until they refuse to co-operate with you that you're in real trouble.

NOTICE: If within your marketplace all agents are best friends, rivalries do not exist, and nary an agent speaks a disparaging word, then disregard the text to the left.

A Serious How-to Manual with a Sense of Humor

1 STATS

Everyone loves a guy or gal who can rattle-off market statistics like their favorite pizza toppings.[343] Throw in some personal stats, and you're boasting now, pardner.[063]

2 PRESS

Stir-up some coverage with a press release. Publications may be interested when you list a unique property or when you change brokers or whenever you need a boost in morale. Be sure to throw-in some of those aforementioned statistics.

3 TESTIES

The best braggarts get someone else to do it for them. So, round-up past clients who yee-haw about you and ask 'em for a video testimonial.[314] Promote those good reviews to prospects large and small. Online peer-review is the next big thing in agent vetting, so it's time to send in the cavalry.

4 RADIO

Call local stations and promptly toss your hat into the ring. Volunteer as an industry voice or vie for your own show. Otherwise, call-in whenever they're talking about real estate; you just might rustle-up some interest in yourself.

5 PODCAST

If them varmints won't let you on the public airs, then create your own radio station on the intarwebs. Promote your digital gabfest via email signature, newsletter, website, and any other giddy-up you can find. Keep it mostly real estate, but add some flavor to keep your listeners interested.

6 WEBSITE

On the *About Me* page of your site, be sure to list your achievements in education and citations within the industry. And don't bother mentioning your young'uns nor that old hound dog. This glory is yours, so show off your skills instead.[071]

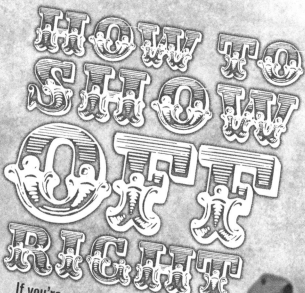

HOW TO SHOW OFF RIGHT

If you're gonna strut your stuff, you might as well make it memorable.

Chapter 7 Quiz

Which services do brokers provide for free?

1
  a) nothing is free
  b) yard signs
  c) sales meetings and networking events
  d) advice

Which of these tasks may not be performed by an unlicensed assistant?

2
  a) database management
  b) hosting an open house
  c) creation of marketing materials
  d) errand running

What should you do when you spot mortgage fraud?

3
  a) tell those involved of your suspicion and decline participation
  b) offer a lawful alternative
  c) tell your broker about it
  d) do all of these things

How can a listing agent avoid parachuters?

4
  a) with a slingshot
  b) with carefully-worded contracts
  c) by ignoring them
  d) parachuters are unavoidable

How should you stay motivated?

5
  a) by adhering to a business plan
  b) by purchasing an expensive, new car
  c) by taking a consistent day-off
  d) by any and all means that work for you

When an agent gets fired, who is the ultimate decider in what happens next?

6
  a) the agent
  b) the agent's broker
  c) the client
  d) none of these

Before implementing zany, new ideas, with whom should you seek approval?

7
  a) your broker
  b) your client
  c) your spouse
  d) all of these people

Which part of real estate sales never changes?

8
  a) the principles of scrupulous salesmanship
  b) the terms of your independent contractor agreement
  c) the time required to achieve competency
  d) everything changes

Which of these is not a typical catalyst for negative gossip?

9
  a) hunger
  b) jealousy
  c) rivalry
  d) boredom

Why are scripted, video testimonials preferred?

10
  a) for brevity and convenience
  b) for believability and accuracy
  c) both of these are right
  d) neither of these are correct

Find the best answers throughout this chapter and on page 323.

Classified

HELP WANTED

Smooth Operator — wanted for performing my listing presentations for me. Paperwork, script practice, web design & picking-up dry cleaning are taking all my time. $5/appt. My name goes on the yard sign. NO exceptions! Box 55

Masticator — seeking food chewer. Business is booming; got no time to gnash my nosh. Three meals per day, M-F, 10¢/bite. No vegetarians. Box 42

FOR SALE

Yard Signs — old and faded, like my career. $2 each or will trade all for bucket of chicken. No judgement. I've gotta eat. You pick up. Box 01

Website — seems broken. Only gets leads from Donald Duck and Seymour Butts. $1 Box 58

REAL ESTATE

Basement Apartment — for rent. Immediate availability. Deadbeat son finally moved out after getting married to his broker. $150 per month

due to leftover stench of despair. No windows. Box 81

For Sale by Owner — 157 Elm Street. 1 bedroom, hot plate, outhouse. Better Hurry. Selling cheap: $1,000,000. No agents. Box 07

ANNOUNCEMENTS

Open House — 678 Maple Ave. Cookies and tea served. Bring your grandmother; she'll appreciate the decor. This Sunday only: 2:15-2:30pm

OFFERINGS

New Broker in Town — agents pay $10 per transaction. You'll enjoy no desk duty, no fees, no dues, no help, no questions asked, no questions answered. Go figure it out for yourself. Box 99

Cleaning Service — we'll make your listing shine so bright that no one will ever notice how over-priced it is! Box 28

Removal — lose your load. Junk, funk, stumps, humps: we haul it all. No questions asked. $15 per burden. Box 14

PERSONALS

Real Estate Wife — seeking woman to replace the one who left me. She kept the staff. I kept the name: Team Paramour. Let's rendezvous! Box 46

Soulmates — seeking sellers to love me and my ways. We'll list at your price and I'll work for free. I just want my sign in your yard. C'mon. Let's play nicey-nice. Box 89

EVENTS

Class — learn how to sell real estate without talking to anyone, doing any paperwork, or leaving home. One-time event, Saturday only at the Civic Center. Noon-1pm $5000

MISCELLANEOUS

Iguana — to a good home. Left behind by my sellers. Eats bugs and BLTs. Answers to the name Larry. FREE. Serious inquires only. Box 12

Self-Help Book — on topic of real estate sales. Makes me feel strange inside. Long-winded and not funny. I'll pay you to pick it up! Box 32

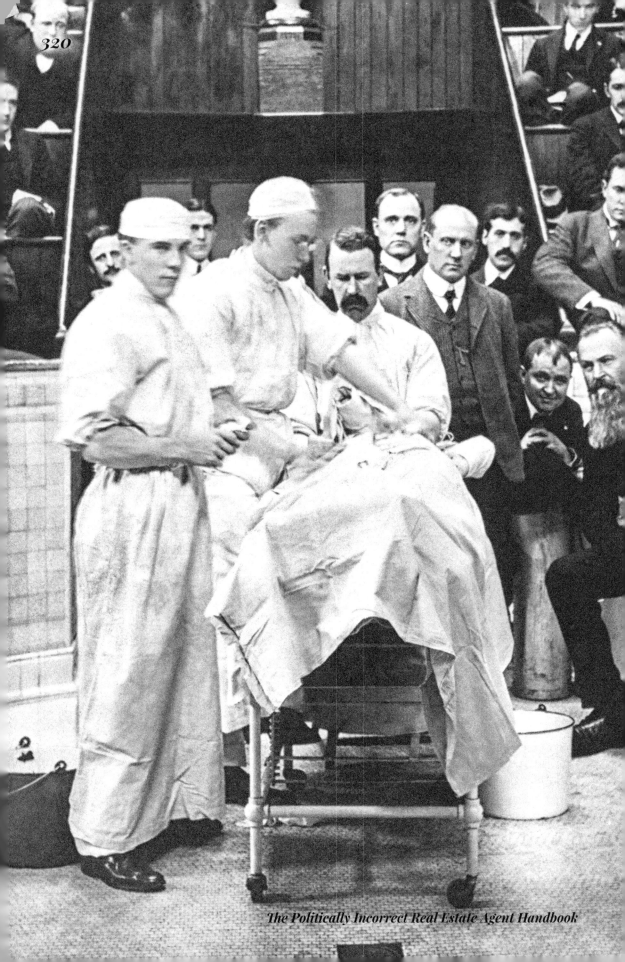

APPENDIX

CONTENTS

A Serious How-to Manual with a Sense of Humor

These pages contain the answers to each chapter quiz and other silly real estate conundrums. If your answers don't jibe with the ones here, then try again.

Logic (from page 165)

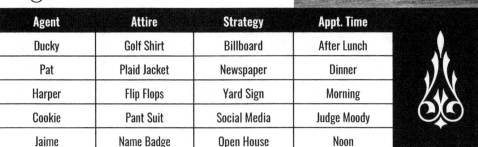

Agent	Attire	Strategy	Appt. Time
Ducky	Golf Shirt	Billboard	After Lunch
Pat	Plaid Jacket	Newspaper	Dinner
Harper	Flip Flops	Yard Sign	Morning
Cookie	Pant Suit	Social Media	Judge Moody
Jaime	Name Badge	Open House	Noon

Note: If you took the time to work the Logic Puzzle,[165] you would have figured that Pat was the agent who promised to place a newspaper ad. However, this puzzle doesn't ask about some dumb newspaper ad; the question posed to you was:
Knowing all the details,
which agent should Ms. Loutfire hire?
The first paragraph mentions that you (the puzzle solver) have been her real estate agent/neighbor for ten years. Therefore, *you* are the agent Ms. Loutfire should hire (unless you just don't get along with the old bat, that is).

A Catchy Tune
Oh where, oh where,
 can my listing be?
My Seller came:
 took it away from me.
It's gone to Melvin,
 so I cursed them real good.
Over-priced listings always
 leave me so whirled.

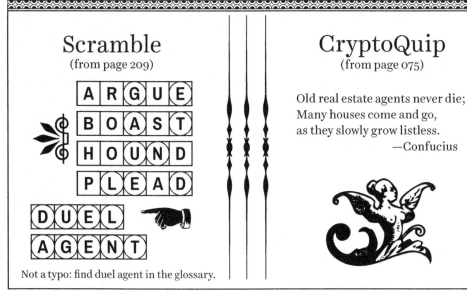

Scramble
(from page 209)

A R G U E

B O A S T

H O U N D

P L E A D

D U E L

A G E N T

Not a typo: find duel agent in the glossary.

CryptoQuip
(from page 075)

Old real estate agents never die;
Many houses come and go,
as they slowly grow listless.
—Confucius

Quizzes

Chapter 1—Basics 1:c 2:d 3:d 4:d 5:d 6:c 7:c 8:b 9:a 10:d

Chapter 2—Prospecting 1:c 2:b 3:c 4:a 5:d 6:c 7:d 8:c 9:a 10:d

Crossword (from page 247)

B	L	A	B			S	M	A	C	K			T	M	
P	A	P	A		C	O	U	P				L	I	E	N
O	P	E	N	H	O	U	S	E			A	M	M	O
	E	N	D		N		C		N		D	E	E	D
	L		I		V	A	L	U	E		E	S		
T			T	H	E	R	E		O		H	E		
H	A	M		G	Y	M		E	N	C	L	A	V	E
O	R	C	A			O	W	N			A	R	E	A
R	A	M	B	L	E	R		N	E	E		E	R	R
	B	A		X		S	U	S	H	I				N
	N	P		A	T	T	I	C		N		G		
C	A	S	A		M		O		R		K	E	R	
M	A	I	L			F	L	O	O	R	P	L	A	N
A	H	O	Y			M	E	O	W		O	S	S	A
	S	N			S	I	N	H			T	E	S	T

Word Search (from page 123)

AGENCY
AGENT
BOUDOIR
BROKER
BURBS
CARPORT
CLOSING
COMMISSION
CONTEMPORARY
CONTINGENCY
CO-OP
CRAFTSMAN
DRIVEWAY
FEE SIMPLE
FIXER-UPPER
FIXTURE
FORECLOSURE
GEORGIAN
GRANTOR
HALF BATH
INSPECTION
KICKBACK
KITCHEN
LISTING
LOCK BOX
MLS
OPEN HOUSE
PREVIEW
PROSPECT
SCRIPT
STAIRCASE
SUBAGENT
TOWNHOUSE
TREND
TURNKEY
VICTORIAN

Quizzes

Chapter 3—Valuation   1:d   2:d   3:a   4:a   5:d   6:d   7:b   8:c   9:a   10:b

Chapter 4—Presentations   1:c   2:d   3:a   4:b   5:d   6:b   7:b   8:d   9:c   10:d

Chapter 5—Agency   1:d   2:b   3:c   4:a   5:b   6:d   7:c   8:d   9:c   10:a

Chapter 6—Contracts   1:a   2:b   3:c   4:d   5:d   6:c   7:a   8:d   9:b   10:b

Chapter 7—Potpourri   1:a   2:b   3:d   4:d   5:d   6:b   7:d   8:a   9:a   10:c

Quiz & Puzzle Answers

Glossary

EXPLANATORY NOTES

Most, but not all, of the terms defined herein may be found within the body of this book; the aforementioned orphaned terms are included here to enrich the reader's real estate vocabulary.

Acronyms are listed on page 340.

GLOSSARY KEY

form. = formula
max. = maxim
n. = noun
stat. = statistic
sys. = system
test. = test
tool. = tool
v. = verb

A

absorption rate *form.* one divided by months of inventory; a measurement of the rate at which listing inventory changes, turns over, or is otherwise *absorbed* by the market; aids in the determination of a buyer's or seller's market, and in forecasting sales of the near future.

acceptance *n.* the act of creating a contract by signing an offer, without making any changes to that offer.

ACTIVE (see *listing status*)

addendum *n.* any document that is attached to a contract for the purpose of adding terms or providing clarification of terms; *examples*: disclosure statements, survey, legal description, list of fixtures, long-winded contingencies; also called *exhibit*; more than one addendum is *addenda*. *important:* do not confuse addendum with amendment: attaching an *addendum* to an already-existing contract requires an *amendment*.

advertising *v.* the act of an agent calling attention to their services or their listings by means of print, internet, radio, or television announcement.

advocate[1] *n.* one who willingly endorses a real estate agent to others; one who freely and often gives referrals to an agent.

advocate[2] *n.* an agent who takes his fiduciary responsibilities seriously.

agency *n.* the representation of another, in their quest to either buy or sell real property.

agency agreement *n.* a contract between agent and client, delineating the duties of each, length of term, and the agent's compensation; required by law in most states as pre-requisite to providing agency.

agency checklist *tool.* list of agency-related services; tool used to emphasize and clarify the benefits of agency.

agent *n.* any person licensed by the state to represent brokers; one who represents real estate clients by broker's proxy; two types: *active*—one whose license hangs with a broker, and *inactive*—one whose license hangs with the state.

agent caravan *n.* a grouping of agents who carpool (or otherwise travel together) for the purpose of touring listed properties; typically, agents will caravan to broker open houses.

agent grapevine *n.* agent-to-agent method of spreading oral tradition, tall-tales, gossip, information, news, and events; the figurative place where an agent hears such news; to be used as entertainment and for bringing awareness, but not to be relied upon.

agent station *n.* the conspicuous display of flyers, marketing packages, and other pertinent information for a listed property, located within that listed property.

agent statistics *n.* the numerical measure of an agent's past performance, used to predict his current ability; the metrics of an individual agent's prospecting and market performances, for the use of comparison to other agents, to the marketplace, or past performance. (see also *market statistics* and *property statistics*)
common agent statistics: AVG. DOM, AVG. SP/LP, AVG. SP/SQFT, CTR, DTR, PTR and other conversion ratios/turnover rates.

agreement (see *contract*)

amendment *n.* an official change to a contract, which requires the process of offer and acceptance to enact.

appraisal *n.* an opinion of value by one with

an appraiser's license; a third party's inter-pretation of a subject property; required by lenders as a condition of loan approval.

adjustable-rate mortgage (ARM) *n.* a loan whereby the interest rate changes (either monthly, quarterly, or annually) based upon an index or other outside barometer; also called *variable-rate* or *tracker mortgage.*

B

back-up contract *n.* a P&S contract that is secondary to a primary P&S contract; a contract that is contingent upon the termi-nation of another contract; leverage used by a seller to encourage the primary buyer to either perform or cancel their contract; a place in-line to purchase.

back-up offer *n.* an offer to secure a back-up contract; often confused with back-up con-tract, but definitely not the same thing.

beauty contest *n.* a grouping of ACTIVE list-ings, judged by buyers and agents on price, pictures, and provided data; the MLS.

best practice *n.* the preferred method of action; the way a subject-matter expert would proceed.

bidding war *n.* a situation in which two or more buyers knowingly compete to pur-chase the same property.

binding contract (see *enforceable contract*)

bottleneck *n.* any step in a process that slows down the operation of that process; can be identified by tracking conversion ratios and turnover rates.

broker *n.* any person licensed by the state to represent real estate clients; a person with whom agents hang their licenses; three, main types: *associate broker*—one who acts as another broker's agent; *managing broker*—one who is in-charge of a broker-age, who enforces policies and facilitates brokerage services to its agents; *qualifying broker*—one who is legally liable for a bro-kerage and its agents.

broker open house *n.* a gathering of agents and brokers at an ACTIVE listing; a place to eat a free lunch.

broker price opinion (BPO) *n.* a valuation method that is more involved than a CMA, but less involved than an appraisal, which is typically used by institutions to gather information about foreclosed and short sale properties; lenders and banks often employ agents to conduct such research.

broker reciprocity *n.* an agreement between brokers to advertise each other's listings.

brokerage *n.* a business that assists buyers and sellers with real property transactions; a place where agents hang their licenses; a list of types may be found on page 029.

buffoon *n.* an agent who habitually wears-out his welcome and/or routinely jeopardizes the well-being of his clients.

business plan *n.* the written account of an agent's business goals and turnover rates, calculated to forecast the daily activities necessary for goal achievement.

buyer *n.* one who is either considering, cur-rently pursuing, or actively engaged in the process of acquiring real property; in the aggregate, the demand of supply and demand.

buyer flow chart (BFC) *sys.* a diagram of boxes, arrows, and questions, meant to guide an agent through the tasks required to successfully navigate the steps of a buyer transaction: from pre-qualification to pre-sentation to showing property to signing a P&S contract to closing.

buyer hijacker *n.* an agent who converts another agent's unsigned buyer-prospect into a client.

buyer presentation (see *presentation*)

buyer's market *n.* one in which the supply is much greater than demand; typically, more than five months of inventory; one that benefits the buyer during negotiations.

buyer's remorse *n.* a sickening feeling felt by some after making an important decision; self-doubt; second-guessing; may be abated by preparation, information, and comfort; can be felt by sellers, too.

buying signal *n.* an outward gesture or dis-play of interest, which may be overt or concealed.

buying the listing *v.* the act of an agent quot-ing a high price to a seller, for the express purpose of encouraging the seller to sign an agency agreement; falsely claiming the ability to sell a listing for more than other agents could, just to get a listing; a tactic employed by listing sluts.

C

call reluctance *n.* an inability to prospect due to the fear of rejection or stage fright; fear of talking to prospects via telephone; the feeling that accompanies unpreparedness; agents with such condition are not usually agents for long.

call-to-action *tool.* written or spoken words used to provoke an audience's specific response; *examples:* "call now," "click here," and "sign here, please."

campaign *sys.* a systematic process to convey an ongoing message to targeted individuals; the means by which an agent converts prospects into presentations.

capitalization rate (see *rate of return*)

chasing the market *v.* (in a market of decreasing values) the process of putting a high price on a listing, then (as time passes and FMV drops) reducing the price to one that is still too high to attract offers; the act of continuously reducing list price to one that would have attracted offers previously, but at this time is still over-priced for the marketplace.

client *n.* any person receiving agency by written agreement.

client time *n.* part of an agent's day that is set aside for working directly with clients.

client turnover rate (CTR) *stat.* the total tally of an agent's closed transactions divided by the total tally of that agent's clients; the measure of an agent's ability to successfully convert clients into closings. (see also *conversion ratio* and *turnover rate*)

CLOSED (see *listing status*)

closing *n.* the ceremony at which a seller conveys real estate ownership to a buyer.

closing costs (CC) *n.* specifically, all the costs associated with closing a transaction; generally, all the costs associated with the acquisition a loan; listed on page 135.

closing script *n.* words used to provoke action of another; words used to induce a negotiating opponent to sign an contract.

clouded title *n.* any claim, lien, encumbrance, or break in a chain of title that brings into question its holder's ownership or his right to convey that title without issue.

coach *n.* a real estate expert who offers personalized training to agents, tailored to their needs; an accountability partner; one who keeps an agent motivated to prospect; one who dictates the actions of new agents.

commission *n.* money earned by brokers and agents for services rendered through the representation of clients, referrals given, or retainer fees charged.

commission breath *n.* the foul stench of over-eagerness that leaks from the lips of agents hard-up for cash or clients; words that convey a sense of desperation.

commission schedule *n.* a written description of services-offered in exchange for fees-paid.

commission split *n.* the exact division of earned commission dollars per transaction, shared between broker and agent, as dictated by their ICA.

comparable market analysis (CMA) *tool.* a means by which a subject property is compared to similar properties, in order to interpret its FMV; a macro CMA is comprised of three micro CMA, and a metro CMA is comprised of every macro CMA in a metropolitan area (the entire town).

comparable property *n.* any property whose condition closely resembles that of the subject property; also called *comparable* or *comp.*

concession (see *seller concession*)

condition *n.* all things related to a subject property that are not listed price; the totality of a subject property's condition is comprised of hard, soft, and peripheral conditions: *hard conditions*—those that cannot be changed, or whose change would require significant labor and expense. *examples:* roof, siding materials, and floor plan; *soft conditions*—those whose change would not require significant labor nor expense. *examples:* cleanliness, paint, and curb appeal; *peripheral conditions*—those that cannot be controlled by its owner. *examples:* crime rate, school district, and proximity to shopping.

conditional function of salability *n.* a set of potential list prices, each of which will generate a reasonable purchase offer within a reasonable time frame (for a given subject property).

conformed contract *tool.* a re-drafted version of a P&S contract, meant to clarity the terms of the original contract; a clean version of a muddy contract; the version of a contract that is shared with lenders, closers, and other third-parties; also called *clean copy* or *working copy*.

consideration *n.* something of value given in exchange for something else of value; money and/or real property traded for real property; required for contract enforceability.

contingency *n.* any contractual condition that must be met before a transaction can be closed; a contractual condition that, if un-met, allows either buyer or seller to cancel their agreement.

continuing education (CE) *n.* classes that are required by the state to maintain an agent's licensure.

contract *n.* a mutual obligation to perform; whatever its parties want it to be; *contract* and *agreement* are interchangeable terms.

contract-to-close *n.* time between signing a P&S contract and closing (also called *contract term*); the process by which contract principals prepare themselves for closing.

conversion ratio *stat.* shows the number of times an agent must do one thing to get another thing; the measure of an agent's effectiveness in turning presentations into clients or clients into closings; the inverse of turnover rate; *example*: if, over a given period of time, an agent represents twenty clients and has ten closings, then his clients-to-closings conversion ratio is twenty to ten (20:10), and the inverse of this ratio is ten divided by twenty, which is a client turnover rate of 50%. (see also *turnover rate*)

conveyance *n.* the act of transferring title and ownership of real property from one party to another.

co-operating agent (co-op) *n.* with relation to a listing agent: the buyer's agent; the agent representing the *other side*.

copy *n.* the written description of a listing; advertised words meant to draw attention.

counter-offer *n.* an new offer, made in response to a previous offer.

covenants, conditions & restrictions (CC&R) *n.* the documents that supercede zoning and other laws which regulate an owner's use, maintenance, and appearance of his property; property rules that are enforced by a neighborhood or HOA; the rules of an HOA (when combined with bylaws).

crazy van *sys.* prospecting activity whereby several agents drive around together, happily hunting FSBO and EXPIRED listings.

curb appeal *n.* the overall visual look of a property from the street, including the front elevation, landscaping, and surrounding views; part of a property's condition.

customary practice *n.* habitual practices that are passed from one generation to the next; concerning the social niceties of real estate sales; any one of many routine practices which have been rendered obligatory by its participants; part of the rules of real estate, but are not laws or the ethical standard; *examples*: buyers posting earnest money and buyer agents leaving business cards on countertops.

customer relationship management (CRM) *tool.* computer software used to organize names and their corresponding contact information, for the purpose of waging campaigns; a database.

D

daily flow chart (DFC) *sys.* a diagram of boxes, arrows, and questions, meant to guide an agent's day; a systematic approach to an agent's daily tasks; a fun system to promote daily prospecting; home base.

database *tool.* a list of ongoing relationships from which an agent may prospect for clients and referrals; a place where names, phone numbers, email addresses, and notes are kept, and campaigns are managed.

datasheet (see *MLS datasheet*)

days on market (DOM) *stat.* the number of days an individual property is FOR SALE before accepting an offer; the number of days between listing and going under-contract to sell; the number of days a listing is ACTIVE; the amount of time that passes between a seller listing her property FOR SALE and signing a P&S contract to sell it; **when averaged: (AVG. DOM)** the average number of days all properties within a (micro, macro, or metro) market were listed FOR SALE before accepting an offer of purchase; used to compare a subject property or an agent's performance to the marketplace; may be a market statistic or an agent statistic.

Dear Seller Letter *tool.* a letter drafted by a buyer which explains that buyer's desire to purchase a specific property; a cover letter to an offer; a display of goodwill and earnestness; a negotiation tactic meant to start-things-off on a pleasant footing.

deed *n.* a legal instrument that proves ownership of real property.

designated agent *n.* any agent representing a principal client, whereby the opposing principal client is represented by an agent from the same brokerage; term used to describe the individual agents assigned to a buyer and a seller, whenever a single broker represents both buyer and seller.

directional sign *tool.* one that points passersby to a listing; used to attract and guide people to an open house; when balloons are attached, it becomes eye-catching.

discloser's razor *max.* when in doubt, disclose your ass off.

disclosure *n.* the act of providing otherwise unknown information to another.

discrimination *n.* the act of choosing clients based upon their merit, and not by arbitrary traits of race, gender, or other dumb (superficial) reasons.

discussion turnover rate (**DTR**) *stat.* the number of presentations given divided by the number of real estate discussions had; the measure of an agent's ability to turn discussions about real estate into presentation appointments.

dual agency *n.* the seemingly impossible task of providing fiduciary service to two, opposing principals; banned by some states and brokers; when employed, requires written disclosure to and from all.

dual agent *n.* one who represents both sides of a transaction by means of dual agency.

dual rate commission (see *variable rate commission*)

due diligence *n.* a thorough investigation of a subject property, including hard, soft, and peripheral conditions; contingency period of P&S contract, during which investigations ensue.

duel agent *n.* one who shoots his mouth off during listing presentations; one who, when facing challenge, attacks a competing agent's reputation instead of explaining his differentiation of service; a mud slinger.

E

earnest money (**EM**) *n.* money posted by a contract principal (typically, the buyer) to demonstrate serious intent of transaction completion.

effective age *n.* the difference between the actual age of a structure and the economic age of its systems; *example*: a house built fifty years ago which just received a new roof and new plumbing is effectively younger than if the same house was not renovated/ updated.

effectiveness *n.* the degree to which performed tasks are successfully accomplished.

efficiency *n.* the measure of time and money spent while performing a task.

elements of enforceability *n.* contract parts that are required to hold one or more of its principals accountable to their agreement, including written offer and acceptance, the principals names and signatures, mutual consideration, a legal description, and a closing date.

enforceable contract *n.* one that includes the elements of enforceability; one that gives its principals the ability to compel other principal parties to perform (through legal action); one whose principal parties are bound by its terms.

equity *n.* the FMV of a property minus all loans; the portion of a property's value that an owner may realize upon its sale; *example:* a property worth $100K with an outstanding loan balance of $80K has $20K in equity.

escrow[1] *n.* an account that holds other peoples' money, usually deposit/earnest monies.

escrow[2] *n.* a neutral, third-party to a transaction, who holds contract documents, EM, and deed, and then executes the closing, once all contract conditions are met.

estimated sales *form.* (for a macro market, over the next thirty days) absorption rate times the total number of ACTIVE listings (the total number of new, PENDING listings will likely equal the same number as are estimated sales).

ethical standards *n.* a set of behaviors considered appropriate by a society, group, or profession of people; in the real estate sales industry, the code of ethics written by NAR is widely accepted as the standard.

example flow chart (XFC) *tool.* a diagram of boxes and arrows, meant to familiarize an agent with the flow chart system (the XFC is found on the last page of this book).

exclusive-right agency agreement *n.* one which guarantees the agent's compensation, regardless of whom or what is the procuring cause of sale; one in which the agent has an exclusive right to get paid.

executed contract *n.* one in which all parties have fully performed their duties, and closed the transaction.

executory contract *n.* one that is signed now, but not set to close until later; one in which its parties have yet to perform their respective duties; one that is not fully executed; not yet closed.

exhibit (see *addendum*)

EXPIRED (see *listing status*)

F

fair market value (FMV) *n.* the price an informed buyer should be willing to pay for a particular property; this term may apply to a single, subject property or a grouping of properties in a macro or micro market; the AVG. SP/SQFT of a subject property's micro CMA; also called *market value*.

farm *n.* a grouping of prospects by geographic or niche boundaries; a place where an agent routinely prospects for clients in the same location.

Federal Housing Administration (FHA) *n.* United States government agency whose primary purpose is to insure private mortgages.

fee simple *n.* the highest form of freehold land ownership.

feedback *n.* the written or oral description of a buyer's reaction to a viewed listing; information used to monitor a marketing strategy.

fiduciary *n.* one who provides fiduciary care to another.

fiduciary care *n.* the collection of duties an agent is legally-required to provide to clients, generally being disclosure, skilled

care, loyalty, confidentiality, obedience, and accountability.

fixture *n.* real property that was formerly personal property.

fixture test *test.* a method to discern between real and personal property by analyzing an item's method of attachment, its adaptation/customization, and/or the intention of its use.

flow chart *tool.* an easy-to-follow diagram meant to stream-line a complex workflow; examples of agent flow charts can be found on the last pages of this book.

flyer *n.* a handbill used to advertise a listing; a take-away reminder for a listing's lookers.

for sale by owner (FSBO) *n.* a seller attempting to sell real property without the representation of an agent.

forecast report *tool.* (with regard to a macro marketplace) guesstimations of estimated sales in the next thirty days, the number of ACTIVE listings (including which ones, in particular) will go PENDING in the next thirty days, and the current number of shoppers.

Friend Script (The) *n.* a script to teach friends, so they may help their agent-friend get referrals: *My friend is a resourceful real estate agent. Would you be offended if s/he called you?*

front elevation *n.* the facing view of a real property structure from the street, consisting of the front door, front windows, siding material(s), and structural style.

G

good faith estimate (GFE) *n.* official documentation that must be provided by a lender to a borrower which outlines all the expenses, fees, and costs associated with the loan (as required by RESPA).

grantee *n.* one who receives property ownership; a buyer.

grantor *n.* one who gives property ownership; a seller.

gross commission income (GCI) *stat.* the total dollar amount of all commissions earned by an agent, before paying his commission split; may be stated as a single, monthly, or annual figure.

H

hazard insurance *n.* an insurance policy that covers residential property; also called *homeowners insurance.*

hickor *test.* a mnemonic device used to remember who is whom: the one who gives.

home equity line of credit (HELOC) *n.* a mortgage, whereby the lender extends a line of credit based upon a property's existing equity; mortgage money that may be spend by the borrower on anything, not just to improve the real property; because a HELOC is akin to cash in a bank account, it is often over-looked by sellers when calculating net-to-seller; a second mortgage.

home owners association (HOA) *n.* a private organization of elected property owners, who set-forth and enforce real property rules for the collection of its owners.

I

independent contractor agreement (ICA) *n.* the documentation of an agent and broker officially agreeing to affiliate with each other; contract that sets-forth commission split and limits on an agent's activities.

influencer *n.* one who holds sway over another's real estate decisions (usually, a friend or family member).

internet data exchange (IDX) *n.* a computer system that delivers MLS listing data to various websites via the internet.

inventory *n.* all the FSBO and ACTIVE listings in the market; all the properties that are currently FOR SALE; all the listings currently held by a brokerage; all the listings currently held by an agent; the supply of supply and demand.

investment property *n.* any parcel of real property whereby its owner draws income from another's use of that property.

invitation to bargain *n.* a seller's declaration of interest to entertain offers: an ACTIVE listing, a FOR SALE sign, or an open house.

item of value *tool.* any thing that enhances a prospect's life, while simultaneously demonstrating an agent's competency.

J

Jekyll & Hyde Agent *n.* one who is a good boss, but a bad employee, or vice versa.

K

kickback *n.* a rebate or payment given to agents by vendors for shared business ventures, or to clients by agents for referrals or "just because"; some kickbacks are legal but others are not, so an agent should carefully consider the law before engaging in such activities.

L

lead (see *prospect*)

lead generation *n.* the process by which an agent searches for prospects (see also *prospecting* and *advertising*)

lease/option contract *n.* a set of three, simultaneously-signed real estate (lease, P&S, and option) contracts, whereby a tenant agrees to rent a property until either his lease expires, or he exercises his option to purchase the property.

lease/purchase contract *n.* a set of two, simultaneously-signed real estate (lease, P&S) contracts, whereby a buyer agrees to rent a property, and then purchase that same property immediately after the rental term ends.

legal description *n.* a way of describing a particular piece of real property beyond reproach; an element of enforceability.

lessee *n.* one who receives a lease; a tenant.

lessor *n.* one who gives a lease; a landlord.

list *v.* the act of signing a seller-agency agreement; to place descriptive data into an MLS.

listed price (LP) *tool.* a tool used to either attract or repel offers.

listed price per square foot (LP/SQFT) *stat.* a property's listed price divided by its square footage; when averaged: (AVG. LP/SQFT) the average LP/SQFT of all properties within a market, used to compare a subject property to its comparable marketplace.

listing *n.* the MLS publication of a property's description through words, photographs, supplementary documentation, and status.

listing presentation (see *presentation*)

listing extension *n.* an amendment to an agency agreement for the purpose of lengthening its term; a second (or third) chance.

listing inventory (see *inventory*)

listing slut *n.* a derogatory term used to describe an agent who will do anything to get a listing; an agent who agrees to any and all kinds of listing terms, regardless of the likelihood those terms will lead to a sale; an opportunist looking to leverage listings solely as a means to attract additional listings or buyers who will purchase other listings; an agent who routinely lists over-priced listings; an agent who takes advantage of seller-clients.

listing status *n.* a property's current position in the marketplace, as assigned by its MLS; the state of a listing's affairs.

common listing statuses:

ACTIVE—one that is FOR SALE; a listing in search of a buyer.

CLOSED or SOLD—one whose transaction is complete; no longer FOR SALE.

EXPIRED—one whose agency agreement has ended before going PENDING; a seller without an agent.

PENDING—one that is under contract to close; often has sub-classifications such as PENDING-CONTINGENCY, or PENDING-LENDER APPROVAL.

WITHDRAWN—one whose owner has fired his agent prior to going PENDING or EXPIRED; a seller without an agent.

listing syndication *n.* the automation of listing data, shared through an IDX; the automatic sharing of listing data with numerous consumer and agent websites; an advertising tool used to expose a listing to a large number of eyeballs via the internet.

loan-to-value ratio (LTV) *n.* mortgage term used to describe the percentage of a property's value that is represented by its loan; *example:* an $80K loan on a property worth $100K is said to be at 80% LTV.

lockbox *n.* a strongbox which contains the key to a listing; usually secured to real property so that it cannot be stolen, but may be accessed by anyone with a lockbox key or code.

looker *n.* any person who visits a listing, commonly being an agent, buyer, prospect, influencer, or neighbor.

low-ball offer *n.* one that is considerably lower than the listed price; a negotiation tactic used to identify desperate sellers.

M

macro CMA *tool.* the zoomed-out view of a subject property's marketplace, used to interpret an approximate FMV; consists of three micro CMA; all properties within a macro CMA share the same hard conditions. (see also *CMA*)

market[1] *n.* a grouping of potential buyers; a grouping of specific, ACTIVE listings; may denote all properties FOR SALE, or only the specific properties which are comparable to a subject property; markets are defined by property condition and geography (price range is a result of these two factors).

market[2] *v.* to proffer a listing FOR SALE.

market absorption (see *absorption rate*)

market activity report *tool.* an organized display of all listings, sorted by status and statistic; a snapshot of the current happenings within a marketplace.

market statistics *n.* the metric calculations of multiple properties within a market, for the use of comparison to individual properties, to other markets, or to an individual agent's results. (see also *property statistics* and *agent statistics*)

common market statistics: AVG. DOM, AVG. SP/LP, AVG. LP/SQFT, AVG. SP/SQFT, trend rate, and absorption rate.

market trend[1] *n.* the rise, fall, or leveling of property values over time. (see also *trend rate*)

market trend[2] *n.* the aesthetic preferences of contemporary buyers, including (but not limited to) property types and styles, construction materials, and the use of rooms and spaces.

market value (see *fair market value*)

marketing package *tool.* a collection of all information relevant to a subject property, used by a listing agent to attract offers.

marketing strategy *n.* listing agent/seller's plan to attract offers; the extent to which price, pictures, and information are exposed to prospective buyers.

marketplace *n.* the figurative place where buyers and sellers meet. (see also *market*)

marketplace dashboard *tool.* a valuation report that consolidates market activity, absorption, and trend reports into a single, 'quik-look' report; when generated on a monthly basis, the dashboard allows an agent to quickly assess his niche marketplace by comparing this month's statistics to those of months past; an example may be found on page 343; also called *the dashboard.*

mentor *n.* any person who lends insight, perspective, and/or suggestion to an agent on a routine basis.

micro CMA *tool.* the zoomed-in view of a subject property's marketplace, used to interpret absolute FMV; three types: *top, middle,* and *bottom* ranges of a macro CMA; all properties within a micro CMA share the same soft conditions. (see also CMA)

MLS datasheet *tool.* all the information about a particular listing, displayed on a single page, which may be printed and carried into the field, where it is used as a reference tool when showing real property.

MLS hotsheet *tool.* a daily report which displays all the listings that have changed status, whether from ACTIVE to PENDING, PENDING to CLOSED, or PENDING to ACTIVE; useful tool for tracking the market on a daily basis.

mobile open house *n.* the mass showing of several, similar listings to a bus-full (or car caravan) of buyers; a prospecting method of considerable coordination.

months of inventory *form.* the total number of ACTIVE listings (current inventory) divided by the average number of sales per month. (see also *absorption rate*)

mortgage *n.* a promise to repay a loan.

mortgage fraud *n.* the participation in hiding or misrepresenting any transaction facts or details from a lender.

mortgage insurance *n.* an insurance policy that is meant to protect a lender from a defaulting borrower; required by most lenders when the borrower's LTV is in excess of 80%; called MIP (mortgage insurance premium) when the loan is FHA insured, PMI (private mortgage insurance) when the loan is conventional; insurance that is paid-for by a borrower, to protect his lender from default.

mortgagee *n.* one who receives a mortgage; a lender.

mortgagor *n.* one who gives a mortgage; a borrower.

mortgagor's razor *max.* whenever a buyer is obtaining financing, *all parts* of his transaction must be disclosed to the lender(s)—no exceptions.

multiple listing service (MLS) *n.* a private organization of brokers, whose intent is to share listing information with each other; a private website whereby agents list property and find tools to aid in the interpretation of market value.

multiple offers *n.* an event whereby a single listing simultaneously receives more than one purchase offer. (see also *bidding war*)

N

National Association of REALTORS® (NAR) *n.* an organization of real estate professionals, whose purpose is to regulate ethics, foster education, and lobby government; comprised of state and local chapters.

need *n.* a desired property condition or P&S contract stipulation that a buyer classifies as "must-have." (see also *want*)

needs analysis *sys.* the process by which a buyer-prospect and an agent mutually discover exactly what that buyer desires.

net listing *n.* an seller-agency agreement, whereby the agent's commission is the difference between the listed price and the sales price; illegal in most states, due to the ease by which a dishonest agent may take advantage of an ill-informed or naïve seller; *example*: suppose a seller desires only $100K from the sale of her property, but her agent knows it's worth more. Under a net listing, if the agent lists at $100K, and then sells the listing for $120K, his commission would be the difference: $20K.

net operating income (NOI) *form.* annual rent minus annual expenses; a calculation used by investors to analyze property value.

net present value (NPV) *form.* net operating income divided by rate of return; a valuation method used for investment property.

net-sale *form.* sales price minus seller expenses minus seller concessions; the net proceeds from a sale before the seller pays-off lean and loan obligations; SEBLLP. (for an example, see *net-to-seller*)

net-to-seller (seller-net) *form.* sales price minus seller expenses minus seller concessions minus lean and loan payoff; all the leftover money from a sale that goes into a seller's pocket; *example*: if sales price = $100K, seller expenses = $1K, seller concessions = $4K, and lean & loan payoff = $80K, then the net-sale is $95K, and net-to-seller is $15K.

newsletter *tool.* a monthly demonstration of an agent's value to prospects and clients; a written analysis of newsworthy events and the dissemination of relevant, community information, targeted to a specific audience of subscribers.

niche *n.* an agent's specialty of practice, prospecting method(s), and/or the geographic boundaries within which he conducts business.

nickname *n.* a word or phrase that describes a particular listing; a tool used to aid in the memory of specific properties during future discussions; a fun way to build rapport with buyers, while fostering clear communication during conversations of previously-shown property listings.

notice *n.* the formal means of communication between parties of a contract.

O

objection *n.* a script roadblock; an agent's impediment to getting their way; a chance to build rapport through discussion; often confused with rejection, but the two are not the same. (see also *rejection*)

offer *n.* a thing that—*if accepted*—becomes a contract.

offeree *n.* one who receives an offer.

offeror *n.* one who gives an offer.

onion peeling *sys.* the process by which an agent asks a series of probing questions, meant to discover the true core of a buyer-prospect's needs and wants. (see also *needs analysis*)

online valuation calculator *n.* the internet's version of an appraisal of value; an algorithm that guesstimates the FMV of a subject property, which is often grossly-incorrect due to the lack of human interpretation

of relevant data, that is the cause of client confusion and thereby agent consternation.

open house *n.* a party to showcase a listing; an event whereby lookers are invited to view a listing without a previous appointment; a listing agent's opportunity to speak directly with prospects.

opponent *n.* any person with whom an agent negotiates.

P

parachuting agent *n.* one who enters an agency agreement at the same time their client is entering a P&S contract.

PENDING (see *listing status*)

personal property *n.* all property which is not land or affixed to the land; chattel.

PMI/MIP (see *mortgage insurance*)

pocket listing *n.* one that does not appear in the MLS; property that is "quietly" marketed to select buyers only; a listing that is held "in the pocket" of its agent, and thereby hidden from most buyers in the marketplace.

Porcelli Principle (The) *max.* whatever happens to me and my business is a direct result of my actions and inactions.

posse *n.* a grouping of individual vendors whom an agent recommends to prospects and clients; an agent's extended team of professional service providers.

pre-approval *n.* (pertaining to a loan) the state of a borrower who has remitted all requested documentation to a lender, and whereby that lender has informally committed to giving a loan to that borrower.

pre-listing package *tool.* a collection of materials sent by an agent to a seller, prior to a scheduled listing presentation; literature meant to sway a prospect's opinion before a formal meeting.

pre-qualification *n.* (pertaining to a loan) the state of a borrower who has answered some lender questions, and whereby that lender has conducted a credit check and declared that the borrower is a good candidate for receiving a loan, so long as requested documentation confirms the borrower's previously-stated answers; (pertaining to agency) the state of a buyer or seller-prospect who has satisfactorily answered an agent's questions regarding that prospect's motivation and likelihood to actually buy or sell real property.

presentation *n.* the meeting of an agent and a prospect to mutually discover whether or not to engage in agency; the discussion of a prospect's needs and wants, current market conditions, the transaction process, marketing strategy, and agency services, all meant to set mutual expectations.

presentation turnover rate (PTR) *stat.* the number of clients signed divided by the number of presentations given; the measure of an agent's ability to turn presentations into clients.

preview *v.* the act of a buyer's agent visiting a listing before showing it to his buyer; a way to save clients' time, by ensuring a listing meets their stated needs and wants; the act of an agent visiting listed properties for the purpose of marketplace awareness or valuation research.

price reduction (price improvement) *n.* the act of changing a property's listed price, in response to the market's lack of interest.

principal[1] *n.* any person who is under contract to buy or sell real property.

principal[2] *n.* any person who is represented by an agent; a client.

principle/interest/taxes/insurance (PITI) *n.* the sum of each of these expenses equals a monthly mortgage payment; acronym of the four components of a mortgage.

principles of value *n.* the fundamental and guiding truths of real property valuation, primarily being the laws of supply and demand, substitution, externalities, conformity, balance, anticipation, and highest and best use; definitions for each principle may be found on page 136.

procuring cause *n.* person, thing, or event that causes a transaction to originate or come into being.

property statistics *n.* the metrics of a single, individual property for the use of comparison to its comparable marketplace. (see also *market statistics* and *agent statistics*) common property statistics: DOM, SP/LP, LP/SQFT, and SP/SQFT

prospect[1] *n.* any person who is a potential candidate for agency.

prospect[2] **(prospecting)** *v.* the act of exploring the marketplace for new clients; the act of an agent calling attention to his services or listing inventory by face-to-face, telephone, or electronic or manual correspondence for the purpose of finding clients or selling his listings.

purchase and sale contract (P&S) *n.* a contract to transfer real property title and ownership from seller to buyer.

R

rate of return (R) *form.* net operating income divided by net present value; a calculation used by investors when analyzing property value; also called *capitalization (cap.) rate.*

real estate commission[1] *n.* a government (state) body that oversees the licensure of brokers and agents through regulation, meant to protect the public interest; sometimes called *board* or *bureau.*

real estate commission[2] *n.* monies earned conducting real estate duties and activities. (see also *commission*)

real estate fee (see *commission*)

real estate owned (REO) *n.* an alternative term for foreclosed property; a term used to differentiate between listings owned by individuals and those owned by banks or corporations; a balance sheet entry used by banks or other institutions to show the total value of their real property holdings.

real estate roller coaster *n.* refers to an agent's income when it comes in waves; an affliction caused by inconsistent prospecting, whereby an agent goes through spurts of activity, followed by bouts of inactivity, over and over again.

Real Estate Settlement Procedures Act (RESPA) *n.* United States law, enacted to protect the public while shopping for real estate services (loans and closings); primarily meant to regulate and standardize disclosure regarding lending and settlement, and to eliminate hidden kickbacks.

real property *n.* land and all that is attached to land as a fixture; *real property, real estate,* and *realty* are interchangeable terms.

REALTOR® *n.* one who belongs to NAR.

referee *n.* one who receives a referral.

referor *n.* one who gives a referral.

referral *n.* a prospect who is introduced to an agent by a mutual acquaintance.

referral buddy *n.* an agent with whom another agent frequently trades referrals.

referral fee *n.* the commission earned by an agent for introducing a referral to another agent; may be paid in arrears, once the referral's transaction closes, or upfront, once the introduction has been made.

referral flow chart (RFC) *sys.* a diagram of boxes and arrows, meant to guide an agent through the tasks required to successfully trade referrals with other agents.

Referral Script (The) *n.* a script used to elicit referrals: *Hi. I need your help. Who do you know that is currently looking to buy or sell real estate?*

rejection *n.* a denial to continue further; NO!; absolute stoppage; often confused with objection. (see also *objection*)

retainer fee *n.* the upfront payment of money by a client to an agent; money used to offset an agent's expenses and/or to act as a demonstration of earnestness from his client, which is often times discounted from future sales commissions earned.

reverse offer *n.* one that is originally drafted by a seller, which takes into consideration the targeted buyer's unique needs and wants; an unconventional (but highly effective) way to begin P&S negotiations.

Right Price (The) *n.* (subjective to each property) any listed price that generates at least one reasonable purchase offer within the AVG. DOM of the subject's comparable marketplace.

robot voice *n.* a cold, scripted delivery; the monotone sounds of a speaker reading, whether or not that speaker is actually reading; a disingenuous presentation.

role-playing *n.* the act of practicing scripts in simulated, live-action situations.

rules of real estate *n.* the collective laws, regulations, customs, and ICA terms that govern an agent's actions.

S

Saint Joseph *n.* the patron saint of buyers, sellers, and real estate agents; buried statuettes of the saint are said to promote a successful transaction.

salability differential *form.* one minus AVG. SP/LP times FMV; the variance from FMV a property's listed price may be, yet still attract reasonable and timely offers.

Sales Formula (The) *form.* price plus condition plus exposure equals salability; $f(\text{price}) = \text{salability}$.

sales price *n.* the price on a P&S contract.

sales price to listed price ratio (SP/LP) *stat.* sales price divided by list price; shows the percentage of change between a property's listed price and its sales price: when more than one (>100%), the listing sold for more than its listed price (a premium), and when less than one (<100%), the listing sold for less than its listed price (a discount);

when averaged: (AVG. SP/LP) two types: (as a market statistic) the average SP/LP of all SOLD properties within a market, which shows whether the average property in a market is currently selling at a premium or a discount; (as an agent statistic) the average SP/LP of all SOLD listings by an individual agent, which shows whether the average property listed by that agent sells at a premium or a discount.

sales price per square foot (SP/SQFT) *stat.* a property's sales price divided by its square footage; **when averaged: (AVG. SP/SQFT)** the average of all SP/SQFT of all properties within a market; denotes FMV of a particular market; used to compare a subject property to its comparable marketplace.

sales volume *stat.* the total dollar amount of all sales prices of all transactions of which an agent is a party; *example*: an agent who conducts three sales at $100K each, has a sales volume of $300K.

salesman *n.* a scrupulous person who helps others make informed buying and selling decisions.

scratch 'n' sniff *n.* a method of written counter-offer, whereby an offeror uses an ink pen to strike-thru and/or add terms to a previously received offer.

script *n.* a preconceived sequence of words to effectively communicate an idea.

seller *n.* one who owns real property, and is either considering its sale, has an ACTIVE listing, or is otherwise engaged in the process of selling real property.

seller concession *n.* time, money, or effort spent by a seller to sweeten the deal for a buyer; for a list of specific concessions, see page 135.

seller earnings before lean and loan payoff (SEBLLP) (see *net-sale*)

seller expenses *n.* as part of a transaction, a seller's own tax, commission, and closing cost obligations, as well as property condition improvements that were completed and paid-for prior to listing.

seller flow chart (SFC) *sys.* a diagram of boxes, arrows, and questions, meant to guide an agent through the tasks required to successfully navigate the steps of a seller transaction: from pre-qualification to presentation to market exposure to signing a P&S contract to closing.

seller's market *n.* one in which demand is much greater than the supply; typically, less than four months of inventory; one that benefits the seller during negotiations.

selling a listing *n.* the act of successfully bringing a buyer and a seller to agreement, but not yet closing; the act of a buyer and a seller entering into an executory contract; a phrase used to describe the moment a listing goes into PENDING status.

settlement statement *n.* the official documents used to close a real estate transaction, which include an itemized list of all settlement credits and debits for each, buyer and seller.

sharp axe *n.* a clear mind; an agent without undue, mental burden.

shoppers *n.* all the buyers in a particular marketplace who have yet to sign a P&S contract; potential buyers; the number of shoppers in a macro market may be estimated to equal the total number of macro CMA sales in the last ninety days.

shopping zone *n.* the geographic boundaries by which most buyers shop; commonly: MLS area, zip code, school district, or county lines; shopping zones are the geographic boundaries of macro markets.

short sale *n.* any real estate transaction whereby the sales price is less than the seller's lean and loan payoff; any P&S contract whereby the seller lacks the funds needed to payoff their loan, and their lender's approval to payoff a lesser amount is sought through contingency.

short seller *n.* one whom lacks the funds to make-up the difference between the sales price and his lean and/or loan payoff obligations.

showing *n.* an event whereby a buyer visits a listing; a time when a listing is being judged by its lookers.

SOLD (see listing status)

spec home *n.* real property that is built for the average buyer's taste; not customized.

special stipulations *n.* terms added to a contract that are in addition to (or override) the document's pre-printed terms.

staging *v.* arranging furniture and other adornments to showcase a listing's features.

stale listing *n.* one that has been over-priced for so long that buyers and agents now ignore it; one that has been listed for much longer than the average listing.

status (see *listing status*)

subagent *n.* one who represents a listing agent; one who assists a listing agent with his seller representation duties; traditionally (before buyer agency) a subagent was the one who brought the buyer, but represented the listing agent and (through that relationship) the seller; the practice has been abandoned by most in modern times.

subject property *n.* a piece of real property that is being discussed, investigated, or is otherwise the matter at hand; also called *subject* or *the subject*.

super macro market *n.* all the macro markets in an agent's niche; denotes the entire geographic area of a particular agent's business.

survey *n.* an examination of a parcel of land and all structural improvements upon it, typically drawn as a map and limited to boundaries, measurements, elevations, gradations, types of soil, location of utilities, and the site of its structures; may be used as a legal description.

survival of the agreement *n.* a contractual clause within a P&S contract that states certain obligations may be completed post-closing.

syndicated website *n.* one which receives IDX from an MLS; any website that displays listing data, piped-in via the MLS. (see also *listing syndication*)

system *tool.* an organized assemblage of subtasks, utilized to complete a complex task.

T

task *n.* a piece of work.

term¹ *n.* a length of time, usually referring to the duration of a P&S contract or an agency agreement.

term² *n.* contract language.

testimonial *tool.* the act of a past client endorsing an agent; used by agents to flaunt their services and accomplishments.

third-party website (see *syndicated website*)

time limit of offer *tool.* the expiration time and date of an offer.

title *n.* ownership interest in real property.

title insurance *n.* an insurance policy that covers financial loss associated with defects in the title of real property ownership.

top-three list *n.* a method to prioritize shown listings, meant to help a buyer decide.

transaction *n.* the process in which a buyer and a seller each prepare for and then execute the conveyance of real property.

transaction agent *n.* one who helps to facilitate a real estate transaction, but does not represent either principal party of that transaction.

transaction brokerage *n.* one whereby its agents pay to the brokerage a fixed transaction fee per closing, and not a percentage of the commission earned; not to be confused with a *transaction agent.*

trend allowance (TA) *form.* trend rate times the subject property's square footage; used as a factor to consider the market's trend rate when pricing a listing.

trend rate (TR) *form.* AVG. SP/SQFT now minus AVG. SP/SQFT then, divided by the number of months between then and now; the average dollar amount each SOLD listing (of a particular market, over a given period of time) either increased or decreased in value each month, expressed as SP/SQFT; used to forecast FMV in the near future and to calculate trend allowance.

turn-key *adj.* a property which is in perfect condition, requiring no improvements or updates; such properties are said to be turn-key because the new owner must only "turn the key" in the door and then enjoy the property as it is.

turnover rate *stat.* calculated by dividing one real estate activity by another, to show a success rate; inverse of conversion ratio; common turnover rates include client turnover rate, presentation turnover rate, and discussion turnover rate. (for an example, see *conversion ratio*)

V

valuation *n.* the process of determining the value of real property through the analysis of comparable properties, market absorption, trend rate, current market activity.

valuation flow chart (VFC) *sys.* a diagram of boxes and arrows, meant to guide an agent through the tasks required to successfully interpret either FMV, create a monthly marketplace dashboard, or calculate the *Right Price* for a listing.

value *n.* the sense of worth a person puts upon a thing.

variable rate commission (VRC) *n.* one in which the seller agrees to pay a listing agent one amount if that agent is the procuring cause of sale, and a different amount if a co-operating agent is the procuring cause of sale; when utilized, a listing agent should disclose VRC within all marketing materials and advertisements; also called *dual rate commission.*

vendor *n.* a person or business that provides products and/or services to brokers, agents, and/or real estate principals; a member of an agent's posse.

W

walk-thru *n.* the act of briskly investigating a subject property, with attention paid to specific things; called a *final walk-thru* when conducted on the eve of closing.

want *n.* a desired property condition or P&S contract stipulation that a buyer classifies as "would-be-really-niceta-have." (see also *need*)

web syndication (see *syndicated website*)

WITHDRAWN (see *listing status*)

About the Author

Creating this book[001]
has been my
grandest presentation,
thus far.

thus far.

Time for a victory lap...

The Politically Incorrect Real Estate Agent Handbook

I was born at an early age, and quickly became the eldest of four siblings. We had wonderful parents—an army officer and his doting bride—who kept moving us around the map every few years. Wherever we lived, Mom and Dad sponsored our passions, fostered our creativity, and championed our causes. As a curious child, this environment meant endless discovery.

Right away, I discovered the art of the argument. A few stages of development later, I fell for entrepreneurism, although I didn't know that word back then. I just knew that running a business was fun. My childhood concerns were washing cars, mow/snow/leaf blowing lawns, paper routes, selling school supplies from my locker, flipping yard sale items, and various ventures on-the-side. In college, I studied business administration and managed a bar, which got me revved-up. With a real estate license, I sped-off.

At first, I sold houses to investors and college buddies. Next was FSBO and EXPIRED listings. Then came brokerage management and ownership.

The whole time—from childhood, throughout—I've loved prospecting. Most agents hate it, but not me. I love riding in the proverbial cockpit, out-steering obstacles, and racing for the checkered flag. I think victory is in client conversion. The rest is mostly procedural. Soon, I began teaching agents fun and effective ways to find clients and sell real estate. It's been good for them, and I quite enjoy it, too. They frequently ask for a book. And now, after a brief pit stop, here it is.

A Serious How-to Manual with a Sense of Humor

ACR	AVERAGE COMMISSION RATE		LTV	LOAN-TO-VALUE RATIO
AIR	ACKNOWLEDGE/ISOLATE/RESPOND		MLS	MULTIPLE LISTING SERVICE
ARM	ADJUSTABLE-RATE MORTGAGE		NAR	NATIONAL ASSOCIATION OF REALTORS ®
ATP	AVERAGE TRANSACTION PRICE			
BFC	BUYER FLOW CHART		NOI	NET OPERATING INCOME
BPO	BROKER PRICE OPINION		NPV	NET PRESENT VALUE
CC	CLOSING COSTS		PITI	PRINCIPLE/INTEREST/ TAXES/INSURANCE
CE	CONTINUING EDUCATION			
CMA	COMPARABLE MARKET ANALYSIS		PMI/ MIP	PRIVATE MORTGAGE INSURANCE/ MORTGAGE INSURANCE PREMIUM
CRM	CUSTOMER RELATIONSHIP MANAGEMENT			
			PTR	PRESENTATION TURNOVER RATE
CTR	CLIENT TURNOVER RATE		P&S	PURCHASE AND SALE CONTRACT
DFC	DAILY FLOW CHART		RESPA	REAL ESTATE SETTLEMENT PROCEDURES ACT
DOM	DAYS ON MARKET			
DTR	DISCUSSION TURNOVER RATE		SD	SALABILITY DIFFERENTIAL
EM	EARNEST MONEY		SEBLLP	SELLER EARNINGS BEFORE LEAN AND LOAN PAYOFF
FHA	FEDERAL HOUSING ADMINISTRATION			
FMV	FAIR MARKET VALUE		SEO	SEARCH ENGINE OPTIMIZATION
FSBO	FOR SALE BY OWNER		SFC	SELLER FLOW CHART
GCI	GROSS COMMISSION INCOME		SP	SALES PRICE
GFE	GOOD FAITH ESTIMATE		SP/LP	SALES PRICE TO LISTED PRICE RATIO
HELOC	HOME EQUITY LINE OF CREDIT		SP/SQFT	SALES PRICE PER SQUARE FOOT
HOA	HOME OWNER ASSOCIATION		SQFT	SQUARE FOOT (OR FEET)
ICA	INDEPENDENT CONTRACTOR AGREEMENT		RFC	REFERRAL FLOW CHART
			TA	TREND ALLOWANCE
IDX	INTERNET DATA EXCHANGE		TR	TREND RATE
LO	LOAN OFFICER		VFC	VALUATION FLOW CHART
LP	LISTED PRICE		VRC	VARIABLE RATE COMMISSION
LP/SQFT	LISTED PRICE PER SQUARE FOOT		XFC	EXAMPLE FLOW CHART

These acronyms are found within the text and in the glossary.

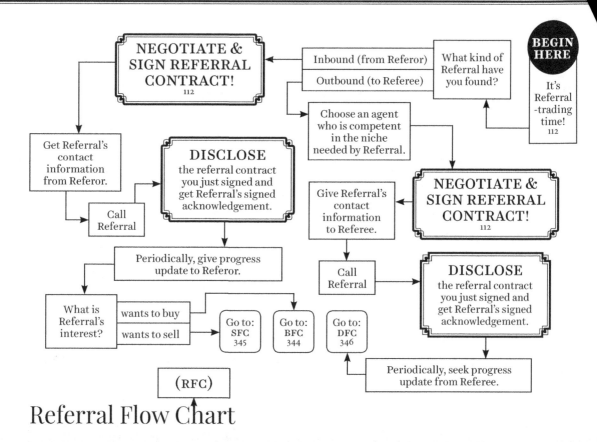

Referral Flow Chart

Stay on Track
with the

FLOW CHART SYSTEM

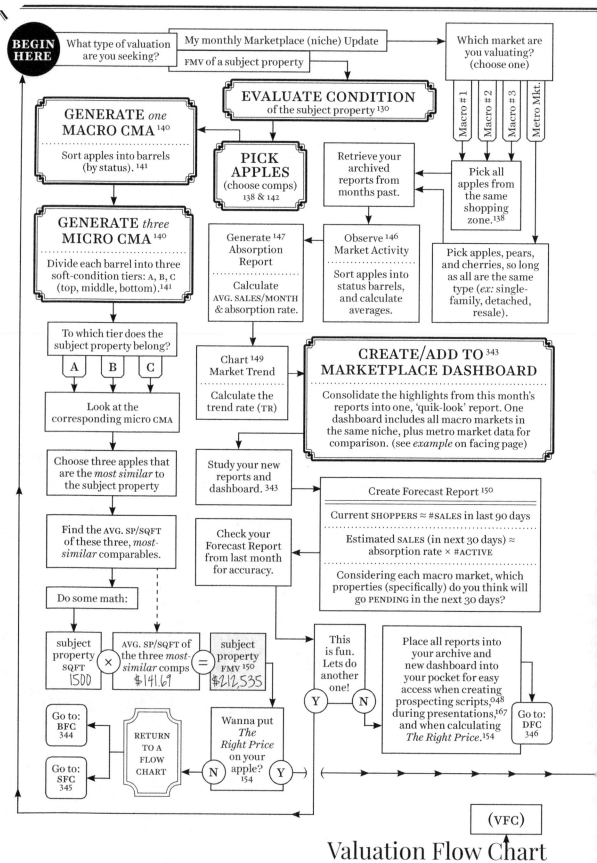

BEGIN HERE

What type of valuation are you seeking?

My monthly Marketplace (niche) Update

FMV of a subject property

Which market are you valuating? (choose one)

Macro #1 · Macro #2 · Macro #3 · Metro Mkt.

EVALUATE CONDITION of the subject property [130]

GENERATE *one* **MACRO CMA** [140]

Sort apples into barrels (by status). [141]

PICK APPLES (choose comps) 138 & 142

Retrieve your archived reports from months past.

Pick all apples from the same shopping zone. [138]

GENERATE *three* **MICRO CMA** [140]

Divide each barrel into three soft-condition tiers: A, B, C (top, middle, bottom). [141]

Generate [147] Absorption Report

Calculate AVG. SALES/MONTH & absorption rate.

Observe [146] Market Activity

Sort apples into status barrels, and calculate averages.

Pick apples, pears, and cherries, so long as all are the same type (*ex:* single-family, detached, resale).

To which tier does the subject property belong?

A · B · C

Chart [149] Market Trend

Calculate the trend rate (TR)

CREATE/ADD TO [343] **MARKETPLACE DASHBOARD**

Consolidate the highlights from this month's reports into one, 'quik-look' report. One dashboard includes all macro markets in the same niche, plus metro market data for comparison. (see *example* on facing page)

Look at the corresponding micro CMA

Choose three apples that are the *most similar* to the subject property

Study your new reports and dashboard. 343

Create Forecast Report [150]

Current SHOPPERS ≈ #SALES in last 90 days

Estimated SALES (in next 30 days) ≈ absorption rate × #ACTIVE

Considering each macro market, which properties (specifically) do you think will go PENDING in the next 30 days?

Find the AVG. SP/SQFT of these three, *most-similar* comparables.

Check your Forecast Report from last month for accuracy.

Do some math:

subject property SQFT 1500

× AVG. SP/SQFT of the three *most-similar* comps $141.69

= subject property FMV [150] $212,535

This is fun. Lets do another one!

Y · N

Place all reports into your archive and new dashboard into your pocket for easy access when creating prospecting scripts,[048] during presentations,[167] and when calculating *The Right Price*.[154]

Go to: DFC 346

Go to: BFC 344

RETURN TO A FLOW CHART

Go to: SFC 345

Wanna put *The Right Price* on your apple? 154

N · Y

(VFC)

Valuation Flow Chart

MONTHLY MARKETPLACE DASHBOARD

March		Macro #1	Δ	Macro #2	Δ	Super Macro	Δ	Metro	Δ
from Market Activity Report	#SOLD	28	↑3	30	↓4	156	↑29	25,478	↑3014
	AVG. SOLD PRICE	$238k	↑$2k	$235k	↑0	$241k	↑$1k	$298k	↑$2k
	AVG. DOM	78	↓5	73	↑1	75	↓2	81	↓5
	AVG. SP/LP	96%	—	97%	—	96%	—	94%	—
from Absorp. Report	#ACTIVE	90	↑8	112	↑12	571	↑48	128,456	↑214
	AVG. #SOLD/MTH	25	↑1	26	↑2	138	↑10	23,458	↑451
	MTHS OF INVENTORY	3.6	↓.3	4.3	↑.5	4.1	↓.9	5.5	↓1.4
	ABSORP. RATE	27%	↑3%	23%	↑3%	24%	↑2%	18%	↑4%
Trend Rpt.	TREND RATE (TR)	$0.495/sqft	—	$0.621/sqft	—	$0.524/sqft	—	$0.210/sqft	—

Δ = change since last month; ↑↓ = direction of change

Notice that even though both charts on this page include the same shopping zone (MACRO MARKET #1), the statistics in the CMA BREAKDOWN are not the same as the statistics on the MONTHLY DASHBOARD. This is because a CMA focuses on a subject property and is comprised of comparable data from the last several months, while the DASHBOARD is comprised of all similar properties in a shopping zone, and shows last month's data only.

In the *example* shown (the hand-written numbers):

DASHBOARD: ALL MACRO MARKETS includes only ranchers:
- 3 or 4 bedrooms,
- 2 or 3 bathrooms,
- with or w/out a basement.

CMA BREAKDOWN: MACRO MARKET #1 is for a subject property:
- 3 bed, 2 bath,
- w/out a basement,
- 1500 square feet,
- in Micro B.

subject property FMV [150] $212,535   ×   *from micro CMA* (1– AVG. SP/LP) One minus 95%   =   salability differential (SD) [154] $10,627

subject property SQFT 1500   ×   *from DASHBOARD* trend rate (TR) [149] $0.495   =   trend allowance (TA) [154] $743

In this case, *The Right Price* is any price lower than: $223,905

subject property FMV [150] $212,535   +   trend allowance (TA) [154] $743   =   One end of the middle price range $213,278   +   salability differential (SD) [154] $10,627   =   Other end of the middle price range $223,905

Go to: SFC 345

Prices come in three ranges: high, low, and in-between. [154] To find the middle range, do some math:

Use CMA data to create a CMA BREAKDOWN. (see *example* at right)

CMA BREAKDOWN

April 17th	Micro A	Micro B	Micro C	Macro #1
AVG. SP	$250k	$225k	$200k	$232k
AVG. LP	$260k	$237k	$206k	$244k
AVG. SP/LP	96%	95%	97%	96%
AVG. DOM	74	83	60	76
AVG. SQFT	1562	1588	1638	1575
AVG. LP/SQFT	$166.45	$149.24	$125.76	$154.92
AVG. SP/SQFT	$160.05	$141.69	$122.10	$147.30

(VFC)

Valuation Flow Chart

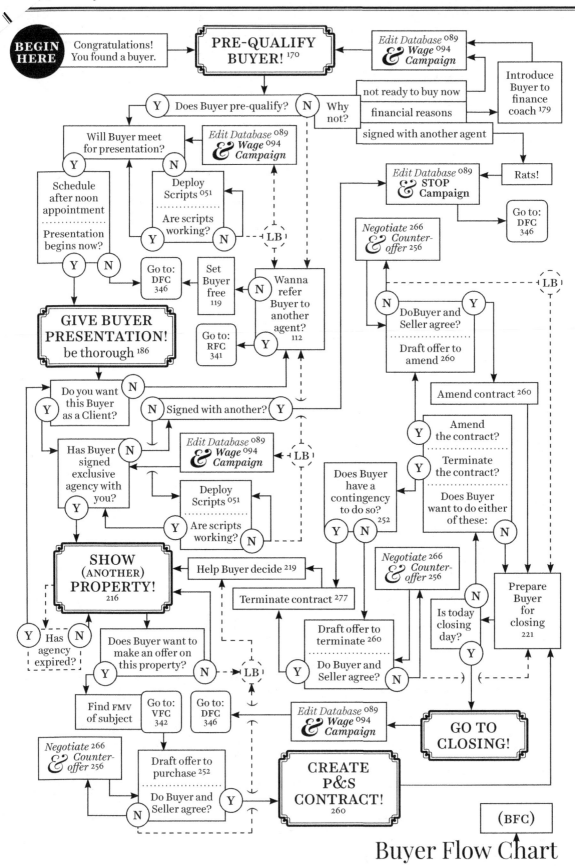

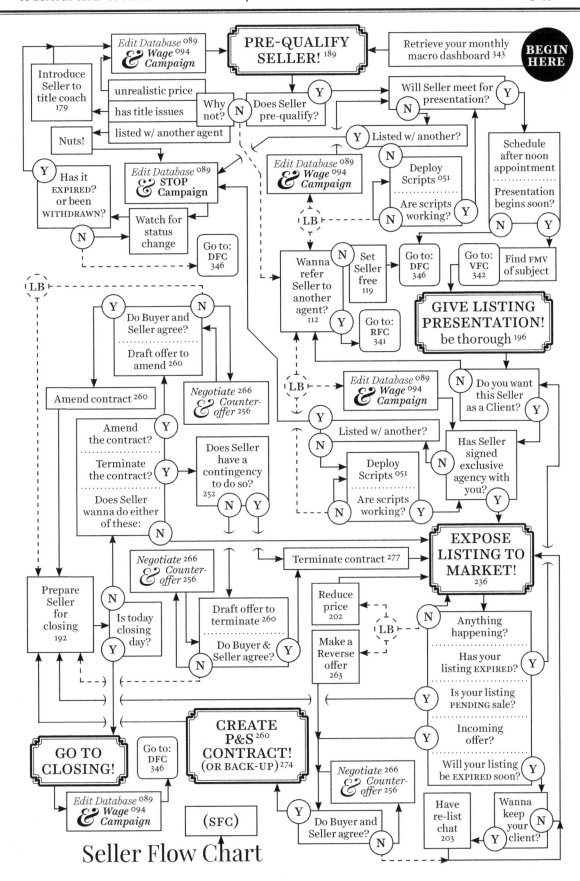

Seller Flow Chart

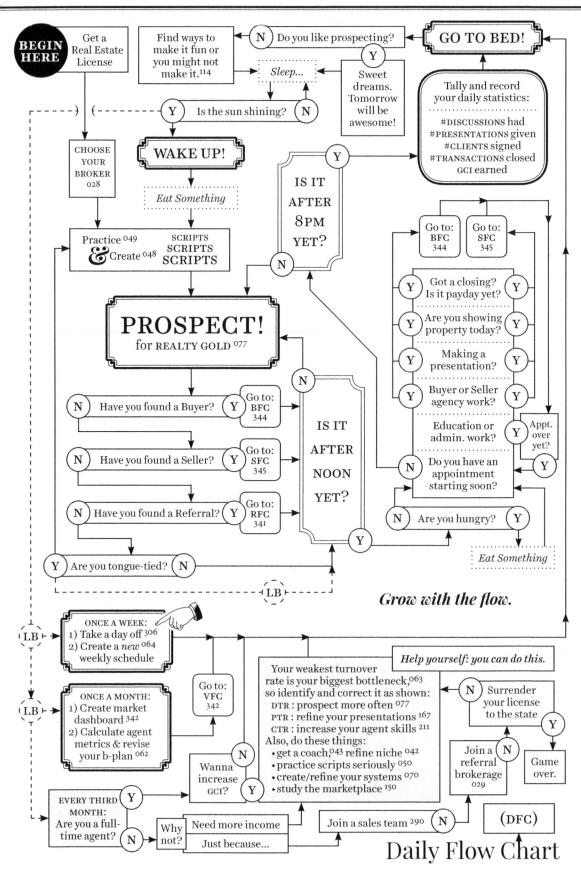

BEGIN HERE — Get a Real Estate License

CHOOSE YOUR BROKER 028

Practice 049 & Create 048 — SCRIPTS SCRIPTS SCRIPTS

WAKE UP!

Eat Something

Is the sun shining? Y / N

Sleep...

Find ways to make it fun or you might not make it. 114

Do you like prospecting? N / Y

GO TO BED!

Sweet dreams. Tomorrow will be awesome!

Tally and record your daily statistics:
#DISCUSSIONS had
#PRESENTATIONS given
#CLIENTS signed
#TRANSACTIONS closed
GCI earned

IS IT AFTER 8PM YET? Y / N

PROSPECT! for REALTY GOLD 077

Have you found a Buyer? N / Y — Go to: BFC 344

Have you found a Seller? N / Y — Go to: SFC 345

Have you found a Referral? N / Y — Go to: RFC 341

IS IT AFTER NOON YET? N / Y

Are you tongue-tied? Y / N

LB

Go to: BFC 344 — Go to: SFC 345

Got a closing? Is it payday yet? Y / Y

Are you showing property today? Y / Y

Making a presentation? Y / Y

Buyer or Seller agency work? Y / Y

Education or admin. work? Y — Appt. over yet? Y

Do you have an appointment starting soon? N / Y

Are you hungry? N / Y

Eat Something

Grow with the flow.

LB — ONCE A WEEK:
1) Take a day off 306
2) Create a *new* 064 weekly schedule

LB — ONCE A MONTH:
1) Create market dashboard 342
2) Calculate agent metrics & revise your b-plan 062

Go to: VFC 342

Wanna increase GCI? N / Y

Your weakest turnover rate is your biggest bottleneck, 063 so identify and correct it as shown:
DTR : prospect more often 077
PTR : refine your presentations 167
CTR : increase your agent skills 211
Also, do these things:
• get a coach, 043 refine niche 042
• practice scripts seriously 050
• create/refine your systems 070
• study the marketplace 150

Help yourself: you can do this.

Surrender your license to the state N / Y

Join a referral brokerage 029 N / Y

Game over.

EVERY THIRD MONTH: Are you a full-time agent? Y / N

Why not? — Need more income / Just because...

Join a sales team 290 N

(DFC)

Daily Flow Chart

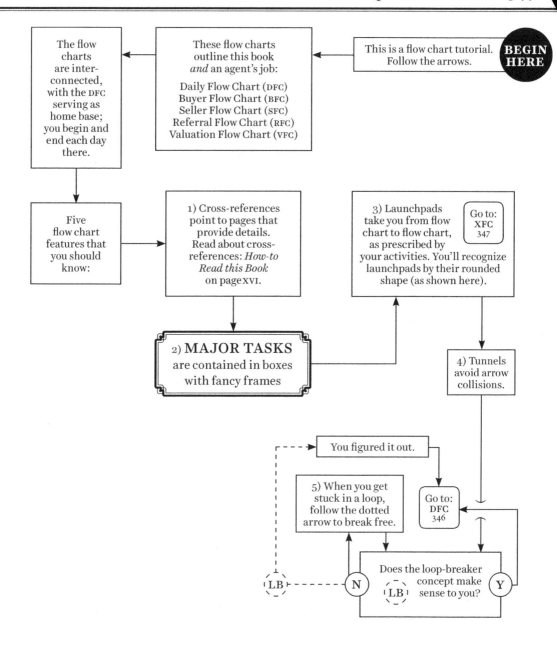

This is a flow chart tutorial. Follow the arrows. **BEGIN HERE**

These flow charts outline this book *and* an agent's job:

Daily Flow Chart (DFC)
Buyer Flow Chart (BFC)
Seller Flow Chart (SFC)
Referral Flow Chart (RFC)
Valuation Flow Chart (VFC)

The flow charts are inter-connected, with the DFC serving as home base; you begin and end each day there.

Five flow chart features that you should know:

1) Cross-references point to pages that provide details. Read about cross-references: *How-to Read this Book* on page XVI.

3) Launchpads take you from flow chart to flow chart, as prescribed by your activities. You'll recognize launchpads by their rounded shape (as shown here). Go to: XFC 347

2) **MAJOR TASKS** are contained in boxes with fancy frames

4) Tunnels avoid arrow collisions.

You figured it out.

5) When you get stuck in a loop, follow the dotted arrow to break free.

Go to: DFC 346

Does the loop-breaker concept make sense to you?

LB   N   LB   Y

FLOW CHART TIPS

• Fold this page under the book, so the DFC is viewable when prospecting by telephone.[078]
• Rely on these flow charts to shepherd you through this book *and* guide you in the field; they're in the back for your convenience.
• Although each flow chart may seem complicated at first glance, they're really quite simple to read and navigate. Go on, now—get to know them better.

(XFC)

Example Flow Chart

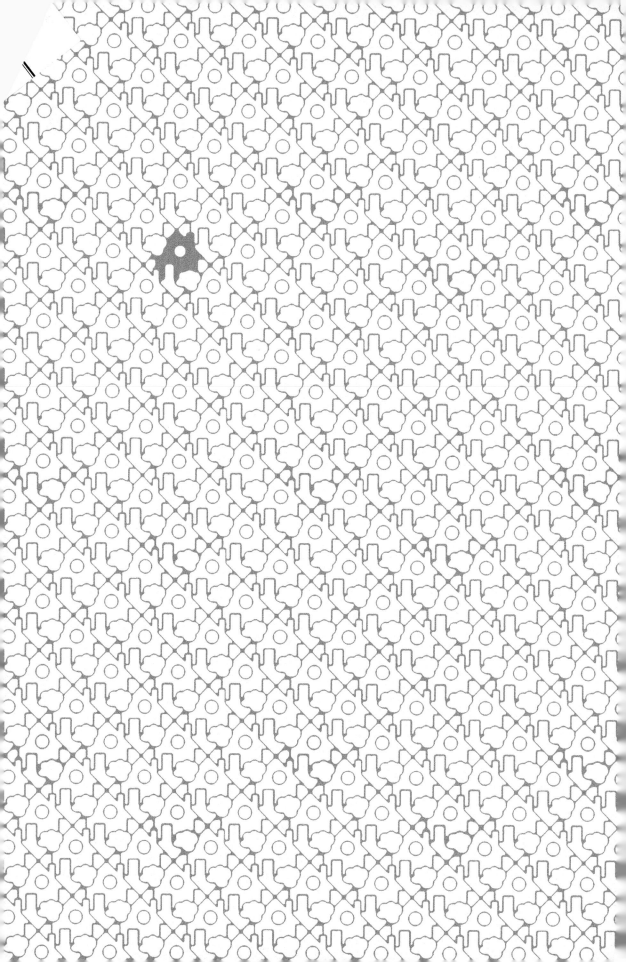

Made in the USA
Columbia, SC
22 July 2018